Memorializing Pearl Harbor

GEOFFREY WHITE

Memorializing Pearl Harbor

UNFINISHED HISTORIES AND THE WORK OF REMEMBRANCE

Duke University Press · Durham and London · 2016

© 2016 DUKE UNIVERSITY PRESS
Printed in the United States of America on acid-free paper ∞
Interior design by Courtney Leigh Baker; cover design by Natalie F.Smith
Typeset in Whitman by Westchester Publishing Services

Library of Congress Cataloging-in-Publication Data
White, Geoffrey M. (Geoffrey Miles), [date]
Memorializing Pearl Harbor : unfinished histories and the work of
remembrance / Geoffrey White.
pages cm
Includes bibliographical references and index.
ISBN 978-0-8223-6088-9 (hardcover : alk. paper)
ISBN 978-0-8223-6102-2 (pbk. : alk. paper)
ISBN 978-0-8223-7443-5 (e-book)
1. Pearl Harbor (Hawaii), Attack on, 1941. 2. World War,
1914–1918—Monuments—Hawaii. 3. War memorials—Hawaii.
4. Collective memory—United States. 5. Memorialization—United States.
I. Title.
D767.92.W475 2016
940.54'26693—dc23
2015035370

Cover art: Pearl Harbor survivor Ted C. Clinard presents USS *Maryland* wreath.
December 7, 1995. Photo by author.

CONTENTS

ACKNOWLEDGMENTS

If books are journeys, then this one is best described as an odyssey—a project that at first seemed quite modest in scope but eventually turned into twenty-five years of increasingly immersive involvement with the national memorial to the Pearl Harbor bombing attack. What began as a project with casual observations in 1991 and a small grant for fieldwork at the USS *Arizona* Memorial in 1994 developed, perhaps inevitably, into multiple projects and collaborations. Along the way I was invited in 2001 to join the nonprofit organization that partners with the National Park Service (NPS) to assist in the development of education programs associated with the memorial, opening up opportunities to work with an even wider range of people and organizations. Needless to say, it is not possible to summarize this journey in any simple way, except to say that this sort of long-term, engaged fieldwork spawns many friendships and collaborations that can't be adequately acknowledged.

One of the arguments of this book is that memorial sites and activities are fundamentally social in nature. A corollary of this argument is that insight into the operations of the kinds of "collective memory" that emerge from such sites requires engagement with the people and communities involved in the memory-making. The research for this book has its roots in the open attitude toward research among members of the National Park Service at the USS *Arizona* Memorial (and currently the World War II Valor in the Pacific National Monument), as well as the Pearl Harbor survivors and others who work there as volunteers. Among the latter, Everett Hyland, Richard Fiske, Bob Kinzler, Ray Emory, Richard Husted, Stanley Igawa, Joe Morgan, Herb Weatherwax, Sterling Cale, and Jim and Yoshie Tanabe, became friends as well as consultants.

The members of the National Park Service who helped out with information and advice are too numerous to name individually, but a few stand out. The support of a sequence of superintendents—Donald Magee, Kathy Billings,

Doug Lentz, Frank Hayes, and Paul DePrey—proved critical to sustaining the project. In the early phases of this work, the support of the memorial superintendents Donald Magee and Kathy Billings laid the groundwork for my research in 1994, conducted with Marjorie Kelly and supported by a grant from the Wenner-Gren Foundation. Daniel Martinez, chief historian at the memorial, has been a good friend and constant source of insight throughout. As principal architect of the fiftieth-anniversary symposium in 1991, which brought scholars and veterans (American and Japanese) together into a historic program, Martinez has been at the center of many of the activities documented in this book.

Among the important developments at the memorial in the 1990s were the efforts of Japanese veterans of the Pearl Harbor attack to develop friendships with their American counterparts and engage in ceremonies of reconciliation. Given that I have no background in Japanese studies (specializing rather in Pacific Islands studies), my research on these transnational dimensions of memorialization has benefited from the scholarship of a number of close colleagues in Japanese studies, including Pat Masters and her early work with Japanese visitors at the memorial, Yujin Yaguchi's research on that subject in the 2000s, collaboration with Takashi Fujitani and Lisa Yoneyama on the politics of remembering the Pacific War, and with Marie Thorsten on Pearl Harbor films and veterans' commemorative activities. Conversations with these colleagues have added immeasurably to my interpretations of the tangle of U.S.-Japan relations in memorial space.

My location in the 1990s at the East-West Center, a federally funded organization established to strengthen relations between the United States and countries of Asia Pacific, proved fortuitous. The mission of that organization was a good fit for facilitating active involvement with the efforts of veterans, especially Japanese veterans, to engineer reconciliation events with their American counterparts. With the East-West Center available to act as a "community sponsor," I found myself working with veterans, particularly the Japanese naval veterans organization, Unabarakai, to arrange for a major ceremony hosted at Punchbowl National Cemetery in 1995 to mark the fiftieth anniversary of the end of the war. In that context I learned about the impressive efforts of the local historian John Di Virgilio to document oral histories of Japanese veterans of the attack and came to know and appreciate their dogged pursuit of reconciliation. Leading up to the Punchbowl event in 1995, the Unabarakai invited my wife and me to participate in their own ceremony at a memorial park in the Japanese Self-Defense Forces base in Tsuchiura, Japan. I am grateful to the Unabarakai president Takeshi Maeda, Secretary Jiro Yoshida, and their associate Hiroya Sugano for hosting a visit that allowed me to glimpse the Japanese side of memorialization examined in this book.

My constant presence around the memorial in the 1990s led to my appointment in 2001 to the board of what was then called the *Arizona* Memorial Museum Association, opening up all sorts of opportunities for bringing research and education into conversation with one another. Notable among these were summer programs for high school and college teachers that I coorganized with Namji Steinemann at the East-West Center, supported with grants from the National Endowment for the Humanities between 2004 and 2010. As a member of the board of the *Arizona* Memorial Museum Association (now Pacific Historic Parks) charged with advising on the development of education programs, I not only learned about the institutions that help to make public history at Pearl Harbor, but I gained a more personal understanding of the social milieus that make it possible. Here, too, it is not practical to name all those in the organization with whom I've worked over the years, but George Sullivan, Neil Sheehan, Colette Higgins, Tom Shaw, Paul Heintz, and Laurie Moore deserve special mention. Ray Sandla provided advice on maps and photographs that have made this book more visually effective than it might be otherwise.

Perhaps the largest and longest project undertaken by the NPS and its partner at the USS *Arizona* Memorial while I was conducting this research was the fundraising and redesign of the new visitor center and museum opened in 2010. Invitations to participate and consult on museum planning from Lynn Nakata, head of the NPS museum redesign project, curator Scott Pawlowski, and members of the Aldrich Pears Associates consulting team (Phil Aldrich, Doug Munday, and Sheila Hill) offered a chance to learn about museum planning by participating at several levels. At an early stage, for example, we worked together to mobilize small teams of graduate students from the University of Hawai'i to conduct pilot research on visitor attitudes and expectations in ways that might inform the design process. I am grateful to Margaret Bodemer, Peter Hourdequin, and Noa Matsushita for their foray into visitor interviewing in 2006, as well as Karen Kosasa, professor of American studies, for facilitating a second survey in 2007, involving her students in the University of Hawai'i Museum Studies Certificate Program.

As someone living in Hawai'i and working in Pacific studies I have come to understand that Pearl Harbor as both geography and history is deeply entangled with Native Hawaiian geographies and histories of the area, termed *Pu'uloa*. Although fishponds have been filled in and names overwritten, the area is dotted with cultural and sacred sites that have renewed significance in the context of movements for Hawaiian sovereignty. I have learned much from my colleagues Ty Kāwika Tengan, Jonathan Kamakawiwoʻole Osorio, and Kyle Kajihiro, among others, about some of the ways those histories affect and are affected by the harbor's military history. Although this book does not engage with these longer histories and memories in any depth, I hope this project will inform future work by Native Hawaiian scholars and others that will bring more attention to these connections and their importance for Pearl Harbor as well as Puʻuloa.

Although most of the research for this book has been undertaken as "home" work without the expenses of distant fieldwork, grants from the Wenner-Gren Foundation and a National Park Service task agreement provided support at key moments. For the latter, Superintendent Paul DePrey facilitated support for research on Native Hawaiian military experience and Chinese visitor perceptions conducted, respectively, by my University of Hawaiʻi colleague Ty Kāwika Tengan and then masters student Kuan-Jung Lai. The Department of Anthropology at the University of Hawaiʻi provided assistance with transcribing and indexing research materials, making available a rich archive of texts for this project. Here I would be remiss in not thanking Matt Loui and others for their careful and patient work with transcription. Finally, the larger forms of institutional support for the summer teacher programs from the *Arizona* Memorial Museum Association, the East-West Center, the Freeman Foundation, and the National Endowment for the Humanities made possible a set of multinational and multilateral dialogues that both inform and unsettle the arguments that follow.

Support for writing has come from several sources, including a sabbatical leave from the University of Hawaiʻi in 2013 and a monthlong fellowship with the International Forum for U.S. Studies (IFUSS) at the University of Illinois, Urbana-Champaign. The IFUSS fellowship offered the chance to spend time with my colleagues Virginia Dominguez and Jane Desmond, who have been interlocutors for this project longer than I can remember. I thank them for the invitation to spend time together at a crucial time for the writing, and especially the chance to interact with the tourism scholars Edward Bruner and Jonathan Skinner.

Parts of several chapters in this book have their origins in earlier papers and publications, several of them coauthored with colleagues who have been part of this odyssey. Chapter 4's treatment of the memorial film draws from the paper "Moving History," published first in *Positions: East Asia Cultures Critique* (1998) and then in revised form as a chapter in the book *Perilous Memories: The Asia Pacific War(s)* (2001). That paper benefited from the work of Marjorie Kelly, as well as perceptive comments from the filmmaker Lance Bird. And I first developed the analysis of the documentary *December 7th* in a paper written with Jane Yi titled "*December 7th*: Race and Nation in Wartime Documentary." Additionally, what little I know of the production and reception of Pearl Harbor films in Japan is owed to Marie Thorsten, especially the opportunity to work together on the essay "Binational Pearl Harbor?: *Tora! Tora! Tora!* and the Fate of (Trans) national Memory," published in *The Asia Pacific Journal: Japan Focus* in 2010.

The discussion of tourism and the theming of Pearl Harbor in chapter 5 builds upon analyses of Pearl Harbor tourism in several papers delivered at conferences and invited talks. I first started thinking about Pearl Harbor as a theme park when invited to participate in a panel on theme parks at the meetings of the American Anthropological Association in 1997, presenting a paper titled "On Not Being a Theme Park: Pearl Harbor and the Predicament of National Memory." A few years later I wrote about similar issues in a paper focusing on an exhibit controversy at the Pacific Aviation Museum, "The Battle of Ni'ihau: Theming the Good War in Pearl Harbor's Military Tourism Complex," presented at the meetings of the AAA held in 2009. Here I need also to thank Fumiaki Fujimoto for his work on the Japanese side of the story of Ni'ihau, begun when Fujimoto was a participant in one of our teacher programs. More recently Takashi Fujitani invited me to give a talk at the University of Toronto on "Touring America's Good War: From Pearl Harbor to D-Day"—an occasion that proved especially useful in locating Pearl Harbor in a wider context of war memory and tourism.

Chapter 6's account of the politics of pedagogy in teacher programs incorporates elements of a paper given at meetings of the Organization of American Historians held in 2006 ("The Pearl Harbor Workshops: Memorials, Museums, and the Politics of Pedagogy") and later developed as a chapter for a volume of essays by Japanese participants in the teacher programs, *Narrating Pearl Harbor: History, Memory, and Education* (2011), edited by Yujin Yaguchi and colleagues Takeo Morimo and Kyoko Nakayama, who coordinated Japanese participation in those programs.

Finally, for advice on writing and revising this manuscript, I am indebted to a number of colleagues who read all or part of earlier drafts of this book. Kathy Billings, Donald Brenneis, Eric Gable, Michelle Lipinski, Daniel Martinez, Nancy Montgomery, Jim and Yoshie Tanabe, Ty Kāwika Tengan, Marie Thorsten, Yujin Yaguchi, and two anonymous reviewers for Duke University Press. At the Press, Ken Wissoker's early interest and guidance in responding to reviews provided an experienced hand that has much to do with the clarity and focus of the book.

To conclude by returning to the start, my wife, Nancy, and son, Michael, have been with this project the whole time. Whether in the evocative questions and comments of a child swept up in fieldwork or the shared involvement of a partner, they are part of the story in ways that only they know.

Introduction

MEMORIALIZING

HISTORY

The presentations had gone well. For an evening event held in the middle of the week at the memorial's visitor center, a respectable audience had turned out. They listened appreciatively as a panel of museum specialists offered their critiques of the new museum opened in December 2010 as part of a $58 million makeover for the World War II Valor in the Pacific National Monument, home to the USS *Arizona* Memorial, the national memorial to the bombing attack on Pearl Harbor, carried out in 1941, that killed over two thousand and triggered America's entry into the war.[1] The question-and-answer period generated discussion that surely pleased the representatives of the National Park Service who oversee the memorial and were on the panel to present their views of the project and solicit comments. As the panel facilitator asked if there were any further questions, a middle-aged man raised his hand and stood to give his comment.

> I do have a question. My name is Keoni Wong[2] and when I saw the exhibit I was pulled by the . . . very obvious story that is being told but [pause], of the Hawaiian perspective, I saw nothing. [Voice cracking.] I've lived in these islands for sixty-three years, born and raised, and this is my first time to come to Pearl Harbor. My parents witnessed, my

grandparents witnessed the event and they told us the stories. But as a Hawaiian coming to this exhibit and searching for a framework, some text that is sensitive to we the indigenous people, two hundred and fifty thousand, perhaps, claiming to be Hawaiian living in these islands. There was very little. . . . The way the text was written sort of puts Hawaiians as a footnote in the rear in history. . . . So when you said earlier that this exhibit was for everyone, no. My three children will not come to Pearl Harbor to see this (and they're young; they're five and eight) until this is changed. . . . You are able to tell the story of two larger powers at war that happened over these islands, our island. But you never told our story. You told local stories. You did tell local stories, but not the other. . . . Please address it. It needs to be addressed. Millions of visitors go through this and they walk away without knowing our story. Don't make us the footnote. . . . . Please. (audio recording, March 23, 2012)

Actually the problem such exhibits pose for the story that the speaker wants to tell is even more formidable than he acknowledges. The issue is not just that the designers have left out someone's story, a problem that could be rectified by "finishing the exhibit." Rather, the story of a surprise attack that killed thousands of American servicemen and servicewomen and wreaked horrific destruction upon the United States Navy's most powerful base in the Pacific has been a monumental episode in American public memory ever since the attack became a rallying cry for fighting the Pacific War (Rosenberg 2004). Despite concerns that younger generations might forget the story, the public history of Pearl Harbor has retained much of its force through decades of American memory because it is a story that speaks to core symbols and sentiments in the national imagination, to American identity and patriotism.

A history that is told to honor the sacrifices of American servicemen and servicewomen who died in the first line of battle, victims of a violent attack in a war not yet declared, is one that does not easily incorporate critical histories replete with moral complexity and contradiction. Like the significance of Pearl Harbor for Japanese Americans, many of whom were immediately taken into custody and confined in internment camps, the trajectory of Hawaiian history does not align comfortably with stories that are recounted to honor military sacrifice. To further complicate the issue, the multiple narratives of Pearl Harbor are not simply different ways of recalling Pearl Harbor that run parallel to each other, but are narratives already entangled in history and in public spaces where power and perspective modulate the amplitude of voices that speak about history. As the speaker above intimates with his reference to the

Reciprocity Treaty, the story of indigenous Hawaiians that appears "forgotten" is strongly connected to the story of the United States in the Pacific and the annexation of the Islands with an eye on the strategic value of Pearl Harbor. See appendix 2 for a chronology of postcontact Hawaiian history noting key moments in the transition of the Hawaiian Kingdom to America's fiftieth state and poststatehood moves to restore Hawaiian sovereignty.

Erasure of the history of Hawai'i's indigenous population is one of the consistent consequences of the Pearl Harbor story. For typical American histories of Pearl Harbor, the story of why there was a naval base at Pearl Harbor in the first place, or how Hawai'i, in the middle of the Pacific Ocean, came to be America's fiftieth state simply are not relevant. The standard American history of Pearl Harbor and the history of Native Hawaiian[3] dispossession have been effectively insulated from one another during most of the memorial's development, despite the fact that questions about Hawaiian sovereignty were gaining momentum as the fiftieth anniversary of the war was being commemorated in the early 1990s. In 1993 the Hawaiian movement saw an outpouring of native sentiment around the hundredth anniversary of the illegal overthrow of the Hawaiian monarchy, when Queen Lili'uokalani was deposed by a conspiracy of commercial interests. At times, however, these parallel histories have intersected, with uncomfortable results, as in the Hawaiian speaker's comments at the evening forum. To write a history of memory at the Pearl Harbor memorial is to identify the practices that insulate these histories from one another, as well as to focus on such moments of intersection and the conditions that make them possible.

The literature on memorials is replete with examples of efforts to expand or complicate their histories, which are challenged as inappropriate or disrespectful to the purpose of memorialization. Similar conflicts have been front and center in the efforts to create a museum at the site of the 9/11 World Trade Center attacks (Gopnik 2014). Finally opened in May 2014, the National September 11 Memorial and Museum includes, along with its exhibits, a "remains repository" "located at bedrock," as well as a memorial exhibition "dedicated to commemorating the unique life of each victim."[4] Combining a shrine and a museum that seeks to inform the public about the history of the 9/11 attacks has proven a difficult task even from the early days of planning the museum. A proposal to create an educational center called the Freedom Center foundered in the face of challenges from some of the families of individuals killed in the attack. In a strongly worded editorial, Debra Burlingame (2005) wrote that attempting to teach history "over the ashes of Ground Zero" would be "like creating a Museum of Tolerance over the sunken graves of the USS *Arizona*" (cited in Sturken 2007b, 274). Burlingame's almost off-handed reference to Pearl Harbor, invoked to convey an offensive scenario of desecration was, in fact, almost prescient of developments that were just beginning to unfold at Pearl Harbor.

Cancellation of the Freedom Center echoed the sort of conflict that had been fought over commemoration and education at the Smithsonian's National Air and Space Museum ten years earlier. The Smithsonian's attempt to mount an educational exhibition about the atomic bombings of Hiroshima and Nagasaki on the occasion of the fiftieth anniversary of the bombings is now a textbook case of the collision of commemoration and historical analysis in a national museum (Harwit 1996; Linenthal and Engelhardt 1996). That exhibit, which focused on the B-29 named *Enola Gay*, which dropped the bomb on Hiroshima, aligned military organizations wishing to honor veterans of the Second World War, particularly Air Force veterans, against curators and historians seeking to expand awareness of a pivotal event in twentieth-century history. During debate over the exhibit, some Congressmen argued that national museums are places that, by definition, should affirm and inspire, rather than cast doubt on the national past. In the course of these arguments, the vision of impressionable children coming to the museum to learn about their nation's past was invoked by critics anxious to safeguard national history. Political forces opposed to the *Enola Gay* exhibit were strong enough to cancel the exhibit and force the resignation of the museum director, Martin Harwit.

And yet the same opposition of agencies and structures that have aligned in opposition over the remembrance of America's wars in the past seems only to repeat itself. At present, the Department of Defense plans to commemorate the fiftieth anniversary of the Vietnam War by honoring the sacrifices of American soldiers.[5] These plans have provoked a broad challenge from historians, journalists, and civic leaders who see the focus on honoring veterans as ill-suited to the project's other mission to "provide the American public with historically accurate materials" for educational purposes. A group of some five hundred scholars and veterans, who see their war differently, have sent the Secretary of Defense a petition asking that the commemoration not be a "one-sided" portrayal of a war that proved so divisive in American history.[6]

In the wake of the *Enola Gay* controversy, the historian Edward Linenthal asked, "Can Museums Achieve a Balance between Memory and History?" (1995). Whereas his question continues to be relevant in a broad range of contexts beyond museums, including school textbook controversies, the question is most apt when asked of memorial museums, where the risks (and, I would say, responsibilities) of combining commemoration and education are especially acute.[7] Marita Sturken, who has studied several major American memorial sites, is less than sanguine about the possibilities of mixing pedagogy with memorialization. In the case of the failed proposal for a Freedom Center at the World Trade Center site, she observed that, "anyone with knowledge of the history of memorial museums could have guessed the outcome" (2007b, 274). And yet, some degree of mixing—often unnoticed or unmarked—is inevitable at memorial sites, particularly those that create museums or museum-like spaces within a larger memorial complex. In this study of the USS *Arizona* Memorial, I trace a history of memorial practices in which discourses of education and memorialization continually intertwine, informing one another at times and colliding at others.

With the opening of the first visitor center in 1980 and the development of the memorial as a larger, more complex institution managed by the National Park Service, it began to engage with both memory and history, with the documentation and preservation of history as well as the work of public commemoration. Along with the opening of the visitor center with its museum and collections facility came National Park Service staff, including a park historian and curator, charged with recording historical information and managing exhibitions relevant to the bombing attack. These activities, including the recording of oral histories and education programs like those discussed in chapter 6, opened up opportunities for more wide-ranging conversations with "other" communities of remembrance that would not have been possible in the sacred space of the memorial and its shrine room.

In the case of the new museum discussed in the evening panel, then, how could exhibits in a memorial space devoted to the commemoration of 2,390 military and civilian deaths in the bombing attack on December 7 come to terms with a Hawaiian history that raises questions about the presence of the U.S. Navy in the harbor? Within the context of a memorial created to honor military service and sacrifice, how could one "add on" an indigenous history of displacement and cultural suppression without placing the project of memorialization at risk? From the perspective of postcolonial critiques of Pearl Harbor as a symbol of U.S. military power in the Pacific, the answer to these questions is simple: you can't honor both histories. "Other" perspectives are not forgotten, they are excluded by virtue of the logic of colonization and nationalization (Gonzalez 2013, 119; Kajihiro 2014). One of the things that Pearl Harbor commemoration does is cover over a history of occupation that, from the perspective of many Native Hawaiians today, is even more painful than the calamity of Pearl Harbor for those who suffered losses in the attack. When participating in another panel reflecting on the new museum in 2011, the

Native Hawaiian historian Jonathan Osorio articulated his view of this emotional logic of exclusion:

> The Pearl Harbor museum is a battlefield museum [that] occupies a special kind of role, especially for imperialist nations. It doesn't simply address a public curiosity in a historical event . . . it's there to renew patriotic ties . . . a kind of religious rite of mourning and rededication. . . . There are powerful emotional currents that are connected with that museum for the survivors who return, on both sides, Japanese and American, and also for the survivors' children's children, descendants. And, for any people who are . . . a part of the American nation. In all of these powerful emotions, what kind of place is there for the Native person who is related to people who are descendants of people who own that land, who fished in the fishponds of Puʻuloa . . . hundreds and hundreds years ago? For Native people, whose lands have been turned into military bases, an erasure takes place . . . an erasure of Native names, an erasure of access to that place, there's an erasure of Native rights to that land. (Jonathan Kamakawiwoʻole Osorio, Western Museums Association Conference presentation, September 24, 2011)

Having noted the predicament of indigenous memory at Pearl Harbor, it would be possible to pile up examples of the exclusion and marginalization of perspectives that run counter to dominant narratives of America in the Pacific and the legislated purpose of the memorial. But to tell the story of memory politics at the USS *Arizona* Memorial this way imputes a uniformity and solidity to the institution that misses its complexity as a space traversed by multiple commemorative cultures, all contingent and in motion. The *Arizona* Memorial is less of a total institution than a site of intersection (or perhaps cohabitation) of diverse and often conflicting interests, even though some interests take precedence over others. Whereas the hegemony of military history at an American war memorial is not surprising, military narratives and their values also contend with alternative and oppositional histories. Just which histories emerge most forcefully, for which publics, at any point in time is itself subject to shifting conditions and contexts for the memorial's commemorative culture.

Theories of collective memory routinely approach museums and memorials as "sites of contestation." But what, in practice, do such contestations look like? Very often accounts of memory clashes are cast as conflicts between whole, oppositional narratives—memory and countermemory, dominant memory and marginal memory, as if disembodied narratives were at war. Whether by theoretical design or methodological limitation, much of the scholarship on the ways memorials "remember" tends to miss their internal complexity and, curiously, the affect, agency, and intimacy that are so prominent in spaces of memorialization. Broad-brush views of collective memory at memorial sites tend to homogenize the "official," on the one hand, and to ignore the crucial question of how official histories become meaningful and emotional, on the other. Memorial practices are one of the most public means of marking histories as personal, as matters of felt emotion, whether those emotions are feelings of inspiration and belonging or alienation and resistance (as in the testimony above). Such practices not only express the affective dimensions of history, they can create them by defining and validating feelings in acts of collective representation.

Now listen to the National Park Service Superintendent's response to the Hawaiian speaker's intervention:

> If I could just respond. I appreciate your comment. . . . I'll be the first to say that I don't believe that we had as a goal up front . . . to try and describe what the Native Hawaiian experience was in relation to the United States. . . . We wanted to be sure [visitors] understood that Pearl Harbor had significance before it was a U.S. military facility or before it was an attack site. . . . Our efforts are really to try and ensure that the visitors who come through the site understand the dynamics around the attack on Pearl Harbor and the Pacific War. We certainly do see that in order to do that justice . . . we need to be sure that we emphasize . . . the value and contributions and significance of the Native Hawaiian cultures and traditions and people who are still present here. . . . It is something that we are going to continue to be paying attention to into the future. I want your children to come here. I want you to feel comfortable bringing your children here. I want you to feel as though this is a site that is as open to them as anybody else who comes here. I feel like that's our responsibility, as you know, [that's] the National Park Service's job to do.

I quote this response at length in order to illustrate the manner in which history and historiography are themselves topics of public discussion at the memorial. Much of the language implicitly codes the power and authority of the state to make decisions about what is memorialized, and even to decide how Native Hawaiians will be represented. Thus, as he expresses an intent to recognize "the value and contributions and significance of the Native Hawaiian cultures and traditions," he refers to them as a people "who are still present here." In other words, in this context, Native Hawaiians are located in a narrative of disappearance (within which they are still present), implicating a longer history that in fact is mostly absent in the space of the memorial. Even though there were no Native Hawaiians on the panel, the fact that such a discussion took place at all, involving National Park Service administrators, principal planners of the exhibit, university critics, and museum leaders, along with the broader community, also tells a story about the kinds of conversation about history that can occur in the memorial's public space.

It is important to note that these sorts of exchange, about the purpose of representing Pearl Harbor history, are happening now during a pivotal period of transition. In particular, with the passing of the Second World War generation and, with it, the Pearl Harbor survivors, voices that spoke powerfully in commemorative activities for decades have diminished. The Pearl Harbor Survivors Association (PHSA) was formally incorporated in 1962, the same year the USS *Arizona* Memorial was dedicated. Membership rules stated that anyone who was serving in the military on the island of Oahu on December 7, 1941, was eligible to join. The PHSA was always a major presence in anniversary ceremonies, particularly the five-year anniversaries. As its numbers dwindled, however, the association finally decided to disband. By March 2012 the PHSA had already dissolved itself and the cadre of volunteers who work regularly at the park had shrunk to just four or five regular participants in their nineties. None were on the panel that night and as far as I know none were in the audience.

These changes in the memorial's living memory were happening at the same time that the park service was articulating more clearly than ever its commitments to "multiple perspectives" on the bombing—a philosophy of history that twenty years earlier was a matter of public debate. In his response that evening, the superintendent avowed that telling history at the memorial is always an unfinished story, and that it is the job of the NPS stewards to continually "improve" and update the story so that it will be responsive to different publics. Two points are crucial. The first is that official historiography here is idealistically driven by a philosophy of "balance" and responsiveness to "multiple points of view." The second point, less explicit, is that not all voices speak with the same volume in memorial space. The superintendent's response articulates a remarkable philosophy of inclusion, a commitment to public history characteristic of National Park Service efforts generally to be inclusive and balanced, allowing multiple interpretations and meanings. But what are the limits and contradictions of such a philosophy in a memorial context? And how do such philosophies of history shift through time? There is always a politics to history, to the ability of some stories to be told, heard, and retold in particular places or media at particular times. In matters of public history, hegemony, although usually invisible, is rarely total or sealed. Whereas it may seem obvious and even banal to observe that public history is responsive to the operations of power, it becomes more interesting to ask how those operations work in producing and reproducing history in ways that often go unrecognized.

In many ways, histories of America's "Good War" exemplify the principle that "to the victor go the spoils of history." Certainly the ability to produce one's own triumphal versions of history unhindered by the voices of vanquished former enemies (or others whose stories are not as well aligned with those histories) holds true for the American popular memory of the Second World War (for critical examinations of the American Good War narrative, see Adams 1994; Beidler 1998; Bodnar 2010; Torgovnick 2005; Wood 2006). Having said that, it is simplistic and mystifying to interpret public histories at the national memorial as a product of the invisible hand of the state. Instead, the memorial's history emerges in a web of social relations and daily practices, albeit within the constraints and conditions that make some kinds of knowledge more relevant and valued than others.

In the case of a national war memorial and tourist destination such as the uss *Arizona* Memorial, it should be obvious that complex social, political, and economic forces converge there in affecting exhibits and programs, and that these, in turn, will provoke diverse interpretations from audiences moving through memorial space. Over time, conversations such as that of the exhibit panel quoted here are a kind of gauge or index of shifting perspectives and sensibilities, reflecting the varied sensibilities that intersect at the memorial, each with a different set of possibilities for affecting the official and officializing stories told there.

The Pearl Harbor Memorials: A Brief History

At the heart of the uss *Arizona* Memorial are the actual places, objects, and people, both living and dead, involved in the original attack. These material realities circumscribe the memorial's sacred space. The central, dominant icon in this space is the sunken hulk of the battleship *Arizona*, still located where it exploded on December 7, 1941. The large majority of the 1,177 sailors and marines who died on the ship are entombed there. As with those lost in the violent disintegration of the World Trade Center on 9/11, little or nothing remained to be recovered of hundreds who died in the massive explosion and fire that destroyed the *Arizona*. Forever after, the sunken ship has been a grave, shrine, and cemetery that has been a focal point for military and civilian ceremonies honoring those who died in the bombing. (See appendix 1 for a brief list of the attack force and casualty figures.)

With time, the ship memorial also became a major destination for tourism—becoming the most visited site in one of the world's busiest tourism economies: Honolulu, Hawai'i. In this study I use the term *memorial* to refer to the USS *Arizona* Memorial as an institutional complex that includes not only the shrine but a visitor center on shore with a museum, theater, and gift shop surrounded by a landscape replete with historic markers, located where visitors look out on the harbor. I retain the term *memorial* to be clear that my focus in this book is the USS *Arizona* Memorial site, even though it, and its broader surroundings, are constantly evolving.

During the decade that followed the bombing, the sunken hull of the *Arizona*, with its entombed remains, became a military shrine for naval rituals as sailors on board ships passing in the harbor would "man the rails"—a tradition of lining the deck as an expression of honor for the lost ship and its men. In 1950 the Commander in Chief of the Pacific Fleet ordered construction of a platform on the ship's deck with a flagpole for conducting ceremonies. Then in 1958 President Eisenhower signed legislation creating the USS *Arizona* Memorial, paving the way for federal funding for a memorial structure that could accommodate visitors. The authorizing legislation for the memorial makes the focus of commemoration clear. A bill passed in 1961, PL 87–201, to fund construction of the memorial, said that the *Arizona* memorial and museum were established "in honor and in commemoration of the members of the Armed Forces of the United States who gave their lives to their country during the attack on Pearl Harbor" (for an administrative history of the memorial, see Slackman 1986). The USS *Arizona* Memorial was finally completed and dedicated in 1962, more than twenty years after the bombing, three years after Hawai'i was formally incorporated as the fiftieth state of the United States.

The rapid growth of Hawai'i's tourism economy in the 1970s and 1980s transformed the memorial and its environs into a tourism destination that today includes an entire harbor complex of historic sites, military museums, and amenities, all located on the Pearl Harbor naval base (see chapter 4, map 4.1). As the development of transportation and communication links between Hawai'i and North America (as well as Japan) brought a rising tide of visitors in the 1970s, the navy had to rethink its management of the memorial. The solution was to construct a visitor center and museum, operated by the National Park Service, that could provide the services required for a major tourist "attraction." The visitor center that opened in 1980, with its small museum, orientation film, and bookstore, accommodated visitor traffic that would continue to rise until it, too, had to be rebuilt and expanded in the late 2000s. Today about 1.8 million people visit the memorial annually.

FIGURE I.1
Aerial view of the World War II Valor in the Pacific National Monument
visitor center and surrounding harbor area.
Photo by Vito Palmisano.

The value of the Pearl Harbor memorial for the U.S. Navy is evident in the
regular round of official visits, ceremonial enlistments, and commemorative
events sponsored or cosponsored by the navy. From the 1960s onward, as the
USS *Arizona* Memorial was becoming the most visited site in Hawaiʻi's tourism
economy, the naval base that hosts it—the hub of the U.S. Pacific Command—
also expanded in size and sophistication, supporting America's wars in Korea,
Vietnam, and the Middle East. Within this mix of military base and tourism
destination, tourism and military activities mutually affirm and validate one
another, each lending historical authenticity to the other (Gonzalez 2013, ch. 4).

The visitor center is not only about visitors—it is also a space for commemorative activities, with a ritual calendar focused on the December 7
anniversary, as well as Memorial Day, Independence Day, Veterans Day, and
other national occasions. The organizers of the fiftieth anniversary of Pearl
Harbor, in 1991, proudly noted that more American media organizations registered to cover that event than covered the first Iraq war that same year.[8]
It was around this time that I first took an interest in the memorial, seeing
a connection to research on the memory of the Second World War that I'd

been pursuing in more traditionally anthropological places in the South Pacific (Lindstrom and White 1990; White 1995; White and Lindstrom 1989). After attending the symposium organized to commemorate the fiftieth anniversary of the Pearl Harbor attack, in 1991, I began doing fieldwork at the memorial, initially with my colleague Marjorie Kelly, studying its interpretive programs and interviewing those most directly involved in producing its history—park service staff and volunteers, especially Pearl Harbor survivors.[9]

Because the 1990s were a time in which veterans of the Second World War were particularly active in American remembrance of the war, our research focused especially on the activities of veterans at the memorial, and the nature of interactions between visitors and veterans. Not long after the visitor center opened, the NPS superintendent and historian began to recruit Pearl Harbor survivors resident in Honolulu to volunteer at the center as honored guests and volunteers in the Volunteers in the Park program. During the 1990s and 2000s these veterans were a popular and visible element in the memorial experience, with several present on the visitor center grounds on any given day. The survivors (mostly members of the national Pearl Harbor Survivors Association) proved to be popular with visitors who would seek photos, autographs, and stories for their own memories of a memorial visit (White 2004b). At a memorial service in 2013 for one of the leaders of the group of survivor volunteers, someone giving a eulogy said that he must have signed his name on books and pamphlets of tourist visitors "several million times" during the previous three decades. At present the number of survivor volunteers has dwindled to just a handful, a mostly vanished presence at the visitor center.

By the mid-2000s it was clear that the level of tourist visitation had exceeded visitor center capacity. Spurred on by engineering problems in the original construction (on landfill in areas that had once been Native Hawaiian fishponds), a major fundraising campaign was launched to build an expanded museum and visitor center facility. This expansion at the *Arizona* memorial came on the heels of the construction of other military museums on the Pearl Harbor base: the USS *Bowfin* Submarine Museum and Park, in 1981, the Battleship *Missouri* Memorial, in 1999, and the Pacific Aviation Museum Pearl Harbor, in 2006. With these facilities all seeking paying visitors, the renovation of the *Arizona* visitor center turned it into an architectural "gateway" for an entire complex of military tourism destinations (Gonzalez 2013, ch. 4).

As plans for rebuilding the *Arizona* memorial visitor center and museum were just beginning to take shape in the late 2000s, another major change occurred in 2008, when outgoing president George W. Bush created a new entity in the national park system, the World War II Valor in the Pacific National Monument—now the official name for the National Park Service unit that manages the *Arizona* memorial.[10] For the park service managers of the memorial, the administrative change entailed a change in mission, expanding the scope of interpretation from the Pearl Harbor bombing to the entire war in the Pacific. Bundling together nine historic sites of the Second World War, this change initiated a profound shift in thinking about the context and purpose for representing history at the memorial. The superintendent's point, quoted above, that historical exhibits at the memorial continue to evolve reflects this ongoing transformation. The official histories coded in the exhibits of the new museum opened in 2010 were designed to incorporate stronger representation of civilian, and particularly Japanese American, experiences around Pearl Harbor than had been evident in earlier decades, when the memorial concentrated on telling the military history of the attack on the ships and the losses of uniformed personnel. The panel registered this new emphasis by including the director of the Japanese Cultural Center of Hawai'i among its speakers.

War Memory and National Imagination

The two World Wars of the twentieth century irrevocably shifted the historical imaginations of the warring powers. Scholars of nationalism have long pointed to the role of war in producing uniquely effective and affective bonds of national belonging (Mosse 1990; Winter 1999; Winter 2006). At the center of Western scholarship on collective memory, the specter of the Holocaust haunts not only postwar efforts to address genocidal violence, but the entire realm of scholarship on the politics and poetics of war memory (Carrier 2005; Maier 1997; Novick 2000; Sion 2010; Young 1994; Young 2000b). Research on the commemorative cultures of the states and empires that went to war identifies war memorials and their memory practices as crucial sites for linking past wars to present-day politics (Buruma 1994; Golsan 2006; Igarashi 2007; Niven and Paver 2010; Schwenkel 2009; Yoneyama 1999). Among the important insights to emerge from this literature is the significance of war memorials, and their commemorative practices, as tools for forging national subjectivities, linking individual sentiments to larger historical imaginaries (Echternkamp 2010; Herf 1997).

   The history of memory at the USS *Arizona* Memorial traces a complex genealogy relevant for multiple communities of remembrance. One way to characterize the memorial's path of shifting relevance is from a narrowly focused military shrine to a site seeking to represent multiple national (and international) perspectives responsive to postwar sensibilities and global tourism. And even this simplified genealogy is by no means a linear sequence of distinct phases. A more apt analogy would be a series of paths that converge and diverge at various points, intersecting in ways that affect what counts as collective national memory.

When I began work at the memorial in the early 1990s, the superintendent characterized its importance by telling me that it was the most controversial historical site in the national park system. Evidence for this could be found in the shelf full of binders with letters of complaint to congressional offices, the great majority of which were about aspects of the museum or film that seemed to be "soft" on the Japanese, or about the presence of Japanese visitors or Japanese language signage. Confirming findings of research at the visitor center by Patricia Masters (1991), Marjorie Kelly and I found that park rangers during that time had innumerable stories about anti-Japanese behaviors and sentiments. One recalled a complaint about Japanese-language signs by an American visitor who said, "They [the Japanese] had no trouble finding it in 1941." Another ranger noted that, to his dismay, some American visitors objected to Japanese Americans' ("Orientals") working at the memorial.

The timing and volume of complaint reflects the spike in anti-Japanese sentiments associated with increasing Japanese economic power. At that time, in the 1980s and 1990s, the topic of U.S.-Japan tensions had so permeated popular culture that the Hawaiian comedian Andy Bumatai even recorded a comedic dialogue mimicking American puzzlement that Japanese would be spoken in Hawai'i. That bit, released on CD and included in the audio programming of United Airlines flights in and out of Honolulu, has Bumatai speaking in stereotypical Japanese dialect to perform the confusion of American tourists flying in from the U.S. mainland: "You're cruisin' along and suddenly you hear, [unintelligible Japanese words in exaggerated guttural tone]. [Then, in standard English] "Uhm, where is this plane going? I've already seen Pearl Harbor." Don't get nervous now. The Japanese do not bomb us anymore. Now they buy our land and timeshare it back to us, okay. We got Japanese executives in Waikiki going, [in Japanese accent] "Ano, let's see them make memorial out of this one, ho, ho." [Laughter.] "What fun."[11]

Whereas a Hawai'i-based comedian might be able to joke about anxieties and tensions in American perceptions of the Japanese, superintendents at the memorial were nonetheless busy answering their letters of complaint. Based on anecdotal evidence from my own Japanese acquaintances, the atmosphere of tension they felt in visiting the memorial seemed to diminish during the decade of the 1990s. As one friend recalled, "When I visited Pearl Harbor over twenty years ago, I did not have the nerve to get on the boat to the *Arizona* Memorial. There was some atmosphere there those days which made me hesitate to be there as a Japanese. This time (1999), no such atmosphere any more." (e-mail to the author, December 10, 1999).

One way of answering the question, Why so controversial?, is to point to the historical evolution of the memorial from a place of military burial and ritual remembrance to one of public history and education as well as global tourism. This evolution opened up more possibilities for conflicts between the memorial's multiple roles and identities, including tensions between its original purpose as a national memorial honoring those who died in military service and its move toward a wider relevance as a historic site and educational institution for global audiences. Histories of war, even when presented as strategic or diplomatic histories, are always, at some level, about the valorization of identities—personal, local, regional, ethnic, national, and so forth. International wars are also moments of domestic crisis that expose conflicts already present in national histories of immigration, in ethnic and gender struggles over equality, and in the politics of citizenship generally (Fujitani 2011). The commemoration of war, often governed by a binary logic of nation-states and their enemies, tends to bracket or occlude more localized conflicts, as in the case of Hawaiian or Japanese American memories of Pearl Harbor. Writing a history of American patriotism, John Bodnar (1992, 16) observed that "because numerous interests clash in commemorative events they are inevitably multivocal. . . . In modern America no cultural expression contains the multivocal quality of public commemorations better than the idea of the nation-state and the language of patriotism." And no cultural practice expressing the values and sentiments of patriotism is more well established than the commemoration of war and the valorization of military service.

Seen from the vantage point of Hawai'i, the most striking observation about the postwar career of the *Arizona* memorial, up to the point of the new museum's opening, in 2010, was the absence of the local. While the memorial is the most visited tourist site in the state it is also one of the least visited places for local residents. A survey in 2000 found just 2 percent of visitors to the memorial to be local, from the "Hawaiian Islands" (National Park Service Visitor Study 2000). Although the memorial is located in Hawai'i it has not been, historically, of Hawai'i. In line with its legislated purpose, the USS *Arizona* Memorial is first a national memorial for national audiences (White 1997a). Local residents of Hawai'i simply don't go there very much, unless acting as tour guide for visitors. Because it is located on a U.S. Navy base (although with easy public access) and is operated by a federal agency, the National

Park Service, locals have tended to see it as a military place for tourist visitors. By the mid-2000s, as the new museum was being planned, this absence had become well recognized, to the extent that exhibit designers stated explicitly the need to increase the amount of local content. During museum planning sessions, meetings of stakeholders emphasized this point. Notes from a session in January 2007 indicated that one of the priority "interpretive areas" should be to "find context that will speak to local visitors," noting that the "story of Hawaii is missing from current visitor center" (Munday and Hill 2007b, 4).

Despite its status as an ordinary place-name (one that displaced the Native Hawaiian name for the harbor, Puʻuloa), the phrase *Pearl Harbor*, for most Americans, signifies an event more than a place.[12] The place, however, is part of a geographic locale, entwined in indigenous and local histories that both precede and continue on from the bombing attack. Insofar as the memorial is primarily focused on remembering the event—an event well known in American popular culture precisely because it was circulated nationally in radio broadcasts, newspapers, and newsreels to audiences across the country (said to ask, Where is Pearl Harbor?)—it also works to displace the place with its own social, cultural, and political histories (Kajihiro 2014; Osorio 2010). The tendency of national media to tell a national story that leaves out the local was reproduced when Disney Studios released the blockbuster film *Pearl Harbor*, in 2001, with essentially no depiction of the local, mixed-race society—a fact that was not lost on Hawaiʻi's population, who came out of theaters bemused to see that, once again, local society and history were missing in action.

In addition to the fact that, historically, Pearl Harbor is a national story told by national media for national audiences (from the time news of the attack was broadcast over the radio on a Sunday in December 1941), there are other reasons why local perspectives and stories have not been very visible at the memorial. These relate to the colonial history of Hawaiʻi that saw the depopulation and displacement of the island's native Polynesian population and the importation of large numbers of immigrant labor from Asia, including Japan, China, and the Philippines. Whereas local and ethnic histories are probably muted in most memorials managed by nation-states, in the case of Pearl Harbor, the local is also a (former) colonial territory, in which local voices have historically appealed to and challenged military authority. In different ways, the well-being of both Native Hawaiian and Japanese American residents has been closely tied to the military development in Hawaiʻi and to the aftereffects of the bombing in particular. For Native Hawaiians, concerned to protect land rights, the expansion of military installations accelerated a process of dispossession that began with the illegal overthrow of an indigenous monarchy in 1893 (Fujikane and Okamura 2008; Gonzalez 2013; Howes and Osorio 2010; Laenui 1992; Osorio 2010). And, for their part, Japanese Americans (and noncitizen residents) suffered especially under the wartime internment act that suspended their civil rights, forcibly confined about two thousand, and cast the entire population under a cloud of suspicion (Falgout and Nishigaya 2014). (See appendix 3 for a chronology of wartime internment and subsequent legal and political responses.)

In this book I argue that, although a national memorial, the practice of remembering at the *Arizona* memorial cannot be understood without a closer examination of local society as context. Despite its reinvention as mainstream America in many of the standard histories of the Pearl Harbor attack, Hawai'i is distinctive precisely because it was not typical America in 1941 (whatever that would be). Rather it was an island colony with large indigenous and Asian immigrant populations, located on the edge of American empire, transformed by U.S. economic and strategic interests. It was precisely the potential value of Pearl Harbor as a naval station that first attracted U.S. interest in Hawai'i (see the chronology in appendix 2). And those interests found willing support among the islands' population of American businessmen and plantation owners looking to find a favorable market for the islands' expanding sugar production. The convergence of strategic interest on one side and economic interest on the other led to the negotiation of the Reciprocity Treaty of 1875, which gave island plantation owners unfettered access to U.S. markets and laid the groundwork for U.S. access to Pearl Harbor as a naval base, formalized with the extension of the treaty in 1887. As much as any other single factor, it was the strategic value of Pearl Harbor as a site for a naval base that first focused U.S. interest in Hawai'i at the end of the nineteenth century.

The confluence of U.S. designs on Hawai'i gained momentum at the same time as the Native Hawaiian population was suffering a population collapse fostered by decades of epidemics that decimated Native communities (Stannard 1989). Those demographics, with the shift to a plantation economy, weakened the Hawaiian monarchy and led to the illegal overthrow of the Hawaiian queen Lili'uokalani, in 1893. Initially disavowed by U.S. President Cleveland, the republic proclaimed by the coup plotters was eventually endorsed when the Congress voted to annex Hawai'i in 1898, a year that saw the expansion of U.S. colonial territory in the Pacific in Guam, Hawai'i, and the Philippines. Once the plantation economy was on a path for rapid expansion, it needed labor, leading to the importation of tens of thousands of laborers from Japan, with smaller numbers from China, Portugal, and Korea, with a last large migration from the Philippines in the early twentieth century.

As Hawai'i was becoming an outpost for U.S. economic and strategic interests in the Pacific, it was also developing a distinctive multicultural society in which the mix of Native Hawaiian and Asian immigrant populations would form the basis for an emerging sense of "local," set in opposition to continental (white) American interests represented in Hawai'i's business and military establishment. Throughout its history, this mix of Native Polynesian and Asian and North American settler populations has given Hawai'i a distinctive identity and role in the eyes of mainstream America. Where these points of difference brought doubt and suspicion during the war, they would be construed and reconstrued as an asset in postwar, Cold War Hawai'i, offering bridges between America and Asian societies across the region. The Asian ancestries and transnational ties that were a matter of concern and suspicion during the war would become an asset in postwar, multicultural Hawai'i, most recently in supporting efforts to address themes of peace and reconciliation at the memorial. Early discussion of the purpose and shape of the *Arizona* memorial in the 1950s, as many in Hawai'i were pushing for statehood, included visions of an educational center devoted to building the postwar peace.

Where many embraced statehood as a means of benefiting from integration in the powerful postwar American economy, others saw it, or would look back on it, as another step in the assertion of American control over a native population that used all available legal and political means to resist the original annexation. Although statehood and the expansion of both tourism and military spending in the islands brought prosperity to many, that prosperity was not evenly distributed, leaving many in Native Hawaiian communities with higher rates of poverty, unemployment, incarceration, and ill health—a set of conditions that gave rise to a resurgent movement in the late twentieth century to revitalize Hawaiian language and culture and rebuild a political basis for Native Hawaiian governance (an effort generally referred to as the sovereignty movement; see appendix 2). Revisiting and rethinking Hawai'i's colonial history has been at the center of this broad-based movement in the Native Hawaiian community. Whereas the sense of "local" has been a historical point of solidarity between indigenous and immigrant Asian communities in Hawai'i, the rise of sentiments for Native Hawaiian sovereignty has also repositioned Hawai'i's Asian minorities as "settler colonists" (Fujikane and Okamura 2008).

Given the history briefly sketched here, the politics of cultural identity and citizenship for Native Hawaiian and Japanese American residents in Hawai'i have been particularly acute in the memorial spaces of Pearl Harbor. Discussion at the evening panel cited above illustrates well these fault lines in public memory. To focus on these conversations is not to ignore the overriding force of the memorial's original and continuing purpose in honoring military sacrifice. Just the opposite, attending to some of these edges of dominant memory works to better understand the core (unmarked) focus of the memorial in honoring those who died in the attack in 1941 and their living counterparts, veteran survivors, and those in active service today.

The Sacred Spaces of Memorial Tourism

With the rise of poststatehood tourism and the construction of a visitor center open to visitors of all kinds, it was inevitable that the memorial, as a social space, would be defined in part by the tensions and contradictions embedded in Hawai'i's social history. Ironically, the position and history of Hawai'i's Japanese American community, surrounded by conflict in wartime, have facilitated opportunities for transnational commemorative activities in the postwar period. Given the memorial's primary focus on military remembrance, the emergence of new narratives and new constituencies inevitably creates moments of conflict in which distinct and at times dissonant narratives collide. This book examines a number of such moments, over a period of three decades that witnessed rapid expansion of the site, in order to better understand the intersections of power, emotion, and memory that make different histories possible, and powerful, in the memorial context.

The incorporation of the USS *Arizona* Memorial within the World War II Valor in the Pacific National Monument has not replaced the institution's original purpose, so much as expanded its scope and context. The fact that the memorial is a military burial site anchors its significance as sacred space—a quality expressed in regular commemorative activities honoring military service. In earlier writings I put the word *sacred* in quotes, but there is nothing metaphorical about the application of the term to the shrine built over the sunken battleship, at least for those who attend to the ship as a burial place.

The sacralization of the memorial's space is evident in its architecture, in ritual practices, in efforts to regulate and direct tourist visitation, and in regular debates and discussion about ways to protect and preserve memory. Both the physical space of the memorial and its ritual practices are surrounded by various kinds of taboo and prohibition that serve to remind the public of their significance. The most obvious way the sacred is made manifest is in the material and spatial arrangements of Pearl Harbor in which the ship, or memorial, and visitor center, also a museum, are physically separated by the waters of the harbor. The experience of leaving the busy visitor center to travel by boat

FIGURE I.2

USS *Arizona* Memorial shrine room, wall of names. December 7, 2005.
Photo by author.

across the harbor to the memorial over the USS *Arizona* creates an experience of passage, of boundary-crossing that further defines the sacred quality of the shrine.

In like manner, the memorial spanning the sunken ship itself offers up yet another spatial opposition that accentuates the memorial's sacred space, by placing the shrine room, with its wall of names of all those who died on the ship, at the opposite end of the platform from the dock where visitors arrive by boat. Stepping off the boat, one enters the structure and walks across the breezy memorial platform before entering the shrine room at the far end, finding oneself in an enclosed, contemplative atmosphere facing the imposing wall of names.

For the attentive visitor who notices additional names added to an unfinished list on two marble benches—the names of crew members who survived the bombing but later in life requested that their ashes be placed in the ship—there is further evidence for the personal significance of the ship for its crew, continuing to the end of life and beyond.

To understand the emotional and political power evoked by the memorial and the constellation of practices associated with it, it is useful to be reminded of the essentially religious nature of state ceremony focused on the remembrance of death in war (Handelman and Shamgar-Handelman 1997; Mosse 1990; Tumarkin 1994). Here is George Mosse on the religiosity of war memorials in interwar Europe: "The burial and commemoration of the war dead were analogous to the construction of a church for the nation, and the planning of such sacred spaces received much the same kind of attention as that given to the architecture of churches" (1990, 32–33). Whether in burial plots, grave markers, inscriptions in memorial walls, or the stories that are reproduced in memorial ceremonies and national media, war dead remain in perpetual service to the nation (1990). Gillis writes that "in the interwar period the spirit and image of the fallen were repeatedly mobilized on film as well as in political rhetoric to serve a variety of causes. . . . They had become the very embodiment of national identities" (Gillis 1994, 11; see also Inglis 1993). To make a similar point, Benedict Anderson opened his classic treatise on nationalism with discussion of cenotaphs and tombs of Unknown Soldiers: "No more arresting emblems of the modern culture of nationalism exist than cenotaphs and tombs of Unknown Soldiers" (1991, 9). The political scientist John Hutchinson, writing on "war and sacralisation," sees these practices creating a "sacred community of sacrifice" (Hutchinson 2009, 401). In short, military burial sites are among the most acute signifiers of selfless sacrifice—that key word and core value in national military culture.

The sacred quality of the memorial shrine is evident in regular ceremonial activities that usually take the form of two-part affairs with a large public event at the visitor center or a shore-side naval facility, followed by a smaller invitation-only event conducted on the memorial itself, in which representatives of the navy and veterans groups make wreath offerings inside (and just outside) the shrine room. It is in these activities that the importance of the memorial as a burial place, evocative of bonds among servicemen and servicewomen, past and present, is most clearly marked with practices and protocols similar to those regularly conducted at America's military cemeteries and memorials. Whereas tourist encounters have their own immediacy and materiality, it is in military ceremony that the USS *Arizona* Memorial most powerfully renders the abstract idea of America personal through remembrance practices and the discourse of sacrifice.

The sentiments associated with violent death and loss evident at the sunken ship are potentially available in the tourist experience as well, depending on the travelers and their interactions with the semiotic landscape of the memorial, including museum exhibits, audio and video narration, and personal presentations. Just as that landscape has changed radically from the 1960s to the 1980s to the present, so the increasing numbers and diversity of people visiting the memorial have inevitably loosened the ways visitors engage with the place and its history. The rapid growth in the number of tourist visitors poses the question, Will tourists even engage at all? Or are they more likely to pass through as one stop on a Hawaiian holiday? For some decades now, Park Service rangers charged with monitoring the memorial have reflected on the challenges posed by tourist visitors who arrive with no idea of the place or its significance.

The extent to which travelers "get" the sacred quality of the place is socially present in people's comportment in and around the memorial itself. For the park service, stipulating proper behavior for that space has been a last line of defense against a tourist mindset deemed inappropriate to a shrine (see chapter 4). When visitors settle into the theater to see the orientation film, a park ranger (formerly a person, now a video recording) conveys the memorial's significance and reminds visitors of the need for respectful behavior. When that message was delivered in person, the memorial's historian drafted this into a standardized set of welcome remarks: "The Memorial itself deserves special respect. The ship after all is the final resting place for the crew of the *Arizona*. It is their tomb. Out of respect for this cemetery-like atmosphere, we ask that you keep your voices low while at the Memorial. It is a place where you can reflect on the past and contemplate the future" (Martinez 1997). It is my sense that stewards of the memorial regarded the absence of meaning (or feeling) as a greater problem in the early decades of the visitor center. But this urgency has dissipated with the passing of generations and the creation of the larger rubric of the World War II Valor in the Pacific National Monument. More recently, there has been some disagreement among site managers about the importance of conveying the "cemetery-like" significance of the memorial to visitors. Whatever the case, these ambiguities, and the discussions they evoke, offer insight into the cultures of commemoration at Pearl Harbor.

Veterans and Survivors: Emotionalizing History

For patriotic sentiments to remain relevant, they have to be given life through practice and performance—practices that imbue national narratives with personal significance. What kinds of experience and what kinds of institutional practice have the power to do that? How do national imaginings become affective and moving, even moving people to sacrifice themselves? Among all the memorial practices at Pearl Harbor perhaps the most potent symbol is the image of the citizen-soldier—the individual person caught up in larger histories of national war. In this context, those killed in the attack become individuals who died "for us." And today's surviving veterans are their living counterpart. In the memorial context, veterans were always the most effective means for evoking personal engagement with histories that otherwise might remain abstract or alien, semiotic tools for thinking and feeling the nation.

Looking across the diversity of modern wars and national military cultures, it is clear that the figure of the veteran has acquired a wide array of valences, embodying diverse possibilities for person-state relations. Of the appropriation of past heroes in Israeli commemorative culture, Handelman writes, "Rituals of commemoration . . . draw on nationalized myths to connect contemporary citizens with past heroes" (2008, 24). In addition to the affirming sentiments associated with heroic soldiers, the figure of the veteran may also condense more ambivalent sentiments, such as the shame associated with a defeated Japan (Dower 2010; Igarashi 2007) or the "spat upon" Vietnam War veteran in America (Lembcke 1998).[13]

In the social realities of the memorial the presence of the citizen-soldier, both those who died and those who survived, is constantly evident. Veterans are the focus of veneration in ceremonial events, honored guests at public functions, the subjects of texts and videos promoted at the site, and, until recently, a regular embodied presence in the person of aging volunteers. Pearl Harbor survivors, during their prime, would speak about their war experience in a variety of contexts and media, opening up a multitude of possibilities for self-fashioning in media, memoirs, and ordinary storytelling. Anniversary ceremonies always included moments of ritualized gratitude directed toward Pearl Harbor veterans and veterans of the Second World War. In recent years, ceremonies have concluded with a "walk of honor," in which aging veterans, many in wheelchairs, are assisted in an applause-wrapped departure from the ceremonies (figure 2.2).

History, even in textbooks, rarely presents itself directly. Most often the past enters awareness through someone's voice, through embodied practices, and through particular modes of representation (Wertsch 2002). The presence of a small cadre of survivors at the *Arizona* memorial in the 1990s and 2000s became a central feature of the institution's "history lessons," an embodied presence in the institution's culture of commemoration that uses semiotic and ritual practices to place citizen-soldiers at the center of emotional narratives of war and national history. When Pearl Harbor survivors speak, the fact of their experience frames their speech as authentic, as having something to say about events of shared national significance. The survivor voice is typically testimonial, speaking of personal experience as a token of larger narratives often familiar to their audiences. Survivors speak with the authority of experience, as "witnesses" who command a certain degree of attention and respect by virtue of the fact of personal involvement in historic events. The frame of "war veteran" identity is so palpable that it is customary for veterans asked to speak about their war service to begin with a disclaimer that they are not heroes, even though the term *hero* is regularly extended to all war veterans.

The presence of survivor testimony in the context of memorials and museums calls attention to the complicated intersections of history and memory that, at times, are read as the difference between professionalized history and personal recollection. Where personal memory derives its authenticity from experience, it also must contend with the assumption that individual memory is given to distortions of bias, perspective, and power. Whereas the registers of academic and public history often speak in a detached, inclusive voice, acts of remembering are most poignantly expressed in the experiential voice of individuals and communities, in the emotional registers of testimonials and witnessing (Linenthal 1993; Wieviorka 2006). Although the immediacy and directness of personal recollection provides one kind of narrative authority, the authority of the speaker is undercut by assumptions that personal recollections are given to both error and bias: error from cognitive limitations and bias from the effects of perspective and power. In the context of the *Arizona* memorial, all of these ambivalences were evident during the 1990s and 2000s when veteran survivors were most active at the memorial.

One of the most commonly heard refrains in descriptions of the memorial is that it evokes strong emotions. At the center of this emotionality is the experience of death and loss, signified by the ship as tomb but also in the narratives of veteran survivors. The Pearl Harbor veterans who volunteered their time at the memorial in the 1990s developed a variety of strategies for expressing their own emotionality as they would tell their own stories and interact with the panorama of people coming through the visitor center. Traces of these interactions would often find their way into comment sheets full of emotive statements from travelers of all kinds, affected by the catastrophic events and ordinary lives represented there.

One veteran volunteer, talking in a recorded interview in 1994, referred to the importance of emotions for the work he sought to do in conveying something of the meaning and importance of the history to tourist audiences. In talking about his effort to get visitors to "feel the real experience" he spoke about his aim in the two-to-three-minute introduction he would make to the film watched prior to boarding a boat to visit the memorial. He said, "I want them [the audience] to see this as an experience; not just as a tourist attraction. I want them to feel the real experience. There is the hurt, anger, and pain, and there are still dead bodies out there in the ship's hull (Visitor Center theater, June 29, 1994). It is clear that the speaker conceives of the memorial space as one that requires active emotion work (Hochschild 1983) to create a "real experience," in opposition to the ever-present threat of trivialization or commodification in Hawai'i's environment of holiday travel and tropical pleasures. In this context, the lack of emotion is read as a sign of detachment, the sort expected with tourism that brings people to the memorial as an attraction that offers a (free) boat ride and outing to a scenic and historic part of the island. In the early decades of the visitor center, the problem of creating a memorial experience in a tourist economy was a constant in discussions of those who manage the memorial.

But what sort of emotions? And how much is enough? Can you have too much? After all, evoking the real experience of war in the context of postwar peace can be dangerous. Indeed, from the very first moments in which the National Park Service began to develop a plan for presenting a history of the attack to tourist travelers visiting the new visitor center, they worried about the potential of the memorial to engender animosity and hatred toward Japan, something that would be contrary to decades of work to build positive relations that support a Cold War security alliance. At a local level, the state economy of Hawai'i looked to Japan as a major tourism market and source of investment, a relationship reinforced by extensive cultural ties between Hawai'i's community of Americans of Japanese Ancestry and Japan. By the 1990s, Japanese visitors to the memorial accounted for about 10 percent of the total (the largest nationality of foreign visitors), evoking both critical comments from some American visitors as well as curiosity about what "they" felt in visiting the place—a question addressed in research by Patricia Masters (1991) and Yujin Yaguchi (2005).[14]

In this context, the standards imposed by the National Park Service for "balanced" interpretations of history that do not "take sides" provided guidelines for presenting Pearl Harbor history in ways that are well adapted to broadening the audiences for the memorial's history in the context of global tourism. The first "Interpretive Prospectus" outlining these issues was clear about the dilemma faced by park interpreters. Describing the mix of "anger and pathos" and "pride" that many Americans associate with Pearl Harbor, and the sensitivities of the Japanese, the prospectus noted that "these factors . . . place an especially heavy burden on the interpretive staff of the USS *Arizona* Memorial to ensure that the interpretive program is forthright, honest, totally accurate, and presented to visitors without a spirit of malice (Cummins 1981, 1). Note that choices among different narratives are here described in terms of emotion (malice). Indeed, during the 1990s and 2000s when survivors were actively talking about their memories of the attack, giving scheduled presentations that used a number of affective styles, their presentations would be reviewed by the park service historian and, where needed, adjusted to be sure that they did not contain content offensive to visitors, both national and international.

But here again, the potential for offensive content in a memorial that honors those who fought in the Pacific War, a war that John Dower rightly dubbed a "war without mercy" (1986) is always there, even if diminishing with the passing of years. To the extent that the goal is to memorialize the actual "experience of war," by those who fought it, the approach of the park service to "balanced history" is easily criticized as a disservice to the sensibilities of those who fought the war.[15] This was precisely the view put forward in an editorial by the columnist Thomas Sowell, a fellow at the Hoover Institute, at the time of the fiftieth anniversary titled "PARK SERVICE TURNS ITS BACK ON PATRIOTISM":

> Now an agency of the government itself seems to have turned its back on patriotism, and on the bodies of more than a thousand young Americans whose bodies are still trapped in the sunken battleships at the bottom of Pearl Harbor. The National Park Service, which is in charge of the Pearl Harbor memorial and of the 50th anniversary commemoration, has bent over backward to give a "neutral" presentation of Japan's sneak attack on an America at peace.
>
> According to an official of the Park Service at Pearl Harbor the agency's role is "not to moralize but to present history without condemning or condoning." Bitter protests by veterans who were there during that murderous attack leave this bureaucrat unmoved.
>
> "These critics want us to say that Japan stabbed us in the back," he said. "We can't say that." If this honcho is too squeamish to say it then surely there must be someone else in the Park Service who puts his country, and the truth, above "political correctness." That someone ought to be in charge of this memorial.
>
> Being nonjudgmental is one of the petty fetishes of our time. But a nonjudgmental monument is a contradiction in terms. We build monu-

ments precisely because we have made a judgment. (Sowell, *Honolulu Star-Bulletin*, December 11, 1991, A16)

Sowell, in his criticism, like critics of the Smithsonian's atomic bomb exhibit a few years later, held up the importance of honoring the war's veterans as the primary purpose of commemoration, expressing values of patriotism and military service. The fuller text of his editorial paints a picture of veterans doing battle with park service interpreters over "patriotic" versus "politically correct" history. The editorial, written in a style that Richard Hofstadter identified decades ago as the "paranoid style" in American politics (1964), speaks at a distance with little knowledge of context. Yet, by assuming, even expecting, the worst of a state agency (the NPS), the author amplifies the voice of grievance and the likelihood of provoking moral outrage among readers. Although the editorial's exaggerated statements miss the close and constructive relations that the park service worked to create with Pearl Harbor survivors over the years, they do capture important elements of the philosophy of history that informs National Park Service programs at national historic sites.

Having said that veterans mounted "bitter protests," Sowell went on to construct a picture of open emotional conflict between veterans and NPS guides: "Park Service guides have gotten into shouting matches with veterans, as those guides have pushed the Japanese side of the story, claiming that an American-sponsored oil embargo helped provoke the attack." While veterans organizations such as the American Legion have weighed in with written complaints from time to time, to the best of my knowledge, there has been only one incident in the history of the memorial (in 1991) when a veteran who vocally challenged work on new exhibits was asked to leave the grounds.[16] In marked contrast to this flash point, the stewards of the USS *Arizona* Memorial have consistently pursued a policy of close cooperation with veterans and veterans groups, particularly the Pearl Harbor Survivors Association and its local "Aloha" chapter in Honolulu, while they existed. As discussed in the next chapter, Pearl Harbor survivors and veterans of the Second World War and other wars have been extensively incorporated into the daily routines of the memorial. While Pearl Harbor survivors were numerous and active, managers of the memorial usually looked to them as a sounding board in developing films, exhibits, and programs.

The gap between editorial charge and the reality of patriotism on the ground at the *Arizona* memorial illustrates the complexity of the memorial as a site of and for national imagination, a place where the stakes of history for the present are argued out in public debates about how "we" remember or should remember. The extent to which veterans are invoked in the Sowell essay is notable, making for a presence that assumes unique rhetorical force in debates about war history and memory. The picture painted in the editorial is one in which the veteran is a locus of authentic memory, whose protests most genuinely challenge distortions in memory at risk not only from foreign pressures (from a vanquished enemy) but also from the state, in the form of an unfeeling bureaucracy that uses "balanced history" for political purposes.

Despite its paranoid reading of what was going on at the memorial in 1991, Sowell's essay exhibits a certain prescience in describing tensions between competing historiographies that would play out in years to come. Where memorializing practices in the immediate aftermath of the attack aimed to put the focus on the American military men and women killed in a murderous attack (evoking the anger and outrage expected in response to a deep national injury), management of the memorial after the visitor center was built sought to broaden and diversify the narrative, while keeping the sacred core. The affective politics of those developments are marked by efforts to broaden the moral and emotional dimensions of the memorial's history, beyond that associated with the death of American servicemen and servicewomen. Here is the NPS historian introducing the orientation film for an audience being prepared to visit the memorial: "For most of you today, this journey back to the days of 1941 will probably evoke some kind of feeling or emotion: sadness, despair, maybe even anger. Places where tragic events unfolded may evoke such feelings. For the people of Hawaii, the United States and the world, lives were changed forever. World War II was now truly global. When the smoke and the dust of the war settled in 1945, nearly 55 million people were dead" (Martinez 1997).

In this exhortation, expressions of emotion index the salience of past events for their audiences, indicating that they are (or ought to be) relevant to anyone in the audience, anyone from around the world visiting the memorial. The speaker, addressing a global audience, states that the story of Pearl Harbor "will probably evoke some kind of feeling or emotion." Of all the kinds of emotion mentioned, the "anger" of wartime, inscribed so prominently in the call in 1941 to "Remember Pearl Harbor," to fight a war, is now a last possibility ("maybe even anger") after "sadness" or "despair." The contrast in possible emotions reflects shifts in postwar memories of Pearl Harbor associated with an expanding community of remembrance, from Americans in military service to "the people of Hawaii, the U.S. and the world." In this idealized vision, the memorial becomes a global memorial. The tensions involved in this transformation are coded, bureaucratically, in the transition implemented by the park service from memorial to monument.

Just as the audiences for the memorial have been expanding in social space, so have they been changing with time. The most important change at the time of writing this book is the passing of the Second World War generation. The war generation might be expected not simply to "gaze" on the history of the memorial, but to connect personally, as a pilgrimage, marked by ritual offerings and personal feelings. As the generation that knew the war as part of their own experience passes away, what are the consequences for public memory and the work of memorialization? Most obviously, no longer will people arrive at the memorial with the kind of background knowledge acquired of events that occur in one's lifetime, already understanding the magnitude and importance of those events for world history, or family biographies, or both. Will engagements with history at the memorial become, at best, academic or, at worst, simply superficial? With the passing of generations, what is the potential for national history to become part of personal history? What is the role of memorial practice or historical discourse in answering that question?

The disappearance of the veterans who fought in the Second World War has been noted by various writers and filmmakers for well over a decade. (In his seven-part documentary *The War*, which aired in 2007, Ken Burns observed that one thousand veterans were dying each day.) The war generation, of course, was always a core constituency for the memorial, particularly veterans of the Second World War and Pearl Harbor survivors. Not only are veterans held up as objects of veneration, but their voices speak loudly in contexts of commemoration where it is their service and their relations with lost comrades that position the veteran as an embodiment of ideals of sacrifice. If, as Thomas Sowell implied, veteran and survivor memory have been a kind of patriotic litmus test for the authenticity of memorial history, will the passing of the generation of Second World War warriors relax the constraints on what is possible in the memorial context? Indeed, some of those working at the memorial suggested something like this in the 1980s and 1990s, when hostility toward Japan peaked in the veteran community. Would the generation of Second World War warriors have to pass from the scene before it would be possible to further expand and develop the memorial in ways that would embrace multiple perspectives, including even that of the former enemy turned ally?

Although subsequent developments in commemorative practices associated with the transition from memorial to monument suggest just such a path, closer attention to the role of veterans in memorial activities and events explodes the view that veterans speak with a singular voice or share the same subjectivity in regard to war memory and emotion. Emily Rosenberg described this diversity in her account of activities during the fiftieth anniversary of Pearl Harbor, when efforts to engineer expressions of reconciliation met with both acceptance and resistance in the American veteran community. Reviewing these conflicting moves, she concluded that "the commemorative year of 1991 drew lessons to suit every persuasion" (Rosenberg 2004, 103). Considering this rainbow of possibilities, we might ask further what conditions enable different types of historical sentiment and commemorative practice. More specifically, in relation to the *Arizona* memorial, what is the role of memorial sites in facilitating transformations in the emotional meanings of history? In fact, the interest of Japanese and American veterans in expressions of reconciliation began precisely in the context of a conference at the fiftieth anniversary of Pearl Harbor, in 1991. And these interests would later develop into a series of exchanges and ceremonial events, at the memorial as well as in Japan, ultimately leaving one of the most remarkable legacies of the Pacific War.

Whereas some might read the passing of the generation of Second World War veterans as opening up new possibilities for memorializing the war beyond the original focus on the sacrifices of American servicemen, an alternative reading asks what happens to memorialization when witnessing is done without (living) witnesses, where the subjectivity of veterans will be mediated by electronic distillations in the form of recorded testimonies, memoirs, historical texts, documentary film, and so forth. Many scholars of Second World War remembrance, particularly in regard to the Holocaust, have pondered these sorts of questions. James Young, in his book *At Memory's Edge*, finds that the post-Holocaust generation of descendants is troubled by questions of memory and representation. In the work of artists and writers such as Art Spiegelman (author of *Maus: A Survivor's Tale*), he finds a "generation no longer willing or able to recall the Holocaust separately from the ways it has been passed down." In particular, he asks, "What happens to memory when it ceases to be testimony?" (Young 2000b; and compare Hirsch on "postmemory," 2008). In particular, we might ask, how will electronically mediated witnessing affect the construction of national histories, sentiments, and subjectivities in future historiographies and commemorative activities?

On Memorial Ethnography

Insofar as the word *memory* in ordinary language usually references individual memory and the psychology of recall, talk of collective memory seems problematic. In the social sciences, at least, it is surrounded by suspicions of reification and misplaced concreteness. Maurice Halbwachs's (Coser 1992) notion of social frameworks of memory is cited positively by those who seek to rescue memory from individual minds, and negatively by those who assume that real memory is essentially about individual cognition. Writing on the eve of the so-called boom in memory studies (Berliner 2005; Klein 2000; Radstone 2008), two historians asked the question, "Collective Memory—What Is It?," quoting Amos Funkenstein to the effect that "consciousness and memory can only be realized by an individual who acts, is aware, and remembers. Just as a nation cannot eat or dance, neither can it speak or remember. Remembering is a mental act, and therefore it is absolutely and completely personal" (Gedi and Elam 1996, 34). The authors argued that the term *collective memory* could only be metaphorical.

Braving the dangers of this mystical realm, my approach to collective memory looks precisely outside the individual to the social and semiotic processes that represent the past. I find those performative and interactional moments to be a good place to ask how representations of history acquire their potency, both political and emotional. I focus particularly on the ways people interact with history's inscriptions in the landscape, including museum exhibits, film, ceremonial practices, and tourism. In my usage, memorial history is neither individual nor collective, but rather a contingent achievement, constantly re-created in the contexts and constraints of the memorial as a certain kind of institution.

With this in mind, my approach to studying memory and memorialization is at base social and cultural. Much of the literature on monuments, memorials, and museums uses textual and visual modes of analysis to examine them through their architecture, exhibits, and ceremonial speeches. Anthropological studies of tourism tend to be more interactive, looking at the ways travelers engage with historic sites (for example, Macdonald 2009). In this study, working primarily in the institutional spaces of memorial memory-making, I focus on social practices through which representations of history are produced, understood, and critiqued (compare to Connerton 1989; Connerton 2011). Despite the expansion of museum studies in anthropology (Clifford 1997; Karp et al. 1992; Kirshenblatt-Gimblett 1998), very few projects have pursued long-term fieldwork in museums and memorials as institutions (for exceptions, see Handler and Gable 1997; Price 2007), much less the domestic spaces where intimate, local, and cosmopolitan memories intermingle (but see Kwon 2006).

Here I argue for an approach that is both historical (capable of tracing transformations through time) and ethnographic (focusing on the creation of meaning and emotion in everyday interaction), utilizing sustained fieldwork to identify contexts and connections that give histories their significance.

Memorials do not consist of disembodied symbols that somehow speak for themselves; rather they are sites in which multiple agencies actively produce representations of the past that are themselves in history. Whereas much of this work can be done, and is done, at a distance, it also requires being present, listening to and interacting with the people who speak about the histories represented, as in the case of the speakers quoted at the beginning of this introduction. Doing close-up ethnography attempts to understand the affective and experiential valences of memorial practice by attending to the things that people say, do, and feel in memorial spaces, and listening to the small "negotiations" that occur in ordinary interaction, while not losing sight of larger structures that continually influence memorial institutions.

The challenges of my previous fieldwork in the Solomon Islands, which included producing a dictionary of a vernacular language (1988) and writing an ethnographic history of colonial transformations (1991), seem more straightforward than those encountered in the homework I've been doing at Pearl Harbor. Pursuing an ethnographic study of an institution that is intensely public, both highly regulated and embedded in transnational and global circuits of culture, requires choices—choices of what to look at, who to talk to, where to be, and so on. When the field is also home, one is constantly aware of the flow of activities and events that are outside the scope of research, making one more aware than ever that ethnography is always to some degree a patchwork of opportunity. And yet, the longer the involvement, the more likely it is that larger contours emerge from a multitude of minute moments.

Some of the choices involved with my fieldwork and my representation of what goes on at the memorial are constrained by the very same relations of power that shape its representations. I have developed my understanding on the basis of work on site and relations with the National Park Service and its nonprofit partner, Pacific Historic Parks. On the other hand, I've had only minimal involvement with military and corporate interests that are clearly also important in shaping the institutions that memorialize Pearl Harbor. Working at Pearl Harbor, one is continually reminded of the military and corporate interests that support memorialization at Pearl Harbor. It is not difficult for the casual visitor to glimpse these on donor boards displaying the major contributors to the fundraising campaign that built the new visitor center or the list of sponsors who supported making a new orientation film in the 1990s, the majority of whom are major defense contractors, including the Northrop Grumman Corporation, Boeing, General Dynamics, and the Raytheon Company. The same names appear as major donors for the other ship and plane museums of Pearl Harbor, as well, the USS *Bowfin* Submarine Museum and Park, the Battleship *Missouri* Memorial, and the Pacific Aviation Museum Pearl Harbor. Chapter 4 tells the story of the navy-directed expansion of military museums that unfolded in the 1990s and 2000s, punctuated with an account of my own involvement when I was invited to serve on an exhibit review panel for the Pacific Aviation Museum. That account serves as a glimpse of the contrasts to be found between the historical practices of the National Park Service as public agency and smaller, private enterprises focused more narrowly on legacies of the military service branches.

In my case, research at Pearl Harbor over a span of decades facilitated the development of relationships with many of the principals involved with the memorial, especially veteran survivors and a number of National Park Service staff. From the time I first began fieldwork, in 1994, the interest and cooperation shown by the National Park Service afforded opportunities for involvement that would not have been possible without that agency's openness. Those relationships, in turn, led to an invitation in 2001 to join the board of directors of the *Arizona* Memorial Museum Association (later renamed Pacific Historic Parks). As one of the few academics on a board that originated with navy veterans and now exemplifies a cross-section of Honolulu's business community, my role with that organization quickly gravitated to the development of educational programs. These professional involvements opened windows and doors for ethnography, creating opportunities for the kind of engaged research that informs analysis of the social dimensions of memorialization. At the same time, gaining access also means locating and bounding fieldwork in ways that ultimately shape my own perspective. I've attempted to write the chapters that follow with enough reflexivity to remind the reader of these locations.

The story told in this book is organized around the narrative of my own fieldwork, tracing a path of memory-making from the intensive national spotlight placed on Pearl Harbor in the 1990s (a period of fiftieth anniversaries), through the appearance of other military museums around Pearl Harbor at the turn of the century, to the construction of an expanded visitor complex and the creation of the World War II Valor in the Pacific National Monument in 2008 and the new museum in 2010. Although I did not originally conceive of this project as a history of memory, it has become that simply by virtue of the passage of time. The sequence of topics taken up in the chapters that follow reflect that history of remembering, with early chapters focusing largely on the representation of Japan and Japan-America relations, followed by debates about the way Japanese Americans have been included in memorial histories. It is only in the later chapters, when I discuss the design of the new museum and the creation of educational programs, that I return to the question of Native Hawaiian histories and perspectives, reflecting their relative absence during the early decades of the memorial.

The longue durée of this project opens up a perspective on memorial history-making as a process—a process that becomes most visible in moments of institutional change, as in making a new film or the creation of a new museum. In addition to these critical junctures of institutional change, the longitudinal perspective of this project also makes it possible to examine a number of moments of controversy in which memorial history and its representation became objects of criticism and debate. In separate chapters, I explore changing commemorative practices, the production of a new documentary film for the visitor center, the reconstruction of the visitor center itself, including the design of a new museum, and, finally, the organization of teacher programs— all multiyear projects in which Pearl Harbor history and its representation became subjects of discussion, debate, and controversy. Focusing on these moments of negotiation brings home the book's core arguments that memorial memory is, first, thoroughly social, and, second, surrounded by diverse alterhistories that leave behind their own influences on historical sensibilities, even if they are not inscribed in memorial architecture.

When the messages of memorial history are challenged directly, as they were when Japanese American citizens objected to the depiction of Japanese Americans in the memorial's documentary film (see chapter 3), or in an exhibit about the crash landing and killing of a Japanese pilot on the Hawaiian island of Niʻihau (see chapter 4), we are reminded that history, especially memorial history, is never fixed in words or images but depends on an active interpretive process that may produce quite different moral and emotional readings among different constituencies. The penultimate chapter discusses a final case of controversy that also serves as a reminder of my own position as ethnographer and actor in this story. On Veterans Day in 2010 the Sean Hannity Fox News program characterized a teacher program that I had directed as an insult to the U.S. military, reminding me and other participants of the fraught environment in which educators take up memorializing histories, however respectful of their commemorative value.

One

With the rise of tourism in Hawai'i and the construction of a visitor center to accommodate tourists, the memorial became an institution that not only honors the dead, but also elaborates on the history of the attack. The process of expanding the scope and reach of the memorial, begun in 1980, would only accelerate in the decades to come, with the redesign and expansion of the visitor center in the 2000s (see map 1.1). Despite the growth of these expanded facilities (discussed in chapter 4), the basic interpretive "tour" offered by the National Park Service is much the same today as it was when the first visitor center opened. Then, as today, the principal axis for a visit involves arriving at the center, viewing the twenty-three-minute documentary film, and then taking a boat operated by the U.S. Navy out to the memorial spanning the sunken battleship. Additional time may be spent in the museum or wandering the landscape with its wayside exhibits overlooking the harbor. This axis establishes a spatial opposition between the secular activities of the visitor center, onshore, and the "sacred" site of the memorial. It is this mix of sacred and secular, of commemoration and education, navigated in diverse ways by visitors from around the world, that has framed much of the work of memorialization (or "remembrance") at Pearl Harbor as multiple constituencies and stakeholders interact with the site.

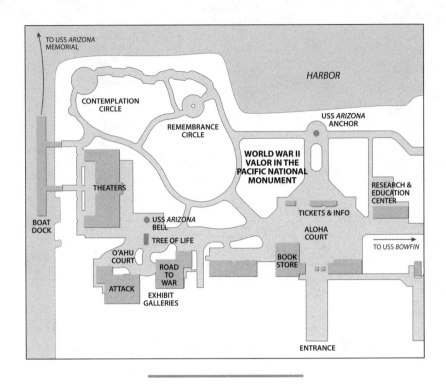

MAP 1.1

World War II Valor in the Pacific National Monument, visitor center.

The one major difference since 1980, and one that has had repercussions that are still being absorbed at the memorial, is the accelerating disappearance of Pearl Harbor survivors (primarily, but not entirely, military veteran survivors of the attack). Everyone visiting the USS *Arizona* Memorial in the 1990s and 2000s would have noticed the prominent presence of Pearl Harbor survivors. By 2010, when the new visitor center opened, that presence had diminished dramatically as the number of able-bodied veterans of the Second World War volunteering their time decreased to just a handful, with none on the premises much of the time. As noted earlier, the disappearance of veteran survivors at the memorial was happening at the very time that the visitor center was redesigned as a gateway to the gallery of museum and memorial sites around Pearl Harbor. The convergence of these factors meant a transition from a smaller space in which the presence of veterans loomed large to a more expansive, architecturally complex area in which veteran survivors are mostly encountered through audio and video presentations in the center's museum and audio tour. What are the implications of this transition, combined with the generational shift in visitors themselves, for the ways visitors come to understand and feel the past at the memorial? In considering this question, I begin with a close-up look at activities around the memorial visitor center in the 1990s, a period of heightened national interest in Pearl Harbor and memories of the Second World War. My account draws on conversations with veterans and observation of their presentations, as background for discussing the transition to an era of virtual witnessing.

The importance of veterans of the Pearl Harbor attack for the work of the *Arizona* memorial during its early decades exemplifies a more general phenomenon common at war memorial sites, where firsthand witnessing often figures centrally in the modalities through which the past is presented, understood, and experienced. In such places former combatants or survivors, civilian or military, participate in the narrative re-creation of historical events in the first-person, "I was there" voice of personal experience. In doing so, they describe events in terms that facilitate empathy and identification with historical actors. The extensive literature on witnessing at sites of violence suggests that the voices of survivors and veterans are uniquely effective in creating moral and emotional meaning for audiences interpreting historical events.

Scholarly discussion of the discourse of witnessing war and violence is most developed in relation to the Holocaust (Hoffman 2004; Wieviorka 2006; Young 2000a). Even though Holocaust victims and survivors have come to epitomize the suffering of civilians in the Second World War, the Holocaust literature shows that the ability to recall, narrate, or publicly perform memories of war is itself shaped by shifting social conditions that were not, and are not, always favorable to narratives of victimization. Here is Eva Hoffman on the shift in societal interest in Holocaust survivor stories and the multiplication of public spaces for their telling:

> After years when social allusions to the Holocaust were greeted with embarrassed silence or sternly nipped in the bud, every dinner party for a while seems to revert to this somber subject, as if it were an irresistible, darkly compelling magnet. Survivors, so shunned in earlier decades, are sent to suburban high schools, interviewed, begged for their tales from hell. Their children, after having the most part succeeded in blending indistinguishably with their peer culture, become an object of respectful interest. We had been close to the real thing. Our parents had those kinds of stories. We had been touched by horror, by hardship, by history. (2004, 154)

In contrast to the turn toward memorializing civilian experience in the Second World War throughout much of Europe and Asia and the Pacific (Williams

2007; Winter and Sivan 1999), American memory of the war has remained steadfastly focused on the experience of military veterans. For most Americans, the Second World War was experienced through battles fought elsewhere. It was not a conflict that raged through U.S. cities and towns as it did in Europe and Asia and the Pacific. Hence Americans more often recall the war through the eyes and stories of the military veterans who fought overseas—veterans whose experience brought the war into the domestic spaces of American families. Pearl Harbor is importantly ambiguous in this respect. Even though Hawai'i was a U.S. colony ("Territory of Hawaii") and not a state at the time, the attack is always recalled as an attack on America, as if Hawai'i had already been a state. Whereas the attack killed forty-nine civilians and wounded many more, and led to four years of martial law that brought constant hardships to the civilian population, the raison d'être of the memorial and the primary focus of its memorial mission is the sacrifice and service of U.S. military servicemen and servicewomen. This veteran-focused logic was reinforced by the fact that the attack was planned and executed as a precision attack on military bases. In fact, it was so well executed that virtually all of the forty-nine civilian casualties were a result of "friendly fire."[1]

This focus, although shifting with the creation of the bigger World War II Valor in the Pacific National Monument, was always made real through the embodied presence of Pearl Harbor survivors at the memorial visitor center. For battlefield tourism, particularly the battlefields of America's Second World War, veterans have played a central role in shaping national memory. American (and Allied) commemorations of the war's fiftieth anniversaries, in the 1990s, witnessed the emergence of talk of the "greatest generation"—a discourse that refers to combat veterans as the heroes of history, veritable rock stars in the spotlight of public interest and excitement. This phenomenon, evident especially during Pearl Harbor anniversaries described in chapter 2, was on display daily in the visitor center during the 1990s and 2000s as veteran volunteers, easily visible in their green shirts and veteran caps, became magnets for curious visitors interested to interact, pose for photographs, and collect autographs. That same degree of heightened interest, repeated daily in excited clusters of visitors gathered around the day's volunteers, also emerged in education programs and just about any context that offered opportunities for meeting the war's survivors.

For visitors, the embodied presence of veterans, and the experience of being present with them, often captured in photos, could make connections between their lives and larger imagined communities. Their presence in memorial space brought a personal reality to collective history (White 2002). How then

FIGURE 1.1
Visitor poses with Pearl Harbor survivor Herb Weatherwax. August 24, 2014.
Photo by author.

do we account for the emotive aura associated with America's veterans of the Second World War, and Pearl Harbor survivors in particular, during this period? Even asking the question may seem odd, given that the war was, with the First World War, the pivotal event of the twentieth century and remains a focal point for postwar generations reflecting on their own place in history. Aging veterans—parents and grandparents to many in the United States—provided a living, personal linkage between the ordinary lives of individual families and the grand sweep of something larger, of national and world history. Whether relevant in their own families or not, anyone coming through the reception areas of the *Arizona* memorial visitor center might well see the Pearl Harbor survivors as that same kind of living linkage with history. Indeed, many interactions with them took the form of joking and familiarity characteristic of more intimate relations.

To understand why these encounters became memorable moments for many travelers, we might, in an almost literal way, apply the cognitive psychologist's idea of "flashbulb memory" (Brown and Kulik 1982; Neisser and Harsch 1992). As is the case for the entire experience of "being there" on a battleground or burial ground, encounters with veterans constituted a moment in which a traveler's personal biography intersects with the narratives of national history. According to the theory of flashbulb memories (normally applied to big events such as the Pearl Harbor attack itself, or the assassination of JFK), such moments tend to be readily and vividly recalled in all their contextual details, much as people can report on the circumstances in which they first heard the news about the September 11 attacks (or, for the war generation, the Pearl Harbor attack). Thus, when American travelers engaged Pearl Harbor survivors in conversation, many would tell the survivor about their own family's involvement in the war or in the military. As an example, here is a woman talking to Richard Fiske, a Marine bugler and survivor from the USS *West Virginia*, who was a constant presence at the visitor center in the 1990s: "My dad was a lieutenant commander on a submarine. And that's why we're here. We're leaving tomorrow morning and my Dad asked me to come by and pick him up a tie tack. I came all the way out here" (audio recording, May 26, 1997).

Embodying History in Pearl Harbor's Memoryscapes

Like most museums located on the historic sites they represent, the memorial's exhibits, artifacts, and volunteers are emplaced in history by virtue of their location in the very landscape that is itself the object of representation. At the same time, just as the visible and tactile presence of the harbor authenticates historical representation, so the exhibits give historical significance to today's military base. Until recently, the most distinctive element among this array of historical icons has been the veteran volunteer as a living link to the Second World War. Given the requirement of the Pearl Harbor Survivors Association that members have been on active military duty on the island of Oahu on December 7, 1941, the great majority of survivors in the 1990s were aging, white, male veterans. Whiteness in this context went unmarked, as it did in the segregated military of the Second World War. Servicemen of color in the memorial context are often held up as emblems of diversity, such as the black mess mate, Doris Miller, decorated for heroic action on the USS *West Virginia*, sent on recruiting tours in wartime America, and subsequently included as an image in nearly every film made about the attack (see chapter 3). Nonetheless, within these constraints, the presence of veteran survivors allowed visitors to interact with history and forge their own connections with the subject of Pearl Harbor.

From the early moments of the opening of the first visitor center in 1980, the park service managers recognized that the military survivors were a special constituency and made efforts to recruit a number of them to work as Volunteers in the Park, a park service designation for individuals from the community given positions to assist with park operations. A small population of survivors living in Honolulu and available in retirement were recruited to be present one or more days a week to meet visitors, tell stories, and assist with various tasks running the center. They were, after all, the living counterpart of the servicemen who died in the attack and whose memory is the memorial's mandated purpose.

Just a few years after the climactic events of the fiftieth-anniversary commemoration in 1991, park service efforts to encourage local veterans to volunteer their time were in full effect. While not all of the veteran volunteers were survivors of the bombing attack, a changing group of a dozen or so survivors resident in Honolulu (and members of the Aloha chapter of the Pearl Harbor Survivors Association) volunteered to talk about their experiences and help out in other ways. Visitors arriving at the reception desk of the previous, smaller visitor center would be greeted by a park ranger in the NPS green and grey uniform, recognizable in national parks throughout the country. Through the 1990s and first decade of the new millennium, they were also likely to see one or more veterans at the reception desk or nearby on the grounds.

The presence of each day's crew of veteran volunteers was prominently displayed on an announcement board just inside the front door, with photos and full-page bios of the individuals volunteering at that moment. On any given day, two or three survivors could be found at the center helping out, giving talks, answering questions, posing for photos, and so on. As volunteers, they would wear the green volunteer shirt issued by the park service. More important, their status as a veteran, Pearl Harbor survivor, or both was most visible from their caps, the distinctive veterans' cap characteristic of American veterans organizations with embroidered designation of their service unit and, in most cases, a host of pins, badges, and insignia indicative of individual careers. For members of the Pearl Harbor Survivors Association, the words *Pearl Harbor Survivor* were stitched on the side. Each volunteer developed ways to present his own story and otherwise engage with visitors. Richard Fiske, the Marine

FIGURE 1.2
Volunteer bulletin board, lobby of the original visitor center. August 24, 1994.
Photo by author.

bugler, used to walk the grounds of the visitor center with a blue binder full of photos and clippings about his war experiences and postwar friendships with Japanese veterans. He, like most, was willing to talk with anyone who would listen. The binder mediated his interaction with people who wanted to talk and pose for photos, just as books, pamphlets, and flyers do for other survivors up to the present.

During the time of the smaller visitor center (1980–2008) and its greater emphasis on in-person interactions, the veteran survivors were a presence larger than their numbers. If visitors themselves didn't realize who they were, park service rangers and guides would often point out this special feature of the memorial's history. Here is a ranger speaking on the boat bringing visitors back from the memorial: "In addition, I would like to mention that we are one of the few parks in the National Park Service to actually have participants of past battles with us. Today we have three Pearl Harbor survivors with us and they'll be wearing bright green park service shirts. If you would like to get some information regarding the attack on Pearl Harbor or if you would like to talk to someone who has actually been there, feel free to drop by the museum area and there will be one or two Pearl Harbor survivors available" (audio recording, January 27, 1994).

In addition to casual encounters with visitors, veteran volunteers also had the chance to talk about themselves and their war experience in more depth, thus bringing their life stories into national history. The two ways this was most commonly done in the previous setup were brief introductions of the documentary film and talks given in or around the museum.[2] In the past, as today, visitors view a documentary film before boarding navy boats to travel out to the memorial. With two theaters running staggered showings of the film to groups of 150 or so in each theater, there was always time for a brief welcome and introduction by a park ranger or volunteer. In the course of our research we found considerable diversity in the topics covered, even as the presence of survivors focused attention on the experience of military personnel on duty on Oahu that day.

Presentations in the theater by rangers and volunteers were scripted, rehearsed, and approved by the park service historian before they went public (something the park service felt necessary to ensure that personal remarks didn't contravene historical facts or fly in the face of the value of "balanced history"). They also, however, introduced a significant degree of diversity as a result of individual differences, reflecting different points of intersection between personal life stories and the Pearl Harbor story. These different conjunctures point to the different meanings of Pearl Harbor for diverse American (and international) publics, such as the Japanese American experience or that of Native Hawaiians. Such elements of diversity, however, emerge around the edges of the dominant type of personal experience represented in the life stories of veterans and Pearl Harbor survivors. Veterans speaking to various audiences at the visitor center would always begin with remarks about their own personal identity, routes into the military, and their location at the time of the attack.[3] Here is an example of a veteran survivor, Robert Kinzler, who passed away in 2013, introducing himself when welcoming theater audiences:

> I do want to welcome you this morning. You're the guest today of the National Park Service and the United States Navy. My name is Bob Kinzler. I'm one of several volunteers at the memorial. I'm a retired army officer. I have been retired now for thirty-two years, following twenty-two years of service. On December 7, 1941, I was a nineteen-year-old soldier in the regular army. I had been in Hawaii for a year and a half.

This coming June it will be fifty-four years since I enlisted and came to Hawaii as a private, a Morse code radio operator in Headquarters Company 27. (audio recording, March 3, 1994)

Straightforward and unsurprising for travelers visiting Pearl Harbor in the early 1990s, these introductions reference key elements of survivor identities: military status, mainland American origins, and presence at Pearl Harbor on the day of the bombing. Most of the speakers would name the state they lived in prior to the war, calling attention to the fact that the bombing affected families all across the United States, something that might resonate with family histories for many in the audience (about 65 percent of visitors in 1991 were from the U.S. mainland, 5 percent from Hawai'i, and the remainder international [NPS visitor statistics for 1991]). The most skilled presenters would look for connections with the audience (such as by asking who in the audience was from their home state), constructing a momentary social tie to frame the occasion as a collective experience.

As the (mostly white, male) embodiment of the American military who bore the brunt of the attack, survivors and veterans often spoke in the collective voice of the national "we"—a subject positioning that could be rhetorically extended to the majority of Americans in visitor center audiences at that time. Richard Husted, a survivor of the battleship *Oklahoma* (that experienced the second highest number of casualties on December 7), would regularly give a twenty-minute talk in the museum that covered the Pearl Harbor attack through the battle of Midway (where "the tide turned" in favor of the United States) (White 1999). He would introduce himself as a veteran survivor, but then talk in a register much like that of a public historian—matter of fact, with an emphasis on details of the attack. The main difference was that he would talk in the plural, first-person *we* to describe both Pearl Harbor and American actions in the Pacific. Thus, he once described the sinking of one of the Japanese midget submarines as follows: "And one of the destroyers, the *Monaghan*, had gotten under way from one of these nests over here [pointing to photograph] and rammed it. So we sank that little sucker right there." And then, concluding his presentation, he and the collective national voice were back in the narrative: "Now we had them on the run, we chased them as far as we could. We inflicted as much damage as we could. And the Battle of Midway was the turning point of the battle for the Pacific of World War II. From that battle on, we were the attackers and they were the defenders. And thank you for your attention" (audio recording, USS *Arizona* Memorial museum, March 8, 1994).

By locating themselves in history, veterans and survivors personified larger narratives about "world-changing events," and in so doing created a framework in which their audiences, especially Americans, might potentially find personal meaning in collective history. Beyond the question of what sort of feelings might be evoked, however, lies the potential for diverse and even contradictory moral lessons from the highly individual nature of the personal experiences recounted by veterans and survivors.

Personalizing National Memory

The growth and redesign of the visitor center, culminating in the opening of the new complex in 2010, completed the replacement of personal talks with video kiosks and audio tours—a process under way for years as visitor numbers increased and NPS staff was stretched thin. Thus, where once park rangers talked with visitors during their boat ride to the memorial, visitors would listen to a recorded audio program. The memorial experience today, minus the presence of survivors, relies on historical artifacts, images, and texts to invite visitors to "find their own meaning" (in a museum environment that, not surprisingly, strongly encodes a canonical Pearl Harbor narrative, a "preferred story," told largely in the recorded voices of historical figures). Given the individuality and variability of survivor witnessing at the memorial, the passing of the war generation has had the ironic effect of narrowing the kinds of testimonies encountered by visitors. This narrowing comes at the very time in which curators and historians had expected to find more latitude to interpret the war beyond the dominant military narrative of "be prepared." While that is true in terms of the range of topics now introduced into the memorial space, the passing of the war generation has also meant the passing of voices that would talk about moral conflicts or predicaments that they experienced during and after the war, often worked through in highly individualized ways.

Whether the short introductions of welcome in the theater of the visitor center or longer talks given in the museum, survivor presentations always wove together personal stories and Pearl Harbor history. Although the park service administration would review and approve presentations for historical accuracy, there was plenty of latitude for personalized talks, covering a wide range of subjects, to enter the memorial's public history—topics such as internment, religious experience, or reconciliation that were not, at that time, present in the memorial's museum exhibits or documentary film. Although park superintendents and historians would keep an eye out for anything that might offend the visiting public, such as political or religious views that could turn a historical presentation into something overtly ideological, the narratives of veterans and survivors covered a wide variety of experiences, ranging beyond the events of December 7. As much as these talks were primarily presented to affirm and expand dominant histories of the attack, they also came with the risk of unsettling generic narratives with individualized histories ripe with moral ambiguity and complexity.

As examples of the social histories that were routinely woven into veterans' presentations, consider Joe Morgan, an enlisted navy man at Pearl Harbor on December 7, and Stanley Igawa, a Japanese American high school student in California that day. Both were speakers among the cadre of regular volunteers at the visitor center in the 1990s. Joe was on Ford Island during the attack and Stan, after being interned with his family, served in the army in the Second World War, Korea, and Vietnam.[4] In different ways, both Joe Morgan and Stanley Igawa greeted Pearl Harbor visitors with stories about their experiences and, in the process, served up personal reflections about deeply felt religious and ethnic identifications. Consideration of their presentations, augmented with interviews, illustrates some of the ways religion, race, and nation may intersect in public memorial space.

Reverend Joe Morgan was chaplain of the Oahu chapter of the Pearl Harbor Survivors Association and was frequently asked by the National Park Service to perform the role of chaplain at commemoration and burial services. Joe would also present his own twenty-five-minute talk about once a week at the visitor center. In his talks he focused on his experience on December 7, but then went beyond to reflect on the emotion work he did in transforming his feelings about the attack, and about the Japanese, because of his postwar meeting with the Japanese pilot who commanded the aerial attack, Mitsuo Fuchida (Prange, et al. 1990).[5] Fuchida, it turns out, was a remarkable historical figure, not only because of his role in the Pearl Harbor attack, but because of his conversion to Christianity and dedication to the cause of peace after the war—a personal mission he pursued traveling in the United States and speaking with church groups throughout the country. After narrating his harrowing experiences during the bombing attack, Joe would turn his story toward his relationship with Fuchida, presenting his story as a moral lesson about the transformation of wartime anger and hatred to forgiveness.

In opening his talk, Joe would identify himself much like the survivors mentioned above, and make a bid to connect with his audience. Standing in front of a large display with an aerial photo showing a panoramic view of the harbor at the time of the attack, he would take a moment to locate the audience in the landscape of the harbor, and the spaces of history—telling his audience where

FIGURE 1.3

Joe Morgan giving his talk in the visitor center museum. March 16, 1994.
Photo by author.

they were currently standing in relation to the *Arizona* and his own location on the morning of the attack:

> "The Eyes of Texas Are Upon You." Can't anybody sing that for me this morning? You all know, recognize I'm from Texas. I was brought up in Texas but I've lived in Hawaii more than I've lived in Texas, so I call myself a kama'aina (local White person) now. My name is Joe Morgan and I'm a retired navy chaplain, and also an honorary chaplain of the National Park Service. Occasionally when men who survived the *Arizona* have subsequently passed away, they often request that their ashes be buried with their shipmates. When that is requested, I am asked by the park service to conduct those memorial services out on the memorial while the divers take the ashes and put them in the number four turret space out there. However, in 1941 I was an enlisted man, a white-hatted sailor stationed with utility squadron two on Ford Island. [pointing to the large aerial photo of Pearl Harbor behind him] Here is where you are over here and here is the *Arizona*. And here is where squadron two was housed in 1941. (audio recording, March 16, 1994)

After talking about his experiences during the bombing, Joe continued his story to talk about his meeting with Fuchida in 1956, about his own transformation as he listened to Fuchida tell of his own conversion experience at a local Methodist church:

> In his [Fuchida's] testimony he said that before he became a Christian, he hated Americans and thought it was a great honor and privilege to take part in the attack on Pearl Harbor. After he became a Christian he said, "I realized I was wrong and I asked God to forgive me, and now I'm coming to ask Americans to forgive me." And you know, God gave me the grace to forgive that man right then and there. Not because I was so great, but because God is great. After his talk was over, I went up and introduced myself to him as a survivor of the Pearl Harbor attack. In his polite Japanese way he bowed his head and said, "Gomenasai," the Japanese word for "I'm sorry, please forgive me." He reached down to shake hands with me and as our hands clasped, all that anger, hatred, and animosity left my heart. Not because I was so great but because our God is a powerful god of grace and mercy. (audio recording, March 16, 1994)

Joe Morgan would conclude his museum talk by holding up a poster-size photo of himself with Fuchida so that he could talk about the meaning of that encounter for his own life. That story served to establish the theme of reconciliation on a personal level, much as others were doing with commemorative activities during those same years (see chapter 2). From that point Joe would shift back to the present to urge his audience not to visit the memorial "with feelings of anger or rancor in your heart":

> Ladies and gentlemen, someone snapped this picture of Captain Fuchida and yours truly, shaking hands there in front of the Lahaina Methodist Church where he spoke that morning. This has become a symbol to me. The power of God's grace, able to help us forgive our enemies. I realized that this is really the true answer, bringing world peace to our world in our time. Thank you and have a good tour and God bless you. [pause] As you go out [to the memorial], don't go with feelings of anger or rancor in your heart. Really go with gratitude to those people who still lie in that watery grave, nearly a thousand of them who paid the supreme sacrifice so you and I could be free today. Thank you. Have a meaningful tour while you are here. (audio recording, March 16, 1994)

Joe Morgan's use of the phrase "rancor in your heart" borrowed the phrasing that President (and Second World War veteran) George H. W. Bush had used in his speech during the fiftieth anniversary, phrasing that the park historian also appropriated for use in the audio tour narration. When I interviewed Joe Morgan I asked him where he got the word *rancor* and he replied without hesitation, "George Bush."

Joe Morgan's presentations were frankly religious, conveying the importance of religion in his life and in his coming to terms with the meaning of the attack for him, particularly its emotional meaning. By extending his narrative beyond the moments of the attack and the war, to his postwar life as both a survivor and a chaplain, as someone whose feelings about war were changed by "the power of God's grace," Joe Morgan presented a Pearl Harbor story that he hoped might inspire his audiences to transform sentiments of anger and hostility associated with Pearl Harbor and the war. By telling a story of emotional transformation, Joe Morgan offered up a discursive means for reimagining relations with Japanese, and, in his words, "bringing world peace to our world in our time."

His somewhat lengthy explanation of his identity as both a retired navy chaplain and an honorary chaplain with the park service was a way to validate his presence in light of uncertainties about the appropriate place of religion in the context of a national park—something that my colleague Marjorie Kelly and I would learn more about in interviews with him. When we asked him how his audiences reacted to his talk, he commented on the resistance he sometimes encounters to his mixture of god and nation. In response to Marjorie's question, How do you find your audiences' responses to your talk and are audience members attentive, are they surprised by what you have said today, he responded by focusing on this sometimes controversial aspect of his presentation:

> I have noticed this and it has not bothered me. Every time I start talking about God, I'll have some people get up and walk away. Especially before I began to announce that I am a chaplain. Sometimes I maybe lose up to 15 percent of my audience, talking about God. . . . One person made an informal comment on paper. A lady. And the second one he came up to me personally and was angry. He said, "You don't have any right to do this here. This is government property." I said, "Hey, man, for ten years the government paid me to do this on board a government ship." [laughter] But since then I have made the announcement at the beginning of my talk that I am a retired navy chaplain and I'm honorary chaplain of the park service. Then I give a little explanation of what that means, that I conduct funerals out there on the memorial for the park service and I also participate in their ceremonies here as their chaplain. Since then, I have very, very few people leave when I start talking to them about God. (audio recording, June 29, 1994)

The challenges to Joe Morgan's religious theme illustrate the risks involved in using personal narrative to talk about national history in a national space. Stories that draw upon personal experiences and identities (such as Joe's Baptist faith) may not work in the larger arena of national community, where others may challenge points of difference. The tension between national and religious identities was troubling enough for Joe that he would resolve it by emphasizing his role as a chaplain recognized by the park service, making it clear that his religious activities were sanctioned by the state, in particular for burial services at the *Arizona*.

The second example of a veteran volunteer who presented a personal story at the memorial during the 1990s and 2000s is Stanley Igawa. In his theater introductions, Stanley would begin with his own memory of first hearing the news of the attack—a moment that, as for so many veterans of the Second World War, was followed by enlistment. But the patriotic narrative in his case was complicated by the fact that he was Japanese American and his family and friends were instantly entangled in the mass internment set in motion by Franklin Roosevelt's Executive Order 9066 in February 1942. As was the case for Joe Morgan, Pearl Harbor was a turning point for Stanley Igawa. But the pivotal importance of Pearl Harbor began with the story of forced confinement, to be followed later by military service.

When speaking to audiences in the 1990s (more than fifty years after the bombing), Stan would begin by asking his audience how many of them remembered "7 December 1941." He would then recall his experience as a high school student living in California, listening to the radio as President Roosevelt delivered his declaration-of-war speech to Congress. While his flashbulb memory may have been similar to that of most Americans of his generation, the immediate consequences of the news could hardly have been more different. Here he is greeting visitors who have taken their seats in the theater:

> Good morning. On behalf of the National Park Service, the navy, and volunteers, we wish to welcome you to the USS *Arizona* Memorial Visitors Center. My name is volunteer Stan Igawa. . . . I would like to ask the question now, How many of you remember 7 December 1941—may I see the hands? Thank you. There are quite a few of you, almost two dozen of you. On that day, I was living in Los Angeles, California. I had gone to an ice-skating activity with my classmates. Upon our return, we learned about the Pearl Harbor attack. The following Monday, the following day was a Monday, and the entire student body of John Marshall High School in Los Angeles, California, sat out in the bleachers to hear the famous day of infamy speech given by President Franklin D. Roosevelt. A few months later, our family was disrupted. We moved to a place called Pomona, California, where they established an assembly center for Japanese Americans. A few months later, again, we moved further inland to a place called Heart Mountain, Wyoming—near Cody, Wyoming. This became a relocation center for Japanese Americans. (audio recording, March 1, 1994)

Stanley Igawa's presentation was a hinged story, coupling together two narratives: one of racism and confinement and one of patriotism and enlistment. Indeed, his account encapsulated a story line about "fighting two wars," against racism and against foreign enemies, that was emerging in the 1990s with the increasing renown of the highly decorated 442nd Regimental Combat Team.[6] In Stan's story, the accomplishments of the 442 on the battlefield were made personal in his remembrance of two classmates who were killed in the fighting in Europe. Here is how he put it: "They both volunteered for the now-famous 442nd regimental combat team that fought in Europe during World War II. This unit uniquely comprised only Japanese-American volunteers. This unit still today is considered to be the most highly decorated unit in the United States Army. Unfortunately, both of my classmates were killed in combat fighting with the famous 442nd regimental combat team in Europe. When I received the news, it deeply grieved me and perhaps some of you may have encountered similar episodes in your lives" (audio recording, March 1, 1994). Without the story of military service and sacrifice and, most important, without his own life story of military service, it is unlikely Stanley Igawa would have joined the ranks of volunteers talking at the visitor center. By telling that story, he brought the contested history of race relations into a memorial context that otherwise sought to avoid overtly political discourse, much less a story that had the potential to subvert one of the primary themes of Pearl Harbor's mythic history, that it unified America.

In this respect, Stan's presence at the memorial, as an interned Japanese American and veteran of three wars, posed an interpretive puzzle for many in his audiences. Even with the account of the loss of his friends in the 442nd, in the memorial context of the 1990s the internment story remained out of sync with the memorial's narrower focus on the December 7 bombing attack. In those years, and through the 2000s, the story of internment, like much of the wider context of the attack, was excluded from the main interpretive program conveyed in the visitor center museum and film. When the *Arizona* Memorial Museum Association undertook the production of an educational DVD in 2004, collecting oral histories, images, and newsreels as a resource for schoolteachers, editors briefly considered the topic of internment but decided to leave it out as not relevant for the project. As evidence of which parts of Stan Igawa's story were deemed most relevant for the memorial context, when speakers had to reduce the time of their welcome and introductions because a new, longer film was introduced in 1992, Stan made the decision to focus on the theme of military service rather than internment. The resulting simplification, eliminating a point of contradiction with the dominant Pearl Harbor history of unification, illustrates the way national memory selects for stories that align best with dominant narratives and institutional purpose—in this case honoring military service.

The story that disappeared in Stan's reduced presentation was about a female friend of their family who had two sons, one of whom resisted the draft to protest internment, and the other who enlisted and became a war hero. The former was imprisoned for resisting the draft and the other received a Purple Heart for battlefield injuries. When required to shorten his talk, Stanley removed this story in order to retain the account of his two friends killed fighting with the 442nd regiment. But the predicament of the mother with two sons who made different choices—a predicament that would become a major postwar debate within the Japanese American community—remained for him a strong personal memory, and one that in conversation he described as a justified response to the injustice of internment: "I can still remember mom consoling Mrs. Takayama. She was so saddened. But when you look back, the younger son had every right to declare the fact that he didn't want to enlist in the army or volunteer. So that's part of what I talked about" (audio recording, July 19, 1994).

Even though removed from this small part of the memorial's history-making, Stanley Igawa's Pearl Harbor story about wartime prejudice remained relevant in the present (and continues to be in the post-9/11 world). Just as the original Interpretive Prospectus for the park (1981) noted that some visitors felt that the memorial should not hire Japanese Americans to work as interpreters, in the 1990s park rangers were still fending off racially charged comments about "Japs" at the visitor center, including Japanese Americans and Asian Americans. Stanley talked about these issues with us on the basis of his own experiences at the visitor center, described with anecdotes about racial hostilities and misperceptions that pointed to entanglements of race and nation that are also at the heart of the Pearl Harbor story:

> GEOFFREY WHITE: One of the questions for you is, working here as an
>   American Japanese, what kinds of questions do you get about that?
> IGAWA: It's amazing, because generally speaking, I have to be frank,
>   Caucasians when they see an Oriental, they're not able to dis-
>   tinguish between a Korean, Vietnamese, Japanese, Chinese, you
>   know. So those that, I should say in quotes, are "prejudicial" essen-
>   tially, discriminatory, or they have some hang-up being angry that
>   we were at war with Japan, say, "What are all these Japs doing here?"
>   And sometimes I have to tell them, "Hey, sir, can you distinguish
>   an Asian? Those are not Japanese, those are Chinese. They are from
>   Taiwan or they're from Korea or some other country." But to them,
>   it bothers them that they see these Japs here viewing the memo-
>   rial or visiting the memorial and coming here on a tour. Of course,
>   that's not the majority of them, but there are a few of them; and that
>   bothers me—that really bothers me. Being a Japanese American and
>   thinking that all Orientals are Japs.
> GW: All blended together by people who don't know the difference.
> IGAWA: They don't know the difference. Ignorance, huh? [Yeah.]
>   Really ignorance. So in their eyes these Orientals are slant-eyed
>   Japs, coming here. That really irks me.

GW: Do you sometimes get these comments yourself? Obviously people see you with your VFW cap and so on.

IGAWA: They wonder, of course. "What's this slant-eye Oriental doing here?"

GW: They might almost—so, have you had incidents or things that led you to—

IGAWA: Yeah, a couple of times. They see me, they come up to me and say, "You're wearing the VFW hat. What are you?" So I tell them, "What do you mean, what am I? I'm a veteran. I don't wear this hat because I want to." Yes, I want to, but I'm a veteran and I'm permitted to wear it. They look at me. One time he says, "What army did you serve?" [Laughing] I've had, in fact not too long ago, I had an Oriental come up to me and he says, "What army were you in?" I said, "I wasn't in the Japanese army. I'm a Japanese American who served in the American army." That was unusual because an Oriental came up to me. . . . So there were a couple of incidents or where I can overhear. There was a German and one day he was saying, "Well, these damn Japs. What the heck are they doing over here?" He had a slight accent. After a while I found out he was from Germany. He had the gall to criticize the Japanese when we were at war with the Axis powers too. That annoyed me. He said it out loud. I don't know if he did it purposely to get me angry. (audio recording, July 19, 1994)

When Stan Igawa spoke with us about anti-Japanese or anti-Asian sentiments he encountered at the memorial he also mentioned the importance of his status as a veteran. Although in his talks he did not emphasize his own war experience (the Second World War, Korea, and Vietnam), he did wear the cap of the Veterans of Foreign Wars (VFW) organization.[7] Like the caps of the Pearl Harbor Survivors Association worn by other veteran volunteers, Stanley's VFW cap made him easily recognizable as a war veteran. The relevance of his own military career was always there, as in one incident that he related, in which the park superintendent had received a written complaint about his theater talk from an individual who identified himself as a navy ensign. The ensign complained that his talk was "condescending," which Stan interpreted as a reaction to his focus on Japanese American experience:

Yeah, I really wondered what he (the ensign) meant. He disliked what I talked about. Maybe it was because of the fact that I talked about the Japanese American. But I talk about them serving the country and serving it well. I don't know what "condescending" meant. He used that word. I was going to write to him, but I got to a point where—let it be. Here's this ensign. Probably out of either Annapolis or a young officer, and I don't think he realized that I served in World War II, the Korea War, and part of Vietnam. I said, "Oh heck [forget it]." (audio recording, July 19, 1994)

Here Stan talks about his military career as a kind of antidote to the exclusionary politics of race in hierarchies of remembrance. If only the ensign had realized that he had been in three wars, he might have thought differently. In commenting on that moment, Stan went on to mention that the park service had reviewed and approved his talk, just as Joe Morgan, aware of the conflicts over the religious content of his lecture, wanted to be clear that his talk had been sanctioned by the park service.

In concluding his talk, Stan artfully expanded his focus from his own grief to that of the young men's parents and finally to the mothers of the war's fifty-five million casualties: "When I received the news, it deeply grieved me and perhaps some of you may have encountered similar episodes in your lives. Of course, when both parents heard about their son's death they were in deep sorrow. About this same time, there were approximately 55 million other mothers throughout the world who perhaps may have endured similar miseries and heartaches" (audio recording, March 1, 1994). Much like the way Joe Morgan concluded his talks, Stan Igawa also wanted to move from his own story to the larger significance of the memorial. Using a rhetorical device recommended in park service training, he cited a prominent leader to make his point, quoting a U.S. senator speaking about war memorials:

I believe the majority of you are going to return from the memorial with positive thoughts and reflections. And I also believe that most of you are going to relate positively to a speech given by former senator Frank Moss from the state of Utah in which he so beautifully and eloquently expressed his thoughts regarding the dedication of memorials. And I wish to take time now to quote him: "While we are here today to honor those that have given their fullest measure of devotion, we hope and pray that we no longer dedicate memorials to men who die in battle, but to dedicate memorials to men living in peace for all nations and for all men." (audio recording, March 1, 1994)

As in his reference to mothers around the world, the scope here is inclusive; the circle of relevance in the senator's speech is "all nations." In this respect, Stan Igawa's presentation anticipated the increased inclusiveness of the memorial's historical narrative that would begin to emerge some years later with the establishment of the World War II Valor in the Pacific National Monument.

If Stanley Igawa or Joe Morgan, speaking as veterans, stretched the horizons of the memorial's Pearl Harbor story, so too did other speakers, park rangers, and volunteers, who also drew on personal stories to welcome visitors in the theater introductions or other short talks (in the museum and on the boats going to and from the memorial). Not surprisingly, most of the park rangers recruited in Hawai'i also had personal connections to the history of the bombing and some even to communities located in the environs of the harbor. Like the veterans who referenced their military genealogies, these speakers, also, would begin their remarks by locating themselves in the story. Examples include the park historian who talks about his grandfather who was working at Pearl Harbor at the time of the attack and mother, who on that day was a nine-year-old girl sitting in church, or the ranger who talked of being from Iowa, near the hometown of one of the crew of the *Arizona* who died in the attack and who had been engaged to the sister of the five Sullivan brothers (all of whom perished with their ship in the Solomon Islands), or the local Native Hawaiian ranger who talked about her family's experience that day.

The last, a local Hawaiian woman whom I will call Melehana, used her grandmother's diary to convey a quite different sensibility than that of military survivor narratives that made up the bulk of introductions at that time:

> Aloha awakea kakou. Good afternoon, ladies and gentlemen, I am Melehana and on behalf of the National Park Service, I'd like to welcome you to the USS *Arizona* Memorial. . . . Now how many of you were alive on December 7, 1941? Do you remember what you were doing, where you were going, and also what your day was like? I know someone who is very special and very dear to me, who was here on that day. And before I begin the film, I'd like to share with you what was written in my tutu wahine's diary. For those of you from out of town, tutu wahine is the Hawaiian word for grandmother.
>
> [Reads excerpt from grandmother's diary.]
>
> My tutu and her family never sat in the pews, never sang their songs, never said their prayers that morning, because halfway to the church, they had to turn around because of a tremendous noise that echoed in the valley. Now from her car, my tutu saw a house that was ripped in half and engulfed in red flames. She was very scared and very confused.

Her heart pounded against the walls of her chest and her eyes filled with frightened tears. The sirens were ringing in her ears and the people on the streets mirrored her own frightened expression. It was at this point that she realized Hawai'i was somehow in the middle of the war. To the peace and tranquility came the Japanese planes, bombs, and torpedoes causing death, destruction, and of course fear. She also writes in her diary, "I'm afraid for my family, what will happen to us. My husband George, my three children, June, Malia, and Kahala, and of course my unborn child, what will happen to us?" She also writes in her diary, "I will not forget the pained faces, the death, destruction and also my fear. I will not forget this day, the day war began." Mahalo. (audio recording, October 8, 1994)

This talk was given shortly after the park service had, for the first time, compiled a list of civilian casualties from the bombing attack, and fifteen years before the visitor center would open a museum with exhibits pertaining to civilian experience. In her brief introduction this ranger offered a perspective for visitors to ponder the meanings of the bombing for local, Native Hawaiian residents, much as did the Hawaiian speaker quoted in the introduction. Her talk might have caused some to realize that the category "Pearl Harbor survivor" could also be expanded to everyone on Oahu who survived the attack that day. Although she did not talk directly about Native Hawaiian culture and history, Melehana's use of Hawaiian words to greet visitors (even pausing to translate *tutu wahine*) and reference to *akua* (ancestral gods) called attention to the importance of Native Hawaiian society as a culturally distinct community with its own Pearl Harbor memories, different from the canonical story of military sacrifice.

As veterans of the Second World War both Joe Morgan and Stanley Igawa affirmed the narrative of patriotic military service at the core of the memorial's history. At the same time, however, they brought their own experiences, which involved religious convictions and cultural commitments conjoined with that same history. In this respect, their voices were not different from those of others who, although not military veterans, conveyed personal connections to the history represented there. When narrating history as personal experience, these speakers were also, in their own way, calling attention to the fragility and conditionality of history, from an abstract representation of images and texts to a mode of embodied knowledge that, in its moral dimensions, is always subject to reinterpretation or contestation. Although each of these speakers was deeply affected by Pearl Harbor, each also refashioned their experiences with personal stories that expose some of the contradictions and uncertainty of mythic history.

The high degree of public interest in meeting survivors and listening to their stories in and around the visitor center raises questions about the role their stories have played in shaping the memorial's history. Whereas the primary purpose of memorials is to honor and remember, memorials also require History, with a capital "H," as an authoritative representation of the past to validate the work of remembrance. These combined functions are most clear in memorial museums where the professional apparatus of museology is done in an overtly memorial context (Williams 2007). This book's introduction discussed briefly oppositions of history and memory as contrastive modes of understanding the past that often collide in and around museums and memorials (Linenthal 1995). Even though history and memory overlap and intersect in complex ways, they can be set in opposition, as in the difference between museums that make the presentation and analysis of history a primary objective and memorials that use history to honor the past, rather than make it an object of critical scrutiny. In either case, the National Park Service is very much concerned with the status of history at its historic sites, seeking to develop standards for programs of historical interpretation to make public history reliable, inclusive, and fair. When historic sites are also memorials, those efforts can be seen as contrary to the core purpose of the memorial. As may be recalled from Thomas Sowell's editorial (1991), cited in this book's introduction, the National Park Service's attempt to present balanced history at the *Arizona* memorial has been criticized as "turning its back on patriotism."

To further complicate matters, the *Arizona* memorial is not a pure space of memorialization. Like many large memorials, the *Arizona* memorial encompasses both secular museum and sacred shrine, functioning simultaneously as shrine, museum, tourist destination, and classroom. Such spaces, like the World Trade Center today, generate controversies that often turn on conflicting assumptions about the nature of history, about epistemology and historiography, as much as disputes about facts. As many scholars of history and memory have observed, academic histories push for abstraction and objectivity while memorial histories are generally embedded in social relations and communities of remembrance—reinforcing and valorizing desired social realities. At the same time, it is important to look beyond these categories to the everyday realities of historical practice that turn out to be much messier. In the memorial context, history and memory are almost always intertwined. Despite the ease of asserting different missions for memorials and museums, the activities and representations one finds in either type of institution very often work simultaneously to memorialize and historicize, to foster remembrance along with education, preservation, and so forth—all in the same institutional space.

The presence of Pearl Harbor survivors, with personal connections to the site, embedded history in specific social relations and situations, creating opportunities for engagement, while diminishing critical distance and analysis. At the Pearl Harbor memorials, as at most American war memorials, monuments, and museums, veterans speak with a distinctive kind of authority— one that garners attention and respect, especially in commemorative events. Even if historians frequently regard oral histories as unreliable because they are deeply personal points of view, that very same personal quality infuses veterans' testimonies with the authority of experience, and the power to engage ordinary publics through the accessibility of personal narrative.

The distinction between professionalized history and personal recollection lies behind the common perception that survivors' talk is "real," in the sense that it is personal and experiential, but possibly not accurate, in the sense that it is not professional documentary history. Hence survivor memory occupies an ambiguous position in the context of a public institution that is both a site of remembrance and a place for public education. Personal memory derives its authenticity from experience, from the I-voice of someone who witnessed events. The immediacy and directness of experiential narrative provide one kind of authority, but it is an authority undercut by the very same premises that give it force. Experiential positioning also implies a limited field of vision (literal and metaphorical).

One of the features of discourse that often differentiates these contrastive types of historical narrative (objectifying history versus memorializing history) is emotion. Histories that claim social, scientific validity, making themselves open to critical analysis and revision, regard emotion as a sign or symptom of involvement that makes critical self-scrutiny difficult or unlikely. On the other hand, detachment and distance—the ability to hold history at arm's length, to gain perspective—increase confidence that those representing the past do so without first filtering or reshaping it to fit prior expectations and desires. Of the speakers we recorded presenting narratives of Pearl Harbor history, those who talked about its moral significance tended to do so with emotional language. References to grief or sadness associated with death were common, as were references to anger and hostility in talks concerned with the possibilities for reconciliation.

Talk of emotion here does more than describe feelings. It is pragmatic; it actively seeks to create meaning and change ways of feeling. Thus, when

Joe Morgan urged his audience not to go to the memorial "with any hatred or rancor in your heart," he was urging them to conceptualize, and reconceptualize, the Pearl Harbor story in a way that does not evoke anger. In his interview with us, Joe Morgan reported that members of his audience frequently expressed appreciation for his efforts, saying, "You helped me get the right perspective." His own account of what he was trying to do, and the varied responses to it, show that he himself saw his presentations as aimed at doing a certain kind of emotion work. He talked about his audiences' responses by saying that some would come up and give him a hug:

> MORGAN: Even today I've had people come up and hug my neck and
> say, "I thank the Lord that you have the privilege of doing this." One
> man came up this morning, one of my reasons here is to help people
> who are harboring anger. I had one man came up to me my first talk
> today and hugged my neck and he said, "Thank you, I was harbor-
> ing anger and you have helped me very much." My last talk, a man
> came up here and he said, "I can't help what you say, I'm still angry."
> [Laughter]
> GW: Have to work on him some more.
> MORGAN: I told him, I'll pray for you. But anyway, I'm here to be used
> to help people to get over their pain and encourage those who
> have a faith. I don't degrade any denomination. (audio recording,
> June 29, 1994)

While emotions are constantly present in the social life of the memorial, this same emotionality seems to run against the park service value of balanced history (one that is not overtly political, particularly in regard to racial hostilities, domestic or foreign). Thus, in supervising talks given by rangers and survivors, park service managers take an interest in the alignment of affect and memory. Stan Igawa, who worked as a ranger as well as a volunteer, talked about this in recalling the training he received in developing his own presentation:

> When you're hired as a ranger here, they give you the latitude and flex-
> ibility to put in your own personal thoughts and experiences. We are
> evaluated . . . at the theater prior to our actually giving a talk. So that
> if they feel that it's maybe not in order, we should change it or alter it.
> But they thought that with my personal experiences and what I included
> in the rest of the talk, they felt that that was okay. But they do want you
> to express your feelings and your thoughts, so it is good in that way.
> (audio recorded interview, July 19, 1994)

One of the reasons that the park service managers are interested in cultivating expressions of feelings is their concern that many people come to the memorial as just another tourist attraction on a holiday itinerary. People involved with the memorial occasionally speak about the Disneyland problem and the need to define the context in a way that maintains the dignity of a memorial, shrine, and tomb. In this sense, evoking an emotional response from visitors is regarded as a sign of personal involvement. Joe Morgan was particularly clear about his intentions to do this with his talk, saying, "I want them to see this as an experience not just as a tourist attraction. I want them to feel the real experience. There is the hurt, anger, and pain and there are still dead bodies out there in the ship's hull" (audio recording, June 26, 1994).

By the same token, the park service did not want to stir up emotions for emotion's sake, especially if they might rekindle wartime hostilities—something that would be contrary to U.S. efforts to build a strong relationship with Japan as a postwar (and Cold War) ally, as well as efforts by the state of Hawai'i to cultivate Japanese tourism and investment in the economy of Hawai'i. Whereas Joe Morgan wanted visitors to "feel the real experience," he also had a quite specific idea about the kind of emotional experience that would be most desirable—the kind of transformation that he spoke of in his museum talk, one that contributed to healing and reconciliation rather than a perpetuation of hostility and conflict.

Significantly, however, the theme of reconciliation was not part of the permanent exhibits or the original documentary film shown at the memorial, but rather emerged in more fleeting survivor performances. In this respect, survivor presentations were a clear reminder that the performative dimensions of memorials do not simply mirror messages encoded in their architecture and fixed media. Whereas today's World War II Valor in the Pacific National Monument has made the theme of postwar peace central to its programs, past acts of reconciliation at the *Arizona* memorial tended to occur in the margins of official commemorative activities, largely the initiative of veterans, both American and Japanese, and usually conducted outside the boundaries of official ceremonial time and space (see chapter 2). Indeed, the inventive rituals of reconciliation discussed in chapter 2 stood in a kind of tense, ambiguous opposition to more anti-Japanese attitudes prevalent among many mainland-based veterans and veterans groups.

While most of the Pearl Harbor survivors who volunteered at the memorial participated in rituals of reconciliation at one time or another, they often did so without the blessings of the national Pearl Harbor Survivors Association (PHSA). Here again one can see the importance of Hawai'i as the societal context for the memorial. Even though it was made up of mostly mainland-born white, male veterans, the Aloha chapter of the PHSA included some local-born veterans, including at least two with Native Hawaiian ancestry, and a majority of individuals who had settled in Hawaiʻi after the war and, after years of residence (many marrying local women), were clearly influenced by the high value placed on intercultural understanding associated with Hawaiʻi's diversity and history of racial mixing. But their more tolerant views were not characteristic of the majority of national PHSA members. Joe Morgan was aware of the difference and indicated his own frustration in the lack of response when a group of Japanese veterans proposed joining together in a reconciliation ceremony at the memorial the year after the fiftieth anniversary (1992). Joe was one of only six members of the local Pearl Harbor Survivors Association who participated (out of sixty or so members). According to him, "they [the Japanese veterans] tried to get the national [involved] but the people in the national, they wouldn't touch it with a ten-foot pole" (audio recording, June 29, 1994).

For Americans of any sort, whether veteran or nonveteran, Hawaiʻi-based or mainland-based, memory of the attack and associated views of the Japanese were inevitably produced in a larger context, where the meaning of what was said obtained its moral significance from contrasts with competing histories and emotions. Thus, Joe Morgan, who was regularly involved with activities of the Pearl Harbor Survivors Association, was aware that his story of forgiveness and reconciliation worked against the more antagonistic views of many other veterans dominant during those years. In similar fashion, Stan Igawa, in giving his presentation, was well aware of the prevalence of racial ideologies that ran counter to his narrative of Japanese American loyalty. His accounts of problematic interactions with people who knew little or nothing about Japanese Americans, even failing to distinguish between Japanese visitors and Japanese Americans, created the dialogic context for his presentation.

It is in the face of these differences, then, that the survivor narratives recalled here can be seen as active interventions attempting to do a certain kind of moral work. In this broader context, talks like those of Joe Morgan or Stan Igawa were more than projects of self-affirmation; they also aimed to transform. They envisioned their audiences as part of a larger public, a public that could be both unforgiving and sympathetic, that could draw exclusionary circles that separate Americans and the Japanese or that marginalize Japanese Americans or other minorities while still respecting the speakers as veterans. In talking about his presentations, Stan described his talk in terms of its effect on "the public," of what he would like the public to know, think, and feel:

And essentially I wanted the public to know that we Japanese Americans were basically loyal and served our country proudly. Because a lot of them come up to me and say, "I didn't realize there was a Japanese outfit, the 442 and the 100 that served in the war." I said, "My goodness, the most highly decorated unit in the United States Army." . . . I feel it more so because of when I talk about my two friends and I don't bring the name out but the student body president was Fred Takayama and my classmate was Harold Shoji who did all of our annuals. I still keep my '44 annual, 1944, when I graduated. He did all the ink drawings in the annual. Harold was killed also with Fred in the 442. So it becomes so, to me, so—every time I want to convey that these guys were killed, my classmates, fighting for their country. And I want to let the public know that "hey sure we were in camp and we were at war with Japan, but we Japanese Americans served valiantly." (audio recording, July 19, 1994)

As will be seen in the account of commemorative practices that follows, survivor talk at the memorial could be overtly therapeutic, a means of working on conflicts at both personal and political levels. In the case of Stan Igawa's presentations, the performative telling of history seeks to transform the emotional significance of past events. Each survivor who volunteered at the memorial brought a distinct set of life experiences that lent personal meaning to the Pearl Harbor attack. The expressions of emotion and other ways survivors might communicate those personal dimensions of Pearl Harbor history, including their own self-conscious reflections about the importance and impact of those stories, are among the many casualties of the disappearance of embodied history from the spaces of Pearl Harbor memorialization.

Electronic Remembrance

In the first two decades of the visitor center (1980–2000) there was very little in the way of prerecorded material presented to visitors as part of their memorial visit. Even though short staffed, the National Park Service rangers, along with a small number of volunteers, would direct and guide visitors through their tours, which began with the documentary film and the short introductions by a ranger or volunteer. After exiting the theater, groups of 150 or so would board an open-air boat operated by the U.S. Navy to take them across the harbor to the memorial. At each point, visitors would listen either to a ranger or a volunteer provide information, related stories, or both, about the attack, the film, and the memorial.

Eventually, each of the moments for personal talks around the visitor center were replaced by recorded audio and video presentations—first an audio recording played on board the boat as visitors transited to and from the memorial (replacing ranger talks), then an audio guide that could be rented in the fashion of most museums to provide a site-by-site narrative as visitors work their way through the grounds, museum, and memorial. Finally, the short, welcoming introductions given after visitors took their seats in the theater were replaced by a prerecorded video, much like those visitors encounter as they settle into airline seats—an official welcome and introduction from a video of a National Park Service ranger.

Although the folksy style of many of the veterans might seem to have marginalized them in relation to the glossy productions of exhibits, video, or film, their presence resonated strongly with visitors, who would often line up for autographs and photographs with a survivor, capturing their own presence in the memorial's living history. Their stories also enchanted the national media, who would always gravitate toward survivor testimonies in their reporting on the annual anniversary each December 7. Similarly, commercial operations in the business of packaging and selling Pearl Harbor history have often featured Pearl Harbor survivor testimonies. Among countless examples in the outpouring of media products during the fiftieth anniversary was the sixty-minute video sold originally as a VHS tape titled, *We Were There . . . Pearl Harbor Survivors: Eyewitness to History* with both English and Japanese narration.

Understandably, then, as years progressed, talk of survivors as a "disappearing resource" became more frequent. The poignant realization that the generation of survivors was vanishing became a regular topic of discussion around the memorial visitor center. The narrative of disappearance took many forms. It was, for example, coded in a story commonly told about the oil leaking from the sunken hulk of the *Arizona* ("the *Arizona*'s tears"), to the effect that the oil would continue leaking until the last *Arizona* survivor passed away. Veterans themselves would often joke about their precarious status. One commonly made reference to himself and his fellow veterans as an "endangered species." The monthly lunches of the local Pearl Harbor Survivors Association included banter about what they would do with their small treasury when there were too few people left to spend it.[8] The discourse of disappearance began to accelerate after the sixtieth anniversary. During the Pearl Harbor Day commemorations in 2003, the Veterans History Project, based at the Library of Congress, organized a ceremony at Punchbowl cemetery to light 1,700 candles symbolizing the 1,700 veterans of the Second World War said to be passing away each day at that time.[9]

Having featured veterans' experiences and honored survivors in commemorative events, in museum planning, and in program development, the park service managers of the memorial watched and reflected as the number of survivors dwindled, anticipating the moment when there would be none, when the memorial's story would be, finally, history. Here is the park service historian writing about this in program notes for the sixty-third commemoration of Pearl Harbor Day, December 7, 2004:

> At the USS *Arizona* Memorial Visitors Center, a dwindling fraternity of Pearl Harbor survivors share their memories with countless visitors every day. Fortunately, their voices have been recorded for posterity. Sadly, in the future, they will be part of a proud memory. Technology has preserved their voices so that generations of Americans will have the privilege of experiencing their recollections.
>
> We live in a fortunate age. Imagine if we could hear the recordings for those who served with Washington at Valley Forge, or listen to soldiers who stood at the stone wall along Cemetery Ridge at Gettysburg. How lucky we are to have the voices of Pearl Harbor preserved forever. They will always be here to reach out to us. (Daniel Martinez, Program Notes, "Voices of Pearl Harbor," December 7, 2004)

Given the high value placed on the testimonies of military survivors, the park service began to focus attention on recording those testimonies for posterity, as a resource for telling the Pearl Harbor story beyond the lives of the war generation. Here I briefly trace some of the ways those voices have been recorded, represented, and incorporated in public history-making, as modes of presenting history that have progressed from oral performance, to audio and video recording, to Internet-mediated technologies. The genealogy of these technological developments traces the evolution of modalities for producing and distributing memories of Pearl Harbor as virtual remembrances. Whether the VHS technology of the 1990s or today's YouTube and podcast productions, how do these electronic technologies transform memories of Pearl Harbor?

Through the different phases of technological development, the core genre for representing survivor voices at the memorial, with its concern to provide well-documented histories of the attack, is that of the "oral history"—a standard item in the tool kit of public historians, anthropologists, and others interested in the experiential dimensions of historical events. Oral history programs found in national parks around the United States are especially prevalent in sites of war memory, where the testimonies of veterans, survivors, and anyone who witnessed events of war are recorded and treated as a unique historical resource, like artifacts in battle landscapes, to be accessed and made available for purposes of remembrance. One of the most well known projects of systematic recording, archiving, and programming is that of the United States Holocaust Museum with its Spielberg-endowed archive, concerned with preserving Holocaust testimonies (originally circulated in the form of audio cassettes included with fundraising letters, prior to the spread of Internet technologies).

The park service began recording oral histories with Pearl Harbor survivors from the time it received a congressional mandate to manage Pearl Harbor as a national historic site, opening the visitor center in 1980. Stimulated by the outpouring of video productions around the fiftieth anniversary, for broadcast or circulation with VHS video cassettes, the NPS decided to produce its own hour-long videotape of survivor testimonies with the intention of using it for instructional purposes. Because the veteran survivors who volunteered their time at the memorial were always in demand for visits to schools, the park service decided in the mid-1990s to produce a recording that featured highlights of oral histories recorded with a number of veterans with the aim of making the tape available to teachers and schools. The result was a VHS tape that presented the oral histories of eight veterans who had been volunteering at the visitor center—seven survivors plus Stanley Igawa. As the video cassette packaging announced, here were survivors "telling their stories" in brief five-minute accounts of their experience. The tape was subsequently bundled together with a binder of educational materials and made available to schools as a teacher's guide (for grades four to twelve).[10] Placed in this context, alongside historical documents and study aids, the oral histories became part of history, personal testimonies to what happened on December 7.

With the advance of technology, the park service and its museum association soon digitized the entire project and produced a DVD for educational use—a computer-friendly product that combined maps, graphics, and video resources for classroom use. Released in 2005, the DVD contained more than an hour of video including historical footage and the same eight "eyewitness accounts"—seven survivors plus Stanley Igawa. One of the innovations of this project was the expansion of the narrative scope of history to include the first settlement of Hawaiian islands through postwar politics. Still, the survivor testimonials used in the VHS tape (augmented with a few additional oral histories, including the transcript of an interview with a Japanese pilot) remained at the center of the project. Audio and transcripts from the oral histories for most of the speakers could be accessed by clicking on a map that showed their locations on ships or military features.[11]

At about the same time that the *Arizona* Memorial Museum Association began work on the DVD, it also developed a program of video teleconferencing that provided a way to take survivors' storytelling into classrooms anywhere in the world.[12] The first test of the videoconference format, done in February 2003, featured three survivors from the local chapter, described as follows:

> Everett Hyland, USS *Pennsylvania*: His experience in being wounded and spending nine months in the hospital.
> Herb Weatherwax, Schofield Barracks: His experience witnessing the attack from three different locations and then serving in Europe.
> Ray Emory, USS *Honolulu*: His experience during December 7 and his mission to mark the graves of unknown Pearl Harbor casualties. (*Arizona* Memorial Museum Association report, October 2006)

These capsule descriptions place the same kind of tight frame around their subject as video vignettes. The videoconferences also allowed for interaction and questions from the students, some of which went into areas associated with the consequences of the attack and with survivors' lives in a larger context than found in the video oral histories used in previous compilations. When, after three years of videoconferencing, the organizers reviewed the type of questions asked by students, they found that questions ranged beyond the attack itself to its consequences as well as the speaker's motivations for recalling the bombing. As the number of survivors declined, the videoconferencing program shifted to other means to engage students, using historians, curators, and videos instead. The testimonies, however, would live on in audio and video circulated in new ways and, ultimately, incorporated in the new museum.

During the 2000s, when the park service and its nonprofit partner mounted a major fundraising campaign to build an expanded visitor center and museum, they looked to survivor stories as a major resource for fundraising, especially for soliciting contributions at a grassroots level. This initiative led to the first major effort to put videotaped survivor histories online, as the *Arizona* Memorial Museum Association decided to invest in a major new website that would create an online space to "share and immortalize" the stories of Pearl Harbor survivors.[13] That site was similar to the website for the national World War II Memorial, in Washington, D.C., and the Veterans History Project of the Library of Congress, insofar as all of these created an online presence for collecting and archiving stories of military service, of "honoring service" and "sharing stories" with future generations. The World War II Memorial includes an online registry in which veterans and their relatives can add the names of those who served ("To search the electronic World War II Registry of Americans who contributed to the war effort, or add the name of a loved one, click here.").

For the purposes of the Pearl Harbor fundraising campaign, the pearlharborstories.org website stated its mission as follows: "For 65 years America has rightly honored those who gave their lives at Pearl Harbor, but thousands more lived to fight on, defend freedom, preserve democracy and rally a nation. The Pearl Harbor Survivors Project pays a debt of gratitude to the Pearl Harbor survivors from the greatest generation by creating a community to share and immortalize their stories. The initiative remembers the survivors of Dec. 7, 1941 themselves, as well as the freedom they preserved." Defining storytelling as a commemorative act flowed easily into the fundraising goals of the campaign. Giving stories and giving financial support are both ways of enacting a personal connection with pivotal events in the national imaginary, through acts that contribute stories or financial support. These possibilities were all conjoined in the website's invitation to contribute: "The Pearl Harbor Survivors Project is sponsored by the Pearl Harbor Memorial Fund: Remember, Understand, Honor & Give from the Heart. We invite you to share a story, explore the stories of others, and make a donation to the Pearl Harbor Memorial Fund" (www.pearlharborstories.org/about, accessed January 3, 2007). The pearlharborstories.org site attracted a steady volume of activity, peaking during the sixty-fifth anniversary of the attack, in December 2006. The site included four short videos from four Pearl Harbor survivors, including two civilian survivors connected with the museum association.

The fundraising website pearlharborstories.org inspired the National Park Service to make available photos and short, three-to-four-minute videos on the World War II Valor in the Pacific Monument website, using a YouTube channel and a video podcast series.[14] The NPS describes the "Remembering the Pacific" video podcast series as "a video podcast series that presents the personal stories behind World War II's Pacific Theater. Hear American and Japanese servicemen tell their war stories from December 7, 1941 through the war to the ongoing reconciliation between the two countries. Witness the effects on the home front as American and Japanese civilians recount the emotions of the war years and come to terms with loved ones lost, sacrifices made and recognition of civil rights. Hear about the personal importance of the memorials and the lasting impacts of the Pacific War." Although the description refers equally to "American and Japanese servicemen," in fact as of this writing only one of the eight YouTube videos present the recollections of a Japanese veteran. Of the other seven, four present American veterans of Pearl Harbor, one gives views from both sides on the theme of reconciliation, and two are by National Park Service rangers profiling individuals who served—one about Rudy Martinez, who died on the USS *Utah*, and one about the latter-day interment of a survivor of the USS *Arizona* crew. So far these online resources appear to be more of a techno-curiosity than something that has added significantly to the outreach of the USS *Arizona* Memorial. The one video of a Japanese attack pilot (sensationally titled "I sank the *West Virginia*") is remarkable in many ways, but as of February 2014 had a total of 4,100 views—half the number of views for the American oral histories and less than the number of visitors who come through the front gate of the World War II Valor in the Pacific visitor center on a single day.

Despite the still-limited reach of Pearl Harbor storytelling over the Internet, audio and video testimonies are now the primary means through which visitors to the memorial will encounter Pearl Harbor survivors. In the space of a little over fifteen years, the medium for circulating survivor recollections progressed from in-person talks, to oral histories on audio tapes in VHS and DVD media, to Internet circulation available to anyone with a smart phone. How are these electronic transformations affecting the work of memory-making? Just as the veteran survivors were a focal point for oral presentations at the earlier visitor center, so today they are a focal point for video and audio testimonies. One significant difference, however, is that the array of video kiosks and options for selecting speakers now includes a more diverse panoply of civilian and military voices, both Japanese and American, than the preponderant focus on American military veterans speaking in previous decades.

In the earlier era, American veterans of Pearl Harbor and the Second World War were always the featured centerpiece of newspaper and television reporting on the anniversaries discussed in chapter 2, as well as documentary projects of various kinds. The survivors who volunteered their time at the visitor center developed routinized ways of narrating their experience, represented in highly repeatable narrative forms—something linguists call "entextualizing" their experience (Silverstein and Urban 1996). When I first began interviewing Pearl Harbor survivors volunteering at the memorial, I noticed how easy it was to engage them in tape-recorded interviews and quickly realized that this was because most of them were already practiced at telling their stories for public consumption. In conducting interviews aimed at a broader range of subjects, it was sometimes difficult to break the narrative mold established by entextualized narratives. It is, for the most part, these same kind of routinized narratives that are incorporated in oral histories recorded in audio and video.

Beginning with the first official videotapes of survivor reflections, the dominant format for video recordings of individual stories about Pearl Harbor memory is the individual oral history, filmed in a close-up format in which a single person tells "his (or her) story" to the camera. The oral history recording is then edited to play without interruption in a single stream of monovocal narrative, usually relating events in temporal order. This format should be familiar to anyone who has been around contemporary museum exhibits with multimedia technologies used to represent historical experiences in brief, one-to-three-minute recollections. Video testimonies collected for DVD production or online listing show remarkable uniformity in narrative form, moving from identifying information through an account of the attack to a moral coda.

The fact that the era of living survivors was coming to an end weighed heavily on the designers of the new museum (see chapter 5). The redesign of the visitor center included considerable discussion about ways the landscape, architecture, and exhibits could allow visitors to find personal meaning in the events portrayed. The museum planners, with advice from a consulting firm, emphasized "firsthand connections" in envisioning the ideal visitor experience. These firsthand connections emphasized contact with both the material artifacts of history ("direct experience with the real thing") and "one on one with the people who were there"—primarily Pearl Harbor survivors.

Even recognizing that this aspect of the memorial's history would only be possible for a few more years, museum planning continued to feature veterans who survived the attack, even if they would have to be represented in audio and visual recordings. A list of possibilities for AV presentations were outlined in the course of designing a "Visitor Experience Matrix" for the new museum. The matrix asked, "What will visitors to the [memorial] be able to see, touch, hear and do that will create respect for those that lost their lives, stimulate insight into the events before, during and after the attack?" In a column labeled "First Hand Connections" and "One on one with the people who were there," the first example listed in this planning exercise was "Hear a Pearl Harbor survivor story—seeing sacrifice validates my service." Second, "Talk to a survivor." Third, "Share my own experience as a veteran," and fourth, "Take home [the] life story of a 'hero'" ("Visitor Concept Experience," chart prepared by Aldrich Pears Associates for USS *Arizona* Memorial, February 21, 2006). Included in the early plan was a walkway leading back from the boat docks, where visitors returning from the memorial would reflect on the significance of their visit in terms of the theme "Sacrifice and Courage." And it was survivor stories that would facilitate reflection on this core theme: "Sacrifice and Courage: Provides visitors with an opportunity to make meaning of the Pearl Harbor events by seeing and hearing survivors' stories" (Aldrich Pears Associates 2006, 24).

The efforts to use new technologies to inscribe personal experience in the museum come with a certain irony. Just at the moment in which actual encounters with veteran survivors (and others who experienced the attack) are disappearing, the vision for the next generation of museum history features "experience," involving personal, embodied encounters with historical artifacts and stories. As a result, the audio guide is built around a series of sound bites from veterans speaking about their experiences on December 7, and the new museum layout includes multiple video kiosks with touch-screen options for selecting videotaped oral histories. Many of these are gripping in their detail and personal drama. They will, however, remain forever just that: carefully recorded, edited, and archived testimonies that take the place of survivor voices in Pearl Harbor's mythic history, with almost no element of interactivity characteristic of the era of embodied witnessing.

What, then, are the effects of electronic media, particularly video, on modes of speaking and understanding history? Even a cursory review of narratives suggests that as memory goes electronic, frames of speaking get frozen. There are a variety of ways the pragmatics of speaking for recorded oral histories, as an individual testimonial, fix the performative moment in terms of the identity of the speaker, presumed audience, and nature of the speech act itself. Typically survivor testimonials are monovocal, narrated without interruption or other signs of interaction with others. The audience is you, the (generic) viewer. Monovocal speaking tends to strip away metacommentary about oneself or one's speech—the kinds of extrastory comments (often joking) that speakers use to adjust their relation to audiences in the course of interaction. In recorded testimonies, for example, there is little of the humor and irony that were often part of the speech of survivors talking with people around the visitor center.

There is also less commentary, explicit or implicit, about the truth value of the speaker's own account, in-jokes or asides about the potential to exaggerate or distort events, either from faulty memory or an interest in enhancing one's own importance. These are all issues that surfaced repeatedly in survivors' talk among themselves and in addressing friendly audiences. Yet because they are spoken "on the record" for oral history, testimonials take the form of reportage, of eyewitness accounts of dramatic events, with little to indicate other kinds of framing that might shift the relation of the speaker to the events at hand, to the nation, and to the audience.

One of the veterans included in the DVD mentioned above is Everett Hyland, a sailor who suffered traumatic injuries in the bombing of the USS *Pennsylvania* and was hospitalized for nine months. After retiring to Honolulu,

Everett spoke often about his experiences in a wide range of contexts, from volunteering at the memorial, to participating in conference panels and special commemorative events. Whereas his video testimonial is straight reportage (descriptive, detached), his presentations in other contexts were always marked by a sharp sense of wit, irony, and interest in the purposes and contexts of remembrance, especially contemporary relations with Japan and its citizens (indeed, he married a Japanese woman late in life).

The style of his presentations in other contexts contrasted sharply with that of his video witnessing. Here, for example, is the way Everett began his remarks on a panel convened for the sixty fifth anniversary of the attack (audio recording, December 4, 2006). Because he was suffering from a cold that day, he quickly added a comment about his faulty voice as he started his presentation: "If my voice cracks, I'm not getting emotional. I have one granddaddy of a cold. On the morning of the seventh . . ." Everett's reference to "not getting emotional" was a kind of winking at his audience, based on the expectation that survivors often become emotional in recalling traumatic events. Comments such as this, and Everett's statement just a few sentences into his story, saying, "If I ramble here, please excuse it," call attention to the fact that his presentation that day was not a direct replay of his Pearl Harbor experience, it was an account, a constructed version of events mediated by language, memory, and storytelling practice.

About a minute into his conference presentation, Everett also called attention to the problem of exaggeration, an issue commonly recognized and discussed among veterans themselves. As a member of the Pearl Harbor Survivors Association, he was not averse to suggesting, comically, that the imagination of its members "grows with their age." Everett, in comparison, promised to "give it to you straight": "In this organization of Pearl Harbor Survivors Association, their imagination grows with their age. I try to be very careful. I'll give it to you straight. I'll lay off the mayonnaise." Thus, within the first minute of speaking, Everett added a reflexive layer of commentary about the nature of his own speaking. His commentary on the emotionality and truth value of his words adds important frame for the audience to use in listening, evaluating, and feeling in response to his narrative. By adding this sort of commentary, survivors talking about their experiences would remind audiences of their own sense of agency and individuality. Indeed, the issue of exaggeration or fabrication would commonly come up among survivors, even at the monthly lunches of the local chapter or in their newsletter. At about the same time that Everett was adding his qualifications, the newsletter of the Aloha chapter beseeched members, "Pearl Harbor Survivor volunteers at the USS *Arizona* Memorial are advised to be as factual as possible in telling their story and to be careful not to embellish their story to make it sound better . . . [enumerates several examples of recent published accounts unlikely to be "true"] . . . As we get older, the stories get better and better, but that's not better when talking to school kids" ("Pupukahi: Newsletter of Pearl Harbor Survivors Association," Aloha Chapter #1, Hawaii, May 2006, 3).

Everett Hyland, like a number of men in the Honolulu chapter of the Pearl Harbor Survivors Association, was frequently involved in building relations with Japanese veterans through commemorative practices discussed in this book's chapter 2. In other contexts, such as educational panels for high school teachers or videoconferencing (he participated in one special videoconference for an American school group set up with the Japanese bomber pilot Zenji Abe), Everett spoke at length about his relations with the Japanese from the time of war to the present. Those experiences, however, rarely intrude in the videotaped oral history in which he was recorded telling his story, as he was asked to do repeatedly in educational and media contexts. Those experiences outside of the attack are either not mentioned or, in conference settings, brought up in question-and-answer periods. Similarly, the brief video testimony of Richard Fiske, the Marine bugler who devoted much of his elder life to acts of reconciliation, gives no hint of those activities in the DVD released in 2005.

The substitution of video screens for persons who once spoke to audiences in and around the memorial is in many ways the definitive marker of the transition from embodied to electronic memory. One of the sharpest examples is in the visitor center theaters—that darkened space where the orientation film prepares audiences for their trip out to the sunken ship and its white shrine. It is in that space where survivors, veterans, and park rangers (some of them also veterans) used to welcome visitors. With the passing of the survivor generation and the perennially short-staffed situation at the memorial, audiences now hear only from the video-recorded park ranger. I quote from the greeting, less than three minutes in its entirety, to better highlight contrasts in the voices of the memorial, as it transitions into the electronic era. The ranger begins,

> It's the story of life and death, heroism and sacrifice. Today at the USS *Arizona* Memorial, you'll come face to face with the names of some of these individuals, the men of the *Arizona*. The story is a tragic one as the bomb that destroyed the *Arizona* ended their lives even before they knew what was happening. There really is no wartime story to tell about these men. Many others, civilian and military, lived through the attack and for the next three and a half years endured incredible hardship and extreme

horror. Please consider this during your visit today. The USS *Arizona* Memorial is just one of many memorials built to honor the dead and to remember the event. Memorials are places of learning and inspiration, reflection and quiet contemplation. This film will undoubtedly answer many questions, but it will surely raise questions also. Hold onto your questions and when you arrive at the memorial a park ranger will be glad to answer them. Now, as the lights dim, you're going to take a journey to the past, back to December 7, 1941.

> [Fade out to written message:]
> Mahalo nui loa ["Thank you very much."]
> for your generous support to ensure that
> we will always
> Remember, Understand, and Honor
> [followed by sponsor credits][15]

Several points are worth noting. Despite a strongly stated philosophy behind museum planning (chapter 5) and much of the park service thinking about memorialization that attempts to invite personal reflection, rather than impose an official interpretation, this introduction is highly directive. The audience is first told what the story is about—"Life and death, heroism and sacrifice," hitting keywords of heroism and sacrifice that are central themes at American war memorials—before the ranger, speaking in the voice of institutional authority, instructs the audience in the purpose of memorials in general: "Memorials are places of learning and inspiration, reflection and quiet contemplation." Emphasizing the educational aspect of memorials, the ranger informs the audience that the film will surely "raise questions," but they will be questions that can be answered by a park ranger available on the memorial.

The seamless institutional quality of the video presents a stark contrast with the individualized and interactive greetings characteristic of survivors like Joe Morgan. He might have invoked the imprimatur of the park service but generally spoke more simply, in the voice of a person affected by the bombing, not the omniscient voice of a federal agency. The ranger monologue places the audience in a larger institutional context by noting that this memorial "is just one of many memorials built to honor the dead and to remember the event." The final signature of bureaucratic sponsorship is in the video's solicitation of support—a sign of the messy realities of underfunded and understaffed agencies that depend on gift shop sales and, increasingly, direct appeals for donations. Although the memorial received an exception from the legislation that established entrance fees for national parks (because of its significance as a burial place and a sacred site), the real-world pressures for fundraising increasingly intrude into the spaces of memorialization—even into the darkened chamber where an orientation film was made precisely to transition its audience into the sacred space of the memorial (see chapter 3).

BY REFLECTING ON THE history of Pearl Harbor survivors' activities in and around the *Arizona* memorial, across the decades in which they were most active, this chapter has offered a glimpse of the power of storytelling in a memorial context—places where routinized stories and emotions engendered by nations at war form a potent mix. The brief history of memory offered up here reveals a process that, on the one hand, valorizes the stories of military veteran survivors, reproduced and circulated through diverse media, while also facilitating storytelling that attempts to intervene in dominant narratives, reaching for new affective configurations enacted in the performance of personal stories.

In discussing strategies of personalization in historical discourse, I have noted some of the ways that storytelling works to resolve tensions between national identities and other, more specific identifications, whether ethnic, religious, or something else. Perhaps this is what Bodnar (1992, 14–15) had in mind for "public memory" when he wrote that "people can use it [public memory] as a cognitive device to mediate competing interpretations and privilege some explanations over others. Thus, the symbolic language of patriotism is central to public memory in the United States because it has the capacity to mediate both vernacular loyalties to local and familiar places and official loyalties to national and imagined structures."

Drawing on observations and conversations with the survivors who made up the core of speakers at the memorial, many of whom became friends now sorely missed, this chapter has also asked about the transformations in memory associated with the cusp of living history. If there is one obvious conclusion, it is that the personal complexity and richness that is to be gained from conversation is largely lost with the passing of the person and opportunities for interaction. The loss is also a loss in our ability to understand the intersection of personal memory and public memory, of subjectivities and histories. Yes, "we" may lose some details of events that have not otherwise been written down or recorded but, more important, we lose much of the uncertainty, complexity, and subtlety conveyed by speakers attempting to articulate their own thoughts and feelings about the things they spoke about—subtleties often marked by humor, irony, arguments, and ambivalence. When considering the evident emotionality (or should one say humanity?) of memorial sites, feelings expressed by survivors convey a depth of connection between self and history. As survivors, finally, pass away, how are such connections represented in the apparatus of representation and recognition built by the state and its various national agencies?

The expression of affect is part and parcel of memorial discourse precisely because emotions communicate an embodied connection between people and events represented. The act of burial, the very reason the memorial is constructed in the first place, is the ultimate expression of the most intimate of connections between self and nation, through the experience of military brotherhood. This sort of personal connection, signified most intensively in death, is most evident in the decision of *Arizona* survivors to "rejoin their shipmates," by having their ashes interred on the ship after they die. This insight may help us understand why both of the video vignettes posted by the National Park Service on its "Remember Pearl Harbor" YouTube program focus on the death of citizen-soldiers—one a eulogy to a casualty of the *Utah* attack and one a portrait of a survivor's choice to have his ashes interred back on the *Arizona*.

Two

C U L T U R E S   O F

C O M M E M O R A T I O N

At the outset of 1994, as Marjorie Kelly and I were first beginning fieldwork at the memorial, I was going through the routines that most visitors do—getting tickets for a showing of the orientation film and viewing the film before boarding a navy boat to cross the harbor to the memorial. Everyone arriving at the memorial makes their way up the steps of the dock, enters the memorial through its main entrance, and then, after lingering in the open-air middle part of the platform, with its views across the harbor and down onto the sunken hull, makes their way to the shrine room at the opposite end of the platform. There as you walk through the doorway you find yourself in a solemn high-ceilinged room facing the imposing marble wall with names of all those who lost their lives in the explosion of the USS *Arizona* (figure 1.2). Most who enter stand silently, staring upward, pondering the names. In front of the wall, a set of chrome stanchions cordon off the wall itself, so no one can walk up and touch the wall. Rather, the cordon and stanchions serve as an altar for offerings of leis and flowers left just a few feet in front.

On this first occasion of fieldwork on the memorial, I wrote the following in my notebook: "Memorial room: From Japan Katogakuen High School; 8 wreaths on floor." Without any further information or interpretation, the note remained just that, a jotting about objects that had evidently been part of a presentation from a visiting Japanese high school. My next observation duti-fully recorded the more permanent inscription etched in the middle of the shrine room's marble wall of names of the dead: "Memorial inscription: To the memory of the gallant men here entombed and their shipmates who gave their lives in action on December 7, 1941 on the U.S.S. *Arizona*. This memorial was installed and rededicated by AMVETS April 4, 1984."

Looking back on those notes, on one of the first few pages of my spiral notebooks, it's possible to see that those objects tell a more complicated story about the entangled history of commemorative practices at the USS *Arizona* Memorial. Whereas much has been written about the architecture and sym-bolism of the memorial, there is much less about the activities, events, and performances in which people of all sorts construct their own connections (or lack thereof) to the place. As observed in chapter 1, even the talks given by Pearl Harbor survivors at the visitor center had a more variable and fleeting quality than the exhibits, film, and plaques inscribed in the memoryscape. In the shrine room, the contrast between the temporary and intriguing Japanese offering, which would be removed by the following day, and the permanence of the marble inscription conveying the legislated purpose of the memorial, sponsored by a major American veterans organization, reflects a complicated story of commemorative activities, official and unofficial, formal and informal, that have been evolving from the time the memorial was first built.

Of all the ways collective memory is reproduced, commemorative prac-tices are a uniquely public means of making a statement that certain histo-ries matter—to those engaged in remembering, certainly, but also to broader imagined constituencies (like national populations). Not only do commemo-rative practices produce statements about what's important in history to some imagined community, they reproduce the social reality of those communities through acts of collective remembrance (Connerton 1989, 2011). Further-more, there is rarely a simple one-to-one relationship between the original "official" purpose of a memorial and activities that take place there as a space of performance. The fact that, at a single memorial, some commemorative practices are more visible and routinized than others says something about the social and political realities that undergird (or oppose) those practices. Some of those practices are quite literally outside official commemorative space, and so go largely unrecorded in mainstream media. At the same time as the fiftieth anniversary, for example, a protest by nearly one hundred dem-onstrators organized by church groups and Hawaiian organizations stood out-side the front gate of the naval base and visitor center, the protestors holding banners calling for attention to the violence associated with America's just-

FIGURE 2.1
Sendai Higashi High School offering, memorial shrine room. December 7, 2005.
Photo by author.

launched invasion of Iraq. Their actions received no television coverage—a fact that only surfaced in the media in the form of a letter to the editor of one of the local papers (*Honolulu Star-Bulletin*, December 15, 1991, A13).

In mapping some of the multiple commemorative activities conducted at or in connection with the *Arizona* memorial (and World War II Valor in the Pacific National Monument) throughout much of the postwar period, this chapter also charts transformations in the social and political contexts for memorializing the Pearl Harbor attack and the Pacific War. At the *Arizona* memorial, the institutional context for remembrance has progressively widened in concert with the memorial's expanding memoryscape, marked first by the construction of a visitor center in 1980 and then, decades later, the establishment of the World War II Valor in the Pacific National Monument and its larger visitor center complex. At each phase, these developments have expanded the range of commemorative activity at the memorial, reflecting a wider, more diverse range of visions of the meaning of Pearl Harbor.

The existence of the memorial as a public institution open to international visitation proved critical to the evolving interactions between American and Japanese veterans. James Clifford's suggestion that we look at museums as "contact zones" (1997), where multiple narratives or ideologies of culture intersect, applies equally well to memorials. In fact, in the case of memorials, those intersections are more likely to fold into definitions of the institution's purpose and politics. For memorials that become destinations for global tourism, it is not unusual for diverse and even contradictory narratives and affects to comingle, or, to use Marita Sturken's term (1997), to become "entangled." War memorials, by definition, enshrine histories of conflict between multiple national constituencies. In an era of postwar tourism, then, memorials as contact zones become sites of intersection for multiple national narratives—places where complex, contested national imaginings interact, even if that interaction only involves the way one imagines the other (compare Yoneyama 2001).

At the *Arizona* memorial in the 1980s and 1990s, the appearance of Japanese veterans in a space where Americans were honoring American veterans and war dead created one such entanglement that would set in motion some years of transnational memory work. Despite tensions during the 1980s (or perhaps because of them), a few aging Japanese veterans of the Pearl Harbor attack found their way back to the memorial, seeing it as a place to honor former enemies and comrades alike, through various kinds of reconciliation or friendship events. After the fiftieth anniversary of the attack, in 1991, Japanese veterans, intent on promoting reconciliation among surviving veterans, initiated a remarkable series of ceremonial events. The formation of personal relations between Japanese veterans and some of their American counterparts (those inclined to participate in reconciliation activities; not all were, obviously) proved to be an important catalyst for these developments. In that era, those interpersonal ties largely sustained these unsanctioned activities in the absence of more official recognition or sponsorship (outside of the generally hospitable reception given by staff of the National Park Service).

The fact that such practices were not only possible at the memorial, but actually facilitated by the memorial as a global institution, is an important reminder that national war memorials can readily become sites of transnational remembrance. More recently, with the establishment of the World War II Valor in the Pacific National Monument, the park service shifted to a more active role, sponsoring events with different kinds of Japanese participation, and promoting the theme of postwar peace—a theme associated in Japan with the memorials to the atomic bombing victims in Hiroshima and Nagasaki. Events such as the dedication of a museum exhibit in 2013, displaying one of the paper cranes folded by the fourteen-year-old girl whose story of dying from radiation sickness has become a children's story known around the world (Coerr and Himler 1977), dramatize shifting commemorative practices indicative of a larger national memory in transition.

This chapter briefly traces this history of interwoven commemorative activities, focusing first on the most visible official events commemorating the December 7 anniversaries, and then considering the stream of activities involving Japanese veterans that unfolded largely in the margins of the memorial in the 1990s and 2000s, before taking up more recent activities of the World War II Valor in the Pacific National Monument that seek to develop the interpretive theme of postwar peace.

The December 7 Ceremonies: Military Memory as Ritual Process

Reenlistments, burial services, official visits, anniversary ceremonies, and national days of remembrance (Memorial Day, Veterans Day, Independence Day) make up a busy slate of ceremonial activity at the *Arizona* memorial, and the World War II Valor in the Pacific National Monument. The largest commemorative activity at the memorial each year is the annual anniversary ceremony on December 7, proclaimed "National Pearl Harbor Remembrance Day" by the U.S. Congress in 1994.[1] Whereas commemorative activities, large and small, are performed daily at the memorial, it is the institutionalized ceremonies that mobilize the ritual apparatus of the U.S. military branches that are in some way definitive of the state of national memory, as enacted in national space (a U.S.

memorial on a U.S. military base), by state officials (hosted by naval commanders and, since 1980, park service officials). Looking at these ceremonial activities over time, it is possible to trace both continuities and transformations. The protocols of military memorial ceremony give the December 7 events a high degree of consistency and continuity. That continuity is etched in the shrine wall, in the story of military identities and careers enacted in ritual practices honoring those killed in battle (as well as their living counterparts, military survivors and veterans). At the same time, however, tracing those activities across several decades affords a view of their articulation with shifting contemporary concerns, especially present-day military engagements.

The largest and most publicized moment for ceremonial activity each year is the commemoration of the anniversary of the bombing attack on December 7. Everything about the ceremonies—the place, the time, the people—iconically reproduces connections to the historical event recalled. In fact, those very parameters work to define what the event recalled is—fundamentally, a bombing attack that inscribed images of shocking destruction in the concentrated, bounded area of the harbor and in military installations on Oahu. The ceremonies at Pearl Harbor recall the attack in the same landscape as the bombing itself, timed to begin at the same time the attack began, and conducted by and for military personnel much like those who died in the attack—including, throughout decades of postwar commemoration, the Pearl Harbor survivors who provided a living link to the events recalled.

As years have passed and the structure and composition of commemorative activity expanded, broadened, and transformed, it is useful to keep in mind the origins of memorialization with the men who survived and the military units most involved. It is their embodied presence, their ability to enunciate their stories that provided much of the focus for official (and mass mediated) memory of Pearl Harbor as a military story. By the same token, as the survivor generation diminished, and the memorial complex evolved, commemorative activities also transformed. The continuities and changes in December 7 ceremonies over the past two decades tell a story about the power of the Pearl Harbor mythos to reproduce itself while also adapting to changing circumstances.

Among the constancies of Pearl Harbor anniversary ceremonies are the parameters of space and time for commemoration. Ceremonies are either held on the memorial or within eyesight of it, in the same military landscape where the bombing occurred in 1941, with a program that marks the time of the start of the attack (7:55 a.m.) with a moment of silence and a flyover of military aircraft. I have been attending and recording December 7 ceremonies each year since 1994. During this time, the core ceremony has followed a similar, tightly scripted sequence of presentations and performances structured by the protocols of military tradition. The continuity is evident in the similarity of the program for the dedication of the newly constructed memorial on May 30, 1962, with that of all the December 7 anniversaries since. Compare the dedication in 1962 with a recent ceremony on December 7, 2013:

1962	2013
	Hawaiian Blessing
Jet Flyover	Flyover
	Presentation of Colors
National Anthem	National Anthem
	Hawai'i Pono'i [state anthem]
	Prayer for Peace
The Invocation	
Introduction of Dedication Speaker	Guest Speakers [introductions]
Dedication Address	Keynote Speaker
The Memorial Prayer	
	Branch of Service Wreath Presentations
The Navy Hymn	
The Benediction	Benediction
Rifle Volley and Taps	Rifle Salute Taps
	Retire Colors
	Walk of Honor

The ceremonial constancy across half a century reflects the ability of ritual practices to locate remembrance in a more timeless realm of tradition and values—to continually re-create military time and space. With each performative act, the pilots, chaplain, band members, honor guard, and bugler all reinscribe the moment with a larger significance coded in the familiar sights and sounds of military ceremony. The attendees, in turn, enact their own place in this community through their participation in singing, praying, applause, and collective silence.

These consistencies through time are particularly remarkable in light of some of the institutional changes that have taken place since the dedication of the memorial in 1962. With the opening of the visitor center, in 1980, the National Park Service began sponsoring its own anniversary events each

December 7, hosted on the lawn of the visitor center, while the navy maintained its smaller ceremony with invited officials and dignitaries on the memorial itself. And in 2006, at the time of the sixty-fifth anniversary, the park service and the navy joined forces to cosponsor the December 7 ceremony in a form much like that which takes place today. With plans for renovation of the visitor center on the horizon, the ceremonies were moved from the lawn of the visitor center to a large warehouse facility in the middle of the naval base, looking across the harbor toward the memorial. The new arrangement limited access for security purposes. Sharing the stage, the superintendent of the National Park Service (NPS) gave welcoming remarks, while it was the commanding officer, Naval Station Pearl Harbor, who acted as the master of ceremonies.

Through all these permutations, the ceremonies have continued to have much of the look and feel of the events sponsored by the navy. The park service adopts the same military protocol to conduct its ceremonies (color guard, flyover, rifle salute, taps) as the navy and, like the navy, places Pearl Harbor survivors at the center of their commemoration. In addition to the similarities of the NPS and navy ceremonies, however, there are also some notable differences in the NPS-hosted programs. These include a Hawaiian blessing that has been a feature of NPS commemorations since 2003, the Hawaiian state anthem, and a "prayer for peace" that has been presented by a Japanese Buddhist organization since 1981, shortly after the visitor center opened. The presence of Hawaiian and Japanese voices reflects the mandate of the National Park Service to engage a diverse public in its programs. The park service invites a broader range of local organizations to participate in its events—events that are also open to the public, including onlookers who might be visiting that day. The Hawaiian prayer, or blessing, typical for public events in Hawai'i, is indicative of those connections, as is the Japanese prayer, presented each year by a Japanese peace group based in Hiroshima. A locally based member of that organization asked about participating when the visitor center first opened, and was invited by the superintendent at the time. They have been part of the NPS ceremony ever since.

While these culturally different elements, particularly the Japanese prayer, might seem discordant to some, they in fact function more as rhetorical devices that actually mark off and accentuate the dominant narrative of American service and sacrifice. The primary anchor for constancy in Pearl Harbor ceremonies is the focus on citizen-soldiers, past and present, who have been ready to serve and, in some cases, die in service to the nation. This central defining concept is the theme of sacrifice, repeated often as a cornerstone of military ceremony. The value of military service, embodied by survivors, veterans, and active-duty military personnel, is evident in the entire ritual process. Ritual practices linking past and present military service have been carried out at Pearl Harbor since the immediate aftermath of the attack, when the crews of navy ships passing the sunken *Arizona* would line up on deck, a practice termed "manning the rails"—a U.S. Navy tradition of sailors recognizing other sailors (and Marines) killed in battle. Like that practice, commemorative ceremonies at Pearl Harbor create an embodied linkage between the past and present, especially between those who "made the ultimate sacrifice" in the nation's service and those who now serve in the U.S. military.

Even if their presence in the ceremony has contracted to a handful, veteran survivors continue to be the focus for collective acts of remembrance, acts that frame the purpose of the ceremony. In these events, veteran survivors occupy a dual position as both agents and objects of ritual remembrance. On the one hand, they participate in commemorative events to honor those who died in the attack. Yet, as years went by, they increasingly became primary objects of commemoration. In this role they embody patriotic citizenship, icons of military service in wartime. As such, they were (and continue to be) given an honored position at the front of seating arrangements, formally acknowledged at the beginning and end of the ritual process. At the beginning of the ceremony, survivors are asked to "stand as able" so that they may be recognized, something that, since at least the 1990s, has turned into a standing ovation. In recent years ceremonies have added a "walk of honor" at the conclusion of the ceremony, when the audience again applauds the survivors as they exit, assisted by active duty military who steady them or push wheelchairs, if needed.

This is then elaborated in one or two additional stages in which all other veterans of the Second World War are asked to stand, followed by "all veterans," receiving the same appreciative applause. Here is the master of ceremonies for the sixty-fifth anniversary ceremony, asking veterans to stand and be recognized in a manner that has been repeated in every December 7 ceremony for the last twenty years: "Would all Pearl Harbor survivors please stand as able. . . . [Applause] Ladies and gentlemen, I would also ask all other veterans, foreign and U.S., please stand as able, and be recognized. . . . [Applause] It is because of you and others like you that we enjoy the freedom and liberty we have today" (audio recording, December 7, 2006). At each juncture the audience responds with a standing ovation. In this manner, all military veterans come to inhabit the same position as Pearl Harbor survivors, exemplars of military service for the nation. In the act of honoring the larger group of veterans, everyone present, veteran and audience member alike, performatively locate themselves in a community of remembrance honoring military service (W. Cole 2007b).

FIGURE 2.2
Walk of Honor as Pearl Harbor survivors exit the December 7
anniversary ceremony. December 7, 2014.
Photo by author.

In addition to these ritualized means for connecting military past and present, the December 7 ceremonies create connections between Pearl Harbor history and today's military in speeches and presentations that honor military service. Through time, these statements continually invoke the memory of Pearl Harbor to honor men and women serving in wars from Vietnam to Afghanistan and Iraq. Thus, on the twenty-fifth anniversary of Pearl Harbor, in 1966, Admiral Roy Johnson, Pacific Fleet commander, made comparisons between Pearl Harbor and other famous battlefields such as Lexington and Iwo Jima. He also spoke about the significance of Pearl Harbor for the generation that was again being called upon to fight in Vietnam. Addressing his speech to the assembled veterans of Pearl Harbor, he noted that younger men and women now bear the "heavy responsibility of maintaining peace, freedom and the dignity of man which you discharged with such valor" (*Honolulu Advertiser*, December 8, 1966, A6).

During the decade following the 9/11 attacks, the anniversary ceremonies increasingly included references to the Middle East wars, bringing the narrative of the "good war" to bear on the conflicts of today that otherwise are surrounded by higher levels of public doubt and disagreement (Dower 2010; Rosenberg 2004, ch. 10; White 2004b). In particular, the figure of the citizen-soldier (or sailor or Marine), embodied by the veterans of past wars and the active-duty servicemen and servicewomen of today, make history personal and relevant through the presence of both aging veterans and today's uniformed military personnel. The connection of Pearl Harbor remembrance with more recent wars emerged with greater force in the December 7 ceremonies after the 9/11 attacks, in 2001. By the time of the sixty-fifth anniversary, in 2006, military installations and communities across the United States had built up large and growing numbers of veterans of service in Iraq and Afghanistan. Honoring their military service also became a more direct part of the agenda of the Pearl Harbor anniversary ceremonies. In the sixty-fifth anniversary ceremony, the navy chaplain giving the benediction opened the program with praise for veterans of the Second World War but moved quickly to asking for prayer in support of active-duty military personnel serving in Iraq and Afghanistan:

> Please join me as we pray together . . . may we be inspired by the valor of the brave men who first defended our freedom in World War II. Now on this day, 65 years removed from that momentous attack, we still live in a world wrought of danger and the threat of terror. We pray for our fellow countrymen around the world who, like the Pearl Harbor heroes before them, are subject to sudden and violent attack. Please protect them. Bring them success in their missions, and return them soon to their homes, in this we pray. We are particularly thankful for the Pearl Harbor survivors present here today, pray for continued blessings upon them, the armed services from which they came and the great nation we serve. In your wonderful and strong name we pray. Amen. (audio recording, December 7, 2006)

In concluding his benediction, the chaplain asked for blessings directed to the Pearl Harbor veterans, and added that the same should be given to the armed services as a whole and indeed to the "great nation we serve." This is the time-honored work of ritual, to create and validate felt connections to an imagined community larger than the immediate time and place of remembering. Even if that community is always in some measure a phantasm, it is made real in moments of public performance.

FIGURE 2.3
Pearl Harbor survivor Ted C. Clinard presents USS *Maryland* wreath. December 7, 1995.
Photo by author.

As is typical of Western mortuary practices at burial sites, the memorial ceremonies include wreath presentations made by sponsoring organizations, mostly veterans associations. While easily incorporated in the ceremonies on the memorial as a burial site, wreath presentations had not been part of the shore-side ceremonies until the fiftieth anniversary, in 1991. For the large commemoration in 1991, however, the park service came up with an idea to make wreath presentations to all of the battleships (extending the memorial's focus on the *Arizona*) by erecting a row of yardarms along the shoreline, each one representing one of the "capital ships." Ideally the wreaths could be presented by a surviving member of that ship's crew or, if not, a Pearl Harbor survivor.

Eventually the USS *Utah* was added, as well as the other military stations attacked on the island of Oahu. As explained by the park service superintendent,

These circular wreaths represent an expression of our gratitude and a symbol of our unending appreciation for their service and sacrifice to the United States. With the carriers at sea the battleships became the focus of the attack. It is customary at this observance for Pearl Harbor survivors to place a wreath on the flag mast of each of the capital ships that were in port when the attack took place. We also place a wreath for the USS Utah, which, like the USS Arizona remains where she was moored that day. In addition we also recognize each of the sites on Oahu that came under attack. (audio recording, December 7, 2010)

The presentations are introduced one by one, working down the row of yardarms by calling out the ships' names and the names and titles of the presenters. In their original form, the presentations were made with a park ranger assisting by handing the wreath to a veteran survivor who then placed it on the yardarm, stepped back, and saluted. In this way, each presentation personalizes the work of memorialization by introducing the individual presenters, identified in terms of military status and duties on December 7.

In 2006 wreath presentations were modified in two respects. First was expansion of the list of recipients of wreath presentations to include each of the military service branches along with the battleships (army, navy, Marines, air force, Coast Guard, and even "civilians" of the state of Hawai'i). Secondly, the presentations were made by active duty personnel, with commanding officers for each of the service branches presenting, assisted by a member of that service recently decorated for actions on Middle East battlefields. (The civilian wreath was given, at the sixty-fifth anniversary, by the governor of the state of Hawai'i.) Here is the way the master of ceremonies, Navy Base Commander Captain Skardon, introduced the naval presentation, repeated for each of the other service branches:

> Representing the United States Navy, the 1,999 sailors who died during the attacks on Pearl Harbor and Kaneohe Naval Air Station is Admiral Gary Roughead, Commander of the United States Pacific Fleet. Admiral Roughead is assisted by Hospital Foreman Second Class Fleet Marine Force, Robert Almanado, of the Naval Health Clinic Hawai'i. While deployed at Afghanistan from June 2005 to January 2006, Petty Officer Almanado was wounded with three marines when his vehicle was hit by an improvised explosive device. Petty Officer Almanado managed to get all three wounded marines to safety, render aid, and was credited with the saving of all three lives. (audio recording, December 7, 2006)

At the heart of each anniversary ceremony is a keynote address or speech by an invited dignitary. Here the passage of time and gradual disappearance of the generation of survivors is acutely evident. Between 1991 and 2001, all of the keynote speakers at the anniversary events were Pearl Harbor survivors, with two exceptions (a well-known author who writes about Pearl Harbor, and a rear admiral and commander of the Pearl Harbor navy base). After the sixtieth anniversary, in 2001, the dominant identity of keynote speakers reversed, with only one survivor speaking in the next decade (Mal Middlesworth, in 2011, at the seventieth anniversary). All the rest were navy commanders (five times), federal officials, historians, or media figures (twice each).[2] The shift from Pearl Harbor survivors to federal officials or historians changes the voice of remembrance from that of witness to that of praising and honoring. With few exceptions, elements of self-reflection, often tempered with humor or uncertainty, are replaced with a more monotonic register of honorific language, but in the process reaching for connections between past and present military service that, with survivors, could even go unspoken because the speaker himself embodied that connection.

Two examples from the keynote speeches of the sixty-fifth anniversary ceremony, in 2006, illustrate the tenor of postwitnessing commemoration. In this case, speeches by Admiral Gary Roughead, commander of the United States Pacific Fleet, and Secretary of the Interior Dirk Kempthorne reflect the fact that the ceremony in 2006 was the first to be cosponsored by the navy and park service. While speaking from somewhat different positions (military, civilian government), the core principle that ran through both talks was the connection between veterans and active-duty military personnel—a connection that rests upon a vision of the value of military service to the nation. Admiral Roughead addressed the crowd:

> In September 1942, Admiral Chester Nimitz, in the company of Admiral Bull Halsey, honored the first heroes of the Pacific War here in Pearl Harbor on the USS *Enterprise*. In that ceremony, he recognized chief ordinance-man, John Finn, who is one of fifteen honored with the Congressional Medal of Honor. And we are honored to have him here with us today. We are also honored by the presence of all the survivors and veterans of that infamous day. . . . Their sacrifice and greatness live on in profound ways . . . it lives on in the sailors and the marines and the soldiers and the airmen and the coastguard-men who serve our country. They are the current generation of patriots who go forth in the same way that those who first pledged their lives, their fortunes, and their sacred honor did so many years ago. They carry on with an enduring belief and commitment to the values upon which our nation rests. . . . On behalf of

all who wear our nation's cloth, thank you, and your generation for your selfless service, your profound sacrifice, and your enduring example. Thank you, soldiers. (audio recording, December 7, 2006)

In concluding his remarks with "Thank you, soldiers," Admiral Roughead finds a rhetorical moment to construct veterans as, still today, soldiers—a term that converts a former military status into an enduring quality of the person, a life-long identity that, even late in life or, in this case, especially late in life, merits acknowledgment and praise. Coming from Admiral Roughead as commander of the Pacific Fleet, the thank-you comes, as he says, from "all who wear our nation's cloth"—from the military community and, in one vision, from America. By implication, the expression of gratitude performatively constructs military service as a community of individuals who have selflessly put the nation first, and should be thanked for it.

Whereas Admiral Roughead was speaking from and to the military, the Secretary of the Interior constructs a more historical narrative about military service in American tradition, about and for a wider populace, referring to the role of the National Park Service as custodian of national historic sites, including oversight of eighty-eight national battlefields. Using an image of "the mural of America's military history," he too (like Admiral Roughhead), tells a story about history as a tapestry of individual stories woven together through a common willingness to serve and a sense of individualized personhood given over to the nation:

Historic events such as the Battle of Yorktown and the attack on Pearl Harbor are part of the mural of America's military history. This is a mural seemingly painted with a wide brush with each year's conflicts and triumphs depicted in broad belief as more than two centuries passed. . . . I understand this may be the final reunion in Hawaii of those who survived the attack. . . . I want to assure you on behalf of the Department of the Interior and the National Park Service, that we will continue to be vigilant, and that we will ensure that this site is preserved as eternal memorial to all. . . . To those who fought so nobly and have come back yet again to this hallowed site, we honor you. To those who sacrificed their lives in this place, we honor you. . . . To those who have died defending our country in battle for more than 200 years, we honor you. God bless you all. (audio recording, December 7, 2006)

Whereas December 7 and other key ceremonial days (Memorial Day, Independence Day, Veterans Day) are core moments for celebrating American patriotism, the expansion of the purpose and mission of the memorial as a destination for global visitors created opportunities for different forms of patriotism to be expressed and enacted there (Bergman 2013). One of the most remarkable of these was the arrival of Japanese veterans seeking connections that for them, late in life, would add (or perhaps help validate) a dimension of meaning to their own war memory. Ironically, perhaps, the very patriotism that might have seemed to repel involvement by people of other nationalities attracted the Japanese, seeing a way to be involved in events that conveyed respect for service in the war that they would not find at home, at least not in the manner of highly public national memorializing.

Unlike December 7 anniversaries, however, Japanese commemorative activities in the 1990s and 2000s developed outside official ceremonial time and space. Because the memorial is also a destination for global tourism, it offered a space that could be appropriated for other sorts of activities, fostering interactions and inventive ritual practices that created their own threads of continuity, a genealogy of rites of reconciliation extending across more than two decades until those involved became too frail to enact them. Whereas some of these events attracted considerable media interest, especially in Hawai'i and Japan, few entered into mainstream American media, and one must look closely today to find inscriptions of those events in the more enduring representations of Pearl Harbor history.

Genealogies of Transnational Memory Making

Six months after I had begun fieldwork at the memorial, in July 1994, an unusual delegation came knocking at my door at the East-West Center. Since I'd been making short visits to the memorial for a few years and had developed friendships with some of the National Park Service staff and volunteers, I was not entirely surprised when Richard Fiske, the Marine bugler who survived the attack on the USS *West Virginia*, introduced in chapter 1 of this book, showed up with a Japanese veteran in tow, Jiro Yoshida, a pilot who trained to fly Japan's high-performing Zero fighters, along with another Japanese colleague, Hiroyu Sugano, and John Di Virgilio, a local schoolteacher and historian known for his research on Japanese veterans of the Pearl Harbor attack. Both Yoshida and Sugano had participated in the fiftieth anniversary commemoration of the Pearl Harbor attack, in 1991, among other events, and now were looking to the fiftieth anniversary of the end of the war in 1995 to expand the emergent culture of "friendship" between veterans that had been percolating during the anniversary period. On this occasion, this unusual team was visiting to ask if the East-West Center would be willing to be a sponsor for a commemorative ceremony that would bring American and Japanese veterans together in friendship, marking the fiftieth anniversary of the end of the Second World War. It was an unlikely request to an unlikely sponsor, but one that managed to crystallize a set of interests resulting, eventually, in an impressive ceremony at the National Memorial Cemetery of the Pacific (Punchbowl) one year later.

I had come to know Richard Fiske as one of the Pearl Harbor survivors volunteering their time at the memorial visitor center. And I knew John De-Virgilio from his work interviewing Japanese veterans of the attack and his careful reconstruction of the minute-by-minute destruction of the battleships. Yoshida and Sugano I met for the first time on that occasion. Yoshida, with a reasonable command of English, had gravitated to the position of spokesman for an organization of naval veterans of the Second World War, the Unabarakai. Sugano came with an artifact of war in hand, a kind of sacred relic in the form of a dented (actually, melted) aluminum canteen that had been salvaged from the crash site of two B-29s that had collided while on a bombing run over his home city of Shizuoka, Japan, on June 20, 1945. Growing up in that city, ravaged by fire bombing, he had developed a strong interest in the Second World War and found a personal connection to the memory of the B-29 crew who had died in that fiery crash but been buried with Buddhist rites thanks to the efforts of a devout citizen, Fukumatsu Ito, intent on preserving human dignity, even for the enemy bombing the city. Sugano was a child in 1945 but in time inherited Ito's project of honoring the dead crew, organizing a series "US-Japan Joint Memorial Services" in Shizuoka from 1970. He ultimately reached out to the Pearl Harbor memorial to extend the spirit of reconciliation, attending the fiftieth anniversary and searching for relatives of the deceased B-29 crew (Sugano 2001). That effort led to a memorial service in Japan in 1995 with relatives present and the performance of canteen rituals at the *Arizona* memorial that continue to the present (Meyers 2013).

Cautious at first and knowing little about the people and organizations behind the plan, I and the East-West Center were soon drawn into planning the commemorative ceremony conducted at Punchbowl Cemetery in September 1995. As I eventually came to understand, however, the event in 1995 was part of a longer history of transnational memory-making that dated back to the early days of the memorial and its visitor center. As others have observed, interactions between American and Japanese veterans had crystallized during the fiftieth anniversary commemoration in Honolulu in 1991 (Linenthal 1993; Rosenberg 2004). But those interactions, in turn, were preceded by earlier encounters that had been facilitated by the memorial as a social space traversed by diverse constituencies and interests.

Significantly, most of the goodwill events during the anniversaries of the 1990s were a result of initiatives by Japanese veterans seeking opportunities to express friendship with their American counterparts. As early as the twenty-fifth anniversary of Pearl Harbor, in 1966 (just a few years after dedication of the *Arizona* memorial, but well before construction of a visitor center), the lead pilot of the Pearl Harbor attack, Mitsuo Fuchida, made his way to the anniversary ceremony to make an offering of peace by presenting a Bible to Pearl Harbor survivors. Fuchida, who lived an incredible and charmed life, surviving the war, including his role on the first inspection team into the Hiroshima radiation zone, had become a Christian evangelist after the war and devoted himself to fostering a dialogue of peace between the United States and Japan (Prange et al. 1990). Recall from chapter 1 that it was Mitsuo Fuchida whom Pearl Harbor survivor Joe Morgan met in the 1950s with profound effects on his own feelings about former Japanese enemies. Although an unofficial presence during the 25th anniversary, Fuchida's actions were nonetheless prominently reported in local media. The *Honolulu Star-Bulletin* made this the lead story in their issue on December 7, 1966, featuring a large front-page photograph of Fuchida and Reverend Abraham Akaka, a prominent Hawaiian pastor, standing together holding the Bible with Pearl Harbor and the *Arizona* memorial behind them. Part of no governmental observances (he attended memorial services at Punchbowl National Cemetery as an anonymous visitor), Fuchida was the subject of one of Reverend Akaka's sermons at Kawaiaha'o Church, where he was introduced and bestowed with a lei.

The contacts and exchanges that unfolded in the 1980s and 1990s were facilitated by the existence of the *Arizona* memorial as a kind of international contact zone. As noted earlier, the location of the memorial and its visitor center in Hawai'i has shaped the kinds of commemorative activity that take place there through connections between the memorial and the broader multicultural society of Hawai'i, with its history of transnational social networks connecting the United States and Asia, especially Japan. The fact that Honolulu and Hiroshima have a sister-city relationship reflects a longer set of historical connections that begin in the nineteenth century with migrant labor from Hiroshima prefecture working in Hawai'i's sugar plantations. These relationships are the very same ties that brought suspicion and rejection down on the Japanese community during the war years but in the period of postwar alliance-building proved to be an important basis for reconnecting Japan with the United States. The USS *Arizona* Memorial may be a national memorial, operated by a federal agency for the benefit of a national constituency, but its location in Hawai'i has fostered a certain receptivity to intercultural relations.

With the expansion of the social space of the memorial in the 1980s came greater involvement with individuals, institutions, and organizations in Hawai'i or connected with Hawai'i and its Asian and Pacific heritage—organizations such as the Japanese Cultural Center of Hawai'i, the Spark M. Matsunaga Institute for Peace at the University of Hawai'i, and the federally funded East-West Center. Important effects are also evident in the biographies of key individuals resident in Hawai'i who played a role in facilitating transnational commemorative practices. A case in point is John Di Virgilio, the most active facilitator of Japanese and American friendship activities during the 1990s and 2000s, discussed below. He got his start at Pearl Harbor as a tour guide who was ultimately motivated to pursue his own self-funded historical investigations with encouragement from park service historians. Di Virgilio's family history as the son of a Japanese mother and U.S. military officer who had been with U.S. forces in occupied Japan gave him a strong interest in the Pacific War and U.S.-Japan relations (tape-recorded panel discussion, July 26, 2006). Even the local chapter of the Pearl Harbor Survivors Association had a significant number of members with connections to Hawai'i's multicultural society, through birth, marriage, or longtime residence. In a perceptive analysis of the veterans exchanges between Japan and the United States during the anniversary period of the 1990s, Marie Thorsten has noted that Hawai'i, as "America's most variegated multicultural habitat . . . provided an ironically hospitable venue" for the veterans to meet (2002, 323). Specifically, Hawai'i did this by offering a "more culturally porous milieu . . . away from the mainstream tensions in each of their respective nations" (318). Just how the structures and textures of Hawai'i have affected Pearl Harbor memorialization requires a closer look at the history of specific events and activities.

Daniel Martinez, the National Park Service historian who has worked at the USS *Arizona* Memorial since 1986, recalls the first visit to the memorial's visitor center by a group of Japanese veterans of the attack:

> In 1984 or 1983 the Japanese, about seven or eight of them, came as a group to pay their respects to the memorial. They were very apprehensive of how they would be welcomed. And so they just didn't announce themselves, they just came. And then word got back to the superintendent . . . "We have some Japanese pilots here." And they were so welcomed and escorted to the memorial, did their prayer service and all that they wanted. Somewhere I have that picture . . . they're bowing . . . Among the group was one Zenji Abe. And Zenji was so taken by that experience that he now saw an opportunity for himself to move forward with his

thoughts of connecting with American veterans . . . and he decided to do it on national television with *The Today Show*. . . . And that was the first act of reconciliation. The step toward reconciliation was their visit here. The atmosphere in which they were welcomed compelled them to sense that the USS *Arizona* Memorial would not be a dangerous or hostile place. (recorded interview, March 16, 2006)

The sheer presence of Japanese veterans in the memorial's memoryscape enabled contacts with American survivors of the attack, especially among the group of Hawai'i-based veterans who, in retirement, had begun volunteering to spend time at the memorial, telling their stories. A number of them welcomed the Japanese and showed their own interest to know more about the former enemy, now embodied by these aging veteran aviators looking much like themselves. Richard Fiske was one of these volunteers, as was an army survivor named Bob Kinzler (met in the previous chapter). In 2010 an AP reporter writing about the changes brought about by the memorial and visitor center quoted Bob Kinzler to the effect that it was the opportunity to meet Japanese veterans that initiated a shift in attitudes: "Robert Kinzler, 89, who was a soldier stationed at an Army base north of Pearl Harbor in 1941, said American survivors became more open to reconciliation after their former foes began visiting Hawaii before the 50th anniversary of the attack. 'We started getting Japanese pilots to come through and they were willing to answer any and all questions. And the attitudes began to change,' said Kinzler. 'There's two sides to this war'" (McAvoy 2011).

The core Pearl Harbor mythos, built around the narrative of a violent surprise ("sneak") attack, can easily be constructed around a kind of cardboard, one-dimensional enemy lacking subjectivity or humanity. This, of course, is the work of wartime propaganda, produced to dehumanize or demonize an enemy to be hunted on battlefields where killing is best done to anonymous adversaries. In the absence of contacts with the former enemy during the years after the war, there was little to disrupt or dislodge these sentiments, which, after all, are supported and reproduced in racial imagery (Dower 1986), even after the war ended and was replaced by a postwar alliance. But that started to change, for some, with those early encounters around the memorial decades later.

In some cases, the opportunity to meet and talk with the former enemy as persons initiated personal and emotional transformations that were in fact literally healing (a word that tends to be overused in describing commemorative activities that allow some kind of narrative reworking of wartime conflicts). Here is Richard Fiske, the Marine bugler who, after surviving the Pearl Harbor bombing experienced some of the most brutal combat of the war in Iwo Jima, almost died from an ulcer that his doctor attributed to emotional distress:

> RF: I just, I'd look at the Japanese and I would look past 'em, and trying not to make eye contact, because there was still that animosity. You look at them and [think] "Here you are here enjoying all of this and [look] what your compatriots did." . . . I've never talked about it like this. . . .
>
> GW: You just kept it in all that time.
>
> RF: Yeah. . . . Well it takes, uh, I think it takes someone to, if it'd been by myself I'd probably still be the same, but when you have someone talk to you, and it does it's just like when I was talking to a little bit with Mr. Maeda and Abe, and I got to realize what they went through and Mr. Yoshida. And tears come to my eyes, you know. Because I understand how they felt too, because they were under very strict orders. More than what we were. I mean if they didn't do it, they're gone. (recorded interview, December 7, 1995)

What seemed an anomalous development early on with the arrival of Japanese veterans on a kind of pilgrimage would become, eventually, a more public and visible part of the memorial's commemorative culture, even if always marginal to its primary focus on American veterans. But that work also opened up opportunities for the involvement of Japanese veterans in the mix of commemorative practices that became increasingly elaborate in the 1980s, leading up to the fiftieth anniversary, in 1991.

Beginning in 1986, the *Arizona* memorial began to organize public symposia in connection with the major anniversary years (every fifth year). These events brought large numbers of veterans back for the December 7 ceremonies. For veterans groups, many of whom helped raise funds to build the memorial, the memorial has been an important, even sacred, location for anniversary ceremonies (discussed above) and other memorial events. For all these, Pearl Harbor survivors, along with veterans of the Second World War and military veterans generally, are the primary honored guests and focus of appreciation. At no time was this more apparent than during the fiftieth anniversary commemoration, attended by about two thousand members of the Pearl Harbor Survivors Association—twice the number present for the twenty-fifth anniversaries, in 1966.

In addition to the fact that most American war memorial ceremonies are organized by and for American military constituencies, the possibility of Japanese participation in the fiftieth anniversaries of the Second World War in the

Pacific was made more difficult by public antagonism toward Japan during the preceding decade. In the United States in the 1980s, the discourse of "Japan bashing" extended wartime hostilities fueled by racialized depictions of an enemy that had committed atrocities and perpetrated a sneak attack on "sleeping" victims. Even though exchanges had begun to develop with Japanese veterans around the memorial during the 1980s, the intensification of anti-Japanese sentiments during the years leading up to the anniversary led to a policy of official exclusion of foreign representatives from the fiftieth anniversary events. By 1991 controversies had already drawn attention to the way the attack was being represented in the memorial's museum and film. As noted above, critics were arguing that the park service was distorting history in its efforts to tell a "balanced" story that would not offend Japan (or, from the state's vantage point, Japanese tourists). In this context, government agencies responsible for organizing the anniversary ceremonies worked to avoid open conflict by minimizing formal Japanese presence in the official activities. Proposals made by the park service to include some kind of dramatization of reconciliation as part of the observances of the fiftieth anniversary were dropped.[3] And the Department of Defense and Department of State decided to exclude all official foreign representation so as to avoid the problem of hosting an "unrepentant" Japan.[4]

Accounts of the fiftieth anniversary of Pearl Harbor have all noted the conflicting attitudes and sentiments that collided around the commemorative activities (Linenthal 1993; Rosenberg 2004; White 1997b). At the same time in which public resentments of Japanese economic power were fueling calls for an official apology for the attack on Pearl Harbor some of the survivors, along with Japanese veterans, were beginning to seek ways to show their interest in expressions of friendship.[5] The mix of countervailing sentiments made the efforts at reconciliation all the more uncertain and dramatic—a set of tensions often seized on in media accounts of the war anniversary events. Emily Rosenberg's survey of the commemorative activities and media representations during the anniversary concluded, "In the end, the books, articles, television programs, and speeches during the commemorative year of 1991 drew lessons to suit every persuasion" (2004, 103).

These diverse representations, particularly the seemingly opposed narratives of conflict and reconciliation, do not, however, occur in the abstract or in isolation; they are socially and historically located. Even if kept apart, the very separation of military remembrance from gestures of reconciliation is itself a symptom of the institutional organization of commemorative practice. The at times contradictory representations of Pearl Harbor during commemorative moments are socially (and hierarchically) organized, most often in dialogic tension with one another. As will be seen in the brief history of memorial practices traced here, it has been possible for multiple, contrasting modes of commemoration to cohabit memorial space, distributed across contexts and media capable of telling multiple stories to multiple publics. Indeed, the distribution itself tells a story about the politics of national memory-making.

During the fiftieth anniversary, in 1991, the commemoration, like all the December 7 anniversaries, focused on the primary agenda of honoring American losses, survivors of the attack, and veterans of the Second World War. It also, however, drew attention to a broader history of the attack that included the war's effects on civilian populations, issues of race and ethnicity in the military, Japanese American internment, and themes of reconciliation. On the day of the anniversary, President George Bush (senior) gave two speeches at Pearl Harbor: one on the *Arizona* memorial and one on shore at the naval base. The contrast reflects a spatial coding of memory with military discourse in the sacred center and broader societal themes occupying the more secular spaces of the naval base and visitor center. In his first speech of the day, Bush took on the controversial issue of Japanese American internment. Speaking at Punchbowl National Cemetery, where many Japanese American war veterans are buried, he criticized the flawed policy of internment. In contrast, the ceremony on the memorial focused on veterans and the role of today's military, leaving local experiences and international relations for speeches back on shore. There he delivered a speech in which he famously said that he "had no rancor in his heart" toward Japan—a statement that turned out to be highly quotable, cited often in exhibits and interpretive programs wishing to contextualize wartime hostilities with the contemporary reality of postwar friendship (Rosenberg 2004, 105).[6] His statement was eventually picked up and replayed in the visitor center's audio program as a way of bringing that theme more clearly into the commemorative space of the memorial. It is still invoked in key ritual moments at the visitor center, as in a ceremony in 2013 to install a small paper crane, folded by the young Japanese girl and Hiroshima bomb victim Sadako Sasaki (see chapter 5).

Bush's statement was especially significant because he himself was a veteran of the Second World War, speaking in the authentic voice of a pilot who had survived being shot down in the Pacific. News reporting during the fiftieth anniversary, as during all of the Second World War anniversaries, focused especially on veterans and survivors. Journalists reporting on the anniversaries pursued veterans, first, to elicit accounts of "what it was like" but also to ask how they felt about the war, looking back. Veterans became guardians of memory, the eyes (and minds) through which history could be imbued with personal and moral significance for the larger national community. During the fiftieth anniversary, one of the questions most commonly put to veterans was how they felt about Japan and Japanese people.

Despite the official exclusion of foreign (and Japanese) representation in the main commemorative ceremonies, a historical symposium organized by the park service as part of the anniversary program created another means for fostering some degree of Japanese and American dialogue, in this case in the interest of expanding public knowledge about the details of military history. By 1991, enough contacts had been made with Japanese veterans through the memorial and its work on oral history that a number were invited to speak on a panel in the symposium. While the official commemorative program kept its focus on honoring American veterans, the symposium offered a context for some tentative interactions between American and Japanese veterans. No doubt the preceding years of contacts initiated by Japanese veterans enabled attempts at more public gestures of friendship.

Because the symposia included social occasions and off-stage moments in which participants could meet one another, it provided an opportunity—one of the only opportunities since the war—for former warriors to be introduced to each other. Edward Linenthal, in commentary on the fiftieth anniversary commemoration, noted that "many of the most emotional events of these days were not announced on the formal program" (1991, 249). When both parties showed sufficient interest, they would engage in halting conversations, limited by language but in some cases facilitated by bilingual staff and relatives. (Even Japanese veterans and citizens interested in the war met each other in the anniversary symposium context. Sugano, it seems, met the Japanese Pearl Harbor veterans for the first time in Honolulu.) Just as Japanese veterans were usually in the lead in these developments, in at least one instance Japanese broadcasters worked to arrange an encounter that would capture this moment in evolving relations. One of the most dramatic encounters, set up to take place on camera during the fiftieth anniversary events, involved the introduction of two veterans of the Pearl Harbor attack, Richard Fiske (who would later come calling at the East-West Center) and Takeshi Maeda. In recalling this moment in an interview with me, Fiske described the emotional occasion as if he had been swept up in someone else's script (most likely that of Japanese TV producers):

GW: Tell me about the first time you met Maeda-san, what that was like.
RF: That was the most emotional thing in my whole career. I never, I
    wasn't really sure. See, they kept us apart. Before they introduced us
    they took us out on the memorial on one of the gray [navy] boats.

GW: Now you knew that you were going to be meeting Maeda on this day?

RF: I knew that he was on the boat but I didn't have any idea what he looked like.

GW: Who was it that set that up? How did you first get invited?

RF: I got a hunch Captain Woods set it up. And, so they kept him [Maeda] in the bow of the boat. They kept me in the stern. And they kept blocking my view so that I wouldn't see him. Then when we docked, now this is about nine o'clock at night [December 5], see we went to see the *Arizona* memorial. . . . So they already had the cameras out there. So when we docked, they made me get off first. And took me into the shrine room and put me in the corner. Then they had the TV all set up and everything. . . . And finally they say, "Mr. Fiske, I want you to meet Mr. Takeshi Maeda." And I looked at him. It seemed like about a half hour. It was probably about four or five seconds, I guess. We looked at one another and he looked at me and I automatically saw all of those torpedoes coming in toward the *West Virginia*.

GW: Is that right?

RF: And it was quite a flash back. And it seems like I was reliving that moment. And I, you know, wait a minute, this is not 1941.

GW: Shake yourself out of it.

RF: So then I went over to him. And, I just, it just seemed automatic that I would do this. And he did the same thing. We didn't, like this [extends both of his hands to demonstrate], we just held both hands . . .

GW: You didn't hold out one hand to shake?

RF: No, no. Neither one of us did.

GW: Just clasped?

RF: And we just came together and . . .

GW: Hugged?

RF: Cried. Honest to gosh, we cried. I, uh, we just held on to one another. I mean, it was, I'll never forget it as long as I live. It's just one of those things that we don't forget. And then we backed up, and then we shook hands. And you could see the tears on both of us. And then they asked questions back and forth. And they said "Mr. Fiske, what do you think of Mr. Maeda?" I said I hope that now we can, I said, I hope that we can seal our friendship this way, that we will always be friends. And they told him in Japanese and he did then,

we hugged again. Couple of more tears and . . . they were filming
it for the broadcasting in Japan on the sixth. And after it was over,
I got this picture with the producer, and they gave me this watch.
(recorded interview, November 18, 1994)

While the videotaped meeting of Richard Fiske and Takeshi Maeda may
have been orchestrated, many others during the anniversary were spontaneous, fortuitous encounters. With large numbers of veterans participating in
the symposium, contacts increased during the anniversary week to the point
where the closing dinner became an occasion for an unusually public demon-
stration of goodwill. The park service historian who was principal organizer of
the symposium recalls the unplanned moment when he called veterans from
both sides forward for joint recognition from the assembled audience. The resulting images of handshaking and posing for photographs became iconic images of rapprochement that stood in contrast to the tensions and uncertainties
of U.S.-Japan relations in 1991. For many of the Japanese veterans who had hes-
itated to come in the first place, and who rarely experienced this kind of public
appreciation at home, the experience motivated them to organize future activities around the theme of reconciliation. In this way the symposium experience
laid the foundation for further exchanges in subsequent years.

For Richard Fiske, who would become something of a heroic figure in the
work of reconciliation, the meeting with Maeda on the memorial would not
be the only new Japanese friendship emerging from the anniversary. He also
made the acquaintance of Zenji Abe, a dive-bomber pilot who was perhaps the
most active among Japanese veterans seeking opportunities for reconciliation
with former American adversaries. In thinking back to the anniversary during
an interview with me, he recalled meeting Abe, and forming something of an
odd couple as they sat side by side at the visitor center signing autographs to
satisfy an endless line of curious visitors and anniversary guests. He also recalled a lavish dinner at which both American and Japanese veterans dined out
together after the symposium and were given free champagne by an astonished
restaurant owner. From these anniversary activities, Fiske and Abe formed an
enduring relationship that would ultimately be recorded in countless media
stories and even a children's book (Nicholson 2001).

Abe, who, prior to the fiftieth anniversary, had sought out American veterans willing to make public statements of reconciliation (and who had initially
been rebuffed), seized the opportunity opened by these positive interactions
to set in motion his own ritualized means of sustaining the theme of reconciliation. Given the memorial as a place where individuals of any country are

FIGURE 2.4
Takeshi Maeda and Richard Fiske shake hands in shrine room. 1995.
Photo by author.

welcome to pay their respects to the men who died on the battleship *Arizona*, Abe came up with the idea for a small collaborative ceremony that came to be called the "sister rose ceremony"—a practice that has continued to the present time, past the deaths of both Abe and Fiske. Fiske described the origin of the ceremony in a conversation with Abe just before he left Honolulu to return to Japan after the fiftieth anniversary, in which Abe "peeled off three $100 bills" and said, "Please do me this favor. I want you to put two roses on the memorial, one rose for you and one rose for me, and then also if you get a chance to do the cemetery. And would you play taps" (recorded interview, November 18, 1994). At the time he recalled the start of the rose ritual (in 1994), Abe had just sent him another $300 to continue the practice.

In this informal and always ad-hoc ceremony, Richard Fiske would each month make an offering of two roses in the shrine room of the memorial, followed by his playing taps and making a brief statement about the significance of the event—usually to a curious group of tourists, those who happened to

FIGURE 2.5
Richard Fiske plays taps for rose ceremony, memorial shrine room. July 6, 1997.
Photo by author.

be the people present at the time he enacted the presentation. Usually assisted by John Di Virgilio, the local oral historian and dedicated facilitator of the veterans' friendship events, the elderly Marine bugler would enter the shrine room, set his bugle case off to the side and set about taping two roses to the stanchions in front of the shrine wall. Di Virgilio would then address people gathered in the shrine room to explain the friendship between Fiske and Abe and Abe's wish for reconciliation. Fiske would then play taps to a silent room. After finishing he would say a few words of his own, often tearing up, but seeing it through and then making himself available to any and all in the room. Here is the way he put it just after blowing taps on one occasion in 1997, when he had been doing this for six years and, as he proudly said, "hadn't missed a month" since 1991:

> Ladies and gentlemen, I want to thank you for sharing this moment with me. I do this once a month. One of my very dear friends who was a Japanese pilot who bombed my ship December 7th 1941. We became very good friends when we met in 1991.[7] Before he left to go back to Japan he asked me if I would put two roses on the *Arizona* Memorial, one

for him and one for me. He said, "I realize that the roses are small but," he said that "this is my way of saying I'm sorry." [Choking up] I've been doing this every month since 1991, haven't missed a month. He keeps sending me money to put the roses out here, which I do very gladly. And it's an honor for me to do this. We have become very very good friends. [Showing photo from his three-ring binder] This is what Mr. Abe looked like; that's when he was aboard his carrier *Akagi*. This is Mr. Abe and I together. If you'd like to come and take a picture of it, you're more than welcome. . . . I want to thank you all for coming out here and sharing this moment with me (voice quavers) because as Mr. Yoshida says, if you have love in your heart, there's no room for hate. If you have hate in your heart, there's no room for love. Thank you again. God bless you all. God bless each and every one of you [Pause, followed by applause]. (audio recording, May 26, 1997)

On this day, as in other instances, a number who had listened in a kind of puzzled amazement—the random audience for this unannounced event—then approached Fiske to follow up with questions of their own. In the case of Americans, questions often sought to connect his performance to their personal interests or family histories.

The rose ceremonies of Richard Fiske and Zenji Abe were one of a series of friendship activities that followed the anniversary symposium in 1991, in most cases initiated by Japanese groups. Usually occurring outside official, state-sponsored commemorative events, these activities exemplify the complex (and contested) life of memorials that, more often than not, become the locus of memorializing activities quite unforeseen in founding legislation. In the initial stages, the exchanges between Japanese and American veterans were mostly an individual affair, the result of personal contacts that allowed expressions of mutual respect. But these initiatives broadened out in ensuing years, spawning multiple events and enlisting the involvement of a small but growing number of American veterans (in which Hawai'i-based veterans played an important role). Eventually one of the largest Japanese veterans organizations, the Unabarakai, an organization of Japanese naval veterans, took on the mantle of publicizing and sponsoring friendship ceremonies between American and Japanese veterans in both Japan and the United States (Thorsten 2002).

It was this initiative that swept me up in its wake when Fiske, Di Virgilio, and Sugano came to see me in 1994, seeking East-West Center sponsorship for the end-of-war anniversary event in September 1995. Given the moves toward reconciliation during the symposium in 1991, a number of the actors involved (veterans and historians alike) started to think of the last of the fiftieth anniversaries, the anniversary of the signing of the surrender on board the USS *Missouri* in Tokyo Bay on September 2, 1945, as an occasion for a larger, more formal and public reconciliation event. The idea was to mark the end of the war with a ceremonial event expressing friendship between American and Japanese veterans.

The very fact that the unlikely delegation of Fiske, Sugano, and Di Virgilio came looking for support from an institution as anomalous as the East-West Center (little known outside circles of Asian studies in the Pacific region), was itself a clear sign that the event they envisioned was not part of mainstream commemorative culture. Fiske and his compatriots had already been deflected by the Hawaiian state planning committee charged with coordinating all the end-of-war anniversary activities planned for Hawai'i. The chair of the committee was sympathetic to their aims, but advised them to find sponsorship from local community groups and schedule their event just after the calendar of official activities—which included a presidential visit from Bill Clinton and multiple ceremonies sponsored by the service branches and Hawaiian veterans groups working with relevant federal and state agencies. As an indication of the contentious nature of Pacific War memory at this time, consider that this Punchbowl event was held just one month after the cancellation of the Smithsonian Air and Space Museum's plan to mount a major atomic bomb exhibit on the occasion of the fiftieth anniversary of the bombing of Hiroshima and Nagasaki.

Despite worries about unresolved tensions in U.S. and Japanese war memory, the idea for a reconciliation event involving Japanese and American veterans ultimately produced an extraordinary "friendship ceremony," held September 4, 1995, at Punchbowl National Cemetery, in Honolulu, an American military ceremony operated by the Department of Veterans Affairs. Such an outcome was, however, hardly anticipated in the early stages of planning. Like many of the activities in this genealogy of marginal memory-making, most of the protocol for the proposed event was made up in conversations among interested individuals. Institutions fell in line where opportunities seemed to fit institutional agendas. Even if it would be outside official commemorative time and space, the proposed event crystallized a set of interests with enough support in Honolulu to produce a significant ritual moment in the commemorative history of the Pacific War. In addition to the East-West Center, the planning group found willing sponsors in the Matsunaga Peace Institute of the University of Hawai'i and the Hawai'i Army Museum Society, the nonprofit organization that operates the U.S. Army Museum at Fort DeRussy, in Honolulu.

Members of these organizations, along with the historian of the National Park Service, first imagined an event held either at the East-West Center or the army museum. Talking with the committee, John Di Virgilio came up with the idea of a plaque dedication signifying friendship between Japanese and American veterans. The ceremony would dedicate two bronze plaques, to be installed in both American and Japanese memorial sites. Questions about the place for the ceremony and for installation of the plaque were quickly settled once the director of the Punchbowl cemetery responded positively to the group's inquiry, indicating that the ceremony could be held at the cemetery so long as the event had an American institutional sponsor. With the cemetery as location, the plaque could be placed along its memorial walkway, lined with plaques from organizations that have hosted ceremonies there (a location where the plaque resides today). Approval to hold the ceremony at Punchbowl made it possible for event planners to incorporate a military color guard and band, signifiers of the state sponsorship mobilized by the Punchbowl cemetery location.

The dedication of two plaques is indicative of the transnational nature of the Punchbowl ceremony. Not only did the event involve both American and Japanese participants, but it linked directly to the Japanese veterans' own memorial activities with their Unabarakai organization back in Japan. I had a close-up look at one of those activities when I was invited to be a speaker at a Unabarakai service in 1994, a year prior to the Punchbowl ceremony. Although limited by a lack of language ability, my understanding of that event benefits from the work of Marie Thorsten in Japanese studies, who was involved in a number of Unabarakai activities in both Honolulu and Japan, taking an interest in the question of what parts of veterans' national memories intersect in these "zones of intertextuality" (Thorsten 2002, 328).[8] During the 1990s, at least, the Unabarakai held a memorial ceremony each year in a small memorial park on the grounds of a Japanese Self-Defense Forces (SDF) base in the city of Tsuchiura and generally tried to include an American guest in the ceremony. As I would eventually realize, in participating in that ceremony, I was filling an American slot in a ceremonial structure that validated the strong value placed on positive U.S.-Japan relations. Other speakers who participated in that same event during these years included Richard Fiske, the National Park Service historian for Pearl Harbor, and the director of the Punchbowl cemetery (they were required by their federal agencies to participate "as private citizens").

My participation in that event in October 1994 allowed a more personal insight into the sentiments and motives of the Japanese veterans. As John Dower (1999) and others have described, the calamity of military defeat and civilian suffering in Japan produced strong antimilitary sentiments among the war generation, for whom the military build-up and blind patriotism that took the nation to war in the 1930s and 1940s had proven catastrophic. In line with the skepticism and distrust of militarism shared by many in postwar Japan, veterans were ignored or even denigrated—an inversion of the intense valorization of military heroes during the war itself.

In light of these attitudes, some Japanese war veterans likely saw the American programs as a path to recognition or validation from former enemies, validation not found at home. Indeed, a short statement by Jiro Yoshida, a former Zero fighter pilot and Unabarakai organizer, used in publicity materials for the anniversary in 1995 suggests such a feeling. With words borrowed from the group's American historian, John Di Virgilio, the statement separates "we, the veterans" from the "old warlords" and then asserts that each veteran "served with dignity": "All the old warlords who wanted war are now gone, leaving us, the veterans, with the obligation to stitch together the fabric of friendship. . . . Every veteran put forward his best effort in the desperate struggle throughout the Pacific war. Each served with dignity." The Japanese veterans traveling to Honolulu in 1995 (many with family members) understood that they would be observers of the official events taking place over a weekend, leading up to their own ceremony, in Punchbowl. Even though lacking official invitation or recognition, they nonetheless came prepared to express their sentiments of respect for their former enemies during the official parade, when the American veterans would be featured in a long parade through the middle of Waikiki, in Honolulu. The morning of the parade, a large group of the Japanese visitors assembled along the parade route, Kalakaua Avenue, just outside their hotel. They unfurled one huge banner from the hotel's second floor with a graphic of a handshake and the flags of the United States, Japan, and Hawai'i, saying, "FRIENDSHIP SALUTE. TO THE AMERICAN AND ALLIED VETERANS OF WWII FROM THE JAPANESE VETERANS." And the veterans themselves stood at the side of the street holding another banner with the same handshake graphic and the words "WWII PACIFIC WAR VETERANS. FOREVER FRIENDS. 1945–1995."

If the Japanese veterans were risking rejection in their bid to participate in a joint commemorative activity, so were their American counterparts. A number of the latter had already been challenged four years earlier, during the 1991 anniversary, when a group from Georgia had proposed a veteran-to-veteran ceremony and were roundly chastised by the leadership of the national Pearl Harbor Survivors Association (Thorsten 2002, 321). In many ways the same climate of opposition and ambivalence continued through 1995, with the official commemoration committee declining sponsorship and the president

FIGURE 2.6
Japanese veterans of Second World War hold sign along parade route for fiftieth
anniversary of the end of the war commemoration, Waikiki. September 2, 1995.
Photo by author.

of the Pearl Harbor Survivors Association (PHSA) again writing a letter, this
time to the Honolulu chapter of the PHSA, asserting that none of the members
would be allowed to wear their association shirts or caps—a dictate that most
seemed to ignore.

In this contentious milieu, the "end of war" event in 1995 took on a kind of
hybrid complexion, with numerous elements of official sponsorship and the
ritual apparatus of American war commemoration—evidence that the event
had been quietly excluded from the centers of U.S. military commemoration.
Except for the sponsorship of the Punchbowl National Cemetery (and the
federally funded East-West Center), it was the Hawaiian state context that
enabled a full-fledged ceremony conducted in a national memorial space
(even if not the *Arizona* memorial) and coverage in local news media (if not
national media). Just as it was support from the Hawaiian state commemoration committee (headed by the Hawaiian-born retired admiral Robert Kihune)

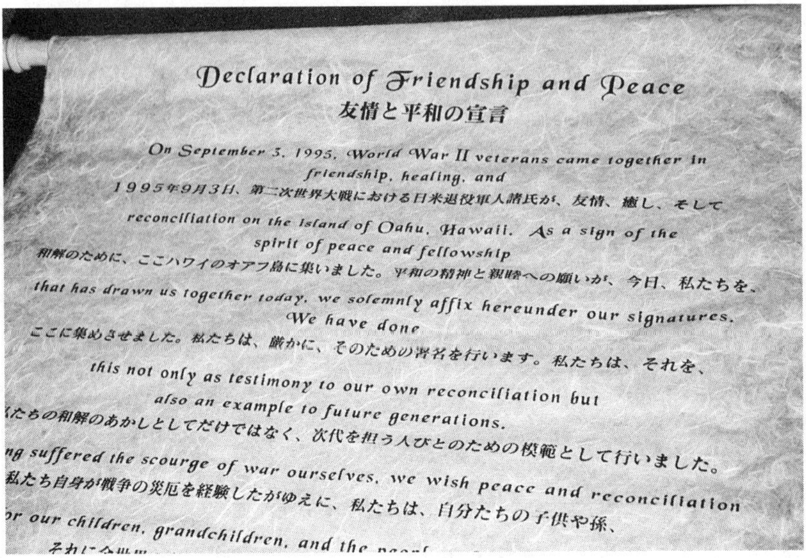

Declaration of Friendship and Peace
友情と平和の宣言

On September 3, 1995, World War II veterans came together in
friendship, healing, and
1995年9月3日、第二次世界大戦における日米退役軍人諸氏が、友情、癒し、そして
reconciliation on the Island of Oahu, Hawaii. As a sign of the
spirit of peace and fellowship
和解のために、ここハワイのオアフ島に集いました。平和の精神と親睦への願いが、今日、私たちを、
that has drawn us together today, we solemnly affix hereunder our signatures.
We have done
ここに集めさせました。私たちは、厳かに、そのための署名を行います。私たちは、それを、
this not only as testimony to our own reconciliation but
also an example to future generations.
たちの和解のあかしとしてだけではなく、次代を担う人びとのための模範として行いました。
ng suffered the scourge of war ourselves, we wish peace and reconciliation
私たち自身が戦争の災厄を経験したがゆえに、私たちは、自分たちの子供や孫、
r our children, grandchildren, and the peopl

FIGURE 2.7
Declaration of Friendship and Peace scroll. September 3, 1995.
Photo by Michael White.

FIGURE 2.8
American and Japanese veterans sign the Declaration of Friendship and
Peace. Hale Koa Hotel, Waikiki. September 3, 1995.
Photo by author.

that first encouraged the veterans, it was letters of support from state political leaders in Hawai'i that filled the official program (letters from the governor of Hawai'i, Ben Cayetano, Hawai'i's senior senator, Daniel Inouye, and the mayor of Honolulu, Jeremy Harris). Significantly, for the Japanese veterans especially, the consul general of Japan in Hawai'i also provided an official letter.

The veterans' friendship events of September 1995 in fact consisted of two days of activities, including a reception at the military Hale Koa Hotel, next door to the army museum in Waikiki, at which participants were invited to personally sign a "Declaration of Friendship" produced in the form of two large scrolls, followed the next day by the plaque dedication ceremony at Punchbowl cemetery. The organizing principle for all these events, particularly the Punchbowl ceremony, was the duality of joint performances and presentations by American and Japanese veterans. Every aspect of the ceremony expressed this duality: national anthems of Japan and the United States, welcomes from American and Japanese sponsors, two keynote speeches by Japanese and American veterans, wreath presentations by pairs of Japanese and American veterans (many of whom had met first at the *Arizona* memorial) and the unveiling of the two plaques by a pair of prominent Japanese and American veterans. Except for the keynote speaker, most of the American veterans in these presentations were Pearl Harbor survivors.

Tea, Roses, and the Routinization of Remembrance

As dramatic and photogenic as the events in 1995 were, they remained outside official commemorative space. That would all begin to change fifteen years later when, at the same time, the voices of survivors were rapidly receding. As noted for the trajectory of December 7 ceremonies, with the shift from survivors as keynote speakers to a diminishing set of elderly veterans to be venerated, it is leaders in military or civilian service who now speak about history rather than from or as history. As a result, the ritual practices for memorializing Pearl Harbor were increasingly expressed in a bureaucratic register—a mode of representation or type of speaking that can be performed by anyone in the appropriate position, according to military rank or political appointment. Such speeches often reach for personal connections in making remembrance "real," affected by experience, but increasingly it is experience outside the frame of December 7, with the speaking authorized by position rather than participation.

Changes associated with the disappearance of the war generation and Pearl Harbor survivors have long been anticipated by the public historians and administrators who manage the memorial, all of whom are acutely aware that while an irreplaceable "resource" is being lost, new opportunities for expanded interpretation are emerging as the veterans, guardians of their memory, pass away. In a turn of events that few had anticipated, however, the presidential proclamation of the World War II Valor in the Pacific National Monument, in 2008, would significantly alter the administrative organization of the memorial in ways that converged with the diminishing presence of Pearl Harbor survivors to accelerate ongoing transformations in the memorialization of Pearl Harbor.

In December 2008 President George W. Bush issued his proclamation creating a new national monument that would bring more prominence to the Second World War as remembered in America by grouping together nine historic sites associated with the war (see introduction, note 10). The monument came at the same time that popular support for the wars in Iraq and Afghanistan was in rapid decline and a new Democratic administration about to take office. The fact that this wider mandate came when the number of Pearl Harbor survivors was diminishing to a small group of frail men in their late eighties and nineties suddenly opened up a variety of topics and approaches that previously would not have been considered relevant for American memory of the December 7 bombing attack. It seems likely that few at the higher levels of government responsible for reengineering the administrative context for the *Arizona* memorial realized that this reorganization would achieve in a single move what decades of contested remembrance could not—situating the Pearl Harbor bombing attack in a broader context of war that includes, in equal measure, civilian and military casualties, as well as the impacts of war for all sides involved. As the short version of the mandate for the new monument on the park service website reads, "World War II Valor in the Pacific National Monument preserves and interprets the stories of the Pacific War, including the events at Pearl Harbor, the internment of Japanese Americans, the battles in the Aleutians, and the occupation of Japan" (http://www.nps.gov/valr/index .htm, accessed September 12, 2013).

Even though the interpretive scope of the monument has yet to be worked out in any detail, the wider framework enables an expansion of historical and educational programs to address ultimately the entire history of the Pacific War. In addition to Pearl Harbor, this includes the internment experience of Japanese Americans and even of a defeated Japan. Recent activities at the memorial show that these developments opened the door to new forms of local, national, and transnational commemorative activity that include topics assiduously avoided in the past, such as the atomic bombings of Hiroshima and Nagasaki and the discourse of "peace" associated with remembrance ceremonies in those cities—cities that have historical ties with Hawai'i's Japanese American population.

Although the declaration of the new monument came too late to affect the basic design and narrative structure of the new museum (where exhibit designs had reached the 90 percent completion phase at the end of 2008, see chapter 5), the formation of the monument had an immediate impact on the kinds of activities hosted in the new space. Even though planning and fundraising had been carried out under the name Pearl Harbor Memorial Foundation when the new facility was opened in 2010, it was dedicated as the World War II Valor in the Pacific National Monument (VALR) visitor center and museum. While the memorial spanning the *Arizona* may be fixed in architectural form, the activities that take place there are not. Also somewhat fixed are the exhibits of the museum and walkways on shore that only undergo change after an extended planning and approval process (chapter 5). In contrast, the events and activities that take place in and around the memorial are planned from year to year and hence more readily accommodate change. With the advent of VALR, once marginal or ambivalent topics that had been present around the edges began to show up in the center of commemorative space, including its sacred center. Thus, Hiroyu Sugano, who had been coming on his own initiative to perform ritual offerings of water poured from the melted B-29 canteen, has for the last few years found himself hosted by an increasingly formalized ceremony of reconciliation organized and presented by the National Park Service.

Coming in rapid succession after the opening of the new visitor center, in December 2010, would be an extraordinary Japanese tea ceremony conducted on the memorial itself in July 2011, and a ceremony accepting the donation of a paper crane from Hiroshima in September 2012, followed by a dedication ceremony for the new exhibit displaying the crane in September 2013. Although quite different in nature (the tea ceremony a one-time ceremonial event conducted on the memorial and the paper crane project focused on a display that would become part of the permanent exhibits of the new museum), both were fundamentally transnational, with ties to Japanese tradition and commemorative culture. Although a tiny addition to the visual displays in the museum, the incorporation of a highly iconic object associated with the atomic bombing of Hiroshima, centered on the story of the fourteen-year-old girl who died from radiation sickness after attempting to fold 1,000 cranes (Coerr and Himler 1977), marks a momentous turning point in the memorial's commemorative culture by linking Pearl Harbor and Hiroshima, two topics closely aligned in history but for decades kept separate in American commemorative practices— an innovation not lost on Japanese commentators (Inoue 2013).

FIGURE 2.9
Hiroyu Sugano, assisted by Daniel Martinez and Takeshi Maeda,
pours water from the B-29 canteen into the well of the USS *Arizona* Memorial.
Photo by author.

Visits of individuals or small groups that once might have been personal visits (as was the case for many of the Japanese veterans in the 1990s) now take on
the aura of a national event with state (federal) sponsorship. Along with larger
ceremonies, such as the tea ceremony or the dedication of the paper crane
exhibit, held in 2011 and 2013, smaller, more transient activities can now be
framed as expressions of a larger theme, as the work of national memory (if
not of the memorial, then of the World War II Valor in the Pacific National
Monument). Thus, the initiatives of Japanese individuals to enlist American
counterparts in the conduct of inventive transnational rituals in and around the
memorial, once relegated to the edges of sacred time and space, have gradually
gained official sponsorship. To take one example, when three members of the
Japanese Diet (parliament) visited Honolulu in January 2014 to strengthen relations with the state of Hawai'i, they made a floral presentation in the shrine
room of the memorial, accompanied by two Hawaiian state legislators, the
local Japanese consul general, and the NPS superintendent. The group marked
the occasion with a photo showing everyone holding roses and standing in

front of the shrine's wall of names, to either side of a floral bouquet crossed with a ribbon with the words "Japan–Hawaii Friendship." Such events have long been commonplace in Japanese official visits to the state or to the navy. However, given recent developments, the NPS superintendent could now describe the visit in an e-mail to the NPS Office of International Affairs as follows, linked to the newly installed Sadako crane exhibit (see chapter 5): "They were participating in a legislative alliance between Japan and the State of Hawaii. After the visit to the USS *Arizona* Memorial, we reviewed the recently unveiled Sadako Sasaki Origami Crane Exhibit in the museum gallery. Sadako Sasaki's story is emblematic of the rise of the peace movement in Japan following its defeat and occupation by the Allied Forces" (Paul DePrey, NPS superintendent, e-mail to NPS Office of International Affairs, January 27, 2014).

While the tea ceremony did not involve a topic as contentious as the atomic bombings, it was in some ways an even more radical activity because it was conducted in the sacred space of the memorial and shrine room. Performed on the platform over the sunken ship, the tea master prepared tea for a distinguished audience on the memorial platform and made a ritual offering in the shrine room to those who died in battle. First and most obvious to note is the fact that tea ceremonies are a quintessentially Japanese activity. Regardless of the meanings conveyed through the ritual preparation and serving of tea, the very fact that a tea ceremony is conducted in that space ritually transforms it into Japanese cultural space, where meaning and value derive from a tradition of Japanese practice. Furthermore, as an activity that requires rigorous training and apprenticeship, tea ceremonies give expression not only to the specialized skill and a refined aesthetic cultivated in the Japanese tradition of tea, they also convey something of attitudes toward Japanese national culture and the value of traditional or high culture, even if one of the proclaimed values was the importance of communicating to all nationalities, "regardless of language, nationality or religious beliefs."[9] Indeed, in this case, the tea ceremony was not just any tea ceremony, it was a ceremony conducted by Genshitsu Sen, a grand tea master of the Urasenke School of Tea, the largest of several Japanese tea schools. As some of the American reporting noted, the eighty-eight-year-old Sen was "the 15th generation of his family to lead Urasenke, which dates to the 1600s" (Associated Press, 2011).

Given the disparity in the significance of a tea ceremony for Japanese and American audiences, and the complex and often intensely guarded nature of commemorative activities on the memorial, how did the ceremony come to pass? Numerous factors had to come into alignment: the National Park Service, Pearl Harbor survivors, and the U.S. Navy would all need to be on board.

FIGURE 2.10
Grand Tea Master Dr. Genshitsu Sen performs sacred tea ceremony on the
USS *Arizona* Memorial. July 19, 2011.
Photo by author.

In each case, the stars seemed to come into alignment: the park service had its new monument, with a broader interpretive mandate, the Pearl Harbor Survivors Association had just the year before formally dissolved their organization, and the U.S. Navy had just completed a successful mission to Japan, assisting recovery efforts after the Fukushima nuclear disaster and were open to a strong expression of goodwill in the service of alliance-building. The origins of the ceremony, moreover, have their roots in the history of Japanese people in Hawai'i and the extensive personal and institutional ties that have developed between Hawai'i and Japan since the nineteenth century. In this case, the individual biography of the grand tea master who performed the ceremony included significant experience in Hawai'i from the time he came to study at the University of Hawai'i, in 1951, after the war, and subsequently founded the Hawaiian branch of the Urasenke School in 1951. Thus, the tea master's own biography and history provided an additional backstory and rationale for the ceremony, already known to a significant segment of Hawai'i's Japanese American community commemorating a sixtieth anniversary for their school.

The idea for the tea ceremony was first proposed by Jean Ariyoshi, the wife of Hawai'i's first Japanese American governor, George Ariyoshi. In their reporting on the event, Honolulu media describe the birth of the idea as Jean Ariyoshi's vision:

> The idea came to Ariyoshi while she and former Gov. George Ariyoshi enjoyed a Pearl Harbor dinner cruise hosted by Adm. William J. Fallon, then head of the U.S. Pacific Command. As the admiral's barge cruised past the USS Arizona Memorial, which straddles the sunken remains of the Arizona battleship, "I had this vision of people getting together, healing together, and honoring the war dead and praying for world peace," Ariyoshi said. "I thought, 'There's no more beautiful place than to do it here.'" (Nakaso 2011)

Ariyoshi's impulse to give expression to themes of peace and reconciliation at the memorial was, in fact, not dissimilar from views of many Japanese visitors to Pearl Harbor who commonly express remorse and a desire to advance the cause of world peace when visiting the memorial (Yaguchi 2005). The fact that the vision comes from Hawai'i's Japanese American community again demonstrates the importance of Hawai'i as the location for the Arizona memorial, bringing the cultural politics of Hawai'i to bear on the memorial's commemorative potential. In this case, as in that of the Sadako crane exhibit, Hawai'i's Japanese American citizens and institutions would play an important role mediating linkages with Japan's discourses of war remembrance.

The conditions for Pearl Harbor commemoration have not always favored such linkages. Indeed, when first proposed six years earlier, neither the National Park Service nor the navy were interested to take on sponsorship, giving reasons such as their preoccupation with building a new visitor center. After the creation of the Valor in the Pacific World War II National Monument and the continuing "Pacific pivot" in U.S. global military strategy, sentiments became more hospitable. Having been put off for a number of years, Mrs. Ariyoshi's proposal finally seemed to resonate with the sponsors' commemorative agendas. In the eyes of the park service and the navy, the project could only be accepted with the understanding that Pearl Harbor survivors would not raise a strong public challenge. Even though the national Pearl Harbor Survivors Association was less and less vocal on the national scene, the park service took steps to preempt possible objections by ensuring that several local survivors would be prominently recognized in the ceremony and by writing in advance to each surviving member of the Arizona crew, as well as by sending formal notice to the Pearl Harbor Survivors Association, explaining the event in terms of its intent to honor those who died in the attack.

On July 19, 2011, Grand Master Sen conducted a tea ceremony on the memorial in a ritual event that combined elements of the December 7 anniversaries discussed above (Hawaiian prayer, U.S. national anthem, state anthem) with the Japanese tea ceremony and, to conclude the event, both Japanese and American bugle calls (a Japanese military melody followed by taps).[10] The program notes make the syncretic nature of the ceremony clear, calling the event "A Sacred Tea Ceremony for World Peace and to Honor the War Dead at Pearl Harbor," subtitled "In commemoration of the Sixtieth Anniversary of Chado Urasenke Tankokai, Hawaii."[11] When Jean Ariyoshi, as mistress of ceremonies, welcomed guests to the "tea gathering," she welcomed them on behalf of "Dr. Genshitsu Sen, 15th generation Grand Tea Master of the Urasenke tradition, the National Park Service, the U.S. Navy, and the Urasenke Tankokai Hawai'i." The guests themselves also constituted a list of navy officers, federal and state officials, and U.S. war veterans, including three from Japanese American units well known for their war service, and finally three Pearl Harbor survivors (from the group of local survivors who work closely with the memorial). When Jean Ariyoshi got to the survivors, the last to be introduced, she slowed her tempo and asked them to rise: "And . . . our very special honored guests . . . Would you please rise. Three Pearl Harbor survivors." They were then greeted with applause as they were introduced by name and thanked by the MC.

The opening prayer and anthems, much like the December 7 ceremonies, were followed by a message from Hawaiian senator Daniel Inouye (in absentia) and remarks from the governor of Hawai'i, the commander of the U.S. Pacific Fleet, a regional director for the National Park Service, and the consul general of Japan in Honolulu. The presence of the Japanese consul general as a keynote speaker at the Pearl Harbor ceremony was first made possible by the tea ceremony. From the time of the decision at the fiftieth anniversary not to invite foreign representation, no representative of Japan had ever spoken in a December 7 ceremony. In this respect, the tea ceremony, as a thoroughly transnational activity, organized with Urasenke and its strong ties to Hawai'i and initiated by a well-positioned Hawai'i Japanese American (Ariyoshi), made possible an event that otherwise would have seemed unthinkable in the ritual traditions of the memorial.

Since the presence of Japanese government representatives in the Pearl Harbor context always raises, for Americans, the desire to hear an "apology," Japanese officials have also avoided situations that would raise contentious issues in domestic politics over issues of war responsibility and culpability. Not surprising, in his remarks the consul general talked about the war in abstract and morally neutral language that might be used to describe a natural disaster ("Hawaii underwent an attack by the Japanese military"), as something that happened to both countries ("who experienced a few difficult years together"), and is primarily of interest as an occasion that, in retrospect, was an opportunity "to become fast friends and solid allies":[12]

> Hawaii underwent an attack by the Japanese military, which triggered a war between Japan and the United States. Today we come full circle, as a Sacred Tea Ceremony is about to be held in that old battleground here in Pearl Harbor. Although the United States and Japan experienced a few difficult years together, once the war was over, our countries became fast friends and solid allies. When the Northeast region of Japan was undergoing a crisis earlier this year due to terrible devastation from natural disasters, the United States Military Forces stationed at Pearl Harbor were the first to mobilize and offer critical aid under the code name "Operation Tomodachi" ["Operation Friend"]. The people of Japan were deeply moved and touched when the United States responded in our hour of greatest need to demonstrate the strength of U.S.-Japan relations.

The consul general's references to the disaster at Fukushima and the response of the United States were reinforced in the remarks of the U.S. Navy commander, Admiral Patrick Walsh. Speaking before the consul general, Admiral Walsh focused all of his comments on that moment of intense cooperation, taking the opportunity to praise the performance of the Japanese Self-Defense Forces working with U.S. forces and "Operation Tomodachi":

> Today, our quintessential gift has been the opportunity for a proud, strong relationship with our counterparts from the Japanese Self-Defense Force. It is a relationship that now exists between families based on trust, mutual strength, and an inner strength understood and respected by the descendants of combatants and warriors and further reinforced by our shared response to modern day challenges and tests. . . . If history ever records a time and a place to witness an impressive operation, to witness a team in action, to witness heartfelt contribution without concern for credit, it will remember Operation Tomodachi as a force that landed on its feet within hours of an unprecedented crisis and proved beyond measure what it means to be a friend. (Admiral Patrick M. Walsh, commander, U.S. Pacific Fleet, audio recording July 19, 2011)

The comments from these keynote speakers, powerfully positioned on both sides of the state-to-state relationship of the United States and Japan, illustrate well the continuing evolution and adaptation of Pearl Harbor memorializing to contemporary circumstances, in this case the articulation of a strong friendship and defense relationship, once enemies in the Second World War but today strategic partners in the "Pacific Century." The convergence of these interests, along with the expansion of the mission of the National Park Service at the *Arizona* memorial made possible an event that was nonetheless controversial.

The controversy, however, remained muted, confined to conversations among some of the survivors who are not reconciled to reconciliation as well as to members of the public who posted comments on local news sites or editorialized online. Thus, political commentator Wesley Pruden, writing in the (less than mainstream) *Washington Times*, called the event "political correctness run amok" and concluded, "A tea party aboard the remains of the USS *Arizona*, however well-meant, is sentiment misplaced, and a little bit creepy."[13] And a political blogger, Gary Graybill, commented, "Regardless of the symbolism and the intention to promote peace and reconciliation, I can not help but think that those sailors and marines, killed without warning that Sunday morning in 1941, whose final resting place was used for the ceremony, would not have approved." He went on to draw a comparison with the controversy of building a mosque adjacent to the World Trade Center.[14]

As the World Trade Center comparison suggests, and as might be expected from the significance of the memorial and its shrine room as sacred space, much of the public criticism of the event crystallized around the problem of venue, of the choice of the memorial as the location for the ceremony that, for some, was seen as a violation, an intrusion of actors, voices, and narratives inconsistent with the core purpose of the memorial as a place for honoring war dead. For others, though, the ceremony was appropriate precisely because it did recognize the sacred significance of ritual performed on "hallowed ground." Online comments on a local article about the ceremony ran the gamut of views: "The Japanese tea ceremony is an ancient, formal ritual that is held in high regard. As such, I can see why it can be a way to acknowledge the past. Still, as I read this article, my gut reaction was that the venue somehow just seems WRONG." "Maybe a Japanese tea ceremony is innocuous to most but the Memorial located at the ship's site is hallowed ground and shouldn't be subjected to even well-meaning events that may re-invoke painful sentiments. I strongly suggest that it be held instead at the *Arizona* Memorial Visitors Center." "While I agree that the U.S.S. *Arizona* Memorial is hallowed ground for all Americans, what better way to demonstrate our acceptance of friendship and reconciliation than to allow a close friend and former enemy to honor our own war dead on such hallowed ground? . . . The Memorial should serve to honor Americans who died during the attack, but it can also serve as a place of healing."[15]

These comments reflect the uncertainties and ambivalences to be expected at a moment in time when institutional practices of and for memorializing Pearl Harbor are themselves in flux, on the cusp of the era of witnessing, ushering in a new era in which the speakers, narratives, and ritual practices are changing. Amid this change, Pearl Harbor survivors remain an important, if shrinking, presence. On this occasion, as in every other memorial event, journalists sought comments from the three survivors who had been invited to participate in the ceremony. Even though all three were from the local chapter, many of whom have been involved in the friendship ceremonies with Japanese veterans (and two of them regular volunteers at the memorial), published comments from one, Ray Emory, reflect the undercurrent of discontent shared by some of his peers. Even though he was among the honored guests at the ceremony, he didn't hide his own skepticism about the event: "Pearl Harbor survivor Ray Emory, who shot at Japanese fighter planes 70 years ago with a .50-caliber machine gun during the attack on Pearl Harbor, attended Tuesday's tea service and struggled to reconcile his emotions. 'Not knowing much about the Japanese culture, it's hard to understand the ritual,' Emory said. 'The Japanese government has always been reluctant to recognize that Pearl Harbor even happened. . . . Maybe, sometimes, it's a little too late'" (Nakaso 2011).

Despite the critical tone, the very fact that Ray Emory participated in the ceremony reflects the longer-term, ongoing shift in the memorial's commemorative culture since Emory, former "historian" for the local chapter of the Pearl Harbor Survivors Association, has at times been a severe critic of the park service management of the memorial—prominently cited in the media at the time of the fiftieth anniversary—and generally kept his distance from the friendship events with Japanese veterans in the 1990s. Since the Tea Master Sen is also a veteran of the Second World War, having served in the Japanese naval air force, his reflections about the meaning of the ceremony gave it some of the significance of the veterans' reconciliation events discussed earlier, activities that have taken place on the memorial and in the visitor center since the 1980s and 1990s. It is more than a little ironic that it was only after most of the Japanese veterans had passed away or were too old to travel that an officially sponsored, transnational commemorative ceremony would be conducted on the memorial itself, with a Japanese veteran preparing tea.

As the veterans themselves declared, the end-of-war ceremonies in 1995 were the last major events in which large numbers of Pacific War veterans would, physically, convene in a joint ceremony. With Japanese economic power declining, veterans aging, and America caught up in the post-9/11 wars in the Middle East, vocal hostility toward Japan and resistance to exchanges with Japanese veterans declined. In its place were more institutionalized activities, including the formalization of some of the informal activities initiated earlier by veterans, such as Zenji Abe and Dick Fiske's rose ceremonies. These new forms of transnationalism were not centered on war veterans but rather express institutionally sponsored themes pertaining to U.S.-Japan relations, themes that sometimes intersect awkwardly with the work of honoring the young men who died (or lived through) the explosion of war in 1941.

The ongoing transformation and adaptation of the rose ceremony is a case in point. Much of the power of ritual, repeated over time, is that the performance can be sustained even if the performers pass on. While the parameters of the ritual may change to adapt to changing circumstances, practices expressing a basic ceremonial purpose persist. Indeed, in this case, the rose ceremonies performed by Fiske had become so well known that a local author, Dorinda Nicholson, wrote a children's book about this unlikely friendship, *Pearl Harbor Warriors: The Bugler, the Pilot, the Friendship* (2001). Published in time for the sixtieth anniversary, in 2001, her book turned their story into a parable for children's learning about war and peace, fixed in published text and images that mesh well with the expanded mission of the World War II Valor in the Pacific National Monument.

Since the deaths of Richard Fiske, in 2004, and Zenji Abe, in 2007, the rose ceremony has been carried on by others, facilitated by John Di Virgilio (longtime facilitator of veterans' friendship ceremonies) as well as the park service historian Daniel Martinez. First, with the death of Fiske, the rose ceremony shifted from a monthly offering to an annual rite, performed on December 7 by Abe with other Pearl Harbor survivors stepping into the role of Richard Fiske (without the bugle). Then, with Abe's passing, Abe's daughter Naomi began to stand in for her father, attending each December 7 ceremony. The December 7 ceremonies in 2007, then, signaled a first major step toward a newly institutionalized activity, in which the Abe-Fiske tradition would be performed and perpetuated with other actors playing the key roles in the ritual process. The new rite was guided by John Di Virgilio, with support from the park service historian and a group consisting of Abe's daughter and a young, local Japanese American girl recruited to play taps on violin (filling in for Richard Fiske's bugle). Here is Di Virgilio, explaining the ceremony:

Since 1992 Mr. Richard Fiske and Mr. Zenji Abe here [referencing a photograph of them] would come out every month, put up a rose for all the fallen Americans and also the Japanese soldiers. It was their belief that it was difficult to forget, but wasn't that difficult to forgive. . . . So each year, Naomi Shin, Mr. Abe's daughter, would come out, and myself, representing Mr. Fiske . . . So for 12 years we've been putting the flowers out; a tradition passed on to the younger generation to come out once a year. [Roses presented, followed by picture taking] Richard Fiske would play the Japanese taps as well as the American taps. Today Allegra will play the violin taps [American and Japanese taps played on violin]. (audio recording, December 7, 2007)

Thus, whereas the rose ritual was initially the work of a single survivor and his Japanese compatriot, conducted outside the frames of official commemorative activities, it would eventually transform into an officially sponsored event—one that invoked its origins in the relationship of Abe and Fiske, with narratives such as that by Di Virgilio, above, aided with a photo of Abe and Fiske embracing, left as an offering with roses.

The rose ceremony, carried on by the small group in 2007, was later incorporated into a larger, institutional format created for the anniversary ceremony in 2010, with the opening of the new World War II Valor in the Pacific National Monument. Noticing the interest of Buddhist groups attending the anniversary ceremonies to offer prayer in the shrine room, the park service created the idea of an "Interfaith Ceremony" in which spiritual leaders of the major faiths (Christian, Buddhist, Jewish, and Islamic traditions) would be invited to pray or chant on the memorial following the anniversary service. The Abe-Fiske rose ceremony is now included in that event, added in as another form of peace offering. These events are guided and presented by the NPS historian Daniel Martinez as an occasion with official sponsorship.

As I was writing a first draft of this chapter, I took time out to participate in the December 7 anniversary ceremonies in 2013, at the VALR visitor center and out on the memorial as well. Without any particular advance planning, I found that my own path through the day's activities seemed to retrace lines of commemorative practice that have been in play for decades, echoing something like the duality evident in the opposition of the Japanese high school wreaths and the AMVETS inscription on the shrine wall. As with all dichotomies, we should be suspicious of making too much of this duality, but rather notice the differences as indicative of a multitude of possibilities cohabiting the spaces of memorialization at Pearl Harbor.

FIGURE 2.11
Rose offering with photo of Zenji Abe and Richard Fiske, shrine room,
USS *Arizona* Memorial. December 7, 2014.
Photo by author.

FIGURE 2.12
NPS historian Daniel Martinez welcomes Buddhist prayer group, shrine room,
USS *Arizona* Memorial. December 7, 2014.
Photo by author.

On the morning of December 7 I ran into John Di Virgilio, emerging from his car as he arrived for the morning ceremony. Prepared for the rose ceremony, he was holding an 8 × 10 photo of Fiske and Abe and a dozen roses. After some small talk, he mentioned that he had just had time to buy the roses on his way but needed to untie them and remove two (one to be presented by him, one by Abe's daughter). I suggested he bring them all. Maybe he could pass them out to other people interested in making a gesture—an idea that ended up introducing a new element into this invented ceremony. He indicated that he was supposed to meet Abe's daughter and that they were going out to the memorial at 10:30 a.m. following the main ceremony. Although I planned to accompany the group, I lost track of them after the ceremony and decided to join the official delegation of wreath presenters that included the naval commander, the governor's representative, and heads of several veterans' organizations as they boarded a boat to present wreaths on the memorial. Their ceremony carried on a tradition of remembrance for core constituencies of Pearl Harbor that has been conducted on the memorial since its dedication.

The contrast of this official delegation of military and political leaders with participants in an interfaith ceremony that included two Buddhist prayer groups as well as Zenji Abe's daughter and impresario John Di Virgilio symbolized to me an elegant binary opposition: national military remembrance on the one hand and transnational peace prayer on the other. The contrast was brought home as I arrived back at shore with the delegation from the navy and the state and received a call from the park historian alerting me to the fact that he was on a boat right next to us, along with the Buddhist groups and Zenji Abe's daughter, about to leave for the prayer ceremony on the memorial. The duality impressed itself on me as I ran from one boat to the next, the only participant who would participate in both events—a moment that illuminated the capacity of the memorial to sustain multiple, compartmentalized worlds of memory-making, just as the reconciliation ceremony in 1995 at Punchbowl National Cemetery had to be scheduled outside official commemorative time and space.

FROM THE TIME the memorial was constructed as a visitor center, it has transformed from an architectural memorial and location for military remembrance to a complex social institution telling the history of the Pearl Harbor attack and the Pacific War to world audiences. As a tourist destination accessible to international visitation, the memorial became a meeting ground that enabled a new line of transnational commemorative activity, without ever declaring an interest in supporting those interactions. It is important to add that in many ways the space for transnational commemorative activity can also be an "empty meeting ground" (MacCannell 1992), one in which veterans frequently had little understanding of each other's intentions and sentiments beyond the value of mutual recognition. Zenji Abe, in his autobiography (2006), wrote approvingly of the Japanese vision of liberating Asian and Pacific countries from the yolk of Western colonialism—something his American counterparts would have roundly rejected, not to mention the skepticism such a vision evokes in East Asia. As Marie Thorsten (2002) discovered in her work with Japanese veterans, some held highly reactive views about the historical truth of the Nanjing massacre, forced military prostitution, or other contentious issues in domestic war memory.

Despite these gaps and silences, the figure of the veteran who fought and survived the war emerges as a key agent and object in transnational imaginings—disappearing now but still available to those who would reconceptualize their own place in histories of war. Even as just a handful of Pearl Harbor survivors continue their routines of signing autographs and posing for photos with visitors, their presence is an opportunity for others to link their narratives of war (and peace) with Pearl Harbor, however construed. An example that relates back to the leis observed in the shrine room in my first days of fieldwork is an account of a visiting class of schoolgirls from Suma-noura High School, in Japan, who arrived at the visitor center on the anniversary day, December 7, 2007. Clearly inspired by the story of Sadako Sasaki and her thousand cranes (Coerr and Himler 1977), as are most Japanese schoolchildren, this group made a presentation of two thousand folded paper cranes to one of the Pearl Harbor survivors signing autographs at the visitor center that day, Mr. Herb Weatherwax. Although a kind of spontaneous ritual outside any formal or scheduled part of the anniversary agenda, this presentation did catch the attention of a journalist who wrote it up for one of the Honolulu newspapers, quoting Herb Weatherwax as saying, "I'm one of those that feel if you want to have peace of mind, you have to forgive" (W. Cole 2007a). This event, fleeting and unnoticed by most people commemorating the anniversary that year, presaged developments just a few years later with the placement of one of Sadako's cranes in a permanent exhibit in the memorial's new museum (see chapter 5).

Tracing commemorative activities associated with the *Arizona* memorial illustrates the importance of the memorial for the work of remembrance—formal and informal, official and unofficial, secular and sacred, individual and organizational. Indeed, the national and transnational projects described so far make it apparent that the memory work of the memorial is not limited to its fixed representations in its architecture, museum, documentary film, or landscape. The array of commemorative and educational activities that takes place in memorial space (on the memorial, at the visitor center complex, or in programs associated with it) exhibits a striking variety and fluidity. Having outlined some of the main social and performative dimensions of commemorative practice, it is important not to lose sight of the power of the memorial's semiotic architecture, with its historic landscape, its multimedia storytelling, and, until recently, its historic actors, all working to give history affective meaning. In the next few chapters, I turn to these core institutionalized representations of Pearl Harbor and war history, beginning first with a close-up look at the documentary film shown to everyone who visits the memorial.

Three

MEMORIAL FILM:
ENVISIONING RACE AND NATION

Despite its flat surfaces, film has the capacity to carry with it a depth of meaning derived from a complex genealogy of script formation, cinematic direction, editing, production, and audience interaction, for starters. As noted already, the centerpiece of historical representation at the World War II Valor in the Pacific National Monument (and the *Arizona* memorial) is the documentary film that everyone sees before visiting the memorial. In the thirty-five years since the first visitor center was built, there have been only two orientation films. The film that plays today was made in 1992 to replace the one that premiered with the opening of the visitor center, in 1980, and has remained the core storytelling device ever since.

There has, however, been one small but significant change in this impressive history of continuity. And it was a change that did not come easily—the deletion of a single image and a few words that some in the Japanese American community deemed offensive. The image in question shows a Japanese American cane cutter, standing along the edge of the harbor, looking up as a U.S. Navy vessel glides by, accompanied by narration that refers to an American commander's fear of "saboteurs hidden amid Hawai'i's large Japanese population." The producers of the film crafted the scene to depict Oahu's large population of Japanese, including both first-generation immigrants legally precluded

FIGURE 3.1
Cane cutter image from *December 7th* (1943), included in the visitor
center orientation film. 1992–2000.

from citizenship and second-generation citizens whom key military commanders imagined were rife with spies and the potential for sabotage. At the point where the cane cutter appears, the film's narrator explains that "General Short [the army general responsible for defense of the island] believed the great danger was not air attack, but saboteurs hidden amid Hawai'i's large Japanese population." The film then goes on to explain that fears of sabotage led to poor tactical decisions that made the island more vulnerable to aerial attack. What the film does not say, and still does not say, is that General Short's fears were based on faulty intelligence and a lack of knowledge of Hawai'i's multicultural society. In fact, there was never an incident of sabotage, never a court case for an act of Japanese American disloyalty in Hawai'i, and only innuendo and one unique exception to disloyal action (discussed in chapter 4).[1] The complaint about that image and the struggle that ensued tell a story that replays a deeper politics of race and nation extending back well before the bombing itself.

To start at the end of this saga, once the park service made its decision to remove the image of the cane cutter, newspapers in Honolulu ran the story

FIGURE 3.2
Cane cutter scene as it appears today in the visitor
center orientation film. 2000–present.

with the headline, "*Arizona* Memorial film is trimmed" with the subtitle "A suspicious isle Japanese cane worker in the film upset Japanese Americans" (Tighe 2000, A3). With that announcement a conflict that had spanned over a year and a half of discussions, involving the National Park Service, the Japanese American Citizens League, veterans organizations, and even Hawai'i's representatives in Congress, came to a close, or almost to a close. The letters to the editor written in response quickly mapped out the fraught terrain of conflicting views of history and identity that would hardly be resolved by adjusting the film—reminding readers of Faulkner's often quoted adage, "The past is never dead. It's not even past"—a reminder that also helps us understand why it is that representing war history at a national memorial is likely to be an unstable and unfinished process. As indication of the continuing relevance of the politics of representation surrounding documentary film in a memorial context, one of the first flash points in the opening of the National September 11 Memorial and Museum at the World Trade Center was a seven-minute film on "The Rise of Al Qaeda," which several advisers to the museum found objectionable. One Imam on an interfaith advisory group resigned, saying, "Unsophisticated visitors who do not understand the difference between Al Qaeda and Muslims may come away with a prejudiced view of Islam, leading to antagonism and even confrontation toward Muslim believers near the site" (Otterman 2014).

In the case of the film shown at the *Arizona* memorial, even news of the controversy seemed to evoke racial antagonisms very much like those of wartime America portrayed in the film. In a letter titled "*Arizona* film shouldn't have been edited," one citizen wrote, "This distortion of history is an outrage. . . . Right or wrong, General Short's perception of a local Japanese threat is what made the Pearl Harbor attack happen the way it did. There is no evidence that Short's belief was wrong. The Japanese people have a history of deception and lies" (letter to the editor, *Honolulu Star-Bulletin*, April 27, 2000). No doubt stunned that a letter confused about the difference between Japanese and Japanese Americans would be published in the Honolulu newspapers, local citizens did write back. Here is Jerald S. Takesono's letter, titled "Japanese in Hawaii were loyal Americans": "I was saddened by [the] April 27 letter to the editor . . . people like [the author] still cannot separate Japanese Americans from the Japanese enemy of World War II. Despite the heroic efforts of the 'local Japanese,' the battle of being accepted as Americans has yet to be won" (letter to the editor, *Honolulu Advertiser*, May 5, 2000).

The story of this conflict can be told in many ways: as the struggle of the Japanese American community to ensure old injustices aren't repeated in the retelling of history, as a government agency caving in to "political correctness," as learning to better tell the story of Pearl Harbor in ways that respond to citizens' sensibilities, or from a Japanese vantage point, as an American argument in which Japan continues to be a distant and voiceless other. The film controversy is a textbook case of a certain kind of American culture-war that becomes especially visible, and vehement, in places where patriotism is on display (Bergman 2013). With the first formal complaints lodged with the park service just four years after I had begun fieldwork at the memorial, I found myself hearing all of these perspectives from actors positioned differently in the organizations involved and across the diverse points of view regarding the problems and merits of the film. Over the two years of discussions and organizational pronouncements on the issue, I was able to sit in on meetings convened to resolve the conflict, interview constituents, and talk informally with a number of those involved. These involvements afforded a glimpse of the memorial as a social space, one in which history is negotiated in exchanges between actors who come to know one another in ways that also affect each person's sense of history and, in the end, the possibilities for actively forming and transforming public culture.

In my assessment, the personal stories about war memory, and the memorial's potential as a zone of interpersonal exchange, were as important as the political forces exerted from outside in reauthoring a portion of the memorial's film.

This controversy offers an instructive lesson in the hermeneutics of historical film, especially memorial film. The first lesson is that film, like most texts, is not deterministic. The film itself does not fix the meanings and emotions it evokes, which rather emerge in interactions between text and viewers. Thus, it was Japanese American viewers who first objected that the film left the impression that there was validity to the suspicions of American commanders that local Japanese (American citizens and residents) posed a serious threat of sabotage. That reading took a while to emerge as a public complaint when one local resident, Yoshie Tanabe, first saw the film and, with her husband, Jim Tanabe, spoke up, gaining support from the Japanese American Citizens League (JACL) to lodge a formal complaint with the National Park Service. The JACL is an organization concerned broadly with civil rights issues that has its origins in the Second World War internment experience. Not surprising, anxiety about the film's racial implications first emerged among those who had personal and family experiences with internment. In their view, the film's silences fed racial ideologies that, in the Second World War, led to the loss of civil rights and extensive suffering among the Japanese American population. When the JACL wrote a letter to the memorial superintendent requesting that certain scenes be deleted, the superintendent replied by acknowledging that history can be interpreted from multiple perspectives, but appealed to the historical accuracy of the film, as well as the fact that it had shown for seven years without any complaints, as justification for keeping the film intact.[2] In her letter, copied to the four members of Hawai'i's congressional delegation, who had been copied in the letter from the JACL, the superintendent added that the film had been developed through extensive consultations with "Navy and National Park historians as well as members of veterans groups and organizations."

The process that led from this initial standoff to, ultimately, a digital remastering of a few seconds of the film tells a story about the practices that govern history at a national memorial. In order to understand the forces at work here, some of which are quite specific to Hawai'i, it is necessary to locate the images and texts under discussion within a longer history of Pearl Harbor memory and, specifically, the institutional frames where those images and texts gain authority. The portion of the film that most upset the JACL focused on the cane cutter and associated images of Honolulu's Japanese American community, along with the narration that General Short was concerned with the threat of "saboteurs hidden amid Hawai'i's large Japanese population."

Whereas all agreed that the characterization of military fears was accurate, the absence of any disclaimer left open the inference that those fears were justified (and, by implication, so was the internment of Japanese Americans under President Roosevelt's Executive Order 9066—something that social and legal history has determined to have been an injustice).[3] The final resolution did in fact digitally remove the cane cutter and the six words "hidden amid Hawai'i's large Japanese population." Reaching that solution, however, would require numerous meetings and letters including, ultimately, pressure from Hawai'i's two prominent Japanese American members of Congress, Senator Daniel Inouye and Representative Patsy Mink.

In retrospect the reasons for the conflicting views of this portion of the film seem obvious. Whereas the park service administration, historian, and curator were concerned to tell the canonical story of Pearl Harbor, focused primarily on the military history of the attack, many Japanese American viewers understand the Pearl Harbor story through the optic of race, specifically of the racial fears and prejudices unleashed after the attack, which became painful memories for many families in Hawai'i and California. These are different Pearl Harbors—narratives and emotions that intersect in complex ways, yielding the potential for multiple and at times conflicting readings of history. For the memorial, as a national memorial, this realization raises questions such as, Whose history is it? How is it possible to present multiple and, at times, conflicting histories in a single film? And what is the role of the state in mediating multiple histories intersecting in the spaces marked as national?

Given that all agreed that the existing film was, on the whole, historically accurate, the primary points of dispute concerned silences and absences— stories not told. Although the Tanabes and the JACL asked pointedly for the addition of a disclaimer, they settled for removal of the cane cutter and the six-word phrase. Ironically, the problem of absences was handled with further erasures. At this level of analysis, the differences involve more than just competing narratives, but rather competing views about what sort of histories are possible and desirable in the conjunctures of public space, where multiple histories intersect and seek not only to represent but to evoke different forms of affective involvement.

In this case, briefly tracing the conversations and negotiations that led to modifications of the film offers a lesson about the practice of history in American memorial space. On August 15, 1998, the Tanabes wrote their first letter headed "recommendation for footage modification" to the memorial's superintendent. In making her initial judgment that the film shouldn't be changed, the superintendent relied on advice from the park historian, one of the principal consultants for the film script. The Tanabes then enlisted the support of the Honolulu chapter of the Japanese American Citizens League to press their point, forming an alliance that also sought support from Hawai'i's congressional delegation, including Senator Daniel Inouye and Representative Patsy Mink (who wrote two letters to the superintendent, February 12, 1999, and June 3, 1999). The face-to-face discussions included two group meetings at the visitor center between members of the Honolulu JACL and NPS staff and volunteers (the first in October 1998 and the second in March 1999).

The first meeting of the Tanabes and board members of the JACL with NPS staff and volunteers took place in one of the visitor center theaters so the assembled group could first watch the twenty-three-minute film in its entirety before discussing the criticisms. The main spokesperson for the park service in this meeting was the park historian, who had worked on the film script and was invested in the integrity of the film. Repeating the concern with "historical accuracy" that had been voiced by the superintendent in her initial letter, the historian had prepared a four-page memorandum providing relevant documentation of the historical details under discussion.[4] To support their position, the park service also invited two of the veterans who were regular volunteers in the park, Robert Kinzler (an officer of the local chapter of the Pearl Harbor Survivors Association) and Stanley Igawa (the post–Second World War veteran introduced in chapter 1). Recall that Stanley Igawa's presentations at the visitor center focused specifically on the tragedy of internment for Japanese American families. One of the first (and last) lines of defense for the NPS to maintain the film in its original guise was support from the Pearl Harbor Survivors Association, particularly those volunteering at the memorial. When some of those individuals began to show sympathy for the position of the Tanabes and the JACL (and as pressure came from the Hawaiian congressional delegation), the park service changed its position to accept the requested change.

Comments made in the first group meeting, in October 1998, illuminate some of the underlying assumptions about history and the role of the memorial's film as both historical documentary and commemoration. The discussions began with the park historian's describing the purpose of making a new film in 1992, to first "broaden the context" but, more important, "to emotionally prepare people to go to the memorial . . . that's why at the end it's very emotional in its appeal, because it's the whole thing of how shall we remember them, and that was the whole idea. So that when they walked out those doors and got on the boat there was no doubt where they were going" (audio recording, October 29, 1998). With these remarks, within the first five minutes of the meeting, the historian set the context for discussion by articulating the purpose of the film as a memorial experience that invited personal, emotional involvement. And, as he said, it is not just any memorial experience, but the experience of a memorial to the men who died on the battleship *Arizona*. At a very basic level, the memorializing work of the film is defined in time and space as a prelude to visiting a sunken ship, focused on memorializing the lost crew and America's military losses in the bombing attack—the purpose written into the congressional legislation that established the memorial in the first place.

As will be seen, however, the film's conclusion attempts, poetically, to expand the scope of memorialization in ways that invite wider circles of empathy. Might that circle also include those of concern to the Tanabes? The Tanabes' complaint focused on a different kind of memorial work, for those who suffered intensified racial discrimination as a result of the bombing and the Pacific War. Whereas it might be said that such memorializing should find a more appropriate venue, telling the military story in a way that even minimally broadens the context (by explaining military decisions made in defense of the fleet) explicitly raises the issue of racial tension and suspicion. In other words, almost any type of context-explaining film or exhibit, prior to honoring the lost crew of the *Arizona*, will already be connected, through the ligaments of historical narrative, to other forms of suffering and loss. How then does the viewer answer the question posed in the title of the *Arizona* film, "How Shall We Remember Them?" when both "we" and "them" are on shifting ground?

One reason that these parties to the film controversy didn't arrive at an early agreement is that they brought different narratives to their meetings, and different ideas about the pragmatics of memorial history. As the party who had brought the initial complaint, the Tanabes often spoke in deeply personal terms, at time marked by tearful emotion. After noting that the film was well produced (and "tasteful"), Yoshie Tanabe spoke about the reasons for her concern, beginning by recounting her own viewing practices (coming to see the film several times) while relating the subject of the film to her own experience growing up in Honolulu, that she "lived through it," but she also was aware that no cases of sabotage were ever proven, so concluded that the film was reproducing images that have proven to be signs of racial ignorance and hostility—signs that the Japanese American community has been determined to be vigilant about since the Second World War. Mrs. Tanabe spoke about the cane cutter scene as the one she found most disturbing, depicting a Japanese man who could easily be engaged in spying on a passing navy battleship. She went on without interruption to recall that she had two brothers who went to war in Europe, one in France and one in Italy, before also describing the pain of her family's experience living under the gaze of racial suspicion, pain that, as a fourteen-year-old girl at the end of war, she felt personally: "[In] 1945 I was fourteen when the war ended . . . after the war began we were 'sneaky,' 'not to be trusted,' 'back-stabbers.' The Chinese used to make fun of us because now they were allies and we weren't. When eleven, twelve years old . . . you don't know much, I wished I was somehow haole [white]. I used to look at my mother and say, 'Why you born me Japanese?'" (audio recording, October 28, 1998).

In this meeting, then, the Tanabes and JACL leaders made their case for modifying the film—deleting the cane cutter and adding a statement that there were no recorded acts of sabotage—and the NPS made its case that the film is historically accurate, the product of extensive vetting by military historians and veterans groups, and had already had seven years of successful showing. The reluctance of the park service to make changes in the film (beyond the expense and technical challenges) followed from their experience weathering challenges from other constituencies concerned that the memorial and film are "too soft" on Japan—sentiments widely voiced just a few years prior, during the fiftieth anniversary. The historian pointed out the controversial nature of the Pearl Harbor site, marked by the volume of letters of complaint sent to congressional representatives.

An important irony, and one never acknowledged by parties to the discussions, is the fact that the offending image was in fact the last remaining bit of Hollywood footage in the current film. The cane cutter scene was originally scripted to depict an act of spying, one of several scenes of dramatized spying strung together to depict the lurking threat from spies within Honolulu's Japanese community, as imagined by producers of *December 7th*, the first propaganda film made about the Pearl Harbor attack (see below) (White and Yi 2001). Remarkably, the only scene to have been included in all of the official Pearl Harbor films, from the first documentaries made after the attack to the two orientation films shown at the memorial visitor center, is the cane cutter sequence. The persistence of that image suggests an almost ghostly ability to carry desired meaning through decades of film remakes and through shifts in the social and political contexts for remembering Pearl Harbor. Even when stripped of the explicit context for which it was originally made (as a direct depiction of spying), the controversy with the JACL shows that images produced in wartime decades before can still evoke the racially charged implications for which they were originally filmed.

The first effort, in 1942, to rush through a full-length motion picture about the Pearl Harbor attack, with the production of *December 7th*, proved so problematic that the government agency making it decided not to release it (White and Yi 2001). *December 7th* was made under the auspices of the Bureau of Motion Pictures, a branch of the Office of War Information (precursor of the Central Intelligence Agency) charged with coordinating relations between the government and Hollywood. The actual production was handled by a new Hollywood-based navy film unit headed by John Ford, who chose Gregg Toland (cinematographer for *Citizen Kane* and *Grapes of Wrath*) to direct work for the Pearl Harbor film. As it turned out, there would be two *December 7th* films, an original, long film that was never released and a shorter, edited version that received an Academy Award in 1944. (See appendix 4 for an annotated filmography of the official Pearl Harbor films and major features discussed in this chapter and chapter 4.) It would not be until the memorial had been constructed and a visitor center opened in 1980 that another official Pearl Harbor film would be made as the memorial's "orientation film," this time by the U.S. Navy, for showing in the new visitor center operated by the National Park Service. About ten years later, at the time of the fiftieth anniversary, in 1991, the National Park Service decided to make a new orientation film, calling it "How Shall We Remember Them?" The task of remaking the orientation film proved to be much more complicated and contentious than anyone predicted. Making a twenty-three-minute documentary, a project originally estimated to take six months with perhaps three or four script revisions, ended up taking two years and seventeen scripts (Daniel Martinez, USS *Arizona* Memorial Historian, personal communication).

Clearly, the task of crafting a cinematic history of the Pearl Harbor attack that would speak in the voice of the nation has never been easy, despite the seeming moral clarity of the Good War narrative. The difficulty is that war histories are also social histories. As state-sponsored films about the nation at war, each of the Pearl Harbor films in some way represents national subjectivity—what it means to feel American. Whereas the films released in 1980 and 1992 take on a historical perspective, looking back at events some forty or fifty years ago, they also invite the viewer to inhabit the film and see and feel the world from the vantage point of America under attack in 1941. Thus, when the current film uses the jaunty song "Remember Pearl Harbor," released in 1942, in its sound track, showing parades, posters, and eager recruits enlisting in the military in response to the attack, American viewers report feeling moved by the patriotic spirit of post-attack 1940s. By the same token, the Tanabes' plea sought not only to better represent their experience as Americans, but to create a space for their own participation.

The first government-produced documentary about the Pearl Harbor attack, *December 7th*, foundered on the problem of portraying Hawai'i as part of the United States (referenced as "America's suburb" at the end of a second, shortened version of *December 7th*). Contradictions in the film's own representations of Hawai'i's Japanese population, a result of the island's colonial history and plantation economy, reflect the uncertainty of wartime race relations as Japanese American citizens and residents sought to express their loyalty to the United States in the face of pervasive racism. President Roosevelt signed Executive Order 9066, granting authority to the secretary of war to forcibly remove Japanese people from their homes and confiscate their property on February 12, 1942, at the very time that the Hollywood filmmaker Gregg Toland was traveling to Hawai'i to begin filming. And yet, within a year of the attack, federal agencies overseeing film production in wartime America were already more concerned to emphasize themes of loyalty and unification than to display racial fears and suspicions.

One reason the first production of *December 7th* was never released is the contradiction between the depiction of Japanese people in Hawai'i as a hidden menace in the first half of the film and as patriotic citizens backing the war effort in the concluding scenes ("After those disloyal were arrested"). It is particularly ironic that the original, long version of *December 7th*, with all its ethnophobia, offered explicit statements about Japanese American loyalty where the current film offers none. *December 7th*, overtly racist in its depiction of Hawai'i's Japanese population, nonetheless offered the very disclaimer that the Tanabes and the JACL wanted in the current film: "Not one act of sabotage was recorded." Without that, some of the very same race issues that destabilized *December 7th* surfaced again in the film debate fifty years later.

Whereas much of the attention to official memorial films focuses on the portrayal of Japan and Japanese, it is the representation of Japanese *Americans* that ends up the more intractable point in these films. In part this is because, unlike Japanese nationals who have little place from which to speak in American public debate, Japanese Americans speak as citizens in questioning the film's portrayal of them as Americans, just as Yoshie and Jim Tanabe did plaintively in their meetings with park service administrators. While the sincere persistence of concerned citizens was an important ingredient in this case, the possibility of an extended hearing, leading to policy changes in historical practices, would not have been possible without political support—specifically, in this case, the JACL and Hawai'i's congressional leaders.

Even before critical responses to the cane cutter scene in the 1990s, the scene's career in the versions of *December 7th* produced in 1942 and 1943 was already part of a troubled debate about race and nation in wartime film. For the original, longer production of *December 7th*, the same racial hostilities and suspicions that fueled internment also led John Ford and Gregg Toland to devote the first half of their film to a fictionalized portrayal of Hawai'i's Japanese residents as extensively involved in spying. While in Hawai'i for work on the film on April 13, 1942, Ford wrote a letter to William Donovan (head of the Office of War Information), expressing his views about Hawai'i's Japanese residents:[5]

> We are doing the Japanese espionage stuff [in the film] very thoroughly. It's fascinating and quite exciting. Personally, I do not trust any of the Japanese. I honestly believe the majority of them are tainted. It's strange since the "Raid" how very Oriental Honolulu appears—thousands upon thousands of Jap faces. We have been photographing scores of Jap signs to show the character of the town. Now you can hardly see one. They have all taken down their signs and have substituted English lettering. Example; "Banzai Cafe"—beers and liquors—is now the "Keep Em Flying Cafe". . . .
>
> From the best sources they estimate about six hundred active agents still loose on the island. I figure triple that number. Some amazing stories of spying leak out daily.

The images in Ford's letter to Donovan show up with unerring consistency in the first production of *December 7th*. To create images of a "fifth column" among the local Japanese population, Ford and Toland filmed an extended series of scenes showing local Japanese people unobtrusively gathering information about military activities in the course of their daily activities, such as hair dressers listening to the casual banter of military wives, gardeners listening outside windows, photographers snapping shots of military installations, and, yes, cutting cane along the banks of the harbor. The film offered up a visual panorama of paranoia. All of these scenes were scripted, casted, and acted to depict the same thing: local espionage and the subversive potential of Hawai'i's Japanese population. In this context the cane cutter is not simply glancing up at a passing navy ship, he is performing an act of scripted subterfuge, a threat given sinister meaning by a soundtrack of foreboding music.

Even though the entire sequence of spying was edited out of the short version, the cane cutter was retained and relocated to a position in the opening, scene-setting images of the film (about two and a half minutes from the start), located among views of the harbor as the narrator describes its naval armada as a church bell tolls slowly on the sound track (Sunday morning). No doubt it was this innocuous location where later film editors would have picked up the image, to be used as a kind of background shot visualizing Hawai'i's demographic profile. In the second *December 7th*, then, the filmmakers also intended a more benign reading of the cane cutter image, a reading made possible by the elimination of the first half of the original film, with its dramatized scenes of spying. The short version instead accentuated the theme of patriotic response and unification—a narrative desired by the Office of War Information by the end of 1942.

The fact that the cane cutter reappeared fifty years later in the 1992 film, redeployed to convey General Short's suspicions, is testimony to the durability of the original performance of espionage and the power of the image to reinject an element of racial suspicion into an updated narrative. His reappearance is also testimony to the politics of representing Pearl Harbor as a narrative of military attack, adjudicated by military historians and Pearl Harbor veterans, with very little close involvement of other communities of remembrance (such as Japanese Americans and Native Hawaiians). With apologies to Marshall Sahlins (1985), I call this complex of mythic narrative plus the politics of image-making "mythopraxis."

Filmmaking and Pearl Harbor Mythopraxis

Seeing the Pearl Harbor film as more than a simple text, but as a certain kind of praxis in the service of reproducing mythic history, opens a window onto film as a medium that does as much to shape affect and subjectivity as it does to make history. Documentary films about national wars presented to national audiences are clearly doing more than representing history. At the opening of the last episode of *The War* (2007), Ken Burns's epic, seven-part TV miniseries on the Second World War, the film displays an inscription that says, "A thousand veterans of the war die every day. This film is dedicated to those who fought and won." In this manner and in many less obvious ways, the film positions itself as both documentary and memorial. The memorial functions of the film are most evident in the emotionality of speakers who, in recalling moments of loss, enact a certain kind of remembering—evident in intensity of voice and visible expressions of emotion. Such modes of speaking are common in the affect-laden spaces of memorial sites and commemorative events— spaces that envision historical narratives as an invitation to feel.

At first glance, it might seem that the manner in which the *December 7th* films combine historical documentary and commemoration would only produce awkward or forced filmmaking. Yet, if we gauge the success of these films in terms of audience responses, whether in wartime or in the present, one can only conclude that their peculiar mélange of history and commemoration makes for a desirable history, even if the films were produced across a span of decades, for ostensibly different purposes: fighting a war in the 1940s and remembering the war fifty years later. At the core of the Pearl Harbor narrative is the story of an attack that left over two thousand American servicemen dead. The first documentary, made in the heat of war with the aim of mobilizing a national war effort, included a series of testimonials in the voices of servicemen who died in the attack, embodying the object of memorialization that lies at the film's heart. In 1980 and 1992, however, the memorial voice was no longer embodied in ghostly appearances but rather frames the entire film with references to the memorial itself. In the 1992 film the spirit of mourning is particularly evident in the voice of the female narrator (actress Stockard Channing), from the opening shots of the memorial to the concluding reflection about the losses of war.

Whether made originally to support the war effort and mobilize a nation at war, or to memorialize the losses of that war decades later, all of the official Pearl Harbor films have been made to *do* something, to evoke sentiments and mediate feelings connecting self and national history. Just as the wartime films were made to stir audiences to support an ongoing war effort, the orientation films were also made with an emotional agenda, to prepare viewers for a memorial experience—anchored in a burial place and a history of violent death, transformed into an object of moral reflection. On the surface, the contexts and purposes of wartime filmmaking and postwar remembrance appear very different. However, the convergence of narrative and purpose in these films argues for the continuing relevance of the canonical Pearl Harbor narrative in the service of national remembrance.

Whereas the Pearl Harbor story of 1942–43, told in *December 7th*, was a story about the need to support the war effort, the film made for the new visitor center in 1980 conveyed a message relevant to the need for military preparedness during the Cold War years. In that epoch, the film's celebration of contemporary U.S. naval power flowed easily from the principal narrative. By the post–Cold War 1990s, that same militarizing theme struck some as out of tune with the sensibilities of a memorial constructed to honor the losses and sacrifices of December 7. As a result, the National Park Service decided to remake the film to shift its emotional tenor to something somber and reflective, deemed more appropriate to a memorial and cemetery context. The resulting film, launched at the end of 1992, is framed in a more subdued post–Cold War voice of lament for wartime losses than the previous film's more aggressive "victory at sea" tone, celebrating the growth of postwar U.S. naval power.

Even though these Pearl Harbor films were certainly crafted to do a specific kind of emotional work, they were also careful to present themselves as authoritative, documentary history, assuring viewers of their truth-value. In different ways, all of the official Pearl Harbor films signal their claims to historical validity. Even the producers of *December 7th*, which is now labeled "propaganda" by distributors, were concerned to include a statement about the film's veracity within the film itself, opening with a statement announcing, "Your war and navy department present *December 7th*," followed by a display of signed memoranda from the secretary of war and the secretary of the navy calling for the production of a film that gives a "factual presentation" of the bombing of Pearl Harbor.[6] The fact that the film received an Academy Award in 1944 in the short-subject documentary category suggests that the film worked well in its time as documentary nonfiction.

Yet, as one scholar wrote, "*December 7th* is hardly a documentary at all. It is more of a short narrative film, anything but a dispassionate presentation of facts" (Basinger 1986, 128). With the passage of time, "documentary" came to be viewed as "semi-documentary" (Skinner 1991, 510; Smith 1999, 30) or simply as "propaganda." Critic Richard Schickel writing in *Time Magazine* on the occasion of the fiftieth anniversary called the film "a simple-minded patriotic harangue" (1991, 80). One of the great ironies in the body of film about Pearl Harbor is that the most widely seen feature film on the subject, *Tora! Tora! Tora!*, is in fact more "historical"—more concerned with a detailed recitation of documented actions and events—than *December 7th*.[7] In part this is because *Tora! Tora! Tora!* focuses primarily on the attack itself, with virtually no interest in Hawai'i as a place or for sociocultural matters of race, ethnicity, or national sentiment. And because *Tora! Tora! Tora!* was a binational production, released in two languages, in the United States and Japan, it was less able to construct its account as a moral tale for a single national audience (Thorsten and White 2010).

In what follows, I examine some of the discursive means through which avowedly documentary film becomes moral narrative, if not moral imperative. Having traced some of the ways that arguments about "historical accuracy" and memorial practice were entangled in the discussions between the JACL and the NPS on the current orientation film, I now turn to the antecedents of today's film—other "official" Pearl Harbor films—that also combine documentary history with memorial praxis.

The Two December 7ths:
Takes and Mistakes on the National Subject

Newsreel footage circulated immediately after the attack shouted the need to remember. In February 1942 a Hearst newsreel showed in U.S. theaters under the title "*Lest We Forget! The Truth About Pearl Harbor! First Actual Films Now Released by U.S. Navy—Pearl Harbor Ablaze! First Actual Pictures!*"[8] The navy's Hollywood-based film unit, headed by John Ford, took a different tack. With Gregg Toland in Hawai'i developing a script, the initial goal was a feature-length documentary that would tell the story of Hawai'i as America, locating Pearl Harbor in a longer history of the development of Hawai'i as an American military and economic outpost. The film depicts the bombing itself (with studio re-creations to portray a "heightened realism"), the recovery effort, and the patriotic sentiments that fueled it. It concludes with an imaginary scene in which two deceased veterans (one of the First World War, one of the Pearl Harbor attack) walk through a cemetery, talking about the League of Nations and America's international responsibilities in maintaining world order.

How could a distant colonial territory of the United States, where the majority of the population consisted of Native Hawaiians and Asian immigrant labor, be imagined as America? Both *December 7ths* attempt to answer this question with narratives of Americanization. The longer film does this with an extended history of frontier capitalism and modernization. That larger vision would prove to be the film's undoing, as those scripting the film were busy applying John Ford's fearful vision of Japanese people in Hawai'i as a fifth column waiting to assist Japan. Given the central problematic of race for *December 7th*, Hawai'i's multiethnic population and colonial history posed a number of complications for national mythmakers, forcing filmmakers to seek narrative solutions to entanglements of race and nation. In doing so, scriptwriters seem to have been torn between competing Orientalist visions of Hawai'i: that of "paradise," combining fantasies of tropical vacationland and multicultural utopia, on the one hand, and a more sinister vision of a foreboding borderland populated by suspicious foreign ethnicities, on the other. In the end the contradictions between these colliding visions subverted the effort to craft a film that would somehow tell the story of Hawai'i and tell the story of the Pearl Harbor attack. The solution, found in reediting the original film to produce a much shorter version, was to eliminate the story of Hawai'i—something that continued to be characteristic of the memorial's histories up to the time of constructing a new museum (see chapter 4).

In *December 7th*, Hawai'i is first a tropical idyll, an iconic vacationland that seems to exist out of time and history. Beginning with panoramic vistas of an uninhabited, natural landscape of a type often preferred by John Ford, the opening scenes set up one of the premises of the narrative of progress: that lands to be colonized and developed are best if unencumbered by prior settlement by people who have their own cultures and histories. In this narrative, Hawai'i as colonial possession is remade as an extension of America, sited on the "frontier," as undeveloped land awaiting Euro-American occupation and development, the essential ingredient in transforming raw lands into productive societies. The narrator calls it a "pioneering story" that "compares favorably with the opening of the west." This narrative of progress is summed up in the line "where once was a village of grass huts, a modern American city arose." "Modern" Hawai'i is presented as living testimony to the power of capitalist expansion to transform the landscape and create a modern society.

But the narrative goes on to note that the tropical landscape is filled with faces and languages of different ethnicities, calling attention to the dangers posed by the large numbers of immigrant Japanese people in Hawai'i. With uncanny resonance with John Ford's reference to "thousands upon thousands of Jap faces," the camera cuts to close-up shots of Japanese faces, accompanied by sinister background music. Here the sound of dissonant, "oriental" music accompanying a quick succession of shots at odd angles creates a sense of nervous confusion contrasting with the upbeat and inviting world described in the earlier reverie on modernization. Having set the stage with misleading demographic evidence about the persistence of Japanese loyalties, the film moves to the spying sequence that included the cane cutter scene.

The original, long version of *December 7th* sutured together a twentieth-century history of Hawai'i and a military attack movie, presented through a combination of documentary and a Hollywood drama, with actors playing the parts of Uncle Sam and other imaginary characters. Not surprisingly, it met with skepticism and outright rejection when initial cuts were reviewed by sponsoring agencies. In November 1942, when the secretary of the navy asked Lowell Mellett, chief of the Bureau of Motion Pictures in Washington, D.C., to review the rough-cut of the film, he responded that, "this project, as a picture for public exhibition should be stopped. . . . It is a fictional treatment of a very real fact, the tragic disaster of Pearl Harbor, and I do not believe the government should engage in fiction."[9] And again, in April 1943, when the film had been completed, he reaffirmed this view in another letter, adding, "Presentation of fictional propaganda on the subject would seem to be an improper activity for the U.S. Government."[10]

As an agency that aimed to promote national unity in support of the war, the Office of War Information (OWI) was constantly concerned with issues of race and representation in Hollywood films. That office looked to the makers of *December 7th* to project images of a plural nation coming together for the purpose of fighting a war (Doherty 1993; Koppes and Black 1987). In October 1942, just one month before the recommendation to cancel the release of the long version of *December 7th*, the agency noted strong objections to the film *Air Force*—a Hollywood film made in cooperation with the U.S. Air Force—because of its racist depictions of Japanese Americans' committing sabotage at Pearl Harbor and even shooting at the crew of a downed U.S. B-17 bomber. Nelson Poynter wrote a lengthy letter, based on a review of the *Air Force* script, to the OWI head, Lowell Mellett, complaining, "I believe there is a studied effort to make Japanese Fifth Columnists the alibi for our early defeats in the Pacific. Such a picture can certainly be damaging to us abroad and at home. My understanding is that the facts as gathered by Army Intelligence do not support such a thesis. . . . I believe this is an opportune case for OWI to make an issue of the handling of Army and Navy movie relations with Hollywood."[11]

After having made the decision to cancel the release of the film, the parties who had sponsored it recognized the continuing need for a film that would deploy the Pearl Harbor story in support of the war effort. John Ford returned to the film and cut out everything but the story of the attack and recovery. In the editing, Ford removed the fictional Uncle Sam as well as the final graveyard conversation between young and old veterans. Significantly, however, he retained the memorial sequence in which ethnically diverse servicemen killed in the attack speak about family, duty, and country.

The removal of the first half of the original film, with its social history of Hawai'i, eliminated the vision of subversive Japanese residents and amplified the narrative of unification, thus cutting out the most blatant contradictions in the original film. In the process John Ford's editing established a narrative structure for the Pearl Harbor story that is reproduced in both of the memorial's orientation films. In this way, the edited film succeeded in turning the Pearl Harbor story into an inspirational story for America at war, with a more consistent personification of American citizens dedicated to the war effort.[12] Following the attack scene, *December 7th* tells the story of recovery and mobilization as a narrative of national unification in which ethnic difference is subsumed by the overriding interest of a nation at war. The theme of unification emerges in the film's portrayal of efforts at recovery in the aftermath of the bombing. In this portion of the film, Hawai'i's

Japanese are even more important for telling the story of unification, since for them, according to the film, mobilization meant the renunciation of their Japanese ancestry.

In scripting this part of the film, writers seeking images of loyal citizens could see the value of depicting Japanese Americans working for the war effort. One writer noted that "newsreel shots may be dubbed in here of camouflage being set up, anti-aircraft guns being installed. . . . If possible these should include the defense work of loyal Japanese."[13] Ignoring the policies that were violating the constitutional rights of Japanese Americans during this period, the film presents Pearl Harbor as causing local Japanese people to definitively break with homeland culture, implying that loyal American citizenship could be achieved by erasing cultural ancestry. Addressing "Mr. Tojo," the film states, "Yes, your bombs Mr. Tojo brought many changes and in no small measure served to further complicate the already complex life of the Japanese in Hawaii. And so to permanently erase their relationship to the homeland, they wiped out or removed every vestige of the written Japanese word. Closed are the language schools, empty and boarded up the Shinto temples, gone the flag of the rising sun. This young American Japanese gave the best illustration that over Hawaii the rising sun had begun to set." At this point the film shows a scene almost exactly as described by John Ford in his letter, depicting a Japanese American man replacing a sign saying "Banzai Cafe" with one reading "Keep Em Flying Cafe."

The narrations for *December 7th* in both versions deal rhetorically with the contradictions of loyalty and internment by asserting that it was only "enemy agents" who were "forced out of business and interned," while at the same time praising Japanese Americans working for the war effort. As already noted, the film even included a statement to the effect that no acts of sabotage were committed by Japanese Americans: "Yes, all the people pitched in—the Japanese too. They volunteered in great numbers as blood donors. . . . Those that were known to be disloyal or undercover enemy agents were immediately taken into custody. Many were forced out of business and interned. But despite the wild Tokyo inspired rumors, the scuttlebutt, not one single solitary act of sabotage was committed on the seventh." Here, at the conclusion of the film, the narrator corrects the view that Hawai'i's Japanese population committed acts of sabotage. The film implies that the anti-Japanese American hysteria was a result of "Tokyo inspired rumors" rather than domestic racism. It was precisely the absence of such a statement in the current film that led to the formal complaint from the Japanese American Citizens League.

Speaking from the Grave: Memorialization in December 7th

Both films use the language of memorialization to perform a vision of national community. In a sequence of dramatized testimonials, servicemen from diverse backgrounds killed in the attack all speak from the grave with common purpose. To construct this scene, director Gregg Toland carefully selected the names of individuals from distinct backgrounds so as to depict an American "melting pot." He began by compiling a list of Pearl Harbor casualties with ethnically distinct names from different parts of the country so that he could then contact their families and also include them in the film as visual evidence of the diversity of Americans who had already sacrificed for the war. Toland informed military authorities that he wanted these portraits to represent America's ethnic and regional diversity, as well as the different branches of military service: "I want the names of six families whose sons died at Pearl Harbor on December 7th. They should be from various parts of the United States. . . . One colored family, one Jewish family, one Irish family, one German family, one Filipino family, and a Mexican family. . . . I think you get the general idea from the above. I want representative large cities, small towns, all nationalities, and types of names for a sort of melting pot memorial.[14] Toland's superior responded to his request with a list of six navy men, three Marines and five army men. Although the list included a Japanese American reservist, Private Torao Migita, of Honolulu, with four other U.S. Army casualties, Toland chose not to use him, leaving Japanese Americans out of the vision of ethnic diversity displayed in the memorial sequence.[15] The film also makes no mention of the forty-nine civilian casualties that day, most of whom were Japanese Americans killed by antiaircraft munitions coming down in Honolulu neighborhoods.

Toland used seven of the names to craft a memorial sequence, which the narration introduces as follows: "For on this Sabbath day 2,343 officers and enlisted men of our Army, Navy and Marine Corps gave their young lives in the service of our country. Who were these young Americans? Let us pause for a few minutes at their hallowed graves and ask a few of them to make themselves known. Who are you boys? Come on, speak up some of you." In response, as the film displays their photos, each of the seven introduces himself, stating name, branch of service, and place of residence, before also introducing his parents (and in some cases surviving spouse). In this way the film maps the losses of the attack across an ethnically and geographically diverse America (Anglo, black, Hispanic, Jewish families from Brooklyn to North Carolina to Ohio and California). In conclusion the narrator asks the seventh person, Lt. William R. Schick, United States Army Medical Corps, "But tell me one thing, Lieutenant, how does it happen that all of you sound and talk alike?" To which Lt. Schick replies, "We are all alike. We're all Americans," as the scene shifts to a cemetery with soldiers' graves. Against the backdrop of ethnic and geographic diversity, the portraits of seven well-spoken, young, male servicemen who "gave their young lives in the service of our country" construct an inclusive national "we," extended even to the film viewer, with the narrator's reference to "our country."

Making the Memorial Orientation Film (Again)

No longer wishing to mobilize a nation for war, but rather seeking to "remember" in the postwar context of the alliance between the United States and Japan, the opening of the visitor center, in 1980, called for a different kind of film, one made for an interpretive program and visitor experience honoring the American military who died in the bombing, without fomenting anti-Japanese sentiment. In the memorial context, the film acquires a kind of sacred significance as an object that is unique to the site. It can only be seen at the memorial; it is not for sale as video; and it is not otherwise promoted or commercialized. Park service administrators see the film as the most powerful element in the memorial's interpretive program. To quote a previous superintendent, "The film is our central interpretative tool. While . . . not our only interpretative tool, it is the only one that all visitors to the Memorial see. It must also be understood that it is the only interpretive element that all visitors experience that has an opportunity to present a consistent viewpoint. Ranger talks and survivor talks do not, by their very nature, provide for this consistency."[16]

The consistency of the first orientation film served its purpose for about a decade before the park service decided it was no longer in tune with the times. The primary motivations for changing the film were twofold: emotional tone, seeing the need to set a more somber tone for visiting the sacred space of the sunken ship; and historical accuracy, the need to replace an indiscriminate mix of Hollywood footage and archival film. As the NPS curator put it, "The original film was created by the Navy in 1979 and 1980 and was based on information, accurate or inaccurate, that was at hand at the time. [It] is a film that, obviously, since it was made by the Navy, reflects the Navy's point of view. In some ways it is very objective. In other ways there are historical inaccuracies and in some cases . . . the interpretation is not exactly in line with what we know to be accurate today."[17] These concerns of the park service converged with criticisms from outside, which mounted as the anniversary approached and the memorial became a flashpoint for sentiments associated with U.S.-Japan relations (Linenthal 1993, 235–36; Rosenberg 2004, 78; White 2001, 270–73). In the context of 1980s globalization that saw Japan rising as an economic power, some viewers saw the original film's respectful treatment of Japan as evidence that the nation's history was being diluted to appease Japanese interests, particularly in Hawai'i, with the importance of Japanese visitors for its tourist economy.[18] Reflecting American culture wars of the time, the film released in 1980 was seen by some as too soft on the enemy and by others as too militaristic. The convergence of criticisms convinced the park service to invest in making a new film, placing the concern with historical accuracy in the foreground.

With the current film completed just prior to our research, Marjorie Kelly and I had the opportunity to talk with people about its production and explore the process of scripting the film, glimpsing the social context of production and the dialogue and debate that surrounded scripting. Those involved in making the film recognized the contested nature of their topic. In a memo written in response to cost overruns and delays encountered in finishing the project, the film's producer explained, "We are all doing a very difficult thing. We are making a major motion picture to be shown at the most controversial site the National Park Service manages. This site generates more letters to Congressmen and Park Service executives than any other site in America."[19] Listening in on some of the debates that followed shows official history-making to be more uncertain and internally fractured than might be expected if one only approached the film as a fixed representation or expression of the interests of "the state" as a monolithic agency.

Although the memorial is managed by the park service, many official voices speak about history there. Park rangers, veteran volunteers, and navy personnel all participate in representing Pearl Harbor history, as noted in previous chapters' accounts of commemorative events, museum lectures, theater talks, and informal interaction with visitors. It was not surprising, then, when the park service decided to make a new orientation film, that numerous constituencies had to be consulted and involved in developing the script. Production of the film released in 1992 was undertaken as a contract between the film company and the National Park Service (through its nonprofit partner, the *Arizona Memorial Museum Association*). Each party involved brought in a wider circle of individuals and organizations to review scripts and preliminary "rough cuts" of the film. Roughly thirty individuals evaluated and commented on the film. Filmmaker Lance Bird said that he had "never worked with that many people in an oversight relationship . . . there were so many people who had a stake in this thing turning out well, [and] they emerged as the movie got going."[20]

Primary among these constituencies were veterans groups, especially Pearl Harbor survivors. They were constantly referenced as a key audience, a kind of litmus test for acceptability, and also involved in script review. The park historian distributed copies of the script to representatives of the American Legion, the American Ex-Prisoners of War, and the Pearl Harbor Survivors Association, and formed a review committee composed of representatives of the U.S. Navy and veterans groups, including two Medal of Honor winners.[21] The film's director, Lance Bird, commented, "From the beginning one of our goals was to make a film that could not be accused of 'Japan bashing' nor could it be attacked by Pearl Harbor survivors who might feel that the film was trying to justify the attack" (Lance Bird, recorded interview with M. Kelly, April 14, 1994). Superintendent Donald Magee echoed these sentiments when he stated that he hoped the new film, with its use of actual historical footage, would both "better inform visitors" and "appease veterans groups."

Comparing the navy film released in 1980 and the park service film from 1992 yields a picture of both continuities and changes in official history-making at the memorial. The first and somewhat surprising conclusion is that, despite the intent of the producers of the film from 1992 to make an entirely new film without reference to the one being replaced, the two films closely mirror one another in narrative structure. Lance Bird was very clear about the intent to produce something entirely new. When I sent him a draft of an earlier paper on the film, he asserted that calling their project a "remaking" of the previous film was inappropriate. As he put it, "The creative team's view was that we were in no way 'remaking' the existing film. In fact we were consciously trying to make a film that would stand in sharp contrast to the existing film; that effort extended from the look of our film to its tone and the words heard on its sound track. . . . We never studied the earlier film (in fact, I've only seen it about three times)."[22] And yet the parallel in narrative structure is striking. I take the resemblance as evidence of the force of the mythic plotline that emerged in the aftermath of the bombing, telling the story of a nation attacked and going to war that has endured for decades. At the same time, the differences between these films, particularly in emotional tone and moral praxis, illustrate important shifts in American memorializing of the Second World War.

Since both films were made to prepare audiences for visiting the memorial, they both invite viewers to think about the sunken ship with its lost crew. Both films begin with images of the *Arizona* and names of the dead. The film from 1980 took the viewer underwater and whispered the names of crew who died as the camera ran along the length of an encrusted mooring chain. The current film achieves a similar effect by scanning the names etched into the marble wall of the shrine room. Both then ask, How did this happen? and shift to historical chronology, unfolding nearly the same episodic structure and visual imagery (see White 2001 for a more detailed analysis).

At the outset of making the film released in 1992, the NPS curator responsible for the script was intent on supplying prewar context pertaining to the struggle of colonial powers in Asia. Yet, as he put it, "almost all of that ended up being cut out" because "no matter how you tell that story, it's a favorable story from the Japanese point of view. . . . any nation state makes those kinds of decisions all the time. But anytime you talk about that in the context of Pearl Harbor, people in the United States are going to criticize you for sympathizing with Japan. And that's not at all what I was trying to do."[23] Instead, the image that does come across, as it did in all the previous documentaries from *December 7th* through the navy film of 1980, is Hawaiian innocence, the languid complacency of a Polynesian paradise. After providing some historical background, both of the visitor center films insert brief portraits of Hawai'i that resemble *December 7th*'s portrayal of Hawai'i as a tropical idyll and vacationland. As before, the Hawai'i in these films is a serene island paradise where U.S. military forces relax in touristic leisure. Iconic images of palm trees, beaches, hotels, and hula "girls" appear, accompanied by Hawaiian ukulele and big band music. Hawai'i, in these films, is a place where America is at rest, on vacation. Images of young men at play, unaware of the death and destruction about to rain down on them, give little indication that Hawai'i at the time was one of the strongest military and colonial outposts in the world, "Fortress Pacific," as labeled in today's museum exhibits.

During the script consultations, one of the main points of difference between the approach of the park service and that of national military and veteran advisors concerned the use of personal stories and perspectives, as opposed to a more generalized narrative voice. Because of their commitment to a historiography that speaks in the voice of balanced, universalizing history capable of telling the story in terms of the larger sweep of history, the NPS superintendent, historian, and curator emphasized the importance of narrative voice-over. In contrast, both the film company and the military and veteran advisers wished to take a more personal approach and tell the story through the experience of particular individuals, especially those recognized for acts of valor. In this respect, the push to recenter the film in heroic stories reflects the power of personal narrative as an idiom for popular history—evident in books and films that have been telling the stories of the Second World War since the time the war was fought to the present. Examples include Walter Lord's most-read Pearl Harbor book, *Day of Infamy*, John Hersey's best-selling *Hiroshima* and, more recently, Stephen Ambrose's oral-history-style books, the Steven Spielberg and Tom Hanks film productions *Saving Private Ryan*, *Band of Brothers*, and *The Pacific*, and nostalgia-heavy documentaries such as Ken Burns's *The War*.

When the American Studies Film Center sent their first rough-cut for review by the memorial's staff and the museum association, it struck viewers as having too many voices and no center of gravity. In a letter to his superior in the park service administration, the superintendent wrote specifically of the difficulty of including "personal perspectives" in the film script, and the value of the film as a special type of interpretive tool:

> While it has always been considered important to provide a personal perspective to the telling of the story it has never been considered the primary view point from which the story would be told. This is done in ranger and survivor talks, and in books available through the bookstore. The early scripts, while attempting to present the Pearl Harbor story from a "personal" point of view, failed to tell the story accurately not only in the narrative but in the use of visual images. These early scripts and the "rough cut" viewed by AMMA [USS *Arizona* Memorial Museum Association] and park staff lacked a clear voice in telling the story. . . . It was our feeling that a straight forward telling of the events surrounding the attack would best serve the interpretative needs of the park. In support of this we feel that telling the story from a personal point of view has the tendency to exclude everyone else.[24]

One voice in this first cut that was regarded as particularly problematic was a segment narrated by a Japanese woman commenting on the rise of Japanese militarism in Japan. Whereas this met the park historian's desire to put the attack in a larger context, it was out of line with other expectations formed no doubt by the mythic narrative that has guided American memory of Pearl Harbor since the bombing. As the film producer recalled the process, opinion swung, as more and more people reviewed the film, against devoting so much time to "the Japanese side of it": "They thought the key historical points were being left out to give the time to the Japanese side of it."[25]

Whereas there were few advocates for retaining Japanese voices, leaving out the voices of American heroes would not be so easy. Military and veteran representatives consulted by Park Service Chief Historian Edwin Bearss (himself a Marine veteran of the Pacific War) expressed their "major concern" that the revised script conveyed an "overemphasis on death and suffering as opposed to heroism." The "recommended redress" suggested by this group was for the script to include more references to "acts by Medal of Honor winners and others."[26] This recommendation was followed up with a more forceful letter, saying, "The reference to those heroes of December 7 (Ross, Finn, Hill, Dorie Miller, Welsh, and Taylor) that were indicated in our review of the last draft must be included. If cuts are to be made, they should be made elsewhere. These figures represent the common fighting men." To this the panel added, "We must insist on those changes and the following additions that reflect the thorough consensus of all members of our blue-ribbon panel and the desire of [NPS] Deputy Assistant Secretary Salisbury to be responsive to the comments of veterans and veterans' organizations."[27] The insistence here reflects the importance of heroic narrative in war histories by and for veterans groups. Yet the park service held their course to produce the film with a more reflective voice-over narrative and its wide-angle lens, consistent with the goal of using only historic film footage (except for the cane cutter). The new film premiered on December 2, 1992, to generally laudatory reviews, even if viewers continued to find very different meanings in it.[28]

Memorialization in How Shall We Remember Them?

Differences in the moral and emotional tone of the two orientation films are most evident in the way the two narratives represent the subsequent course of the war and its relevance today. The navy film released in 1980 concluded with a drumbeat listing of famous battle sites that mark the string of Allied victories across the Pacific leading to Japanese surrender (omitting Hiroshima and Nagasaki): "Coral Sea, Midway, Guadalcanal, the Gilberts, Marshall Islands, New Guinea, Marianas, the Philippines, Iwo Jima, Okinawa, Japan." This recitation of names in martial cadence was accompanied by a triumphant music score, scenes of ships in combat, and reference to the ultimate result of the war in building "the greatest armada the world had ever seen."

In addition to worries about historical accuracy, the celebratory tone of the navy's film concerned the park service, for whom context was an overriding concern. As stated on many occasions, such as the discussions with the JACL, the film was regarded as a key element in a process of remembrance, a prelude to viewing the sunken ship and contemplating the shrine room's wall of names. When interviewed about the film prior to its completion, the curator responsible for drafting the script described the emotional importance of the film, referencing Pearl Harbor survivors and veterans:

> [The original film didn't] give the visitor a very good sense of what it was they were actually going out and see. By that I mean that it didn't

set much of a tone for the fact that people were going out to a cemetery; that this was in fact not only a sunken ship out in the harbor. It's a place where nearly twelve hundred people lost their lives in an instant. There should be a certain amount of respect and reverence and reflection that occurred when people went out there. . . . If there are survivors, or World War II veterans or something like that, this is very important for their lives; and to have kids running around or . . . visitors hooting and screaming and you know carrying on. It was clear that the message wasn't being transmitted.[29]

The producer echoed these sentiments when he talked about the importance of the film for setting the proper context for visiting the memorial, for giving it an appropriate emotional meaning: "The overridingly important thing about this film was that it prepare people for the emotional experience of being at Pearl Harbor. Because people sometimes literally show up there with coolers of beer thinking they are going to a Disneyland kind of experience, a tourist attraction. You know, sort of goofy stuff and then they are shocked of course when they walk in the front door and see what is going on there."[30]

For the park service historians, the problems had less to do with the "economics of Japanese tourism and business interests in Hawai'i" than with the film's promotion of Cold War attitudes that no longer seemed to fit. In Superintendent Magee's view, the film released in 1980 concentrated too much on the lesson of military preparedness and not enough on remembrance of those who died on December 7. After his views were written up in a feature article in *Smithsonian* magazine on the eve of the Pearl Harbor fiftieth anniversary (Zinsser 1991), he received numerous letters of complaint (White 2001, 274). When the park historian was interviewed for a newspaper story about the change of films, he stated flatly that the navy film "was very much a product of a Cold War mind-set," an attribution that elicited a call from the admiral in command of the Pearl Harbor naval base to the memorial superintendent, objecting to the attribution of a Cold War mentality to the navy.[31]

In contrast to the coda of military triumph and strength that concluded the first orientation film, the current film, as intended, presents the subsequent course of the war in a more somber, melancholy tone, with the narration in the female voice of Stockard Channing (in contrast to Robert Stack's narration of the first film).[32] Instead of the first film's climactic recitation of hard-fought American victories in the Pacific, with images of battleships firing their guns and Marines storming island beaches, the current film shows wounded men on stretchers and a close-up of a young Marine looking anxiously at the camera while taking cover in the sand. These contrasts in emotional meaning signal a broader difference in the moral lessons posed by each film. Located just at the transition point between the memorial's secular and sacred space, where travelers leave the visitor center for the memorial and its shrine room, the film is positioned strategically to do the kind of emotional work imagined by its producers.

The opening and closing segments of these films create a frame within which the documentary narrative becomes an act of memorialization, an emotive institution (White 2004a). Where the opening of the films bear some similarity, the clearest difference between them comes at the end, when each offers a reflection about the meaning and purpose of remembrance. Both films do this by shifting tense and voice and returning the viewer to the present with images of the *Arizona* memorial. The current film devotes more time to contemporary reflection by showing scenes from memorial services held at the visitor center, before closing with the memorial at sunset. The navy film released in 1980 concludes with the following: "If we forget December 7, 1941; if we forget over 1,000 men still entombed aboard the USS *Arizona*; if we forget that a nation unprepared will sacrifice her finest men and women, then we would forget what America stands for and that is why we must remember Pearl Harbor. Homeport still for one of the world's most powerful Naval forces, the United States Pacific Fleet."[33] In contrast, the current film ends with more generalized, mournful sentiments—the very tone that was criticized by the panel of military and veteran advisers who felt the script should include more references to the actions of decorated heroes. (That panel asked that the final lines of the script referring to grief and mourning be deleted.) As it now stands, the current film concludes with the following thoughts about the meaning and purpose of remembrance: "How shall we remember them, those who died? Mourn the dead. Remember the battle. Understand the tragedy. Honor the memory. Let our grief for the men of the *Arizona* be for all those whose futures were taken from them on December 7th, 1941. Here they will never be forgotten."[34] When the film was released, in 1992, park service personnel spoke about the film in terms of its emotional impact. Interviewed by Honolulu newspapers, the superintendent said, "Visitors now come out of it [the film] as somber as they could be. . . . They used to come out a lot more aggressive. We wanted to impress upon them that this thing is more than a pile of concrete; it's a tomb."

Clearly the two orientation films, produced by different federal agencies (U.S. Navy and National Park Service) and shown in different historical epochs, use quite different language to engage their audiences. Both films speak in a collective voice, talking about how "we" remember. In the narration of the film from 1980, however, the *we* is a distinctly American, national *we*. The current film, in comparison, uses a more ambiguous *we* when it asks, "How shall we remember them, those who died?" When park historian Martinez commented on a draft of an earlier article on this subject (White 2001), he underlined this question and the line that follows ("Mourn the dead"), adding the marginal note: "This line was purposeful so that it represented the US and Japan." Like Martinez, others in the scripting process also saw this passage as widening the moral sphere of remembrance. The narration goes on to make this explicit: "Let our grief for the men of the *Arizona* be for all those whose futures were taken from them on December 7th, 1941." The inclusive impulse here is evident in the film's reference to the losses of the Pacific war, described as millions of "soldiers and civilians" who "would suffer and sacrifice before the war's end," accompanied by visual images that move from American Marines on stretchers to piles of helmets of war dead, including some that appear Japanese. The expansion of empathy is accomplished in part through the film's structure of feeling, attempting to replace triumphal patriotic emotion with a more generalized feeling of sorrow for death in war, a shift away from wartime feelings of outrage toward sentiments of loss associated with war in global perspective.

When the film then moves to the present, it changes focus from the objects of memorialization (those who died at Pearl Harbor) to the people who memorialize, concluding in a way that invites viewing subjects to interpolate themselves into the scene. As it does so, it shows a distinctly international retinue of people participating in annual memorial services, further expanding the relevant public for Pearl Harbor remembrance. At a point in the script where liner notes call for "Japanese and American mourners," the film portrays Japanese Buddhist priests at one of the memorial's annual ceremonies: "Every year on December 7th special ceremonies of remembrance are held here at the Visitors' Center. The dead are mourned; the heroes are remembered. People from all over the world honor young men they never knew, whose lives were cut short on December 7th, 1941." This phrasing, while maintaining the memorializing focus on the "young men" of the *Arizona*, expands the sphere of relevance for those who might meaningfully "mourn," "remember," "understand," and "honor" in ways that would become more dramatic and visible twenty years later, with the establishment of the World War II Valor in the Pacific Monument and its broader commemorative mandate.

TO RETURN TO the cane cutter controversy, it is not so much a concern with objectivity as the memorial imperative of these films, focusing on military losses and sacrifices, that consistently selects for a combat narrative that places American servicemen center stage, rendering Japanese Americans relevant only insofar as they appear as a phantasm of the commanders' imagination. While nothing about the film is historically inaccurate (except, incredibly, the cane cutter), it is or was a historically accurate depiction of a moment in U.S. military history, rendered in a PBS-style voice-over narrative scripted on the basis of documentary and archival sources focused especially on the plans and policies of American military leaders and citizen soldiers. In contrast, the criticisms brought by Yoshie and Jim Tanabe were articulated in a deeply personal idiom, identifying problems in the film on the basis of their readings of the film in terms of their own lives, expressed in a language of personal experience and emotion. For them, responding to the Pearl Harbor film on the basis of their own stories about family struggles during the war, the issue of racist treatment of Japanese Americans was and is central to the Pearl Harbor story, not a "minority" issue to be addressed in secondary exhibits or a longer film. The debates and discussions around the modification of the film were not, for them, academic debates, or problems with a historical text that should be more inclusive. The hook that conjoined their personal stories with the Pearl Harbor narrative was most evident in their use of words like "patriotism" and "loyalty." When the Tanabes spoke in meetings with the park service, their speech tended toward testimonial, performing Japanese American subjectivity (Roxworthy 2008). Here is Jim Tanabe, speaking at the second group meeting of the JACL and the NPS, in March 1999:

> When Pearl Harbor was attacked I was nine years old. . . . And we cannot be more proud as Americans. And do you know who started instilling that loyalty in us? Our alien parents who, when they wanted to be naturalized, showed their loyalty [but] were not allowed citizenship until decades later. . . . My reaction to the attack of Pearl Harbor: horror, anger, . . . "Damn the Japs!" My reaction is no different than that of Americans of other racial ancestries. . . . So when the movie talks of the military having great concern about sabotage among the large Japanese population, . . . I feel an urgency to correct this information. (audio recording, March 27, 1999)

The discussions between the JACL and the NPS about the cane cutter image seemed at times to take the form of a kind of Freudian return of the repressed, as endless repetition of the symptoms of a traumatic wound that could be acted out but never resolved (Crapanzano 2013). In the end, however, the social space of the memorial, as a zone of encounter between different communities of remembrance, proved important, as it did for American and Japanese veterans in commemorative events discussed previously. Over the course of a year and a half, dozens of individual conversations and meetings, many of them on the premises of the memorial visitor center, allowed individuals associated with the various constituencies to get a better understanding of the feelings and perceptions of those with opposing views. The superintendent later recalled, "Once everyone started talking and talking about perceptions and what the Tanabes were feeling, and what it caused them to feel . . . [I was] feeling more and more, 'Well I can understand what you're saying, even though I personally don't see it' " (recorded interview with the author, June 30, 2000). She went on to characterize this working-through process as one that in fact marks the ability of the memorial to "learn" from these kinds of dialogue, and change "interpretations" accordingly: "I think it's part of the learning process . . . that perceptions and cultures change and are evolving all the time. . . . We look at things differently than we did ten years ago. We interpret things differently." One of the most important factors influencing the superintendent's decision to change the film, was the perspective of the Pearl Harbor survivors. The park service looked to the small group of volunteers as a line of moral defense. So when some of them who had been sitting in on the JACL meetings began to sympathize with the Tanabes, the superintendent started to think more seriously about changing the film:

> It was really interesting to watch Bob and Everett, who are not Japanese Americans but are Pearl Harbor survivors, listening to their perspective and then really understand why these people were complaining about the film; and not having a problem with the film being changed. I mean that was a real eye opener to me. At that point when I saw the Pearl Harbor survivors moving toward an understanding, it was like, "We as the Park Service have to follow this movement of understanding that's going on. We can't just stand back and say, 'We made it, that's the way it's going to be and it's going to be that way forever.' " (recorded interview with the author, June 30, 2000)

While the combination of cathartic speech and political pressure worked to bring the memorial's public history more in tune with the Japanese American experience of Pearl Harbor, it also further obscures other absences, particularly Native Hawaiian history. The absence of Native Hawaiians in the dominant Pearl Harbor narrative, except insofar as they populate the backdrop of Hawai'i as objects of military tourism, hula girls, and ukulele music, is increasingly noticeable with the passing of time. The erasure has been so complete that viewers have either not noticed or have not raised objections, because they realize they would be met with puzzled looks by those who regard Native Hawaiian issues as irrelevant to Pearl Harbor memorialization. Most visitors remain unaware or uninterested in colonial history. As literary and film theory remind us, the fractured conditions of disempowerment resist representation in retellable stories, making the experience of marginality easy to forget in the public sphere (Connerton 2009; Renov 1991; Tajiri 1991).

Next, chapter 4 traces the continued growth of tourism in the Pearl Harbor area, especially the expansion of other Pearl Harbor military museums, arguing that tourist pleasures pose a similar challenge to such alternate memories as the Japanese American experience with racism or Native Hawaiian colonial history. Whereas the conflict over the cane cutter image occasioned an extended dialogue and debate that led to modifications of viewpoints and a decision to make changes, the institutional culture of the military-entertainment complex (Gonzalez 2013), evident in the museum spaces around the harbor, offers few such opportunities. Chapter 4 looks at a very similar conflict, but this time with quite different outcomes.

Four

THEMING

AMERICA AT WAR

To study the production of history in places traversed by tourist travelers is to ask about the practices that create, in museum parlance, the "visitor experience." At Pearl Harbor, two primary factors work to define the context for the experience of visiting the USS *Arizona* Memorial: the fact that it is located in Hawai'i, a global tourism destination, and that it is inside a U.S. naval base. Due to its success in attracting visitors, the *Arizona* memorial is the state's most popular tourism destination, with about 1.8 million visitors per year, at present. In 2013 it was listed at number three on TripAdvisor's list of "top landmarks" in the United States, based on visitor reviews.[1] Whereas the growth of Pearl Harbor tourism offers an opportunity to "touch" an increasing number and diversity of people, it also risks the commodification and trivialization of memory often associated with tourism. George Mosse noted a similar set of tensions in European memory of the First World War, where "the war experience was sanctified. Yet at the same time, the war was confronted and absorbed in a radically different way, by being trivialized through its association with objects of daily life, popular theater, or battlefield tourism" (1990, 7).

As a tourist destination, Pearl Harbor doubles up on its attraction value by offering both a historic battleground and a functioning military base as objects for the tourist gaze (Gonzalez 2013). Travelers arriving at the visitor center are greeted with a panoramic view of the harbor, home to one of the world's largest naval bases, impressively on display across the harbor. The entire Pearl Harbor navy base was designated a National Historic Landmark in 1964, two years after dedication of the USS *Arizona* Memorial. Architectural features, interpretive signs, and wayside exhibits overlooking the harbor give the visual panorama historical meaning by linking present locations to the sights of December 7, 1941. Maps that set out the arrangement of ships and base facilities as they were in 1941, along with photos of burning and exploding ships, recode the harbor as it was on the day of the attack, simultaneously historicizing the memorial's present and authenticating its past.

The larger context at Pearl Harbor has transformed dramatically in the decades since the memorial and visitor center were first constructed. Since that time, the harbor has seen the appearance of three major military museums, each focused on different military service branches and their respective technologies and histories. The USS *Bowfin* Submarine Museum and Park opened in 1981, followed by the Battleship *Missouri* Memorial in 1999 and the Pacific Aviation Museum in 2006, both located on Ford Island, in the middle of the harbor. These developments changed Pearl Harbor from a place with one memorial to an expansive landscape with four major military museums. Before the arrival of the USS *Missouri* in 1998, a visit to Pearl Harbor meant a visit to the *Arizona* memorial and possibly a stop to see the submarine next door. Today, visitors may choose from an array of museums that expand the theme of the Pacific War into broader histories of warfare, with weapons and displays related to the wars in Korea, Vietnam, and Iraq.

As the new "attractions" took shape, the multiplicity of options for visitors to Pearl Harbor posed a problem of coordination for the managers of these institutions, ultimately fostering cooperation among the museums, who began calling themselves the "Pearl Harbor Historic Sites." One of the primary architectural goals of the renovation and expansion of the *Arizona* memorial visitor center in the 2000s was the creation of a single entryway and ticketing experience for all four museums. The creation of that entryway attempts to turn the four separate museums into a single destination. Today visitors approaching the visitor center, with its wide entrance bordered with flagpoles, pass between two walls on either side of the walkway listing the names of the museums and memorials included within the Pearl Harbor Historic Sites: the National Park Service's World War II Valor in the Pacific National Monument, with its three ship memorials (USS *Arizona*, USS *Oklahoma*, USS *Utah*) on one side and the three nonprofit military museums on the other: the USS *Bowfin* Submarine Museum, the Battleship *Missouri* Memorial, and the Pacific Aviation Museum.

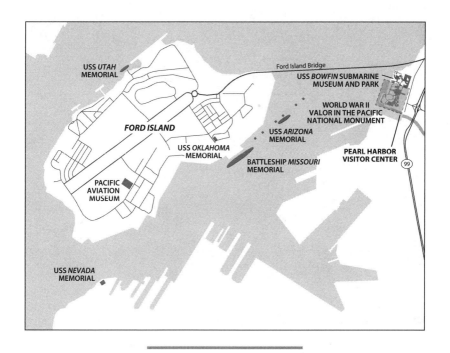

MAP 4.1
Pearl Harbor museums and memorials.

In 2011, a year after the new visitor center opened, the Pearl Harbor Historic Sites issued a joint press release announcing a new "Passport to Pearl
Harbor" that offered a two-day pass to all four memorial museums, "a $115
value for just $65 per adult and $35 per child." This new packaging, oriented
toward more efficient ticket sales, merged the free memorial with the other
paid attractions, thus submerging the special quality of the memorial, recognized by Congress when it exempted it from the requirement that national
parks charge admission (although anyone wanting the audio tour must pay a
fee—something included in the passport package). The press release announcing the new ticket package in 2011, speaking to an American public (about
"our nation"), described the historic sites as an integrated experience that "carries forth the legacies of treasured icons" and honors military service (Kramer
2011): "Pearl Harbor includes several independent memorials and museums—
some under the purview of the National Park Service and others operated
by private, nonprofit organizations. Together, and in partnership with Joint
Base Pearl Harbor-Hickam, they carry forth the legacies of several of our nation's most treasured icons, enduring tributes to the valor and sacrifices of

FIGURE 4.1
Entrance to World War II Valor in the Pacific National Monument and
Pearl Harbor Historic Sites visitor center. May 29, 2015.
Photo by author.

our veterans during a time when the future of our nation and the world truly hung in the balance."

This chapter puts the *Arizona* memorial in this broader horizon by recalling the progressive expansion of military museums in the harbor to the present. With today's close cooperation among the historic sites or "partners," it seems odd to recall, for example, the initial resistance to plans to locate the USS *Missouri* in close proximity to the *Arizona*. Yet in the mid-1990s, as plans for the arrival of the *Missouri* were unfolding, a number of key *Arizona* constituencies argued for a more distant location, fearing that the looming presence of a functioning battleship would detract from the uniquely sacred space of the *Arizona*. In particular, the proposal to locate the *Missouri* nearly adjacent to the *Arizona* memorial was challenged by the National Park Service managers of the memorial, as well as many Pearl Harbor survivors. That challenge, largely forgotten today, can be read as one of many instances in which guardians of the memorial have fought to protect it from forces of development that press in upon the remains of the ship and its shrine.

Although the other ship and plane museums have memorial aspects (as in the name the "Battleship *Missouri* Memorial") or include distinctly memorial spaces (as in the submarine museum's circle of plaques dedicated to lost submariners), they function mainly as museums that offer educational and entertainment activities for paying customers, while also sponsoring commemorative activities honoring military service. As private nonprofit institutions, the military museums differ in mission and governance from the *Arizona* memorial, a public historic site operated by the National Park Service. While each of the three nonprofit museums has its own organizational culture, they are all dedicated to the preservation and promotion of military heritage, led by boards of directors of retired commanders and business leaders. Given their focus on heritage and preservation, the exhibition and interpretation practices of military museums tend to be hardware-driven, focused on the acquisition and display of key artifacts, such as the submarine and battleship, which in turn become vehicles for telling human stories, particularly those of military personnel associated with them. In contrast, the National Park Service, as a federal agency with a mission of stewardship for historic sites, is more engaged with a broader range of social history.

In the final section of this chapter, I explore these differences in the context of one particular exhibit at the Pacific Aviation Museum that became a center of controversy in 2008, shortly after the museum opened. The exhibit told the story of one of the attack planes, a Japanese Zero fighter, that had crash-landed on the island of Niʻihau, triggering a complicated series of events in which the pilot was ultimately assisted by a local Japanese American. Once again, as in the dispute over the film at the *Arizona* memorial, discussed in chapter 3, the controversy was largely a matter of absences. Members of the Japanese American community objected to the way the story was told in the exhibit as evidence for disloyal tendencies in the Japanese American community, without an attempt to relate something of the larger history of internment, with its rich body of historical analysis and debate documenting the overwhelming loyalty of the Japanese American community during the war and the injustices of internment that have been recognized repeatedly in postwar legislation.

Sacred Places, Tourist Pleasures

For many visitors to Hawaiʻi, first contact with the islands comes in the form of the view from an airliner window, looking down upon the island's remarkable volcanic topography. In the approach to Honolulu International Airport, some pilots and flight stewards will offer a running commentary that names islands and visible features of the landscape such as Diamond Head and the beaches of Waikiki as they come into view. The *Arizona* memorial is one of the only architectural features likely to be named in such commentaries, a moment in which the sight of the memorial, as a thin strip of white in the middle of Pearl Harbor, signifies its cultural visibility on the map of Hawai'i's tourist destinations.

But this same prominence can lead to symbolic exhaustion, becoming a part of the saturated landscape of heavily visited sites. A typical travel article on the attractions of tourism in Hawai'i begins, "So, you've laid a lei at the statue of Duke Kahanamoku, the patron kahuna of surfers. You've cruised the beachfront gift shops and sipped a mai tai at Waikiki. You've visited Diamond Head, Pearl Harbor and the USS *Arizona*. Now what?" (Yvonne Daley, *San Jose Mercury*, September 15, 1996). Here, the prose of a travel writer, presumably addressing the seasoned California tourist headed for Hawai'i, locates the memorial in the same discursive space represented in Hawai'i's own travel brochures: nested among a variety of entertainment options that include beach going, shopping, and sipping cocktails in Waikiki. In this short passage, the *Arizona* is presupposed as cliché, as one item in a list of things already done by well-traveled tourists. Where significance is based on entertainment value, depending on novelty, it can be used up, drained out, and emptied of meaning. The writer David Lodge captures just this sense of symbolic exhaustion in his novel *Paradise News*, when he describes a tourist couple, Brian and Beryl Everthorpe, playing the videotapes they have taken of their Hawaiian holiday for a group of friends assembled in their hotel room:

> The film then became tedious again as it began to trace Everthorpe's peregrinations around Oahu. . . . As if sensing the audience's restiveness, Beryl herself requested Brian to "gee it up a bit," and he rather reluctantly pressed the fast-forward button on his remote control. This certainly had the effect of making the film more amusing. At Pearl Harbor, a naval cutter surged out towards the *Arizona* with the speed of a torpedo boat, and disgorged a cluster of tourists who swarmed over the Memorial for a few seconds before being sucked back into the vessel and returning abruptly to shore. (Lodge 1991, 269)

National Park Service staff and others at Pearl Harbor often talk about the challenges of conveying the significance of the memorial to tourist visitors. With the rapid increase in visitation since the 1980s, Pearl Harbor, for many, can be just like it was for David Lodge's Brian and Beryl Everthorpe—one more fast recreational stop on a sightseeing itinerary. Anyone viewing the scene at the visitor center on a busy day as throngs of vacationers mill around (about five thousand per day or 1.8 million per year), taking in the harbor views and museum exhibits as they await their turn to see the documentary film and take a boat to the memorial, can readily understand the difficulty of defining it as a sacred space (Kelly 1996).

Worries about the potential for cultural or historical tourism to destroy its subject matter can be summed up in a single word: Disney (Wallace 1996). Just as Disneyland or Disneyworld are the prototypes for large-scale theme park tourism, the term *Disneyland* is also used as an adjective that implies "superficial"—entertainment that is (merely) recreational and pleasure-oriented. Such a reputation works well for sites defined as places of entertainment, especially those that welcome children's fun and excitement. It works less well for sites associated with violence and tragedy. When park service officials and museum designers sat down to plan the new museum that opened in 2010 (see chapter 5), references to Disneyland quickly marked out the territory they were seeking to avoid.

It was, in fact, Disney Studios that produced the latest Hollywood feature film that managed to turn the Pearl Harbor attack into an entertaining feature for younger audiences. With the release of *Pearl Harbor* in May 2001, Disney knew it would have to navigate a complicated emotional and political terrain. Realizing that production of a film on such an iconic part of American war history, filmed on location, would provoke questions of propriety and respect for the actual history of violence and loss, the producers went to considerable lengths to assure veteran and military groups that they were aware of the need not to trivialize their subject (White 2002). They had their work cut out for them, given that the film's $5 million publicity budget spawned media announcements such as *Entertainment Weekly*'s cover headline "PEARL HARBOR: ROMANCE! HEROISM! STUFF BLOWING UP! Inside Summer's Biggest Movie" (June 1, 2001).

Despite the sensationalism, Disney's public relations office insisted that because of the film's "painful subject matter," they would "steer clear of the marketing strategies that usually surround . . . summer blockbusters." For local audiences in Hawai'i, the very subject of commercializing Pearl Harbor is newsworthy. Just prior to the release of the film, a Honolulu newspaper ran an article under the title, "'Pearl Harbor' Steers Clear of Major Commercialization." The article quoted the chairman of the Walt Disney Motion Pictures Group, saying, "The reverence we have tried to show is vitally important. You won't see any games, toys or anything like that in or around the film. The film is something that we hold very sacred, and is meant to honor, not take away from anything that happened at Pearl Harbor" (Paiva 2008, A8).

The Disney Corporation's strategy in demonstrating its seriousness focused on engagement with Pearl Harbor survivors. During production in Hawai'i, actors and producers staged a ceremony on the memorial in which they appeared with veterans and talked to the press about their feelings. A news story subtitled "Actor Affleck 'Profoundly Touched' by Ceremony's Significance" reported that the movie star was moved "to stand where so many perished for their country" (Ryan 2000). In the end, however, the film became what the Hollywood entertainment industry does best: a film that entertained. It was, by the producers' own description, a love story with a historical backdrop. And that backdrop was built around spectacular special-effect-enhanced battle scenes— imagery not unlike video games familiar to the movie's young demographic. Capping a long process of cooperation between Disney and the U.S. Navy, the film premiered in an evening of spectacle on the deck of a nuclear aircraft carrier, the USS *John Stennis*, which the navy had deployed to Pearl Harbor for the occasion (White 2002). The premier attracted local political and military elites for a gala befitting a Hollywood extravaganza, with dense media coverage of the film's glamorous young actors posing with aging Pearl Harbor survivors, several in wheel chairs.

Despite corporate efforts to convey authenticity and respect, veteran survivors whom I talked with concluded the film was simply irrelevant for them. Historians who had hoped the film would bring attention to Second World War history seemed embarrassed. The twisted path of the Disney film production and reception reflects the moral ambivalence around tourism at Pearl Harbor. For park service officials, historians, and veterans devoted to the memorial's memory work, the pressures of globalization and economic development are both an enticement and a threat, a force that threatens to distort or overwhelm the practice of memorialization. Where some see opportunities to more effectively commodify and sell the "brand" of Pearl Harbor, others see the mutation of history and memory. As a result, the memorial has always been surrounded by a certain amount of anxious monitoring and regulation—by ordinary citizens, by mass media, and by government and military agencies concerned to protect the site from symbolic pollution. Such "contaminants" come in many forms, from loud voices on the memorial to commercialization and efforts to expand the visitor base through corporate marketing techniques.

Such is the predicament for any place that would like to mark off sacred space in the face of a constant flow of visitors who may have little understanding of what sacred would mean. The quality of the sacred is not inherent in the material remains of the ship, the shrine, the museum, or any other part of the physicality of the *Arizona* memorial. It is a feature of the relationship between persons and places—a quality that may or may not emerge as people engage with the site. Problems of commodification and trivialization associated with tourism at Pearl Harbor are compounded by the increasing distance of visitors from the events memorialized. With the passing of generations and the expanding diversity of travelers, visitors are much less likely to arrive with the knowledge or background to engage easily with the memorial's history.

The proportion of international visitors in the Hawai'i tourism economy increased with the rise of Asian economies in the 1980s, making up about 40 percent of "visitor arrivals" in 2012, compared with just 30 percent a few years earlier (Hawai'i Tourism Authority 2012). Visitation at the *Arizona* memorial is somewhat more American in comparison, with about 20 percent international visitors (National Park Service Visitor Study 2000). In the past, Japanese visitors made up about half of that number. And today the Chinese are the fastest growing nationality among the memorial's international visitors. From a somewhat laissez-faire attitude toward Asian visitation in earlier decades, questions about the interests of international travelers are very much on the minds of those who manage the nonprofit military museums, concerned to expand their base of paying visitors among the growing numbers of Asian visitors. In 2014 the Battleship *Missouri* Memorial hired a sales manager to "focus on the China and Japan markets" with the expectation that, in the words of the *Missouri* CEO, "It takes time to build that brand image, give people a reason to want to come and tell them the stories that they want to hear" (Ubay 2014).

Despite park service efforts to reach non-American, non-English-speaking audiences with informational brochures and a (paid) audio tour in multiple languages, there is considerable evidence that, in a significant number of cases, foreign visitors don't engage with desired messages—a failure of communication that shows up in complaints (from American visitors) about unruly tour groups—complaints that also seem to reflect lingering anxiety toward Asian visitors (at times assumed, mistakenly, to be Japanese) in the sacred space of the memorial.[2] For international travelers, the superficiality built into the rhythms of group tours is compounded by gaps in language and culture that make it difficult to understand or relate to historical exhibits and presentations.

International visitors often bring their own national narratives of the Second World War that may or may not intersect with the American story of the attack, as a sneak attack that was the starting point for the war. Tour guides mediate the experience of those on their tours, sometimes leading their groups to museum exhibits relevant to their own national narratives. If time

FIGURE 4.2
Visitor poses with USN sailor in visitor center lobby. August 26, 1994.
Photo by author.

is short, some skip the film and boat ride to the memorial, in favor of photo opportunities around the visitor center and harbor shore. One Chinese tour guide commented, "We don't need the boat trip. You can just put a telescope over by the visitor center. Visitors will be fine with just taking pictures from the other side. It is noisy and hot over here [on the memorial]. Besides, you save the energy and money on running the boat trip" (recorded tour guide interview by Kuan-Jung Lai, September 27, 2010; Page and White 2011, 6).

For obvious reasons, site managers and researchers have given the greatest amount of attention to the experience of Japanese visitors. There have been two in-depth studies of Japanese visitors at the *Arizona* memorial, the first by Patricia Masters (1991, 1992), an American scholar of Japanese studies, in the early 1990s, when tensions between the United States and Japan were running high, followed a decade later by Yujin Yaguchi (2005), a Japanese scholar of American studies, when Japan was more noticeably allied with the United States in the war on terror. Their findings demonstrate changing sensibilities, but also a continuous interest in the memorial among many Japanese visitors, particularly the older generation, who see it as a place for reconciliation (as did the veterans discussed in chapter 2).

More recent research has focused on the expectations and experience of Chinese visitors (Page and White 2011). In a small pilot study, Kuan-Jung Lai and I researched Chinese visitors' experiences at the memorial by following tour groups and interviewing tour guides.[3] In that work we found that older generations, like Japanese visitors, often know well the importance of Pearl Harbor for bringing the United States into the war—a war China had already been fighting for four years, with enormous losses. Since China and Japan have been in almost constant conflict since at least the early nineteenth century, some Chinese travelers see Pearl Harbor as a symbol of Japanese aggression, much the way it is represented in America's wartime representations. Chinese visitors also express interest in the Pearl Harbor of today, as a major naval base projecting American military power in the Pacific. When tour guides talk with their groups at the visitor center, looking out on the harbor, they often describe the area as a vast open-air military museum, fascinating in its array of ships and facilities.

Pacific War Theme Park?

Entering the visitor gateway to Pearl Harbor today, one encounters signs and digital displays advertising the multiple ship and aviation museums that offer choices about how to spend a day touring Pearl Harbor's Second World War "attractions." It seems almost quaint to imagine the early moments of tourism to Pearl Harbor, when everyone came to visit the *Arizona* memorial and, after 1981, possibly the submarine museum next door. The transformation of a large swath of the Pearl Harbor naval base into a more dense cultural space, with historic sites and museums for the touring public, emerged step by step with the addition of two major military museums during the 1990s and 2000s. The first step, coming close on the heels of the *Arizona* visitor center, was the construction of the *Bowfin* museum, with the submarine moored on the adjacent shoreline. Then, with a great deal of media fanfare, came the arrival of the battleship USS *Missouri*, in 1998, followed a few years later by the opening of the Pacific Aviation Museum, in 2006—both initiatives of nonprofit organizations dedicated to preserving battleship and aviation heritage, respectively. And both were located on Ford Island, once reachable only by ferry but henceforth connected by a new bridge that opened it to tourism access. These developments were all part of a wholesale transformation of Pearl Harbor undertaken by the U.S. Navy and by the National Park Service, pursuing their respective, coordinated agendas. The result has been the creation of a tourist destination transformed from a singular historic site focused on the bombing attack of 1941 and the *Arizona* memorial to an entire landscape of museum and memorial spaces telling the stories of the Pacific War and American military history (see map 4.1).

Not surprisingly, that transformation has been marked with periodic conflicts and controversies, struggles over memory and the manner in which it is produced for tourist consumption. The arrival of the park service, in 1980, to manage the USS *Arizona* Memorial visitor center inaugurated the era of large-scale visitor operations at the naval base, and raised the importance of historic preservation and interpretation for redefining the harbor as a historic landscape. This development eased the way for the arrival of a second, historic Second World War vessel, the USS *Bowfin* submarine (nicknamed the "Pearl Harbor Avenger" during the war). The *Bowfin* had been the object of preservation efforts by a dedicated network of submariners who had obtained the vessel in 1979 under the congressional act of 1956 empowering the secretary of the navy to donate decommissioned vessels to parties committed to preservation and education. Once the *Arizona* memorial visitor center was opened, the navy designated the stretch of shoreline immediately adjacent to the center as the location for the new submarine museum and memorial. Although the *Bowfin* has always existed in the shadow of the *Arizona* memorial, the two facilities would henceforth share a parking lot, making it easy for some portion (about one-fifth) of the thousands coming to the *Arizona* memorial every day to expand their Pearl Harbor experience by visiting the submarine, with its museum and array of armaments on display in the surrounding grounds. With the opening of the new visitor center, in 2010, the *Arizona* memorial complex (World War II Valor in the Pacific National Monument) and the *Bowfin* museum became spatially connected, allowing tourists to easily walk to the adjacent submarine museum, where they may go on board the submarine, ponder the circle of memorial plaques to lost submarines, or visit the museum. As they do, they walk by displays of torpedoes and short-range missiles lined up along the sidewalk, with short labels.

From today's vantage point, after the creation of the World War II Valor in the Pacific National Monument and construction of the visitor center gateway to all the partner memorial museums, it is difficult to recall some of the conflicts that marked the emergence of today's historic Pearl Harbor. The first significant public dispute was prompted by the proposal to locate the uss *Missouri* as a floating museum memorial five hundred yards from the uss *Arizona* Memorial. Regard for the sanctity of the *Arizona*, with its wall of names and tomb below, led both the National Park Service and a number of Pearl Harbor survivors to go on record opposing its placement within eyesight of the memorial. Once the *Missouri* was in place, however, along with the Pacific Aviation Museum nearby on Ford Island, the posture of the park service, along with that of the survivors, shifted to one of acceptance and cooperation.

Nonetheless, it is useful to look back at the public debate associated with the arrival of the *Missouri*, an important marker of an even larger process under way, transforming the harbor area as historic landscape. The uss *Missouri* is the most visible of the military attractions among today's partner sites. It is the last of the Iowa-class battleships, the ship on which the Japanese surrender was famously signed, in Tokyo Bay in 1945, and the ship that saw active duty through the first Iraq war (1991). After a long and difficult competition to acquire the decommissioned ship, a Hawaiʻi-based organization, the uss *Missouri* Foundation, succeeded in bringing the *Missouri* to Hawaiʻi. A key to the success of the Hawaiian group was the compelling nature of the historical narrative evoked by coupling the two battleships, the *Missouri* and the *Arizona*. That, at least, was the primary argument put forward by the chairman of the board of directors of the uss *Missouri* Memorial Association in his letter to the secretary of the navy making his case for Hawaii as the best location for the ship:

> World War II in the Pacific is the Navy's story. uss *Missouri*, established as a permanent memorial at Pearl Harbor, will tell that story with dramatic and visual impact that will showcase the Navy's achievements. The 1.5 million annual visitors to the uss *Arizona* memorial are witness to

the opening chapter of the Navy's participation in World War II, and that sunken ship with most of her crew still entombed is eloquent testimony to the consequences of America's military unpreparedness. Adding the USS *Missouri* to the visitors' experience will complete the story of the Navy's role in World War II, and also deliver two important messages: (1) that America, a "peace-loving nation," rose from defeat to victory and (2) brought democracy rather than 'subjugation' to a defeated Japan.

These two distinct stories of America's experience in the war need to be told to future generations, and only USS *Missouri* and USS *Arizona* together can tell them properly. (letter from Edwin L. Carter to John H. Dalton, May 1, 1996, 4, files of the author)

That argument, along with the congressional clout of Hawaiian senator Inouye, carried the day. When the secretary announced his decision, on August 21, 1996, the news reported, "The emotional and psychological pairing of the two U.S. battleships that symbolize the war in the Pacific was a key factor in awarding the USS *Missouri* to Hawai'i."[4] Within two years, on Sunday, June 22, 1998, the USS *Missouri* was towed into Pearl Harbor and moored just five hundred yards from the *Arizona* memorial. The official opening for the ship was held in January 1999, with a large gathering of civic and military leaders. Today the ship draws about 600,000 visitors annually, about one-third of the 1.8 million who visit the *Arizona*.

Although largely forgotten today, when plans for locating the *Missouri* close to the *Arizona* first surfaced, not everyone thought the "emotional and psychological pairing" mentioned above was a good idea. Even though the *Missouri* project is named a "memorial," and its mission is often described that way, as a tourist destination it more often becomes a "gee-whiz" experience conveying the ship's technological capabilities, especially its firepower.[5] Park service officials and some Pearl Harbor survivors argued that the *Missouri* would "overshadow" the *Arizona* and warp the telling of the history of the bombing. As the secretary of the navy was making his decision about where the ship would go, a front-page news story appeared in the *Honolulu Advertiser*, headlining park service reservations about the proposal:

If the USS *Missouri* ever comes to Hawaii, the National Park Service does not want it near the USS *Arizona* Memorial because it would "dominate the area."

Turning the retired battleship into a floating museum in Pearl Harbor would detract from the Park Service's job of presenting the history of Japan's Dec. 7, 1941 attack, the memorial's Lee Wheeler said yesterday.

"We cannot tell the story of all of World War II," Wheeler said. "Our purpose is to tell the story of the attack on Pearl Harbor."

. . . Wheeler said the sheer size of the *Missouri*—nearly 888 feet— "would overshadow" the 184-foot memorial built over the hull of the *Arizona*. (Jon Yoshishige, "Park Service: No to Might Mo," *Honolulu Advertiser*, May 18, 1995, A1)

Despite pressure from the coalition of military and business interests supporting the *Missouri* project, including a call to the superintendent from the office of the Pacific Command (NPS staff, personal communication), park service officials kept up their effort, even after the secretary of the navy decided on Hawai'i.[6] An article in the *Washington Post* quoted the memorial superintendent saying, "In every letter to the Navy we have said we're concerned about the impact of what basically will be a huge tourist attraction right next to a place given to a somber, reflective experience. We don't object to the *Missouri* coming into Hawai'i . . . It's just that putting it so close to the *Arizona* Memorial will change the character of this place. Will they [visitors] still be able to reflect on the loss of life here in the same way? (William Claiborne, "The New Battle at Pearl Harbor: Planned Relocation of USS *Missouri* Ignites Protectors of *Arizona* Memorial," *Washington Post*, August 21, 1997, A3–4).

The media debate between protectors of the *Arizona* memorial and supporters of the *Missouri* played out as a struggle of competing metaphors: with the metaphor of overshadowing going up against the metaphor of bookends representing America's narrative of tragedy and triumph in the Pacific War. Both metaphors sought to stake out a certain emotional terrain, the affective implications of positioning the two battleships in close proximity—one that sees them associated with dissonant narratives (one detracts from the other) and the other that sees them as conjoining to form one grand narrative. By talking about overshadowing, the park service signaled its concern with protecting a space for emotional meaning that cannot be subsumed under a triumphant "victory in the Pacific" narrative. In line with the park service motto to preserve and protect, they looked at the memorial and its historical significance as a cultural resource to be protected through their exhibits and education programs. In the park service view, the looming presence of a different kind of historic object was seen as something that would ultimately redirect the tourist gaze from a historic landscape of tragic violence to an emerging military entertainment complex.

In contrast, the bookends metaphor was deployed early and often by those interested in acquiring the *Missouri*. The symbolic potency of the "tragedy to triumph" narrative was evident from the first moments of the *Missouri* campaign. When the decision was made public, the U.S. Pacific Fleet commander in chief, Admiral Zlatoper, was quoted in a front-page news article saying, "The *Missouri*'s presence at Pearl Harbor 'will create historic "battleship bookends"'" which will represent the beginning and ending of the war in the Pacific" (Murakawa 1996, A1). Former Honolulu mayor Jeremy Harris joined in by calling the *Missouri* a "unique visitor attraction" that would boost the local economy. In his words, "The start and the end of World War II will be within 1,000 feet of each other in Pearl Harbor." The image of a single, easily visited space that tells "the whole story" of the Pacific War is reminiscent of promotions for the Polynesian Cultural Center just across the island of Oahu, where visitors are invited to "see all of Polynesia in a single day" (Ross 1993). And when the *Missouri* finally did arrive in Hawai'i, local editorial writers headlined the event as the arrival of the other bookend: "The 'other bookend' heaves into sight" (*Honolulu Advertiser*, June 21, 1998, A1). A few weeks later, when an anniversary ceremony for the signing of the surrender was held on the ship, Senator Inouye was quoted as saying, "Together at last—the USS *Arizona* and the USS *Missouri*. From pain to pride. From sacrifice to victory. The circle is now complete" (Kakesako 1998, A1). It proved to be a powerful image that still appears frequently in representations of Pearl Harbor, while talk of overshadowing has virtually disappeared.

The battleship icons, linked in visual and symbolic space, facilitate a distinctly American narrative of the Second World War that begins on December 7 and ends with General Douglas MacArthur's accepting the surrender in a much-photographed ceremony on the deck of a floating symbol of American military prowess. One of the consequences of this elegant symmetry is the displacement of longer and messier timelines that might include the war in China or Europe, or draw attention to the American colonization of the Philippines, Guam, or Hawai'i (Gonzalez 2013). This bracketing also deflects attention from the atomic bombings and fire bombings of Japanese cities—highly ambiguous and contested topics in American popular memory (Lifton 1995). When the *Missouri* first arrived, and for more than a decade after, the atomic bombings were nowhere mentioned in the museum spaces of Pearl Harbor, and had even been prohibited from mention in Patricia Masters's research at the memorial visitor center (1991).[7] Although these topics are still outside the purview of most of the exhibits and displays around Pearl Harbor, the National Park Service has taken some first, tentative steps in introducing a newly expanded interpretive theme ("from engagement to peace") by incorporating the Sadako crane exhibit in the new museum (see chapters 2 and 5). Whereas both the story of MacArthur's signing the surrender and the story of twelve-year-old Sadako's folding cranes in the face of radiation sickness could be presented as representative of the themes of peace, the differences in context between the *Arizona* memorial's museum and that of the battleship *Missouri* present very different contexts for their narratives of "peace"—contexts that reflect the broader contrasts in their approaches to representing history.

For all its monumental presence as the most visible addition to Pearl Harbor's historic attractions, the *Missouri*'s arrival would turn out to be one piece of a larger and more elaborate transformation of Ford Island (where it is wharfed) and the harbor as a whole. The context for that larger transformation is the expansion of facilities of the naval base and urban development. In particular, two converging projects would eventually turn the navy's vision for a coordinated space for military history into geographic and institutional reality. The first was an ambitious $84 million plan by the navy to develop base housing, facilities, and "amenities" on Ford Island (see map 4.1)—a process that began in the late 1990s, encompassing plans for the creation of the battleship *Missouri* memorial and the Pacific Aviation Museum. The second was the construction of an expanded visitor center for the USS *Arizona* Memorial (2007–10). The opening of the aviation museum, in 2006, as the first phase of housing development was completed, came just as the National Park Service was realizing that it had to undertake a major reconstruction of the *Arizona* memorial visitor center, with its complex of museum, offices, gift shop, and theaters. The primary point of intersection for these projects was the design of a new point of arrival at the *Arizona* memorial site that would become a "gateway" to all four "Pearl Harbor Historic Sites."

The navy planned for the Ford Island project to include a mix of housing, restaurants, movie theaters, and museums. As an indication of the political and economic importance of the plan, the first major housing contract was signed in a ceremony on the deck of the USS *Missouri* on July 4, 2003, with two of Hawai'i's congressional representatives (Senator Inouye and Congressman Abercrombie) present along with naval commanders and representatives of the company concerned, Fluor Hawai'i LLC. Plans for the development of Ford Island included "a 50,000-square foot waterfront promenade with shops and restaurants, a 16-acre, three-story community of 300 two-bedroom apartments, and a 16-acre development with 130 two-story townhomes with two- and three-bedroom units" (Cole 2003). By 2006, 140 homes had been completed, the first new housing on the island since the 1920s (Cole 2006b).

The Pacific Aviation Museum and the USS *Missouri* now anchor the "cultural" side of these developments. In May 2001, the same month that Disney's

Pearl Harbor was released, naval officials briefed contractors in a presentation that encouraged developers "to provide facilities and services associated with historic visitor attractions, especially on the south side of the island," where the *Missouri* and *Arizona* are located today (Dunford 2001). The collision of development and the interests of "history" surfaced immediately in concerns raised by the National Trust for Historic Preservation, which placed Ford Island, as a historic landmark, on its list of eleven most endangered historic places. When the next year the navy announced its selection of a "medium intensity" model for the housing development, it noted that a "historic visitor attraction," the Aviation Museum of the Pacific, was also "envisioned as part of the private development of up to 75 acres of Ford Island land" (Cole 2002).

The first step in developing Ford Island was the construction of a mile-long bridge connecting the island to the harbor shore. Completed in 1998, at a cost of $78 million, the Admiral Clarey Bridge radically altered the topography and views of the harbor area. It also, however, provided the transportation link needed to transform Ford Island from a sparsely settled base facility, with wharfs, airstrip, and seaplane hangars, to a quasipublic, multiuse area with residential housing. The next year, in 1999, Congress passed special legislation that allowed the navy to grant a developer (Ford Island Properties) property leases in exchange for construction of base housing: sixty-five-year leases to property on Ford Island and key areas along the shore of the harbor, including 6.6 acres in the area between the *Arizona* memorial visitor center and the *Bowfin* submarine museum—a space that would figure importantly in the design of the new visitor center, not yet in the planning stages at that point.

With three military museums visibly on the scene in the middle of the naval base, the design work for the new memorial visitor center quickly made one of its major goals the construction of a large reception area that would create a single entrance point for this new complex, presented as an integrated set of visitor destinations or attractions. Insofar as the *Arizona* memorial and the *Bowfin* are adjacent to one another, the entrance area would also be the place to get on buses going to Ford Island to visit the *Missouri* and the aviation museum. Naval commanders envisioned this development even before design work had begun on the new center. In 2006, Rear Admiral Mike Vitale, commander of Navy Region Hawai'i, stated, "The (initial) plan was an attempt to try and . . . consolidate all of the nonprofits to tell one story, to create for Pearl Harbor this unique, world-class historic attraction that was seamless" (Cole 2006b). The *Arizona* memorial's effort to rebuild and expand its museum provided the opportunity to turn the idea of an integrated, themed environment into architectural reality, building an entryway where visitors would start on their historical journey.

As plans for this vision of an integrated set of attractions was taking shape, however, another player appeared on the scene, a corporation that saw the potential for a more overtly commercial operation to fill the existing void in visitor services at Pearl Harbor—something the navy had stated it wished to do with the Ford Island development plan. The appearance, almost overnight, of a set of boutiques and restaurant kiosks in tents in the parking area between the *Arizona* memorial and the submarine museum showed what a Waikiki-style retail operation could do in the middle of this most-visited Hawaiian tourist destination. Much to the chagrin of the National Park Service and the non-profit military museums, the navy leased the property between the *Arizona* and the *Bowfin* to the Hunt Building Company.

The tent mini-mall offered food and souvenir sales in a Second World War-themed environment, complete with period and island design elements such as thatched roofs and camouflage decor. The operation included eighteen retail and food concessions, with a "1942 Mess Hall," a Second World War Jeep, where one could pose for a souvenir photo, and retail shops selling T-shirts, sunglasses, jewelry, DVDs, handicrafts, and so forth. In this environment, visitors arriving at the *Arizona* memorial encountered tropical kitsch much like that which military personnel during the Second World War would have purchased on shore leave, picking up tokens of their imagined Hawai'i as exotic paradise.

The National Park Service, Pearl Harbor survivors, and Pacific Historic Parks, however, saw the operation as a kind of desecration. A local newspaper story headlined "New Tent at *Arizona* Offensive to Some: Some Say That For-profit Venture Is Inappropriate at the Pearl Harbor Site," reported on the reaction by quoting a few of those expressing objections (Perez 2005):

> As the son of a WWII naval officer, I am simply outraged at the incredibly tacky, for-profit "tourist trap" that has suddenly sprung up—in a carnival-style tent, no less! . . . Has Oahu's real estate frenzy reached such epic proportions that the U.S. government cannot resist parceling out one of the nation's most sacred shrines to sleazy mainland promoters, so they can milk unsuspecting visitors who have come thousands of miles to honor fallen heroes?
>
> Since the tent was erected in mid-December, Ray Emory, historian for the Pearl Harbor Survivors Association, said he has heard from about a dozen survivors who believe the operation is too tacky and denigrating. "They think it's horrible what's going on," Emory said.

FIGURE 4.3
Second World War Jeep in tent mall for souvenir photos. December 7, 2005.
Photo by author.

Anticipating these criticisms, the manager of the new retail operation replied, "I don't want to look like I'm trying to do Disneyland . . . I want to be respectful. I want to do history." History, it seems, is an antidote to crass commercialism. The company putting up the tent mall talked about their operation to the media in terms that sounded like those of the park service next door. They were not just a collection of vendors; they were officially the "Pearl Harbor Visitor Center." To "do history," the company announced it was employing a "docent" to greet visitors and answer historical questions and would even require all employees (called "crew members") to pass a history test assuring Pearl Harbor literacy (Perez 2005).

As months went by, however, there was little sign of historical interpretation as visitors passed through the tent area, enjoying "all-American hamburgers," purchasing T-shirts and jewelry, taking photos, and so on. One of the areas of friction, for existing tours, was how to fit this new commercial setup in tightly timed itineraries that scheduled shopping commitments elsewhere. One tour guide, whom I talked with about a year after the tent mall opened, felt that the vendors were "hustling" her clients in ways that violated the implicit code of conduct for the memorial:

> Like today, when I brought my people, I walked them over [to the tents to buy food] but when we're coming out of the tents they [sales people] were hustling and giving them flyers to come and get a discount. And I'm like, "We're not coming here; we're leaving." So I'll talk to him when I go back and say, "When you see me, don't hustle my group . . . I don't want them to get that hustle feeling." You know, soliciting, being solicited crap . . . This is a memorial . . . I thought it was inappropriate for them to say, "Hey! You can get a real good deal here." I said, "We're going to the *Arizona*. We're not here for a real good deal." (recorded interview, May 18, 2006)

In addition to concerns about decorum, the nonprofit organizations associated with the museums and memorials saw the tent vendors as competition for their own gift shops and snack bars and lobbied to end the arrangement. Indeed, the Hunt company had grand ambitions, hoping to build a permanent visitor center on the shoreline with a plan that included "a pedestrian promenade and a sit-down restaurant" (Perez 2005). That, however, did not happen. The National Park Service and its nonprofit partner, Pacific Historic Parks, were already gaining momentum with plans for the new museum and visitor center. After negotiations involving naval authorities, officials in the National Park Service, and Hawaiian state representatives, the lease for the tent vendors was terminated and the operation closed in May 2007, and disappeared almost as suddenly as it had appeared. At the same time, fundraising and planning for the $50 million park service visitor center next door were in full swing (see chapter 5).

Although a somewhat brief presence in the annals of Pearl Harbor tourism, the appearance of a tent mini-mall, a strictly commercial retail operation, located at the arrival point for the Pearl Harbor historic sites, momentarily transgressed boundaries that had seemed to keep the area's military and memorial solemnity separate from the main centers of Hawai'i's tourism economy, where the forces of commodification reach into every aspect of cultural representation and performance. Many people voiced this view in response to the tent-mall, especially the nonprofit organizations who constantly asserted their intention that plans for the future National Park Service visitor center had no place for "for-profit operations"[8] despite newspaper editorials asserting that "Keeping profit-making operations out of the center would be too restrictive."[9]

Despite asserting the need to respect the sanctity of Pearl Harbor's historic landscape, all of the existing organizations do engage in retail sales. The *Arizona* memorial's nonprofit partner runs a gift shop that generates substantial revenue for the park, and the other three military museums charge for admission and engage in vigorous retail sales and fundraising. All four sites operate shops, sell food, and offer paid audio tours and entertainment options as needed sources of revenue. Both the USS *Missouri* and the Pacific Aviation Museum installed flight simulators that provide visitors the chance to pay for the virtual experience of dogfights and aerial battles. Even before the aviation museum opened up, the same tour operator who complained about the aggressive retail pitches at the tent-mall talked about the *Missouri*'s entertainment offerings as welcome excitement for her groups: "They get so much out of it, you know. It's great; it's fun. Kids love it, you know. They've got a flight simulator. It's a blast; it's great; it's interactive it's wonderful. They also have their gift shop in a Quonset hut, which is way cool" (recorded interview with the author, May 18, 2006).

The battleship, submarine, and aviation museums, which need to raise funds beyond ticket sales, are dependent on in-kind support from the U.S. Navy and fundraising directed to constituencies committed to military heritage. The USS *Missouri*, with the largest maintenance costs (such as an $18 million dry dock overhaul done in 2009), requires donors with deep pockets. Not surprisingly, then, when walking through the entrance approaching the ship, one first passes a large flag-bedecked display listing the honor roll of major donors. At the top of the list are defense contractors, many of whom would have had some association with the ship's history. For companies such as Raytheon, contributions of funding, equipment, or both build a reputation for working in the national interest. The first issue of the *Missouri* association's *Broadside* magazine described such a donation from the Raytheon corporation as follows:

> During the Persian Gulf War, the USS *Missouri* fired 28 Tomahawk missiles in defense of United Nations forces.
>
> A 20-foot model of the weapon was constructed at the San Diego Aerospace Museum. It is prominently displayed at the head of the pier entrance directly in front of the battleship's mid-section and in view of the ship's Tomahawk launchers.

FIGURE 4.4
Flight simulator advertisement, Pacific Aviation Museum brochure. April 2012.
Photo by author.

Dennis Picard, chairman of the board for Raytheon, made the donation as part of a recent visit to the new memorial in Pearl Harbor. "Having a museum like this is just what the country needs and being able to tour this great ship and see where history was made is a wonderful experience."

The model of a Tomahawk missile gifted by Raytheon linked the battleship to the first Iraq war, adding relevance for contemporary conflicts that can be found in the three military museums that make up the other three "historic partners" of the *Arizona* memorial. If travelers visit the *Arizona* first and then take in one or more of the other museums, they will also find themselves moving in time, visiting sites that feature the December 7 story and the Second World War, but that include exhibits, displays, and souvenirs related to all subsequent conflicts, including those in Korea, Vietnam, and the Middle East.

The Pacific Aviation Museum, which opened on December 7, 2006, under a joint agreement with the navy, utilizes three historic hangars on Ford Island to make this time travel through military history explicit. The floor plan for the museum uses the historic hangars to display aircraft associated with the Second World War in the first hangar, followed by aircraft from the Korean and Vietnam wars in the second. Beginning with the hangars themselves as objects of historic preservation, the aviation museum, like the *Missouri*, focuses especially on the aircraft on display, on preserving and interpreting historic artifacts of the Second World War and beyond, "completing the story" begun at the *Arizona* memorial. The aviation museum's start-up collection included fourteen aircraft, including a B-25 bomber, a Stearman biplane "that President George H. W. Bush trained in during World War II," and a Japanese Zero fighter. The original collection is continually augmented as more aircraft are acquired, restored, and put on display.

The visual magnitude of the weaponry of modern warfare draws the gaze of visitors and, aided by guides or docents, evokes stories by and about those who flew, sailed, repaired, or otherwise commanded that weaponry. Unlike the *Arizona* memorial, where the only major weapon is a rusting hulk underwater, all of the other sites offer hands-on, experiential engagement with military hardware, walking into a fire-control room, handling steering or control instruments, putting on a helmet, sitting in a captain's chair, flying a flight simulator. The history in these sites is an embodied, participatory history—just the type that museums everywhere have learned to use in engaging youthful visitors. And, to make their institutions attractive as a destination for local families—military and local alike—they also create educational and social occasions where fun activities are added to the excitement of touring the ships and planes. When the Pacific Aviation Museum marked its fourth anniversary, in 2010, it did so with a celebration that offered food, music, prizes, and entertainment to attract guests from the community as well as tourists. An article about the event titled "Party Like It's 1945 at the Pacific Aviation Museum" (*Honolulu Star-Advertiser*, December 4, 2010), included a photo of the actor Jim Nabors with a broad smile in the cockpit of a Lockheed F-35 flight simulator.

Beyond the issues of trivialization and commodification posed by the military entertainment complex is the question of what kinds of histories are conveyed in commercial tours that visit Pearl Harbor. As in so many tourist venues, the museum professionals who review historical exhibits for "accuracy" (see below and chapter 5), show consternation when they hear about some of the casual histories related by volunteer docents or commercial tour guides. In 1994 I took a popular military tour that offered a one-day van tour of military bases in Oahu. I took the tour just days after the perpetrators of the World Trade Center bombing in 1993 had been convicted, which may be one reason the guide launched into a commentary on internment during the Second World War. The guide began by saying, "I know internment was wrong," but continued, "there are different sides to it." He then proceeded to articulate the same list of falsehoods that the Japanese American community has worked hard to challenge since the war (as discussed in chapter 3 and below). Despite the fact that virtually none of the internees had broken any laws and that thousands of citizens had their constitutional rights violated, the guide observed that "the Japanese were not interned unless they broke the law, for the most part, that is." Not surprisingly, he did not mention the legislation signed by Ronald Reagan in 1988 giving restitution to the internees. He continued:

> If there is a war today somewhere in the world and the United States is involved in it, What do you do with the citizens from that country? If you do not intern them, and the World Trade Center is blown up, who is responsible? For not securing the country, who is responsible? [Tourist: "The government?"] Bingo. So there are a couple of ways of looking at it. And I know internment was wrong, but you've also got to look at the position of the government in this tough situation that they were in. So keep that in mind. There are a number of different aspects to it. (tour guide, audio recording, March 24, 1994)

The differences between what can be said, done, and felt in a museum environment, where commemoration often does become celebration and entertainment, as opposed to a memorial environment, are evident daily to those who transit between the *Arizona* memorial and the other attractions of Pearl Harbor. But what of the histories that are told in these spaces, which also define themselves as memorials to those who served and, especially, lost their lives in doing so? How does the mission of military museums devoted to preserving and interpreting historic military ships and planes affect the way the history of the war is told? My thoughts on this are only suggestive, as the ethnography for this book is focused on the *Arizona* memorial, with only brief forays into the other museum memorials. In one such foray, I found myself in a more intensive discussion about this very question, when, in 2008, I was invited by the chairman of the board of directors of the Pacific Aviation Museum to be a member of a six-person panel of "experts" reviewing one of the museum's exhibits in response to a complaint brought by, again, the Japanese American Citizens League (JACL)—the organization that filed the complaint about the *Arizona* memorial's film, discussed in chapter 3. Like that controversy, the conflict in this case turned out to be a matter of absences in the representation of "factual" histories.

The Ni'ihau (Museum) Incident

The exhibit at issue, originally titled "The Battle of Ni'ihau," tells the story of the crash landing of one of the Japanese Zero fighters on the isolated island of Ni'ihau and the drama that ensued as the pilot, Shigenori Nishikaichi, captured at first, persuaded one of the local Japanese Americans, Yoshio Harada, to assist him in regaining or destroying his flight papers and possibly escaping. The controversy, which I will not elaborate here, not only illustrates the way different constituencies may interpret historical events differently, it also illustrates the basis of those interpretations in assumptions about history itself, about what constitutes historical truth.

The reason that the aviation museum is interested to display what is, basically, a very unimpressive set of metal parts that remain from the crashed Zero, is that the plane functions as a signifier of a unique story involving the pilot and local Japanese and Native Hawaiian residents of Ni'ihau in a conflict that ended with the death of Nishikaichi, the pilot, and Harada, the head of the only Japanese American household on the island with its small population of Native Hawaiians. The events on Ni'ihau might not seem worthy of museum treatment were it not for the fact that the incident received extensive publicity during the weeks following the attack and, over the years, has been held up as evidence of local Japanese disloyalty and the potential threat of Japanese Americans aligning themselves with Japan in the war—the very threat perceived (wrongly) by local commanders in justifying the internment of Japanese residents of Hawai'i (as in California, a smaller proportion of the local Japanese population).

Because the exhibits of the aviation museum are organized chronologically, the Ni'ihau display is positioned immediately inside the door of the museum's first exhibit hall (Hangar 54), devoted to aviation during the Second World War. The Ni'ihau exhibit is, physically, built around the remnants of the Zero, one of twenty-nine attack planes that did not return to the carriers. This one crash-landed on the island of Ni'ihau, an isolated, privately owned plantation island that had actually been designated as an emergency landing and rescue site in Japanese attack plans. Given the astronomic value of Zero fighter planes, very few of which are extant today, the acquisition of even rusted remnants of the plane's skeleton, with its storied link to the Pearl Harbor attack, was irresistible to aviation historians at the museum. Indeed, a recent book about the Ni'ihau incident and exhibit conveys the palpable excitement of curators finding and restoring the remnants of Nishikaichi's Zero (Jones 2014). As one enters the hangar exhibit hall, one faces an intact Zero in perfect condition on one side, repainted in the manner in which Nishikaichi's plane would have been painted, and the Ni'ihau exhibit on the other. But what is that story? And what significance might it have for the larger story of the Pacific War? Answering these questions, it turns out, is not so easy. Even more problematic, constituencies with different collective memories of the war answer these questions quite differently, and not simply due to reasons of bias, spin, or hegemony.

The relic of the crashed Zero acquires historic significance through the dramatic story about the capture of the pilot, Nishikaichi, by Hawaiian laborers resident on the island and the drama that ensued. A remarkable series of events unfolded over the next few days as Nishikaichi persuaded Harada, the local Japanese American caretaker, to aid him in recovering strategic documents, leading to the death of both Nishikaichi and Harada—Nishikaichi beaten to death after he shot one of the Hawaiians and Harada apparently committing suicide. Yoshio Harada's widow, Umeno, in one of her letters about the event, recalled Nishikaichi's saying his plan was to destroy his papers and then commit suicide. Invasion, in any case, was never in Japanese thinking. The most comprehensive account of these events is a slim book, *The Niihau Incident* (1982), by Allan Beekman, a resident of Hawai'i and self-taught historian, who spoke Japanese (he was married to a Japanese woman) and took an interest in investigating the story in more depth. He undertook considerable research, including a trip to Nishikaichi's hometown and several interviews with Harada's wife, Umeno.

FIGURE 4.5
"Battle of Niʻihau" exhibit, Pacific Aviation Museum. September 2, 2007.
Photo by author.

Although not widely known outside Hawaiʻi, and even little remembered there, the Niʻihau story entered briefly into the postattack mythos of Pearl Harbor, highlighting especially the bravery of Ben Kanahele, the Hawaiian man who had been shot and then managed to subdue and kill the pilot. Given that the Pearl Harbor attack was a devastating defeat for the United States, small moments of heroism were seized upon in the media. One of the first news stories to run in Hawaiʻi, just two days after Nishikaichi and Harada were killed, ran with the headline "The Epical Story of Ben Kanahele Hero of Niʻihau" (George Worts, *Garden Island*, December 16, 1941, 1). A few days later *The Honolulu Advertiser* placed a photo of Ben Kanahele in his hospital bed, shaking the hand of an army lieutenant colonel in Kauai, with the caption, "Officer Congratulates Niihau Hero." Indeed, Kanahele was decorated for his actions at the end of the war when the army presented him with a Medal of Merit and Purple Heart in August 1945, giving official standing to the narrative that events on Niʻihau were indeed a battle. Perpetuating the myth that Kanahele was shot three times, the issue of *Reader's Digest* published in December 1942 carried an article about the incident, titled "Never Shoot an Hawaiian More than Twice" (Clark 1942) that focused on the heroism of Kanahele and his struggle with the pilot.[10] A popular song about the event, titled "They Couldn't Take Niʻihau No-how," written by R. Alex Anderson, did the same (not even mentioning the complicating involvement of Harada).[11] The Niʻihau song has been called "America's first World War II victory song" (D'Alto 2007).[12]

In the early days of America at war, characterizing the killing of Nishikaichi in the context of a battle turned the killing of a downed pilot into the defeat of an invasion. Such an invasion is presumed in the title "They couldn't take Niʻihau." Six months after the event, a visitor to the island, David Larsen, a guest of the owners, wrote an extended letter home about the Nishikaichi affair, using the already popular "battle of Niʻihau" label ("While riding with the cowboys this morning the story of the battle of Niihau was told to me by eye witnesses and participants") and described the pilot as "a modern and fully equipped enemy who had gotten the upper hand by treachery" (Larsen 1942, 2): "Thus ended the battle of Niihau—an epic event crowded with heroic deeds, quick thinking and sound judgment. In this battle a naive group of Hawaiians, without modern weapons of any kind, out-maneuvered and destroyed a modern and fully equipped enemy who had gotten the upper hand by treachery. By the time Aylmer [Robinson, the island owner] and the soldiers arrived on Sunday morning, the battle of Niihau was over." Despite the obvious way events are given meaning through wartime rhetoric, Larsen's letter is often referred to as a straightforward description of facts that corroborate the official government report.

While interesting enough as an episode in the military history of the Pearl Harbor attack, the events on Niʻihau have acquired larger significance because of the involvement of Yoshio Harada, presented originally by the museum as evidence of Japanese American disloyalty and, more important, said to have been cited by Franklin D. Roosevelt to justify the internment policy that required the forced confinement of 120,000 Japanese Americans on the West Coast and about fifteen hundred in Hawaiʻi. On this point, though, the facts let the museum down and it deleted reference to Roosevelt's decision when it came to light that Greg Robinson's authoritative study of the subject (2001) has shown that there is no evidence of a Niʻihau effect on White House policymaking on internment. As an indication of the importance of the Niʻihau incident for the internment debate, however, the first chapter of Michelle

Malkin's strident *In Defense of Internment* (2004) is titled "The Turncoats on Niʻihau Island." It presents the Niʻihau struggle as proof of latent tendencies toward disloyalty in the Japanese American community and justification for Roosevelt's executive order. Published shortly after the September 11 attacks, Malkin's book is more than a look at history. It is an attempt to justify internment during the Second World War as a viable precedent for internment policy today. The cover shows photographs of two of the September 11 attackers.

Consistent with the racial suspicions and distortions focused on Japanese Americans after Pearl Harbor, the first newspaper story that ran in the *Honolulu Advertiser* two days after the killings on Niʻihau and before the official report had been made available reported the event in terms of the actions of "the three Japanese," using wartime language that elides differences between the Japanese pilot, the Japanese American Harada, and the local Japanese resident Ishimatsu Shintani (who would later become a U.S. citizen). The article described a scenario that had them banding together as an armed force attempting to control the island (even though Shintani quickly fled the scene and went into hiding with other Hawaiian residents, later telling Harada's widow that he blamed her husband for his troubles): "The pilot is said to have immediately contacted two Japanese residing on Niʻihau, Harada and Shintani, who on Friday following the landing persuaded the natives to hand over the fire-arms including the machinegun. The three Japanese it was reported, thereupon established an armed camp, each standing an eight hour watch to prevent anyone escaping to bring help from Kauai" ("Pilot Clubbed to Death by Hawaiian Pair," *Honolulu Advertiser*, December 16, 1941, 1).

This account invents and rearranges actions to create a battle between a monolithic Japanese enemy and Native Hawaiian heroes. The critics of the exhibit, however, brought different concerns, focusing on the subsequent history of racial discrimination and unconstitutional confinement. For the sake of simplicity, I characterize these two narratives as "victory in the Pacific" and "wartime discrimination at home" (cf. Dower 1995). Whereas the first presumes the categorical alignment of actors as patriots or enemies; the second exposes shifting moral ground such that America's Japanese American population, as minority citizens, are placed under suspicion as potential enemies but then, at a later point in history, become heroes for having endured discrimination.

While much of the conflict over this exhibit has never been resolved to the satisfaction of those who brought complaints, the recommendations that flowed from the exhibit review panel constituted to advise the museum pointed out that the Pacific Aviation Museum, devoted to the preservation and commemoration of aircraft and those who fly them, was ill prepared to present the complex and contested story of Ni'ihau as social history. Small adjustments, such as dropping the title "Battle of Ni'ihau" and eliminating references to the connections between the incident and President Franklin Roosevelt's decision to sign off on the internment of Japanese Americans, indicated recognition that certain features of the exhibit were not supported by the facts. On balance, however, exhibit designers view the corpus of evidence from wartime reports as a factual basis for Yoshio Harada's disloyalty, aiding an enemy in time of war. That core determination then strips away a host of contextual and countervailing factors that lead many, especially in the Japanese American community, to see the end result as highly oversimplified and easily appropriated by racial ideologies that feed wholesale distrust.

How, then, did the Pacific Aviation Museum deal with the relevance of the Ni'ihau incident for issues of Japanese American citizenship and subjectivity and the effect on Roosevelt's policy of internment in particular? The museum originally labeled its exhibit with the same phrase used in wartime newspapers, "The Battle of Ni'ihau," before changing it to "The Ni'ihau Zero Incident" after criticism of the title. Journalist Burl Burlingame, who serves as historian for the Pacific Aviation Museum and was on the exhibit review panel, has said that the incident was "more like a bad bar fight" than a battle. Ironically, however, the very commentary in which Burlingame says the incident was more like a bar fight was published in an article and YouTube video titled "The Battle of Niihau" (Reed 2013).[13]

In designing the exhibit, the museum relied extensively on the facts as compiled at the time, valorizing the heroic efforts of the Hawaiians who killed the pilot and portraying Harada as a conspirator whose actions, it was assumed, provided Roosevelt with an empirical basis for the internment order. The caption for Harada's photo on the exhibit panel read, "Yoshio Harada, a Japanese-American laborer, who conspired with Nishikaichi to take control of Ni'ihau." Here the museum renders a complex and ultimately unknowable set of actions as a plot with the objective of "taking control of Ni'ihau"—language taken almost directly from wartime journalism. Similarly, the exhibit's video soundtrack, although terse and relying closely on details in reports told the Ni'ihau story much as it had been told in 1941. The narration concluded: "Realizing what could lie ahead for him, Yoshio Harada took his own life with a shotgun. Harada's wife would spend the remainder of the war in a prison camp on Oahu. The battle of Ni'ihau had taken its place as one of the first battles in a long World War II."

The museum sought to tell the Ni'ihau story with simple, seemingly well-established facts. Yet, curatorial decisions, guided by an overriding narrative of the Pacific War, made use of some facts (Harada's wife was interned for four years) but not others (she was never charged with a crime, but rather imprisoned under an unconstitutional order and ultimately received the apology and compensation authorized by the Civil Liberties Act of 1988). Such silences may go unnoticed by many visitors, but would stand out to others. Similarly, to make the story intelligible and give it a moral inflection, exhibit writers also attributed unknowable motivations and intentions to the principal actors ("Realizing what could lie ahead for him"). Indeed, when writing as a journalist for the *Honolulu Star-Bulletin*, Burl Burlingame sought to give the story more meaning by filling in a possible basis for the alliance between Harada and Nishikaichi, imagining ways the pilot might have won over Nishikaichi's sentiments:

> Yoshio Harada, whose parents had moved back to Japan, must have been torn between family loyalty and his feelings for the Hawaiians he'd lived with, if not the United States. Like many of the Japanese in Hawaii, he and Irene were closely attached to the Islands. American institutions and ideals were an abstraction.
>
> Thursday, Harada and Nishikaichi talked as they walked together down the beach at Kii. Harada mostly listened. Perhaps the pilot told Harada things would go badly for him when Japanese occupation forces eventually invaded the island. Perhaps he sang the song of the Arawashi, the Fierce Eagle, the symbol of the Imperial naval aviator. Maybe he told of how as he and fellow pilots hiked to build their stamina, they sang and children trailed behind them like streamers, shouting Tennoo haika! Banzai! The striding fighter pilots would swell in pride. Long live the Emperor. (Burlingame 1991a)

History is always more interesting to read when written with literary techniques that provide history's characters with human context. Indeed, the Niʻihau incident has inspired other writers to fill in the blanks by imagining how the actors may have thought, felt, talked, and acted. To date the enigmatic Niʻihau incident has inspired at least one stage production, produced in 1995 (Sutterfield 1992), and one novel (Paul 2006), with other works rumored to be in process.

When it comes to interpreting why facts matter in history, facts don't speak for themselves. Teasing out their significance for audiences today requires filling in things that add subjectivity—human feeling and motivation—things needed to make it a compelling story, one with significance for the historical lessons of war. In the original exhibition of the Niʻihau Zero, the museum presented the facts in the context of the larger narrative of America at war in the Pacific. But that context intersects awkwardly and inconsistently with the history of Japanese American wartime experience, especially historical scholarship on internment (Odo 2004). Without a curator or historian specializing in Japanese American history on the museum staff, and in the absence of meetings with stakeholder groups and the like, there was little chance that the aviation museum's Niʻihau exhibit would do justice to other narratives tangled up with the Niʻihau Zero. Fixing it would prove to be a painful game of catch-up that continually seemed to catch the museum off guard.

Much of the disagreement around the Niʻihau exhibit concerned what the museum did not include in its exhibit. Because the primary concern of the museum is military history, neither the exhibit nor the gift shop offered anything about internment during the war—most likely seen as irrelevant to the museum's mission. A museum engaged with social history might have included more on the postwar debate that exposed the injustices of internment policy, including actions of the courts and Congress. Instead, the incident was presented as a first battle that could be told in the familiar terms of enemies, traitors, and heroes.

Nonetheless, in response to criticisms first aired publicly in state legislative testimony opposing state funding for the aviation museum, the museum responded by conceding that they "erred in making an assumption" about internment that "is apparently still being debated by others," and as a result removed direct references to internment policy. At about the same time, the museum board also voted to remove the sentence referring to the internment of Harada's wife. In noting these changes in a letter to the JACL, museum officials referred repeatedly to their reliance on "available facts" in constructing their displays:[14]

> In telling the story it is our intention to be guided by available facts. . . . The Niihau exhibit which you have criticized was based on extensive research, but we erred in making an assumption which has not yet been documented.
>
> . . . our board voted to remove, as soon as possible, the sentence in our Niihau video presentation which refers to Harada's wife. While factually correct, we have concluded that it is not essential to the telling of the Niihau story.
>
> There is an abundance of official, media, and personal documentation which details the Niihau story. We've been guided by these documents, which you have apparently rejected for the most part.

Looking at the Niʻihau exhibit controversy in retrospect, what appeared as a criticism that might be addressed through the adjustment of problematic signage and video narration in fact unraveled into a prolonged exchange between the museum's board of directors and the complainants. Despite the attempt by the museum to resolve the conflict with the review panel, years later the exhibit remains more or less as it was, with minor adjustments that did not satisfy complainants and must surely have frustrated exhibit designers, a testimony to deeper conflicts between different narratives of the war as well as different assumptions about how to represent history.

One of the notable features of writings about the Niʻihau incident has been the certainty with which so many writers have represented events there. This tradition of telling the "true story," emblazoned in the subtitle of Allan Beekman's book (1982, 93–97): "The true story of the Japanese fighter pilot who, after the Pearl Harbor attack, crash-landed on the Hawaiian Island of Niihau and terrorized the residents," is evident in statements by all parties to the museum controversy, but especially those who designed the exhibit. A recent book about the Niʻihau incident, and exhibit, by the former restoration director at the aviation museum (Jones 2014) is punctuated by references to documentary and oral historical sources of evidence that enhance the accuracy of the account. Access to information from the island's Hawaiian residents is said to "add a final layer of accuracy by including the perspective of the Niihau people" (Jones 2014, 96).

The same emphasis on documentary authority framed a letter from the aviation museum's administration to the exhibit review panel, inviting the panel to review all the evidence and evaluate the factual basis of the exhibit: "A number of investigations were conducted on Niihau immediately after the event, and all the witnesses' stories jibe with each other. Also, there was a private investigation, the documents of which are on file at the Hawaii War Records Repository. The physical details of it concur with the official investigation." The references to "commonly accepted history" and "a number of investigations and testimony" and "physical details" that "concur" convey the underlying assumption that determining what happened is a matter of comparing facts. Such a view of history sees language as a delivery vehicle for information. This is a view of human reporting as unaffected by memory, by subjectivity, by positionality or perspective. Whereas a view of language as political practice might see agreement as evidence of the operation of hegemonic knowledge structures, a more straightforward empirical approach sees the triangulation of evidence. Reading the reports, however, shows that each account is suffused with attributions of intentionality, desire, and motivation for which no confirmation is possible.

The Ni'ihau story is of interest because it has so many potential sources of uncertainty built in and yet is so often seen as one for which the facts have been established. Possible sources of misinterpretation include: The Ni'ihau incident is a story of violence that ends in the killing of two of the principal actors and can provide no testimony about their own intentions or motives; it includes a mix of three or four cultures (Caucasian American, Japanese, Japanese American, and Native Hawaiian) that entail deep differences in cultural psychology; the only written reports were recorded by people who were not present, but elicited oral recollections of others present (a military investigator, the island owner, and, later, a guest of the owner); and, finally, the fact that a war had just been declared as the recollections and reports were being reported would have systematically affected accounts that came from one side about the other—others who by that time were all "enemy."

How do museums handle these kinds of uncertainty? One way, preferred by the aviation museum at that time, is to appeal to facticity, to historical evidence. The first problem for the Ni'ihau case, which can hardly be overemphasized, is that the actions and events on that island at that time can never be known with any certainty. Some particular details, yes, their social and moral meaning, no. In regard to the final moments of violence, in which two people were killed, the only eyewitness accounts are from the people who did the killing (Ben Kanahele and his wife). And their accounts, told through the owner of the island as translator, to U.S. military authorities, would have positioned every action and reaction in a drama of enemies and patriots in an opening engagement of war.

It is difficult to think of a more powerful frame for systematically shaping reporting and remembering than nations at war. It is only decades later, listening to the voices of Japanese American residents of Hawai'i, that an alternative moral narrative can even be considered—not necessarily a true assessment, but one that reminds us of the importance of interpretive frames in making (moral) sense of events. The operation of alternative narratives of the Pacific War is evident in the language used to describe Harada's actions. Burl Burlingame wrote a pamphlet for journalists covering the fiftieth anniversary of the attack, in 1991, with the aim of debunking common myths about the attack. One of the myths he wanted to debunk is the often-stated fact that there were no acts of treason among Japanese Americans during the war (Burlingame 1991b).[15] In his debunking of the myth of Japanese American loyalty, Burlingame described Harada's actions as helping the Japanese pilot "attempt to murder his Hawaiian neighbors": "And Yoshio Harada, a California Japanese-American living on Niihau, helped Imperial Navy pilot Shigenori Nishikaichi attempt to murder his Hawaiian neighbors. Had he lived through the attempt, Harada would certainly have been executed as a traitor" (Burlingame 1991b, 18). In contrast, Japanese American accounts seem to resist identifying motives: "This incident raises questions about possible Japanese American cooperation with the Japanese, in the event of an invasion, though it provides little insight because of the unusual conditions on Ni'ihau and the unclear reasons behind Harada's actions" (Niiya and Japanese American National Museum 2001, 303). "Harada, for reasons unknown, put his borrowed gun to himself and pulled the trigger" (Saiki 2004, 54).

Because military museums generally focus on war weaponry and stories of military service, narratives of victory and defeat in war are generally a good fit for their modes of exposition. By the same token, these same methods struggle with social histories that entail conflicting stories about domestic politics (Fujitani 1997). As at other aviation museums, the primary social aspect of the mission at the Pacific Aviation Museum is to honor the servicemen and servicewomen whose stories are part of military aviation. When the aviation museum opened in December 2006, the museum's director, speaking at a Pearl Harbor sixtieth-anniversary symposium, emphasized the museum's interest in telling "stories of people," not just stories about "airplanes on a piece of concrete," saying that the museum is "peoplecentric" (recorded panel discussion, December 3, 2001) and, in particular "proud to share the historic stories of men and women aviators of the Pacific and pay tribute to those whose bravery helped give us the freedom we enjoy today" (Cole 2006a). Yet, when the scope of stories expands, the attempt to tell larger stories about more complex social histories easily provokes controversy—something discovered by the Smithsonian's Air and Space Museum and its ill-fated atomic bomb exhibit (Linenthal and Engelhardt 1996).[16]

THE RAPID GROWTH of global tourism, and the expansion of interest in sites of violence, warfare, and tragedy in particular (Doss 2010; Williams 2007), evoke all sorts of questions about the purpose and propriety of (war) memorial tourism and the kinds of history that it produces. Who is remembering what for what purpose? What are the tensions between education and entertainment, or between commodification and commemoration?—questions widely raised in tourism research (Edwards 2009). In posing these questions, this chapter has ranged beyond the *Arizona* memorial to glimpse some of the ways the transformation of the Harbor landscape is also transforming the means and methods of representing history. The expansion has been accompanied by the normalization of the word *attraction* to refer to the Pearl Harbor historic sites—a term that conjures up tourism entertainment and is still mostly avoided at the *Arizona* memorial, given its sanctity as a burial site. This chapter's wider horizon, recounting the growth of visitor attractions in the Pearl Harbor and Ford Island area, shows a landscape that has taken on more of the look and feel of a theme park—a term that would likely be resisted by those who manage military museums and memorials and are sensitive to accusations of superficiality or disrespect.

On the other hand, creating a self-sustaining industry of military entertainment requires business models driven by the exigencies of commodification, branding, and marketing. Current advertising for the Pacific Aviation Museum tells the story. In a recent addition of the airline magazine of Hawaiian Airlines, a brightly colored ad invited readers to visit the museum, using the image of a Cobra attack helicopter facing (aiming) forward in profile, with the headline, "Float Like a Butterfly, Sting Like a 4-ton Bee." Underneath the Cobra, the ad continued, "See the history of Pacific aviation come to life in all its glory. Docent-guided tours, vintage aircraft and actual footage of the Pearl Harbor attack offer a totally new and unique perspective," followed by "get a Free WWII Combat Simulator Flight coupon at our website" (*Hana Hou!: The Magazine of Hawaiian Airlines* 16, no. 5: 105).

Given the many alternatives in popular culture in the form of films, video games, interactive websites, what is the attraction of these attractions? Where many theme parks rely on imagination to engage their audiences, military museums such as the USS *Missouri* Battleship Museum offer their audiences the real thing, often in real (historic) locations. Hence, the technology of historical representation tends toward the indexical and iconic, centered on objects that constitute signs of the past, whether the sacred ground of battlefields (Linenthal 1993), the buried remains of war dead, the embodied presence of military veterans, or today's naval weaponry. All of these underwrite what Andreas Huyssen calls "the newfound strength of the museum and the monument" by bringing "the material quality of the object" into an increasingly virtual world of cultural experience (1995, 255).

A tragic measure of the degree to which tourist fantasy and military reality may converge in this themed environment is the accidental sinking of a Japanese training vessel, the *Ehime Maru*, by the U.S. nuclear submarine USS *Greeneville*, operating just outside Pearl Harbor on February 9, 2001. That accident killed nine Japanese crew members, including four young students and two teachers on board for a training cruise. As details of that event emerged, a court of inquiry determined that the failure of the crew of the *Greeneville* to detect the presence of the *Ehime Maru* was directly related to the presence of civilian guests on the submarine, two of whom, it turned out, were at the controls when the collision occurred. John Gregory Dunne's account of the event in *The New Yorker* described the scene inside the submarine as a real-world theme park environment:

> The *Greeneville* was not even supposed to be at sea that day; the trip was laid on for sixteen V.I.P.s and big-ticket political contributors, called "D.V.s," Navy talk for distinguished visitors. On a D.V. cruise, the *Greeneville* was essentially reduced to an underwater theme park, Submarine Land. The D.V.s would sit at the controls, look through the periscope, experience combat training exercise, have lunch with the captain, Commander Scott Waddle. (Dunne 2001, 54; also see Gonzalez 2013, 142–44)

Similarly, one of the admirals on the board of inquiry interrogating Captain Waddle asked him if, in executing the fatal maneuver, he thought his submarine was "the E ride at Disneyland."

All of the sixteen guests participating in the navy's Distinguished Visitor Embarkation program were involved in organizing a celebrity golf tournament to benefit the USS *Missouri* Restoration Fund (Dan Nakaso, "Civilians' Names Break the Surface," *Honolulu Advertiser*, February 18, 2001, A11). In other words, the purpose of supporting the battleship museum had briefly rendered an active nuclear submarine as a space much like that of the battleship itself, where civilians might momentarily occupy the place of military personnel operating one of the most lethal weapons in the U.S. military arsenal. It might be said that activities on shore, in the battleship museum, are a kind of mirror image of this confluence insofar as young tourists who operate the controls of simulators might imagine themselves in command of military hardware or in military careers. In the "D.V. ride" experience, military hardware is rendered as a museum, a fantasy ride, blurring the reality-fantasy boundary in much the same way as travelers, young and old, can do in the military tourism environment of today's Pearl Harbor.

The expansion of war museums on the Pearl Harbor naval base is built upon the availability of historic weapons (and their narratives), now redeployed as symbolic weapons for building public support and interest in military history and tradition. As the history of redeveloping Ford Island shows, the naval past is now on display in museums located alongside the facilities of an active military installation, and the daily activities of maintaining today's Pacific Fleet. The spatial proximity reflects the mutually supporting relationship of tourism and military development, with tourism resources strengthening the production of military heritage, base facilities, and personnel used to sustain the institutions that curate that same heritage. Certainly that was the broad rationale for the U.S. Navy's embrace of the production of the Disney Studios' *Pearl Harbor* in 2001. Just as the film conveys a heroic narrative useful in reaching an important public, the presence of the *Bowfin*, the *Missouri* and three historic hangars housing military aircraft (or, in the case of the Niʻihau Zero, aircraft remains) mobilizes historic artifacts to tell the stories of the U.S. military in Asia and the Pacific—stories that, for the Second World War, convey the narrative of American victory in the Pacific (the Bush administration's original choice for the monument now named World War II Valor in the Pacific National Monument).

As the Niʻihau controversy makes clear, however, objects do not speak for themselves. In fact, even the texts that convey the facts of military history do not speak for themselves. Meaning and value emerge through acts of interpretation, as global travelers traverse the historic spaces of Pearl Harbor, interacting with its semiotic ecology of objects, texts, and activities. This ecology, arrayed across the various military museums, acquires more personal meaning in audio and video commentaries and in the voices of tour guides and docents. A byproduct of these zones of militourism (Gonzalez 2013; Teaiwa 1994) is the naturalization of the role of the military in a state where military families make up about 16 percent of the population, the largest of any state in the U.S. (Ferguson and Turnbull 1998). The foregrounding of twentieth-century military history has the concomitant effect of displacing indigenous and colonial history, dimly visible around the harbor in archaeological formations and Hawaiian place-names that continue to recede from memory (Kajihiro 2014; Osorio 2010; Tengan 2011).

The process of transforming a historic landscape dense with Native Hawaiian archaeological features as well as relics of the Second World War into one developed for tourism has not been easy. The process has been marked by repeated controversies, notably around the arrival of the battleship *Missouri*, the creation of a tent mini-mall, and the design of an exhibit that displays a precious aviation artifact while perpetuating racial suspicions about Japanese Americans. These controversies expose different approaches to history across the various museums and memorials—differences evident in a multitude of ways, as in the contrasts between monumental military hardware and an abstract modernist memorial. Chapter 5 turns to the design and construction of a new museum for the USS *Arizona* Memorial and World War II Valor in the Pacific National Monument, a long and extended process where differing philosophies of history were again much in evidence.

Five

MAKING A NEW
MUSEUM

Just weeks after the National Park Service opened its new visitor center and museum at Pearl Harbor, a local writer, editorializing in *Honolulu Magazine*, characterized his disappointment with the new architecture:

> Subjectively . . . the place just looked-felt-wrong: the colors (Hawaiʻi's now ubiquitous beige); the shed-roof forms, curved like waves; the panel-on-frame construction that lacks solidity. The architecture screamed *retail*, with too many textures and colors reminding me of, say, Waikele Premium Outlets.
>
> To be fair, I went back a couple weeks later for a longer visit.
>
> This time, it didn't remind me of a shopping center. It looked like a really nice elementary school. I don't mean that as an insult. It is an educational facility first and foremost, preparing visitors before they go on to the actual memorial. (Napier 2011b, 96)

This writer, already familiar with the memorial, somewhat awkwardly and apologetically, describes what was, for him, the failure of the new complex to effectively link the shore-side visitor center complex with the sacred space of the memorial spanning the ship across the harbor. To make his point, he invoked that most routine of secular spaces—a shopping center—to draw an analogy before deciding upon the comparison of a "really nice elementary school." It seems the architectural style of the new construction was not, for that visitor, consistent with the experience of a memorial—of visiting the USS *Arizona* Memorial at the World War II Valor in the Pacific National Monument (VALR). These criticisms show how difficult it is to create a space that includes a museum, theater, and bookshop along with a memorial. It is more than a little ironic that the author uses the analogy of a school to express what the visitor center should not be. After a subsequent conversation with the architect, the author reported in a follow-up essay that in fact the school analogy was the intent of the designers: "In Afterthoughts, I wrote that the new facility reminded me of an elementary school. That was the effect the NPS was actually going for, as the center's mission is education and interpretation" (Napier 2011a).

These critical comments must have caused some chagrin among the many planners and consultants who had just spent more than three years and $58 million designing and building the new visitor center and museum. Particularly so since the design team focused a great deal of their attention on designing a specifically memorial space—landscape, architecture, and exhibits that would create a depth of experience appropriate to a memorial on a site of violent death and burial. Since only the museum and shop spaces were being rebuilt, the experience on the memorial itself, and the film that prepares travelers for going there, remained largely the same. Hence, the first challenge of designing the new visitor center was to articulate points of connection between new visitor center landscape and the sacred space of the memorial.

When the design firm contracted to lead the planning process convened the first few meetings with National Park Service staff and others, the problem of conceptualizing transition points between the various parts of the visitor center's landscape as a memorial landscape was front and center. When the facilitator of the first planning meeting asked those sitting around the room to say what most "touched" them when they thought about Pearl Harbor, a park service representative with a long history at the memorial referred to the wall of names in the shrine room, saying, "The wall; for those of us who work here, it always comes back to that. People don't like to get in there [the shrine room], and then [when they do] we have to tell people to move on." Another person, overseeing the building contract, said, "The memorial drowns out everything else. The wall. The ride back is a haze because the power of the memorial is so strong."

Discussion of emotional experience framed much of the planners' early broad-brush thinking about the layout of buildings, spaces, and objects of the new visitor center. In their conversation, emotions were envisioned as coded in the landscape, designed so that moving through the space would render the visit a temporally organized emotional experience, a narrative of engagement and disengagement. As so conceived, the visit narrative was structured around transitions into and out of memorial space, a temporal sequence of emotions evoked by movement through space as well as interaction with particular features in the landscape and exhibits. After two days of discussion, the first planning meeting, in February 2006, produced a spatial layout for the grounds that, in the words of the facilitator, would "order an emotional state we want to lead people through and make open to them" (audio recording, February 23, 2006). The first issue, all agreed, was to prepare the visitor for a memorial experience—something that required departure from the mindset of everyday holiday tourism (in other words, the long-standing issue of making the memorial experience something other than a theme park, as noted in chapter 4). When the facilitator reminded everyone that they were designing a space that would "get the urban clutter out of your head . . . orchestrate or choreograph movement to a goal . . . engender solemnity," his words closely echoed the thoughts of those who produced the new film fifteen years earlier.

Where the film was produced to prepare visitors as they departed for the memorial, the new visitor center also had to address the visitor's return. Here planners used the term *decompression* to describe the emotional transition from the memorial to the visitor grounds, presumably transiting back to the world of secular routines and, for most, a Hawaiian holiday. These discussions focused on the walkway that travelers follow as they come off the boat ramp and head back across the grounds of the visitor center, toward the exit area and gift shop. In these exchanges, the metaphor of decompression found expression in the idea of "contemplation," conceived as an opportunity for travelers to contemplate the meanings of the memorial and the attack as they exited along a walkway on the waterfront toward the entrance and exit area.

The conceptualization of this part of the visitor center landscape proved to be a good match for the NPS historiography of "find your own meaning"—a tenet of NPS interpretive practices that prefer nondirective (or at least not overtly directive) approaches to public history, seeking to provide information in an open-ended and nonjudgmental fashion. The first round of design discussion wedded the idea of contemplation with the interest to personalize the Pearl Harbor story through the presentation of the images and words of people who were involved. Primarily, this strategy focused on Pearl Harbor's military survivors, the veterans who experienced the attack and have been a source of its firsthand oral histories ever since. The walkway envisioned as connective tissue for various elements of the master plan quickly came to be called the "walkway of courage and sacrifice" (see figure 5.1). Phrased in this way, the courage and sacrifice motif maps precisely onto two of the three elements used as defining themes for the memorial museum at the Normandy American Cemetery: competence, courage, and sacrifice. The convergence is not the result of any direct contact between these memorials (the Normandy American Cemetery is run by the American Battle Monuments Commission), but rather the commemorative culture of American military memorials.

In this case, the walkway was conceived as an area for postvisit reflection that would later be implemented by two features of that walkway, the "remembrance circle" and a new area called the "contemplation circle." When constructed, the contemplation circle took the form of an open area with a circular bench and a few inspirational inscriptions etched in the surrounding wall. The designers ended up directing visitors to "contemplate"—an irony not lost on the Honolulu writer above when he came upon the sign "contemplation circle." As he wrote, "The sign just struck me as unintentionally funny . . . this lays it on a bit thick. Contemplate! Now! In this circle!" (Napier 2011a). In another example of this quiet direction toward contemplation, the new visitor center includes a replica of the "tree of life" wall in the memorial's shrine room, located between the museum and theater buildings. At the base of the monolith, a label instructs, "The Tree of life relief was designed and built as a part of the original structure of the USS *Arizona* Memorial. Look for the Tree of Life again when you visit the shrine room on the memorial." Explaining that the architect intended the Tree of Life as a "symbol of renewal to inspire contemplation in visitors to the memorial," the label asks, "What does this symbol mean to you?" I found myself wondering again about the memorial's instructive voice when listening to the new video introduction to the orientation film, in which a park ranger informs the audience about the nature of memorials, presumably as a gentle way to encourage respectful behavior on the memorial itself: "The USS *Arizona* Memorial is just one of many memorials built to honor the dead and to remember the event. Memorials are places of learning and inspiration, reflection and quiet contemplation."

I have opened this chapter about VALR's new museum with consideration of some of the ways designers sought to build memorial dimensions into the visitor center by managing visitors' emotional experience. Although park service staff responsible for interpretive programs draw important distinctions between the memorial and the visitor center, the lines are often blurred in the perceptions and experience of visitors. Thus, the distinction between museum and memorial needed periodic clarification for those planning the new center, as they pondered what could and could not be done in the center's mission of

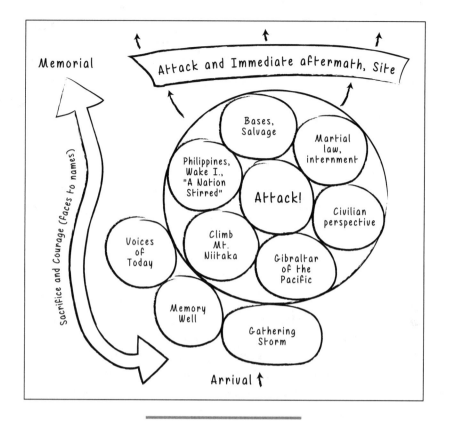

Memorial

↑ Attack and Immediate aftermath, Site ↗

Sacrifice and Courage (Faces to names)

Bases, Salvage

Martial law, internment

Philippines, Wake I., "A Nation Stirred"

Attack!

Civilian perspective

Voices of Today

Climb Mt. Niitaka

Gibraltar of the Pacific

Memory Well

Gathering Storm

Arrival ↑

FIGURE 5.1
Consultant's sketch for planning meeting visualizing museum layout
(author's notebook rendition). March 1, 2006.

"education and interpretation." At one point in the first round of planning, when a group of historians were discussing the possibility of including an exhibit recognizing the Japanese aviators, a member of the consulting team read from the memorial's founding legislation, which mandates "honor and commemoration of the members of the armed forces of the United States, who gave their lives to their country during the attack of Pearl Harbor." To this the park service historian said simply, "Well, the public law applies to the memorial," implying that it does not apply to the visitor center.

That comment notwithstanding, it is impossible to understand the politics of representation at the visitor center without realizing that it is tethered to the memorial and its significance as a burial place for American servicemen killed in combat. As seen in previous chapters, the figure of the citizen-combatant, whether those killed in battle or today's veterans, powerfully organizes the work of interpretation and education as well as memorialization. Just as the Pearl Harbor mythos shaped the making of a new film in ways that made it, in the end, much like the one it replaced (see chapter 3), so the design of a new museum produced a plan that wove in new elements to a plan that became, to a significant extent, a larger version of the original museum. The challenge for any critical analysis of a museum (any museum) as it evolves is to do justice to both the departures and continuities—the new elements, often introduced with self-conscious talk about changing sensibilities—as well as the taken-for-granted assumptions and structural constraints that are built into institutional parameters and politics. In the case of the memorial's new museum, planners introduced significant new elements and themes—each an index of shifting historical and political conditions for the work of remembrance.

Designing a New Museum

The making of a new museum and visitor center, like the remaking of the visitor center's film, opens a window onto unspoken assumptions about what should and should not be represented as history. It is also an opportunity to observe the politics of who speaks, how often, and with what effect in the design and construction process. Asking how new museum ideas are produced through conversations, discussions, and debates carried out in planning sessions, offices, telephone conversations, and so on offers a glimpse of institutional forces that usually remain invisible, behind the surfaces of finished exhibits that present themselves without reference to authorship or to the debates about mission, audience, and politics that bring them into being (not to mention the actions required to fund and construct buildings and exhibits).

Rebuilding the visitor center and its exhibit space required redesigning an expanded landscape with multiple structures, including two large museum buildings, a park service office building, an education and research center, and a gift shop, as well as exhibits and architectural features in the surrounding area (see figure I.1, in the introduction). Designers decided to maintain the existing orientation film that was felt to "remain popular and relevant to today's audience, provide a broad overview of the Pearl Harbor story, and set an appropriate emotional tone for the visit to the Memorial" (Aldrich Pears Associates 2006, 22). Amid all this, the new museum was the main focus for expanding and updating the memorial's history of the attack, consuming much of the attention of park service planners.

The account in this chapter draws from my own participation in discussions convened by the National Park Service in Honolulu, and broader analysis produced in the course of ethnographic work since the earlier 1990s. As the federal agency charged with operating the *Arizona* memorial, the National Park Service took the lead in organizing the planning process, working closely with its nonprofit partner, Pacific Historic Parks (which spearheaded the fundraising campaign), as well as with the U.S. Navy, and other relevant offices in state and federal governments. The NPS initiated the first step in the process by hiring a consulting firm to coordinate the design process, focusing primarily on the museum and its exhibits.

The situation of the USS *Arizona* memorial, with its location inside the Pearl Harbor naval base, implied that designing a new museum would necessarily wrestle with tensions between military memorialization and broader social history.[1] Listening to the discussions that crafted the new museum and its exhibits offers a glimpse of history-in-the-making during a transformative epoch in the memorial's history—beginning before and finishing after the creation of the World War II Valor in the Pacific National Monument. At the same time, by describing the process as one in which individuals with differing views talk about different ways to tell the Pearl Harbor story, constantly referencing what can and can't be done in a national memorial, I also hope to convey a sense of the uncertain and contingent nature of history-making in the memorial context. It is a process that was constantly exploring possibilities while also probing limits, up to and beyond the time ideas were inscribed in exhibit text and images.

A museum expansion had been under discussion for years, but began in earnest in 2005 with the modest goal of shoring up and renovating the original museum that was proving structurally unsound.[2] Once that was determined, the project took on the much more ambitious goal of replacing the entire visitor center (saving only the theater building). The new plan called for doubling the size of the museum to 7,000 square feet of exhibit space, within a visitor center of some 23,600 square feet. The project would take over four years, culminating in the dedication of the new visitor center and museum at sixty-ninth-anniversary ceremonies, in 2010, thus spanning the time the USS *Arizona* Memorial was subsumed in the new federal entity, the World War II Valor in the Pacific National Monument. The project raised $58 million in federal appropriation and private donations, and was implemented with a coalition of agencies and organizations that tapped dozens of subject experts and "stakeholders."[3] The sheer extent and scale of the project is itself a clear measure of the power of Pearl Harbor in the American historical imagination.

As a member of the Board of Directors for Pacific Historic Parks, and as a researcher doing fieldwork in and around the memorial, I joined in as the park service and their consulting firm convened numerous meetings with historians and stakeholders over the next three years. I participated in and recorded close to twenty full-day or half-day sessions from the beginning of the project, in 2006, to the museum opening, in 2010, an involvement that afforded access to draft design schemes and exhibit texts circulated for review to NPS and PHP planners at each phase of project development. The analysis that follows also benefits from interviews, casual conversations, board meetings, and related research work during this time. Having said this, it is important to add that my participation remained limited, particularly in relation to the higher realms of government, military, and corporate interests involved.

One of the insights taken away from my participation is the realization that involvement doesn't necessarily translate into effects. While I was more of a listener than a talker in these meetings, I did occasionally speak about issues and choices, drawing on my experience with commemorative and educational programs at the memorial and in other parts of the Pacific. Having participated in some of the exchanges initiated by Japanese veterans outlined in chapter 2, I jumped in with occasional ideas about ways that the new museum might include a historical perspective on itself, on the evolution of the memorial as a site of commemoration and reconciliation. In the end, however, there is little evidence of that sort of reflexivity in the voices of the museum, which in general did not call attention to its own mechanisms of authorship. This may be one of the limits of memorial history. This chapter concludes with an account of the circuitous discussions that unfolded around the theme of "reconciliation" that ultimately found little place in the final plan, even if that theme would emerge soon in surprising ways, with commemorative activities under the wider umbrella of the Second World War monument (see chapter 2). While it would be easy to attribute the absence of reconciliation in the museum plan to the hegemony of military memory, closer attention to the fractured planning process complicates easy generalizations about "the state" or "the military" as monolithic voices or agencies.

From the start, the museum and visitor center project grappled with issues evident in the longer history of the memorial, as it expanded from being a strictly naval memorial to a space for broader "education and interpretation," reaching audiences beyond the military and beyond the United States. The practice of designing a museum and its exhibits is not just about producing a script; it is itself also an occasion for imagining and enacting national community. Throughout the project, the National Park Service emphasized the importance of an inclusive process that engages diverse audiences with multiple perspectives on Pearl Harbor. Leaders of the NPS regularly reiterated these principles in organizational meetings, informal discussion, e-mail distributions, and so forth, reminding various constituencies that their input was part of a broad outreach process designed to make the new museum more representative of diverse perspectives. One of the leaders of the NPS planning team, herself an American of Japanese ancestry, spoke about these principles to an evening meeting of historians convened during a symposium held in conjunction with the sixty-fifth anniversary of Pearl Harbor, in December 2006. Responding to an open-ended comment from a senior naval historian to the effect that the draft script does much more to represent the Japanese (that is, the attackers') point of view than the previous museum, she responded:

> One of the big pushes of the National Park Service right now is this whole concept of evaluation involving our stakeholders in the planning and design process. And this project, . . . we have been meeting with stakeholders, we've been meeting with local citizen groups, we've been meeting with museum professionals, and we've been meeting with historians and Pearl Harbor survivors. And we certainly haven't met everybody that we need to, but we're constantly trying to find out who are the interested parties and engage them in a dialog as we go through this design process. (audio recording, December 1, 2006)

Assertions such as "involving our stakeholders in the planning and design process" and "getting input from . . . any interested party that perhaps has a different perspective on what the story should be and how it should be told" send a strong message about the values that guide the planning process.

These values were also set out in documents guiding the designers. One of those included a diagram labeled "A Team Framework for Support," showing concentric circles illustrating five levels or types of stakeholder involvement ("USAR Interpretive Media Value Analysis," September 2006, draft, September 5, 2006, 13–15). Under the heading "Who Are the Interpretive Stakeholders?" the document lists the four levels as "core circle" (NPS staff, museum association, interpretive designers), "circle of involvement" (military and Pearl Harbor interest groups, educators and historians, Oahu war experience, specifically, Japanese American individuals and organizations, Hawaiians, and Oahu residents, and tourism and commercial groups), "circle of support" (municipal and state governments), and "circle of awareness" (visitors, American and international, Asia residents, media). The philosophy of outreach to diverse constituencies reflects the role of the National Park Service as the agency that works the front lines of public history in the United States. Although there may be a greater number of federally employed historians working in military service branches than in the park service, their job descriptions largely address the needs of military units and veterans organizations—a far more homogenous constituency than the visitors to national parks and historic sites.

The rise of social history that valorizes multiple perspectives has also been marked by challenge and controversy in America's culture wars, such as controversies around national history standards that have been going on since the 1990s (Nash et al. 1997). Although the effort to give more recognition to a broader spectrum of actors and voices in national history may still evoke occasional criticism as "political correctness," the principle is well established in countless historic sites in the United States. The predicament for public educational institutions charged with representing national histories (state-sponsored textbooks, exhibits, films, anniversaries, monuments, memorials, and so on) is that they become sites of contestation among multiple communities of memory (Wertsch 2002). For agents of public history working in state-sponsored institutions such as the USS *Arizona* Memorial, the need to be relevant to diverse audiences must somehow be worked out within the circumscribed limits of state power (even if state power is rarely monolithic). Here attention to the small conversations of history-making provides an understanding of principles and techniques used to represent controversial subjects, without making the museum itself an object of controversy. Here I mention three related techniques that emerged early and often in planning discussions. The first is the use of the quoted speech of historical actors to represent events, viewpoints, responses, and so forth, as a way of shifting the agency of representation from museum curators to the historical actors themselves. The second is the reliance on personal stories, on the presentation of historical events through the experiential voices of those who participated, shifting perspective from broad, transformative events to experiential narrative. A third technique is the invitation to viewers to "make up their own minds" about the meaning or moral implications of events, rather than include judgmental conclusions in exhibition text. This chapter concludes with consideration of the myriad ways conjecture about possible objections and emotional reactions often bracketed the work of designing an interpretive program.

The first phase of planning convened by the park service and its consulting firm in February and March 2006 sought to establish these parameters to guide the exhibit design process. One of the first axes of debate was between a "just the facts" approach and a "multiple perspectives" approach to historiography. In the former, articulated by a seasoned Pearl Harbor historian, "the museum shows you what happens. And how you interpret it is your thing. And we cannot get into interpretation. . . . I really think that the museum doesn't do that. We're apolitical" (recorded discussion, February 21, 2006). This approach, marked by a wariness of too much interpretation is akin to worries about "revisionist" history that would seek to alter the dominant narrative. Just months before the visitor center opened the National Park Service superintendent said, "One of the continuing pieces of feedback that I've received, from various sources, is 'We've got to make sure it's not revisionist history'" (recorded interview, March 23, 2010). In contrast, the multiple-perspectives approach put forward by several on the planning team acknowledged that "there are lots of different perspectives" and the job of the museum is "to provoke [people] to get them thinking about it. And you can't provoke them with just facts. You have to provoke them with conclusions, different interpretations of those facts" (recorded discussion, February 21, 2006). This latter approach, more or less well established among museum professionals, carried the day. Put simply by a NPS historian, "I think sometimes it's just great to ask them, 'What do you think?'"

A little more than a month after this initial meeting, setting some basic parameters for the project, discussion pushed further into how multiple perspectives might be presented. Notes from the consulting firm summarizing a special meeting of historian consultants convened at the annual conference of the Organization of American Historians, in Washington, D.C., provided a summary list of "general comments" from the meeting. Of the first five points, only one was content-focused ("Interpret the repercussions of Pearl Harbor"). The dominant thrust of advice focused on method, from the practical, "don't attempt to convey too much information," to techniques of representation: "Do not ask, 'what does it mean?'" "Use quotes and let visitors form their own meaning." "Use 'disinterested voice' and present multiple perspectives, carefully chosen." "Use personal stories to turn statistics into people, e.g. Paxton Carter and Zenji Abe."[4]

The list of suggested approaches to representation reveal an underlying philosophy of the museum as a space where past events are not only represented or explained as historically important, they are rendered personal, both for historical actors and for museumgoers encountering them in exhibits. As already noted, the technique of "find your own meaning" is a principle of NPS historiography, evident in invitations to the viewing public to derive their own conclusions and lessons from exhibits. In this approach the word *contemplation* becomes a key word, signifying the viewing subject's ability to, independently and autonomously, derive meaning from objects, photos, and texts. At Pearl Harbor, the renovation of the museum and visitor center became an opportunity to inscribe this philosophy into the architecture and signage of the grounds, as noted in the critic's adverse reaction to the creation of a separate space designated for contemplation, consistent with the find-your-own-meaning rhetoric at work in the interpretive landscape—to the dismay of some survivors who wondered what happened to the primary lesson inscribed in the call to "remember Pearl Harbor" and "be prepared," as emblazoned in their association logo.

The tensions and ambivalences that crisscross the distinct functions of a memorial museum played out in myriad ways during museum planning. A key word in these discussions was *context*. Given that the museum would certainly provide a historical presentation of the basic facts of the December 7 attack, how much additional information should be given to make the attack understandable within the broader and longer forces of history? Here opinions diverged about the best way to answer the question, How much context is enough? Expressing perhaps the frustration of the design company coordinating planning, notes summarizing one of the historians meetings listed "Context" as one of six headings, with two items listed below it: "there is too much context" and "need more context, beginning in Japan in the 1800s." This was followed by the next summary point, "Focus on the attack." In other words, "Don't get distracted" (Munday and Hill 2007a, 4).

Put simply, and no doubt simplistically, those who were primarily interested in the military, memorial function of the monument preferred to keep the interpretive program focused on the attack itself, the ships that came under attack, the servicemen and servicewomen involved, and the events that began and ended on December 7. To add further historical context would risk distraction or dilution of the primary purpose of honoring the sacrifices of those who died and served in the U.S. military that day. In contrast, educators and historians tended to value context as a way to promote education about larger historical events (like the Second World War). In their view, this would add contextual links to a broader range of present-day issues, giving the attack significance for more audiences. On this point it is instructive to compare planning discussions with the controversy around the atomic bomb exhibit at the National Air and Space Museum, in 1995. There, the elimination of a detailed historical exhibit in favor of an exhibit featuring just the principal artifacts (the bomb, the B-29 fuselage) and videos of the Air Force crew were lampooned in cartoons of empty exhibit space ("the air and space museum lives up to its name") and minimal signage ("something really big happened here").

One of the major dimensions of context that emerged early in discussions concerned the importance of local experiences during and after the attack. A number of oral history projects have documented civilian recollections for archival purposes and, in a few cases, produced published accounts (Rodriggs 1991). In particular, the experience of Hawai'i's local, Hawaiian-born Japanese population, which endured suspicion, racism, and in some cases eviction and arrest, as recounted in chapters 3 and 4, has been the subject of a national movement to recognize and learn from the injustices they endured. With the rise of Japanese Americans to positions of political power in postwar Hawai'i (symbolized by Senator Daniel Inouye, Congresswoman Patsy Mink, and activist organizations such as the Japanese American Citizens League or the Japanese Cultural Center of Hawai'i), the twin narratives of racist subjugation and heroic service in Second World War combat units, have elevated the importance and visibility of the Japanese American Pearl Harbor. Hence, when the NPS organized its consultations with stakeholders from a cross-section of community organizations, they received strong recommendations to expand the "local story," often omitted from the mythic narrative of the attack (witness the Disney production *Pearl Harbor*, for which the typical mainland viewer could be excused for thinking that the local community was somewhat like that of rural Iowa). The local story pointed especially to civilian casualties, civilian experience of martial law (Allen 1971), and the wartime experience of Japanese Americans in particular.

When the recommendations of community stakeholders were discussed in the core group of planners, however, the push for expanding the contexts of the attack met with some resistance. December 7 is one of the most elaborately documented battle histories of the Second World War, and its representation in the new museum could draw upon an enormous range of detail about the attack itself and its military and strategic implications in themes such as the "age of the battleship" and "age of aircraft carriers," or the drama of relations between the United States and Japan. Indeed, the focus on the attack was clear from the start, laid out in a visual schematic of topical bubbles with one large, central bubble labeled "ATTACK" (the name given to the second of the two exhibit galleries, with the first named "Road to War"). A meeting in June 2006 reiterated a desire to keep the museum's "primary focus on the events of December 7th itself" (Aldrich Pears Associates 2006, 17). And in subsequent design choices, the "interpretive treatment option" chosen in that meeting called for "more modest treatments of the global context leading to war and differing national perspectives and strategies" and "lesser treatments of local and civilian stories" (Aldrich Pears Associates 2006, 18).

Clearly, then, one of the central axes of conflict in visions for the new museum was between more context, more social history, and a tight focus on the battle. Notes from the next design meeting reflect the underlying dissonance between the two approaches, as four bullet points under the heading "Comments on Stakeholders Meeting" seek ways to contain the distractions of context (Munday and Hill 2007a, 14):

- Can't respond to everyone
- There is a Japanese Culture Centre Museum
  — Tells story of Japanese on Hawaii
- How to reach local community
  — Currently have local stories on tickets and in audio
- Can add local story to waysides and audio

These comments reflect the predicament of museum planners who, on the one hand, began the project expecting to expand the scope of the existing museum, urged on by community stakeholders interested in the local story, while also guided by an iconic battle narrative and the institutional forces invested in it. One solution for handling contextual issues, noted above, was to incorporate them in supplementary media outside the two main exhibit galleries, reflecting a hierarchy of value, with the fixed exhibits in gallery space regarded as the place for priority narrative and ancillary material elsewhere. Indeed, remarks by the memorial's historian during a meeting with historians in December 2006 (assembled for a sixty-fifth anniversary symposium), described the audio guide as a place where the park could experiment with innovations in its interpretive program, suggesting that the less visible mode of audio programming is an area for experimentation and material that might be controversial: "We've been actually silently floating up a trial balloon with this interpretation with our audio program. Our audio program has a lot of edges to it . . . and we haven't had a reaction to it. . . . You know, the survivors are talking to them, we have Japanese pilots talking to 'em. And I can tell you, years ago when I came here, the idea of a Japanese pilot talking in one of our audio programs was probably unheard of, and now we have that voice being heard" (audio recording, December 1, 2006). The historian's remarks here are a reminder that historical representation at the *Arizona* memorial is in motion with multiple media, activities, and streams of development.

The recommendations of some to contain ancillary information coming in from stakeholder meetings reflect an investment in the narrative focus on military service ("sacrifice and courage"). Yet, as the design continued to develop, several aspects of local history and memory would find expression in new exhibits, primarily in relation to the Japanese American experience in Hawai'i, but also in some tentative moves to present aspects of Hawaiian history. The differing fate of these two facets of the Pearl Harbor story in the museum design process illuminates the cultural politics of these entangled histories.

Entangled Histories

One way of looking at the museum design process is as a series of engagements between the mythic story of Pearl Harbor as a surprise bombing attack and other histories that intersect with it. But not all other histories are on the same footing—they have distinctly different degrees of recognition in mainstream American history, and found different levels of representation in the new museum. Consider differences between Japanese American and Native Hawaiian memory of Pearl Harbor (acknowledging that neither of these are singular or homogenous communities of memory). The old museum had devoted almost no footage to Pearl Harbor histories specific to these communities, not to the internment of Japanese Americans, not to the military service of Japanese Americans (except for temporary exhibits mounted on special occasions). Neither was there a place for the early history of Pearl Harbor, the story of how it became a U.S. Navy base, following political intrigue and colonial appropriation (see below). For the Japanese American experience of Pearl Harbor, things would change with the new museum, where two sections of gallery space focus on issues of discrimination, internment, and military service in the aftermath of the attack. In contrast, Hawaiian history is limited to two panels and flip-book displays in a covered outside area. Although some of the content of these panels also represent significant departures from anything in the previous museum, they are often ignored by visitors who sit resting or snacking with their backs to the informational displays. The different outcomes for these two alternative histories reflect differences in recognition in both popular culture and in institutional resources.

By the time the museum project was launched, the Japanese American experience in the Second World War had been the subject of numerous books, films, and exhibitions about internment as well as the military service of Japanese Americans. Legal and policy developments that brought attention to internment history on the national stage included the Civil Liberties Act of 1988, mandating an apology and redress to internees and affected families, a major exhibition at the Smithsonian's American History Museum ("A More Perfect Union: Japanese Americans and the U.S. Constitution" showed for nearly two decades, 1987 to 2004), and the designation of former internment camp locations as National Historic Sites, including Manzanar, in central California (made a National Historic Site in 1992 and opening an "interpretive center" in 2004), and Tule Lake Segregation Center, in northern California (designated a National Historic Landmark in 2006 and included in the World War II Valor in the Pacific National Monument). The transformation of internment locations into cultural destinations within the national park system would prove particularly important, as several National Park Service personnel with Second World War expertise consulting on the VALR project brought that experience with them.

And locally, as seen in chapter 3, the National Park Service staff at the *Arizona* memorial had gained significant experience with local Japanese American perspectives and interest in the Pearl Harbor story through discussion of the film and deletion of the cane cutter scene, as well as awareness of the controversy around the Niʻihau exhibit at the Pacific Aviation Museum (see chapter 4). Those recent discussions about the politics of representation in Pearl Harbor museums brought home the importance of a national theme represented through local community organizations such as the Japanese American Citizens League, the Japanese Cultural Center of Hawaiʻi, and Japanese American veterans associations, not to mention Hawaiʻi's Japanese American congressional representatives, such as the late senator Daniel Inouye and Congresswoman Patsy Mink. As important as these institutional forces were, equally important was the presence of historians, curators, park service staff, and community volunteers who had personal or professional knowledge of Japanese American history. It was apparent from the start that the Japanese American experience of Pearl Harbor would find its moment with the new museum. Observing this, I was aware that just a few years earlier authors of an educational CD about the Pearl Harbor attack produced by the *Arizona* Memorial Museum Association had deemed the topic of internment as irrelevant for that project (Infimedia 2004).

Figure 5.1 shows the layout for the new museum envisioned in one of the first schematics drawn to visualize major topics to be covered in the new museum. A bubble named "attack!" is in the center, surrounded by six other bubbles. Of these, two are about military build-up ("Gibraltar of the Pacific" and "Climb Mt. Niitaka") and two about military response ("Philippines, Wake Island, 'a nation stirred'" and "bases, salvage"). The other two, however, made it clear that the museum would for the first time address civilian issues directly: "Civilian perspective" and "Martial law, internment." But just how extensive or serious this representation would be remained uncertain in the months to follow. As noted above, the preference to keep the focus on December 7 as a battle narrative came with recommendations to scale back on "treatments of local and civilian stories." Thus, the first report from the consulting firm presenting visitor center layout and preliminary details for an exhibit plan included just two paragraphs in a half-page section labeled "Aftermath," devoted to issues of martial law and internment. By the end of the process, however, description of these topics had thickened, producing an extensive display on martial law in Hawai'i and another on postattack prejudice, titled "Looking Like the Enemy: Japanese Americans Fight for Equal Rights."[5] Coming toward the end of the second exhibit gallery, after the attack video, they occupy an important place in establishing outcomes and impacts of the bombing. To bring this point home, an exhibit titled "loyalty questioned," accompanied by a wall-sized photograph of the Japanese American 442nd regiment, occupies the final exhibit room (facing a model of the memorial and sunken ship).

The effectiveness of these exhibits was eloquently represented in a commentary offered by the director of the Japanese Cultural Center of Hawai'i, asked to participate in the evening panel convened at the visitor center, described in the introduction. Her account of her response to the new museum, conditioned by her family's experience with internment and the emotional stigma attached, offers an eloquent example of just the sort of personal engagement sought by museum professionals on the design team:

> My interest in WWII has always been very personal and focused on the impact the war had on my family. Growing up through elementary school, through high school, I dreaded studying U.S. history, I dreaded December 7th and the chapter on World War II and the bombing of Pearl Harbor. I especially hated watching those movies in high school about the bombing of Pearl Harbor and listening to President Roosevelt's voice and his famous words, "a day that will live in infamy." And I can recall that pain of sinking into my seat and feeling that sense of guilt and shame as a Japanese American and my classmates taunting me and asking me if my father was a kamikaze pilot.
>
> . . .
>
> So when I was invited to serve on this panel, I accepted it with very mixed emotions. I took the Pearl Harbor audio tour just last Tuesday and I have to say I was unsure, not sure what to expect. But I was very surprised.
>
> . . .
>
> The strength of this exhibit is the uniqueness of the Valor of the Pacific [exhibit] for me was that it was very inclusive and complete story

of what happened at Pearl Harbor on December 7th. The end of the concluding panels of "loyalty questioned," the panels on disrupted lives, years of internment, I really liked. I liked acknowledging the contributions of the 442, the 100th and the MIS [Military Intelligence Service].

. . .

But it was that closing panel and the quote was, "World War II touched the lives of nearly everyone. The impact echoed through generations of people." And there was a series of three questions. And that last question, "How did December 7th affect you and your family?" For me seeing that was just very profound. It was the first time I felt included. And for the first time I felt my family's experience had a place in the history when we talked about World War II. (audio recording, March 27, 2012)

It is instructive to compare this panelist's statement with that of the Hawaiian participant who spoke from the audience on the same occasion, volunteering his opposite experience of feeling excluded, of disconnection rather than connection. Comparing these two testimonies maps two different points of intersection between personal and community narratives and the history presented in the new museum. The Japanese American experience, told as a narrative of fighting America's enemies abroad and facing racism at home, has not only been woven into the larger fabric of American history, it has served as a lesson in both civil rights and military history.[6] As seen in chapter 3, the theme of America's minorities' rallying behind the war effort, including local Japanese Americans in Hawai'i, was already coded into the first propaganda films about Pearl Harbor, hurriedly reedited to reflect the paradigm shift from racial paranoia to minority loyalty. In contrast, the story of Hawaiians' suffering loss of land, culture, and identity in the face of U.S. expansion finds little common ground with narratives of American triumphalism.

Whereas Japanese people, and Japanese Americans, have always been in the classic Pearl Harbor narrative (however political or problematic their representation), Hawaiians have not, except perhaps in images of hula girls who set the stage for an attack on an idyllic island in the Pacific. Even though Pearl Harbor (as Pu'uloa) is a Hawaiian geographic and cultural landscape, the epic narrative of the attack is a story of nation-states at war, of the "Empire of Japan" attacking the United States of America, with Americans of Japanese ancestry caught up in a politics of suspicion and loyalty. In this sense, the Pearl Harbor mythos is a core episode in American history that is represented in a vast semiotic repertoire of military and mainstream media, usually without reference to the Native population, except in touristic imagery (Rosenberg 2004). From a mainstream point of view, Native history simply isn't relevant to the story of the attack. As others have noted (Gonzalez 2013; Osorio 2010), however, the attack narrative writes over the indigenous history that is entangled with its logic of militarization. Given these structural and political contradictions, one of the significant innovations of the new museum is the effort to include some degree of representation of Native Hawaiian history. The presence of these issues, even in the margins of the memorial, mark the evolution of the visitor center's interpretive space in concert with shifting possibilities for historical representation. The story of how those exhibits, nestled in the courtyard between the exhibit galleries, came to be produced says as much about their marginality as their contribution of a new element in memorial historiography.

The Hawaiian audience member's complaint voiced during the review panel would have been much greater if in fact the exhibits hadn't benefited from last-minute editing and script-writing done in almost serendipitous fashion after the final round of exhibit development was supposed to be complete. That episode illustrates the often surprising and messy way museum spaces are created, through practices that are in no one's manual, much less contained within generalizations about the role of the state or military authorities in shaping the memorial's public history. Here I briefly trace this fractured process as a mapping of one of the edges of memorial history, one that speaks to deeper contradictions in the kinds of memory and countermemory that surrounded the museum design process.

For museum planning, the problem of colliding narratives (American and indigenous) was compounded by the long-standing structural separation of Native Hawaiian scholarship and military institutions in Hawai'i. The lament of Professor Jon Osorio, one of only a few Native Hawaiian scholars who have been involved with education programs at the memorial (as an invited speaker in teacher programs, discussed in chapter 6), expresses well the problems of dialogue between these spheres of Pearl Harbor memory. Despite (or because of) Professor Osorio's involvement, when speaking on a panel convened at the Western Museum Association in September 2011, he noted, "For a Native person to give advice or counsel on what this museum should look like is . . . extremely difficult." Just as he has written that it is hard for him to look out over the militarized landscape of today's naval base at Pu'uloa (Osorio 2010, 5), it was difficult for him to work with the park service museum project, for much the same reason. As noted in the introduction, he commented that, where the naval base is for many a deeply personal "enshrinement," it is, for him and many Native Hawaiians, a place of erasure of ancestral attachments to the land. In language that resonates with the statement of Keoni Wong, quoted in the introduction, he has written that "Puʻuloa has become unfamiliar terrain to us (Native Hawaiians), much like the language of our elders and for some of the same reasons . . . many Hawaiians, unless they join the armed services or the large corps of civilian workers at Pearl Harbor, generally find the place forbidding" (Osorio 2010, 4–5).

For these reasons among others, the National Park Service found it difficult to involve Native Hawaiians in their effort to include diverse stakeholders in museum planning. Although they recognized the significance of Hawaiian history for the Pearl Harbor story, it was never central. In one of the early planning documents, the last of four items under "secondary interpretive themes" was "the site of Pearl Harbor, Wai Momi, has evolved from a place of traditional Hawaiian cultural uses (*ahupuaʻa*, fishponds, and *heiau*) to an active military base" (Aldrich Pears Associates 2006, 5).[7] Despite the wish to include Hawaiians along with other "diverse" groups in the community, the project did not succeed in mobilizing any sustained or in-depth contributions from Native Hawaiian scholars or community leaders. E-mails and attachments were sent out to selected individuals but, without any prior relationship or sustained follow-up, nothing resulted. Unlike dialogue with Japanese Americans that was facilitated by the involvement of organizations such as the Japanese Cultural Center of Hawaiʻi, the Japanese American Citizens League, and veterans' associations of Japanese American units that fought in the Second World War, there were few ties to facilitate that dialogue.

Questions about Native Hawaiian history did emerge in the discussions of museum planners, but without the participation of Native Hawaiians themselves, those topics were inevitably left as passing interjections, rather than topics for sustained discussion. As an example, one of the mainland-based historians from the National Park Service, participating in the first set of meetings in February 2006, wondered, "If anyone ever asks 'how Pearl Harbor came to be a naval base in the first place,'" adding, "I just think that, seen from a Hawaiian perspective it's a thorn in their side." The facilitator at that point responded by asking if the speaker was referring to "sovereignty" issues and then asked, "How far can you go?" Within two turns of speaking, the group's attention had moved on to questions about interpreting the sunken ship and possibilities for constructing a model with detailed visualization of bomb damage.

With no Hawaiians or Hawaiian specialists in the core group of decision-makers, and few participating in the stakeholder meetings, it was inevitable that indigenous history would emerge only around the edges, and then in somewhat stereotypical terms related to the theme of Native disappearance.

Thus, it was left, oddly, to the Japanese scholar asked to review the script for correctness of Japanese language, culture, and historical details, to note the "difficulty" of the section referring to the colonial appropriation of the islands, asking politely if certain additions might add depth and accuracy to the script:

> This (p 239) is a difficult page, isn't it . . . ? But I do think it would be better if somehow we can note that there was a considerable opposition among the Native Hawaiians to give an exclusive right to Pearl Harbor to the United States. And maybe some reference to the secret report by John Schofield, which assessed the merits of Pearl Harbor for the US government? (Yujin Yaguchi, written comments to NPS, August 14, 2008, 2)

For whatever reason, these comments didn't take hold and may even have seemed like "political correctness" to some who preferred the minimal context approach to the memorial's history. Eventually, however, one year later Hawaiian issues would be back on the table, traveling a somewhat circuitous route to gain the attention of exhibit designers.

A critical juncture in the scripting of exhibits about Hawai'i came as those in charge of fundraising began to look to the community for financial support. Once funds had been procured to complete construction of the new visitor center, the fundraising entity, the Pearl Harbor Foundation, turned its attention to exhibit development. Discussion of possible funding sources led to recognition of the need to more adequately represent *local* history—a need that had been recognized from the start with the designation of the outdoor area between the main exhibit halls as the "Oahu Court" (see map 1.1). The need to present even a capsule history of Hawai'i implied the need for some representation of Native Hawaiian history. Seeing this as an aspect of the project that would appeal to local interests, the Pearl Harbor Foundation decided to approach local sources for possible donations. The most well endowed and prominent was the Office of Hawaiian Affairs, a state office with an elected board representing Native Hawaiian interests in the state (see appendix 2 of Hawaiian history). In preparation for that task, a staff member of the Pearl Harbor Foundation, a longtime resident of Hawai'i with a personal interest in Hawaiian culture whom I will call Shirley, began to read through the exhibits on Hawai'i and discovered how unsatisfactory the text would read to Native Hawaiian audiences. The result was a last-minute scramble to redraft those exhibits in mid-2009, at a time when the exhibit design process had otherwise reached 90 percent completion. When exhibits should have been getting a final polishing, these underwent a complete rewrite, coordinated by two people with no exhibit experience, but

KĀNAKA MAOLI

By 1940 only 15 percent of the islands' population was Kānaka Maoli (Native Hawaiians) and sacred areas were being lost to large scale sugar and pineapple plantations, new construction and military use. Access to land and water was important to traditional Hawaiian customs, practices and beliefs. A leader in the Hawaiian community put it this way: *"It is not that the ships and armed soldiers themselves are menacing, so much as it is the sense that they belong to this place and we do not."*

Kamehameha Day, 'Iolani Palace, Honolulu, 195

FIGURE 5.2
Native Hawaiian history exhibit in the "Oahu Court" area, World War II
Valor in the Pacific National Monument museum.
Photo by author.

reaching out to contacts in the community to produce something workable for local audiences (Moore 2009).

The story of rescripting the Hawaiian exhibit panels was one of serendipity and fortuitous connections. Shirley recalls her immediate, negative reaction to reading the texts for the first time. As she put it, she was "thinking of it from a PR point of view . . . picturing opening day, locals coming in and going . . . [grimace]." She felt that the perspective and tone were enough out of line with local sensibilities that the exhibits could not be used to approach local organizations for funding. In her view they were written from a mainland perspective and would not connect with local audiences wary of language that sounded more like the exoticizing rhetoric of Hawai'i's tourism economy. Indeed, the perspective and tone of the exhibit had already been set in the first months of planning, prior to the involvement of local stakeholders. An early draft "walkthrough" developed and circulated in mid-2006 described the exhibit as follows,

In the Oahu 1941 Plaza, today's tourists identify strongly with tourists from this earlier time—drawn then, as today, by tropical breezes and welcoming island life.

Among the natural plantings in this sheltered plaza, visitors encounter a range of abstracted, graphic scenes of Oahu. The scene comes to life through photographs, quotations and the soft strains of popular songs played on ukuleles. Stories are told by Native Hawaiians about Wai Momi, or "Waters of Pearl," and its sacred meaning, and about the influx of defense workers and Marines away from home for the first time. . . . [8]

The Pearl Harbor mythos is in full form here. The draft text reads like a narrative version of the opening scenes of John Ford's wartime film *December 7th*, which begins with a fictional Uncle Sam lounging on his verandah in tropical Hawai'i, imaged as a languid Polynesian lifestyle—all by way of setting up a counterpoint to the reality of war about to descend. The images of Hawai'i here focus on "the antics of some servicemen on shore leave the night of December 6, 1941," presenting Hawai'i through the eyes of military servicemen, for whom the islands are the "first strange place" on military itineraries (Bailey and Farber 1992). The dominant image was that of Hawai'i as a tourist destination. In her retelling, Shirley referred to texts that quoted the words of naval personnel of the day that, however authentic, only seemed to reproduce views of Hawai'i as exotic playland. Examples mentioned included a passage quoting a sailor talking about how the place smelled strange to him and another that described hula in overtly sexual terms. In Shirley's words, "There is no doubt that hula is sensual. There's no doubt about that. But the comment had a lusty tone to it. [I thought] this is not going to go over. I've danced hula for many years. I understand there are sexual connotations to almost every dance. But that's not the primary meaning. And hula now is looked at so differently than just entertainment. Especially now that there is this revival of the Hawaiian culture. You know it's much more of a sacred thing than entertainment, you know, for tourists" (recorded interview with development officer, Pacific Historic Parks, February 26, 2010).

To listen to the story of rewriting the Hawaiian panels is to glimpse the way marginalized histories are produced, around the edges of dominant narratives. At the same time, this story can be read as evidence of an open, permeable process in which someone not part of the museum design team could identify problems and then be authorized to coordinate rewriting. In Shirley's words, the focus of exhibits in the Oahu court on Hawaiian history offered an important opportunity to speak to local audiences in the memorial context: "These exhibits discuss the importance of Ke awalau ʻo Puʻuloa to Kānaka Maoli [Native Hawaiians], the history of Pearl Harbor including the Reciprocity Treaty, the demographic of Hawaiʻi prior to WWII, and how the influx of defense workers created tensions in the islands. Until now, aspects of Native Hawaiian culture and history have not been discussed at this site. The Oahu Gallery and wayside exhibits provide a special opportunity to reach many visitors with these accounts, engage our local community, and preserve a unique aspect of Hawaiian history" (e-mail to author, December 22, 2009). The park service coordinators of the museum project reacted supportively, encouraging Shirley to utilize her local contacts to solicit suggestions and redraft exhibit text. In her telling, she told the team leaders, "We really need to involve the Hawaiian community in this. [My colleague] and I can write as much as we want but it's still coming from a, for lack of a better term, haole (Caucasian) perspective." Since the park service officials said they had tried contacting various Hawaiian representatives, without success, they may have seen this development as an opportunity to get it right. In Shirley's telling, the response was "Let's fix it; let's do what we need to do."

Shirley estimates that she and her colleague contacted and received feedback from eleven individuals known for their expertise in Hawaiian history and culture, most of them Native Hawaiian, making comments and suggestions on an array of panels pertaining to Pearl Harbor and life in Oahu leading up to the attack. The challenge was enormous since the history is so complex, mostly unknown to audiences visiting the memorial, and had to be told in panels with very strict word limits. Exhibit one was two pages long. Some topics had to be "treated in 75 words or less." The process was also made more difficult by the fact that at no point did the Hawaiian consultants meet together or even participate in group e-mail discussions. Unlike the many planning sessions with historians at Pearl Harbor and in the park service, with community stakeholder groups, everything in this last minute consultation on Native Hawaiian topics was done, as Shirley put it, "one on one."[9]

Anyone working on issues related to Hawaiian history knows well that the subject is contested ground. Such awareness may have been a factor in planners' avoidance of more concerted efforts to engage with Hawaiian scholars, many of whom could have been expected to be antagonistic to the project. For these very reasons Shirley was more than a little nervous in approaching people outside her personal network. In describing her first visit to one such person at the University of Hawaiʻi, she recalled feeling like she was "going into the lion's den," that the visit could "go really badly." Instead that scholar wanted to know what motivated Shirley to take on this project, apparently wanting to know more about the context before getting involved. The interaction, she realized, was not only about content, but about relationship-building. As Shirley came to realize, "it was just not knowing the issues and not taking the time, really, that was really necessary for that exhibit. . . . When you work with Hawaiians it's all about the relationship."

In answering that scholar's question about her aims, she recalls saying, "Our intention is to tell this story fairly, accurately, sensitively. And anything here that is not any of those things is because of my own ignorance." It is likely that Shirley's humility counted for more than her invocation of the park service discourse of "fair and accurate"—words often associated with depoliticized histories incapable of engaging Native concerns with justice, structural dispossession, institutional silences, and so on. In this case, however, the bid for cooperation with about a dozen individuals provided enough of an opening to sustain a conversation. Even if some of the consultants remained ambivalent, they did introduce topics that had not appeared in previous interpretive programs, primarily because they were not seen as relevant. When two or more consultants flagged the same topic, those issues generally found their way into the script.

One such topic was population decline. Shirley recalls that, for two key consultants, "it was very important . . . that we used the words 'steeply decreased over the previous 100 years.' That kept coming up over and over. So it's in." The phrase did make it in but in the context of a panel about Hawai'i's multiculturalism that makes it a kind of demographic note to the otherwise upbeat story about Hawai'i's diversity. Another topic that multiple consultants agreed on was the Reciprocity Treaty of 1875, a topic that speaks much more directly to the history of Pearl Harbor as a U.S. naval base. Historians agree that the Reciprocity Treaty, signed in 1875, between the Kingdom of Hawai'i (King Kalakaua) and the United States, was a pivotal turning point, setting the stage for decadeslong political struggles that would ultimately lead to the overthrow of the Hawaiian monarchy, in 1893, and annexation as a U.S. territory, in 1898 (see appendix 2). Those struggles, a subject of close scrutiny in recent Hawaiian scholarship (Osorio 2002; Sai 2005; Silva 2004), show that the strategic military value of Pearl Harbor to the United States was the preeminent motivation for American efforts to bring Hawai'i into the U.S. sphere, a set of objectives that meshed well with American commercial interests looking to North American sugar markets.

According to Shirley, there were just a few points in the script developed with her Hawaiian consultants that were resisted or rejected by the park service, signaling that the agency did have its antennae out for language that could become red flags for complaint. One was use of the word *secretly* to describe the insertion of an amendment to the Reciprocity Treaty in a closed session of Congress. That amendment limited the ability of the Hawaiian sovereign (King Kalakaua) to lease territory to other powers, effectively ceding strategic control of Hawai'i to the United States.[10] Another change in language required removal of the word *insurgents* to describe the plotters who overthrew the Hawaiian queen, in 1893.

More important than these details of history (no doubt beyond the attention span of most travelers) was the inclusion of language that captures the sentiments of a large and growing segment of the Native Hawaiian population. The following sentence concludes a panel about Native Hawaiians (Kānaka Maoli) and Pearl Harbor that, despite its marginal location, gives quiet testimony to the permeability of the museum-making process (see also Osorio 2010, 5):

KĀNAKA MAOLI

By 1940 only 15 percent of the islands' population was Kānaka Maoli (Native Hawaiian) and sacred areas were being lost to large-scale sugar and pineapple plantations, new construction, and military use. Access to land and water was important to traditional Hawaiian customs, practices, and beliefs. A leader in the Hawaiian community put it this way: *"It is not that the ships and armed soldiers themselves are menacing, so much as it is the sense that they belong to this place and we do not."*

Representing Japan

Just as the museum's inclusion of contested events in Hawaiian history represents an expansion of memorial history, so the inclusion of Japanese voices and perspectives in the new exhibits (beyond images of Japanese commanders present in the old museum) marks another edge of the possible, a temporal marker of emergent possibilities and ongoing transformation. Where Hawaiian issues were only dimly present in discussions of museum design, questions related to the representation of the Japanese attackers—the enemy—were frequent throughout. And for obvious reasons. The Japanese are central players in the core narrative of the Pearl Harbor attack, in the Pearl Harbor mythos. They are the "other" to the American "self," the demonic enemy in a bitter "war without mercy" (Dower 1986), remade into Cold War ally. How, then, should Japan and Japanese society be represented in the museum?

This question surfaced repeatedly in planning sessions, in regard to both museum exhibits and the possibility of recognizing the Japanese aviators and submariners who died in the attack. The new museum's major innovation in this regard is the creation of a new exhibit on "State of Mind Japan" that provides a glimpse of cultural attitudes and events in 1930s Japan. This addition was noticeable enough for one newspaper reviewer that she chose to headline her article about the new museum "Snapshots of 1930s Japan Add to Context at New *Arizona* Memorial Visitor Center" (McAvoy 2011).

In fact, the author of that article interpreted the expanded attention to Japan as a sign of a philosophical shift at the *Arizona* memorial, quoting the National Park Service historian who succinctly sums up the implications of this transitional moment in the kinds of memory work done by the institution, itself in a process of transition from memorial to the more museum-like monument:

> Daniel Martinez, the park service's chief Pearl Harbor historian, said it wouldn't have been possible to include the Japanese viewpoint in any official examination of the attack when he first started working at the visitors' center in the 1980s.
>
> "It was just too recent and the wounds were still open," Martinez said. "The idea of exploration of history would have been found unsavory by some of the Pearl Harbor survivors who were still dealing with the wounds of that war."
>
> Martinez said some survivors have understandably wanted to keep the exhibits as more of a shrine or memorial, as opposed to an interpretation of history. But he said it's important for people to grasp a more complex story. (McAvoy 2011)

Despite what sounds like a definitive shift in attitudes and museological possibilities, early proposals for an expanded Japan display, including video testimonials from Japanese military and civilians, met with some skepticism and resistance in design discussions.[11] According to one of the NPS staff involved, it was only at the urging of museum professionals, both in the Canadian-based consulting firm and in the NPS museum facility at Harpers Ferry, that the museum design incorporated a plan that would create a major display on State of Mind Japan. And even after the implementation of this exhibit there are, as of this writing, no Japanese-language labels in the museum exhibits or interpretive signage on the grounds (although a Japanese language audio program and brochure, as well as Japanese language products in the gift shop, speak to the importance of that segment of the tourism market).

The idea for an exhibit on State of Mind Japan emerged as part of an overall plan for the "Road to War" building that called for two parallel exhibits: State of Mind America and State of Mind Japan. In many ways, however, the idea for a more detailed portrayal of Japanese culture challenged the expertise and networking capacity of the design team, with its primary focus on American historians of Pearl Harbor and the Second World War. The initial brainstorming and scripting relied on a small number of American scholars of Japan, along with research by the design firm. The text that emerged tended to use stereotypical images that represented the conflict as a "clash of civilizations" (Huntington 1993) rather than a war between states expanding their military capacity and colonial influence in the region. Given the very limited space available, and the overall goal of representing the mindsets of entire nations, the task pushed representations toward essentialized images of unities with little indication of the internal debates and tensions that government propagandists sought to overcome.

If the museum was to represent "Japan," which Japan? Which "voices" (Japanese people speaking from particular positions and perspectives) would be used to depict an entire national population? A year and half into the planning, the planners could see that this very issue needed to be addressed. In a meeting in September 2007, the facilitator from the design firm observed: we need to "discuss the perspective that the exhibits take in terms of its specific sections, like . . . the state of mind of Japan . . . 'Is there a narrator's voice?' 'Who's that voice?' But also the way that it's presented, which is not just the writing, but [the difference between]: 'This is the view from Japan, from Japanese propaganda' or is it our thought of the view from Japan?" (audio recording, September 12, 2007). The exhibit design reached the final stage with minimal involvement of Japanese consultants. Recognizing the need for more expertise in this area, a scholar based at the University of Tokyo was asked to review the draft script in its final stage. With funding to recruit two advanced graduate students, this scholar submitted three detailed lists of corrections and requests for clarification. Several points pertained to questions of voice or perspective:

> 167 There seems to be a bit of confusion between the quotes taken from [the historian] Ienaga and actual writing of Ienaga. The first paragraph "it is well known. . . ." is not Ienaga writing himself and that needs to be made very clear (he would never agree to such a statement)

> 183 Yamamoto quote—I think it's important to note that Yamamoto was being more sarcastic here than sincere. Yamamoto, a Harvard grad op-

posed to fighting the US because he knew its potential power, of course had no reason to believe that his Navy will take over the White House.

Even though many of the Japanese scholars' points were incorporated in future iterations of the text, one year later the designers recognized that State of Mind Japan was in serious need of revision. One of the NPS leaders asked the same Japan-based scholar for assistance, stating that the design team had "struggled" to portray the Japanese state of mind prior to the attack in 1941 and that the current version (as of May 2009) had "serious problems," including "no balance of perspective" and "too much military point of view." They had concluded that the "entire section needs serious re-doing with more balanced, diverse perspectives, i.e., different quotes from a bigger representative group, better graphic images, and a critical review from a credible, knowledgeable source" (NPS project coordinator, e-mail to Y. Yaguchi, May 21, 2009).

Recognizing these problems, and with higher levels of the NPS hierarchy pushing for "a Japanese history expert [to] provide review/comment," the NPS reached out to additional Japanese scholars closer to home, at the University of Hawai'i, and received comments that again raised questions of representativeness. Which Japan is represented? One of the reasons for the success of Japan's militarization of its population was the relentless use of propaganda in the 1930s (Dower 1986). It seems that images and narratives that once worked well to represent idealized aspects of national character aimed at mobilizing a population for war were also seductive, decades later, for American museum designers seeking to depict an entire national mindset. In particular, a consistent theme in critical comments was that the text "bought into Japan's wartime propaganda and stereotyping" and even the assertion that the "Japanese held communal values above the sense of individualism so revered by Americans" had as much to do with "government exhortation and coercion" as with innate national character (NPS project coordinator, e-mail, June 28, 2009).

Ultimately these rather last-minute consultations with Japanese scholars produced improvements in the sophistication of the State of Mind exhibit. At the same time, however, questions about representing the Japanese killed in the attack surfaced and resurfaced without ever reaching agreement. The uncertainties around this subject reflect conflicting sentiments about representing enemy dead in a national memorial. Even though the distinction between the museum as a secular space for education and the memorial as a sacred space dedicated to American dead might seem to lessen the emotional politics involved, discussions of the new museum show that it is not just the sacred space of the memorial that is guarded by national sentiments.

Reconciling Reconciliation

Although little had changed in the physical architecture of the memorial or the museum during the first thirty years of the visitor center setup (1980 to 2010), the exchanges between Japanese veterans and American veterans in the 1990s and 2000s had introduced some dramatic new elements in commemorative practices (chapter 2). Yet, those activities were sporadic and usually on the edges of official events. Even though the anniversary symposia had previously brought Japanese aviators together with American survivors, the visitor center museum and grounds had never included exhibits devoted to the Japanese attackers as persons (the main exception was the voice of Japanese survivors introduced on the audio tour, available for a fee to those who purchase headsets).[12] How, then, might such an idea affect the narrative and rhetorical strategies of the new visitor center? Would it and the museum move toward including "all those who died that day" (to use a phrase from the orientation film) in its landscape of remembering?

When the first planning group sat down with museum consultants in February 2006, some of those who had been most involved with the memorial and aware of the friendly contacts between veterans wondered if that moment, sixty-five years after the attack, might be the time to include the Japanese attackers (aviators and submariners) in the exhibits. The NPS historian for the *Arizona* memorial introduced the idea as a "factual listing" that would be a timely addition to the educational work of the memorial and possibly have some healing effect ("make us whole"):

> Well we had actually anticipated a wayside that would not have the Japanese story but a listing, just a factual listing of all those casualties and all of that. I'm just saying that it was, this is a huge tragedy for two nations, and the fact that we're on one side honoring ours and remembering those Americans, leaving leis and flowers and all that, and that's part of cultural values and exchange. But it just struck me that here we are going through this and we're still separating sixty-five years with those that seek to keep us separate and not to make us whole. (audio recording, February 23, 2006)

Other historians at the meeting, familiar with battleground sites elsewhere in the United States, added to this suggestion by placing it in comparative and historical perspective. Several made reference to other museums that included more direct Japanese content, and to historic sites that had "evolved" in recognizing the other side. A historian in the park service system noted the way "both sides" are dealt with at other iconic battle sites, such as Little Big Horn and Gettysburg. Of course, in the other sites in the national park system, both sides are now part of the American national community, unlike Pearl Harbor, where the other side is another nation-state. Nonetheless, the sites mentioned as examples of more inclusive memorial practice were also described as places where the politics of memory had evolved through time (illustrating the general principle that the further in time from a conflict, the more possible it is to broaden representation):

> This is going to take courage. When we have a [place for] recognition of the Japanese aviators that lost their lives would there be a place for our Japanese visitors to recognize them? And in doing so would we bring this picture to a closer focus? For a long time they did not recognize southerners that lost their lives at Gettysburg. Eventually that matured. Is this gonna be the time when we finally mature the story and have the courage to do that?
>
> [Representing both sides] at Little Big Horn, you know, it just became a reality three years ago."
>
> . . . even the Admiral Nimitz Museum, for those of you who aren't aware. . . . The fact of the matter is that they built Admiral Togo's teahouse on that property. The Japanese government built it and they hold ceremonies there. That took a lot of personal courage on their part to do it." (audio recording, February 23, 2006)

When the possibility of recognizing Japanese aviators and submariners killed in the attack came up in the first planning session, one of the park service historians, sensing the importance of survivors' views, turned to the one Pearl Harbor survivor at the table and asked pointedly, "What are your thoughts on that? The possibility of recognizing the Japanese casualties. I mean the politics of it." Without hesitating the survivor responded, "Oh, the politics of it. I think it would be a good idea, because of the relationship between the two countries now. But you're gonna have a lot of rednecks who will . . ." The NPS superintendent then interrupted to push for clarification: "There could be a certain percentage of Pearl Harbor Survivors, would you agree, who could be adamantly opposed?" The pointed question drew a pointed answer, with the survivor mentioning that he had a brother-in-law who was on the USS *Lexington* when it went down, who "refuses to come to Hawai'i because the Japanese will be here." Yet he quickly added, "Then again, you're always gonna have opposition, somewhere," a sentiment supported by another NPS official who added simply, "Well we had opposition when we decided to make relocation camps national parks, it didn't stop us from doing it" (Hayashi 2003; Hays 2003). The importance attached to the views of Pearl Harbor survivors, the primary constituency for the memorial, was summed up when the NPS superintendent said that they would be on "safe ground" with the recognition of Japanese attackers by "getting the leadership of the Pearl Harbor survivors to sign off on that."

This early discussion of recognizing attackers moved from the question of including Japanese names in exhibits to a discussion of "memorializing" them by "recognizing the sacrifice of Japanese soldiers." In just a few turns at speaking, planners were asking themselves, What's the meaning of this place for generations that weren't there? The more that discussion moved into language of memorializing, the more the idea raised objections from some around the table, invoking the specter of negative reactions from the public. One of the managerial staff put it succinctly: "It worries me. Our visiting public isn't going to be as forgiving. They're going to jump on it as we're memorializing the attacker." The presupposition is that memorializing the attacker would be inappropriate in a space devoted to honoring Americans killed in the attack. The slippage here reflects the underlying ambiguity in just what museum exhibits and landscape inscriptions are doing in the context of a museum and visitor center linked to a memorial. The discussion started out as a proposal for a museum exhibit, or "wayside exhibit," about the Japanese who died in the attack (these would be names of dead, after all) in the place where they died in military service for their country. In a place such as the *Arizona* memorial or the World War II Valor in the Pacific National Monument, however, just presenting a list of names transgresses distinctions between "museum" and "memorial." Is that a list of historical facts or is it a form of recognition? Clearly, the list of names itself doesn't answer that question.

The assumption that memorializing the former enemy would be problematic is part of the presumptive logic of American war memorials. The dilemma for a national war memorial is the need to honor the wartime experience of veterans while also acknowledging postwar shifts in international relations (and the national culture of former enemies). In such places wartime sentiments mingle with postwar attitudes shifting in the context of new relationships and new historical understandings. As a result, multiple emotional trajectories collide in memorial histories and commemorative practices. Which temporal orientation will govern representation at any given point in time? The question of whether and how to represent Japanese attackers carried a larger implication for which narratives would frame the Pearl Harbor story at that point in history, for which constituencies. In this case, as discussion moved from the level of exhibit to these larger questions ("What's the meaning of this place for generations that weren't there?") a key word was *reconciliation*. *Reconciliation* is a term heavy with moral and political implications, signifying a shift in collective national sentiment away from wartime animosity toward postwar, peacetime solidarity and mutual respect. In the context of a war memorial the term *reconciliation* itself tends to evoke ideological responses that divide along lines of empathy with a former enemy as opposed to a more singular focus on American sacrifice.

The question of whether or not the *Arizona* memorial is a place of reconciliation is crucial to understanding shifts in the institution's identity or mission through its commemorative career. There is no theme of reconciliation in the legislation that created the memorial, nor in the primary thrust of activities there during the first three decades of its existence, especially the 1980s, although the intent in opening a visitor center was always to welcome Japanese visitors along with other international travelers (Yaguchi 2005). Significantly, the acts of reconciliation that did intrude into the public space of the memorial in the first decades of its existence were initiated by Japanese, whether in the appearance of a Japanese peace group asking to present a prayer in the annual December 7 ceremony (something that has been done every year since 1981) or in occasional acts of pilgrimage by Japanese veterans, most notably Mitsuo Fuchida, at the twenty-fifth anniversary (Prange et al. 1990). The uncertainties such demonstrations created continued through the 1990s with the series of unofficial friendship events, discussed in chapter 2. Although those histories were beginning to leave their imprint (as in the publicity surrounding Richard Fiske and Zenji Abe) when planning started for the new visitor center, the theme of reconciliation evoked only a range of contested possibilities. Recall that the museum project began before the creation of the World War II Valor in the Pacific National Monument, with its broader mandate, which has seen such developments as a Japanese tea ceremony on the memorial and the creation of a Sadako Crane Hiroshima peace exhibit.

During the period of museum planning (2006–9), the uncertain possibility of objectifying reconciliation periodically punctuated planners' discussions as they weighed different approaches to the new layout. One month after the first planning meeting raised the possibility of recognizing the attackers, the issue was raised again in a consultation with leading historians convened at an academic meeting in Washington, D.C., and again bracketed with cautionary advice. The notes summarizing those discussions reflect a multiplicity of views, with "Include reconciliation" listed but followed with the caution "Note that not all veterans are in favor of reconciliation; show complexity of views" (Hill 2006). That group concluded that reconciliation was an important theme to be incorporated in the new facility and discussed specific strategies that could incorporate such a theme in exhibits, even observing that "Reconciliation is part of the history of the park."

The first draft of the proposed museum layout and exhibit text took this advice to heart and envisioned an exit walkway where visitors could reflect on big themes in the meaning of Pearl Harbor, for those affected and for postwar history (see figure 5.1). Here the authors adopted the strategy of representing a multiplicity of views and sentiments, making reference to veterans and their diverse emotional legacies, with some open to reconciliation, but others closed: "Exhibit text for this area: WE REMEMBER Sacrifice and Courage. After their Memorial experience, visitors quietly proceed along a 'return' walkway where they view images of Pearl Harbor survivors. Visitors see quotations reflecting tragedy, sacrifice, courage, honor, forgiveness and lingering conflict, and are prompted to consider what insights these may hold for our lives and the world today. They also view Declarations of Peace, the Fuchida story of reconciliation, and understand the anguish of those who cannot forget or forgive (Aldrich Pears Associates 2006, 35).[13] As it turned out, this was more or less the nadir of efforts to incorporate a theme of reconciliation into the museum design. As plans for the exit walkway were scaled back, discussion turned to the seemingly more straightforward possibility of listing the names of Japanese attackers in a wayside exhibit or possibly the "Remembrance Circle," which had already expanded to include civilian names. This idea surfaced numerous times in discussion, with significant support from several in the park service team, but each time evoked opposition, usually through reference to the anti-Japanese sentiments of some segment of the population of Pearl Harbor survivors—a kind of rhetorical trump card.

A meeting of the park service in January 2007 to discuss responses to the current plan continued to make reference to the possibility of including Japanese names, but groped for a strategy. One proposal, briefly entertained, was to include them in the Remembrance Circle, where individual plaques list casualties by ship or base assignments. Notes about discussion of the Remembrance Circle for that meeting include the question "Add Japanese who died in event?" with the added possibility of a separate wayside exhibit along the shoreline: "Do a wayside exhibit about Japanese aviators, midget submarine crews, etc.—mention names of the Japanese fallen." These same notes also mention the need to exercise caution in approaching the issue of reconciliation, making reference, once more, to the attitudes of Pearl Harbor survivors, observing, "Reconciliation story—use caution as not all survivors are reconciled" (Munday and Hill 2007a, 4).

The conversation in the planning meeting shows the uncertainty surrounding the listing of Japanese names—an approach that at least one of the coordinators felt was already accepted, while another concluded that it should be abandoned (audio recording, USS *Bowfin* conference room, January 19, 2007):

> NPS PROJECT COORDINATOR: There is interest on the part of the Park
> and others to include the—the Japanese aviators. . . . I've heard 64
> names—64 individuals. Um, there's an interest to do that, so the
> question is when? Where do we do that? How do we do that? . . . if
> the political climate is right, we're gonna do it . . .
>
> NPS ADMINISTRATOR: Well, . . . I want to get some comments from
> the Pearl Harbor survivors, uh, see how—how our stakeholders
> feel about it . . . before we start taking steps forward, let's do some
> sounding out of stakeholders.
>
> MUSEUM ASSOCIATION ADMINISTRATOR: I mean, how would everybody in this room feel about uh, for whatever memorials are
> being created for 9/11 and the hijackers names were on those
> walls: probably not too good about it . . . And we still have a lot of
> survivors, civilian and military, and I don't think that's gonna sit
> [well] . . . There are some survivors who I've talked to in the 65th
> [anniversary] here who still won't buy Japanese products. It's the
> feeling.
>
> NPS ADMINISTRATOR: We've sort of expanded the scope of why we're
> here just to include the civilians. The memorial was built and the
> legislation . . . for building the Memorial says "for all U.S. armed
> forces that died that day." . . . I don't have a problem with including
> the civilians but we are stretching our scope. And to go to Japanese
> we're really stretching further.
>
> NPS PROJECT COORDINATOR: I think this discussion is good. We
> wanted direction and this was a proposal that was suggested and
> I just wanted to make sure it got a proper airing.

While the clear and direct opposition from some well-placed individuals would seem like the institutions speaking, in fact other well-placed people around the table continued to discuss ways recognition of Japanese killed in the attack might be accomplished. The discussion took up the extent to which the Remembrance Circle was an exhibit or sacred space or both. Some worried if listing names there or even in a wayside exhibit would create a "Japanese memorial" in which Japanese visitors might not just take pictures, but conduct ceremonies: "One of the things about putting up anything that might memorialize the Japanese that lost their lives in the attack is that . . . there will be Japanese that come to use that as a place to remember their relatives. As in Saipan, how they do that by burning incense and burning prayer sticks, we'll have that to contend with too" (audio recording, USS *Bowfin* conference room, January 19, 2007).

The question of recognizing the Japanese aviators recurred throughout planning discussions, but each time was met with opposition, almost as a kind of traumatic memory or return of the repressed, never finding resolution, but never disappearing, continuing to return in unexpected ways. Later that same year (September 2007), more than half way through the planning process, a meeting to review and evaluate a draft museum plan at the 60 percent stage produced an extended discussion about the best way to conclude the museum's exhibits, in the exit area of the second museum building. The topic of reconciliation surfaced again. Discussion ranged over a variety of issues, from the way the museum should articulate with the film to the right balance of emotionality. The exit area posed an opportunity to address the consequences of the Pearl Harbor attack, its historical impacts, and longer-range implications. That discussion quickly circled back on questions about how those involved were affected, especially the Pearl Harbor veteran survivors. It was a short leap of imagination, then, to wonder if the personal acts of reconciliation that had taken place in connection with the memorial since its inception might itself become part of this final phase of the exhibits (audio recording, September 13, 2007):

> SPEAKER 1: One of the most poignant things for me is, well, it was the 65th anniversary, and I know they've done it before, was the zero pilots and survivors . . . sitting, talking.
> SPEAKER 2: Right, yeah, which I always thought was just amazing; reconciliation.
> EXHIBIT DESIGNER: Well, that would be a brief panel though, and a wayside along the Remembrance Circle. Reflection . . .
> SPEAKER 3: That's where—that seems to be the right place for it.
> EXHIBIT DESIGNER: You know, pictures of the zero pilots with survivors next to each other and those kinds of stories . . .

SPEAKER 4: Just being clear that, again, that's not the whole story 'cause there are some people who will never ever . . . drive a Toyota. [Laughter]

SPEAKER 3: I think our Historian points out that the reality—that is something we should have. I don't know if that's the appropriate place to do that, but we could certainly add some sort of reconciliation.

NPS PROJECT COORDINATOR: Well, I think that needs some discussion 'cause the whole reconciliation thing isn't universally embraced by the survivors. I don't know, you know, we need some guidance from you folks about going that route.

This exchange about how and whether to include images that represent the theme of reconciliation oscillate between the appreciation of acts of reconciliation that have occurred at the memorial and reminders of continued resistance among some segment of the Pearl Harbor survivors. The ability to quote Pearl Harbor survivors opposed to reconciliation proved to be the persuasive rhetorical device in this discussion. Invoking the survivor voice put closure on the issue of representing reconciliation at the memorial, even representing the acts of friendship that had been conducted on the grounds of the Memorial by other Pearl Harbor survivors:

NPS PROJECT COORDINATOR: Okay, I'm not clear on the reconciliation thing at all.

MUSEUM ASSOCIATION ADMINISTRATOR: I just wanted to point out how intense some of those feelings are. There are still some Pearl Harbor survivors that will not buy a Japanese-made car. [An *Arizona* survivor] during the 60th anniversary was one. . . . During the reconciliation ceremony he turned to me and said, "I will not shake hands with them. There's a thousand men on that ship that would not want me to do that." So it's still there.

NPS PROJECT COORDINATOR: So your opinion—should we deal with it or not deal with it?

NPS ADMINISTRATOR: It's gonna create more problems, I think, than it solves.

Occasional references to the controversial atomic bomb exhibit at the Smithsonian Air and Space Museum in 1995 punctuated these discussions (Harwit 1996; Linenthal and Engelhardt 1996). After this exchange, there was no further discussion about building reconciliation into the exit space of the museum.

The topic of reconciliation also seemed to have little relevance for the agreed-upon theme of sacrifice and courage that, from the beginning, would be the evocative trope for the walkway along the shore, envisioned as an exit walkway (see figure 5.1). There four inscriptions cast in bronze plaques convey this theme, one from President Franklin Roosevelt and three from Pearl Harbor survivors:[14]

> We are now in this war. We are all in it—all the way.
> Every single man, woman and child is a partner in the
> most tremendous undertaking of our American history.
> *Franklin D. Roosevelt, fireside chat, December 9, 1941*

> Why them and not me?
> *Ensign Paul H. Backus, USS Oklahoma*

> Acts of heroism that day were
> many and not all recorded.
> *Gunner's Mate Third Class Alvin H. Bruene, USS Arizona*

> No matter how severely injured, we will fight for life.
> *Seaman Second Class, Everett Hyland, USS Pennsylvania*

These reflections do the job of capturing the themes of courage and sacrifice outlined in the earliest discussion of takeaway messages that might be inscribed in the walkway area. The quotations, taken together, keep the reader's attention tightly focused on the core elements of the Pearl Harbor narrative: the experience of the American military who suffered the devastating effects of the attack. President Roosevelt's radio exhortation locates the viewer at the inception of the war, while the three veterans reflect on death, injury, and heroism, rendering the themes of sacrifice and courage in personal witnessing.

Without knowledge of the extensive and wide-ranging discussion of other possibilities for this area of personal reflection, the absence of other temporalities and other kinds of witnessing would be hard to notice. Yet, even without insight into background discussions, those who know Everett Hyland, the survivor quoted on the fourth panel, have independently remarked on the choice of that quotation, from an individual who during his years working as a volunteer in the park, came to embody multiple forms of courage: in battle, where he suffered grievous injury in the early minutes of the attack, and in his postwar life, where he married a Japanese woman and actively participated in friendship ceremonies with Japanese veterans, several of whom became friends. When I asked Everett, some years after the opening of the new visitor center, where the quotation came from, he said, "I have no idea." In fact, it was a quotation that had been a stock quotation in NPS literature on the memorial since the 1990s. Whenever it was that he was quoted saying, "No matter how severely injured, we will fight for life," no doubt in one of many talks he has given about his miraculous survival of a bomb explosion on the USS *Pennsylvania*, he had long since forgotten.

As a regular volunteer in the park during the 1990s and 2000s (continuing to the present, past his ninetieth birthday), Everett Hyland is well known to many of the constituencies of the memorial. During the middle of the planning and construction of the new museum, he asked me if the plan was going to finally implement his one wish for the memorial. When I asked what that was, he said it was for the place to include "the other guys; the ones who shot at us." I passed his remark on to the person coordinating the NPS planning effort, who noted it in an e-mail going out to the project team, informing everyone that "Everett said he would like to see the names of the 64 Japanese pilots and submariners added to the list of names . . . it may be a good time to test this idea with the public and larger representative group of PH survivors" (NPS project coordinator, e-mail to planning group, February 1, 2007).

It is doubly ironic, then, that not only did Everett Hyland not see his wish realized (on the basis of invocations of survivor opposition to reconciliation), but he is one of a select few quoted in the walkway inscriptions with a sentiment located firmly in the scene of battle, embodying the designated theme of sacrifice and courage. When Professor Yaguchi was asked to make comments on the draft text, he thought the quotation from Everett Hyland so unusual that he asked if it would be possible to find "a better quote" from him, as a person who had "worked so hard to promote friendship between the US and Japanese veterans." He went on to comment, more generally, that "it seems like 'reconciliation,' which has proceeded since 1991 thanks to the efforts of many including Everett, Zenji Abe (whom you quote in this exhibit) and many others, is out of the scope of the exhibit" (exhibit text comments submitted to NPS coordinator, August 14, 2008, 3).

As consideration for the theme of reconciliation diminished, so did the larger strategy of representing multiple experiences and the diversity of responses among the various communities of remembrance. Recall that the museum consultants, from the outset, recommended an approach that would lay out diverse and even conflicting meanings in the exit walkway, so viewers might ponder a range of experiences in order to reflect on their own. A significant segment of Pearl Harbor survivors over the years had, like George Bush, said they "held no rancor" toward the Japanese, with some such as Richard

Fiske (see chapters 1 and 2) or Everett Hyland actively involved in friendship activities with Japanese veterans. In fact the careers of veterans who had themselves navigated emotional transitions from antipathy to empathy embody much of the emotional complexity of Pearl Harbor memory. Those complex and contradictory sentiments would be hard to find in the memoryscape of today's memorial.

Museums as Unfinished Memory

The new museum opened just after the memorial had been incorporated in the new World War II Valor in the Pacific National Monument. Since planning for the museum was too far along when President Bush created the monument in December 2008, the park service decided not to attempt any last-minute changes in exhibit design, making the museum primarily a memorial museum, rather than a monument museum, a difference that in fact would become apparent very soon after its opening. The significance of that change began to play out almost immediately in commemorative practices, portrayed in chapter 2. The most dramatic of these was the addition of the Sadako crane exhibit, dedicated in September 2013, providing the first material link between the discourse of American Pearl Harbor memory and the peace themes that surround atomic bomb memory in Hiroshima.

Considering that the very topic of Hiroshima or Nagasaki had been essentially banished from the memorial's public programs in earlier years (see chapter 2 and chapter 4, note 7), the creation of this exhibit was an important sign of the transformation brought about by the expanded scope of the Valor in the Pacific World War II National Monument along with the passing of the Second World War generation. After the creation of the monument and the opening of the new museum, the superintendent saw an opportunity to add an element to the museum that would signal the extended interpretive charter of the new monument and agreed to accept the offer of one of the cranes, and to raise funds for the new exhibit—an exhibit added in the last room at the end of exhibit space, a small but powerful index to narratives that had heretofore not "complicated" the Pearl Harbor story.

Perhaps inspired or at least encouraged by the tea ceremony conducted the prior year, in 2011 (see chapter 2), a representative of the Japan Society, based in New York, approached the superintendent of the memorial about the possibility of placing a symbol of peace associated with the atomic bombing of Japan in the memorial museum. The object was a tiny paper crane folded in the Japanese origami style by Sadako Sasaki, who died from leukemia in 1955. Only two

FIGURE 5.3
Sadako crane exhibit, World War II Valor in the Pacific National Monument museum.
Photo by author.

years old when the bomb was dropped, she developed leukemia ten years later and died after a brave struggle that involved folding cranes, according to the belief that folding one thousand could heal her illness. Her story, written up in a children's book (Coerr and Himler 1977), is now part of a global discourse of peace, civilian suffering, and antinuclear activism.

The Sadako crane exhibit, like the tea ceremony, was also an opportunity for the memorial to collaborate with local Japanese and Japanese American organizations—another material representation of the charter to take on a wider range of topics, like Japanese American internment, with more stakeholders, as well. The Japanese Cultural Center of Hawai'i joined with the park service and its nonprofit partner, Pacific Historic Parks, to raise funds for the exhibit, mobilizing Japanese organizations and networks throughout Hawai'i in the effort. The announcement of the gift was made on the anniversary of the atomic bombing, August 6, 2012, a date that is always marked with extensive memorial activities organized and supported by Hawai'i's Japanese American community.

Newspaper reporting on that event by local journalists who had been covering the opening of the new visitor center and museum also commented on the "evolution" of the Pearl Harbor memorial, quoting the head of the nonprofit organization assisting the Park Service: "The meaning of the memorial now goes beyond (Pearl Harbor) remembrance. It has become an opportunity for reflection on life and death, war and peace" (Cole 2012). The same article observed that "The *Arizona* Memorial has incorporated more of a Japanese perspective since the opening of a new $56 million visitor center and museum in 2010," but went on to comment on the limits of this expansion, quoting the same official saying that the new exhibit would not include scenes of devastation at Hiroshima: "'I don't think so. I don't know that, but that's not necessarily the goal,' he said. 'Again, I think the goal is to look at the peace and reconciliation that occurred after the war was over.'"

The park service administration introduced the exhibit as an expression of the new mission. The superintendent, in a ceremony receiving the crane, in September 2012, characterized the manner in which the park service would interpret the crane within a broader end-of-war narrative. His language on that occasion, and speeches that would be made a year later, when the crane exhibit was formally dedicated, maintain a focus on the end of the war, and peace, similar to the bookends metaphor (see chapter 4) that has otherwise been effective in displacing attention from the atomic bombings to the signing of surrender and postwar alliance: "The National Park Service here in Pearl Harbor not only presents the terrible tragedy and conflict but also the development of a peaceful relationship between the United States and Japan. The inclusion of this crane in the museum gallery means that . . . the crane will become part of a special exhibit that will present the ending of the Pacific War and the relationship between the United States and Japan" (audio recording, September 22, 2012). Elsewhere in talking about the delicate nature of representing the atomic bombings at the memorial, the superintendent talked with me about the importance of avoiding any implication that the atomic bombs were in some way retribution for the attack on Pearl Harbor. "We needed to be able to easily demonstrate [closure of the Pacific War] in a way that doesn't equate Hiroshima as payback for Pearl Harbor" (recorded interview, March 23, 2010).

The contested discussions of reconciliation during the planning process, followed by the turn toward Japanese peace discourse in the tea ceremony and Sadako crane exhibit, call attention to the multiple cultures of commemoration that occupy the same memorial space, as discussed in chapter 2. On the one hand, the memorial's built space, with its inscribed texts and images, represented in film, signage, and architectural layouts, carry a permanency in orienting the gaze of everyone who traverses the visitor center and memorial. On the other hand, those spaces are continually host to activities and events that seem, in comparison, more fleeting, less solidified and central to national memory. Chapter 6 shifts attention to another of these fleeting forms of activity—educational programs—where Pearl Harbor histories are made the subject of even more wide-ranging debates and discussions, and so expose institutional narratives to a more expansive range of risks, as sacred history becomes the subject of critical reflection in secular classrooms.

The subtle and not-so-subtle negotiations of exhibit design outlined in this chapter suggest that patriotic paranoia, at least through the first decade of the new millennium, continued to exert a powerful rhetorical force capable of limiting changes to the dominant Pearl Harbor mythos. In this respect the new museum, like the one it replaced, remains true to its original legislated mandate, a memorial to American servicemen (and servicewomen) killed in the attack in 1941, maintaining the focus of a national commemorative culture in which war memorials honor American citizen soldiers. The relative absence of the former enemy in this process seems to reproduce something like the wartime opacity of Japanese as persons—here represented through such devices as an exhibit to understand a foreign mind or the presence of an innocent young girl known more in death than life.

This hurried overview of a four-year design and construction project should be sufficient to demonstrate that history-making at the *Arizona* memorial is not a linear, continuous, or coherent process. On the other hand, the posture of openness that characterized much of the process allowed significant innovation, opening spaces (however marginal) for dissonant and even dangerous voices to speak. Their presence suggests the possibility of future developments with unknown effects on historical memory.

Six

PEDAGOGY, PATRIOTISM,
AND PARANOIA

Veterans Day 2010 provided the ceremonial moment for the Sean Hannity Fox News program to broadcast an exposé about an academic program in Hawai'i deemed an insult to veterans. That exposé exemplifies the highly public and emotional politics of history that surround American war memorial sites and their symbolism of military sacrifice and service. It is also relevant here because the program was one that I organized and directed at the University of Hawai'i with cosponsorship from the National Park Service and funding from the National Endowment for the Humanities (NEH). Here is the way Sean Hannity described the offensive program:

> For our veterans a very disturbing story is emerging about the anti-American agenda being espoused by a taxpayer-funded organization. Now this summer in Hawai'i the National Endowment for the Humanities helped fund a conference for college professors called History and Commemoration: Legacies of the Pacific War. But according to some of the attendants this event was nothing more than an anti-American pep rally that targeted our US military. Now the American Legion's Burn Pit blog has chronicled some of the most outrageous statements included in the conference suggested reading. . . . Now keep in mind this event was held

just miles away from Pearl Harbor and it was all made thanks to your tax dollars. Now we put in several calls to the NEH about this, we're waiting to hear back.

If this controversy had not happened, it would be useful to invent it as an illustration of the institutional forces that surround history-making in relation to a national war memorial. For me, as the organizer of the program who had stitched together cosponsorship from three federally funded organizations: the East-West Center (see chapter 2), the National Park Service (*Arizona* memorial), and the National Endowment for the Humanities (who provided funding from the Landmarks of American History program for college teachers), the episode served as a reminder of the very public nature of national history in national spaces. The program at issue—a one-week program for community college teachers funded by the NEH—was one in a series of summer programs that I had organized or coorganized to put Pearl Harbor on the agenda for the endowment's landmarks program for teachers—a natural fit for that program's interest in stimulating innovative teaching approaches to histories associated with America's historic sites, and a natural fit for my role assisting with the development of educational programs sponsored by the *Arizona* Memorial Museum Association (renamed Pacific Historic Parks in June 2010).[1]

Ironically, my contribution to the agenda of those programs was a presentation about the politics of memory at the *Arizona* memorial, tracing the development of the memorial through different phases of commemoration, and talking specifically about the manner in which the *Arizona* memorial sought to combine education and commemoration without getting embroiled in destructive conflicts such as that which beset the atomic bomb exhibit at the Air and Space Museum, in 1995 (Linenthal and Engelhardt 1996). My argument was, essentially, that the National Park Service had managed to avoid media-driven controversies because they had developed a good working relationship with the Pearl Harbor Survivors Association (PHSA), Hawai'i chapter, many of whom volunteered their time at the memorial. And, indeed, we had tried to build on that formula in the teacher programs by including a strong focus on survivor experiences, involving many veterans from the local PHSA chapter. In my talk, I pointed to the high level of anxiety and complaint that surrounded the presence of Japanese visitors at the memorial in the 1980s and 1990s, but went on to discuss the involvement of veteran survivors in friendship exchanges with Japanese veterans (see chapter 2), as well as the daily operations of the memorial (see chapter 1).

Given that my talk was premised on the existence of strong nation-centered sentiments easily offended by activities that could be construed as unpatriotic, the complaint from one of the program participants who felt that the readings and lectures were anti-American and antimilitary did not come entirely as a surprise. There is not enough space here to address the specific criticisms of that participant. Most of the material found objectionable concerned academic writings about militarization—not "the military" or military service. Even though program speakers gave more attention to militarization in Japan than the United States, the complaint made no reference to that part of the program, nor to the involvement of about fifteen participants from East Asia. The complaint emanated from, and remained confined to, domestic American culture wars.[2]

The episode struck me more as theater than a substantive argument about history or scholarship. But that is not to say the criticism was not important. Certainly the media attack aimed at the National Endowment for the Humanities was an important reminder that work on national memory is never strictly academic and can have injurious consequences for public institutions when things go wrong. Even though by 2010 my colleagues and I had run similar NEH workshops nearly every summer for six years and had received glowing evaluations all along the way, it took just one hostile teacher expressing moral outrage at the perceived anti-American and antimilitary agenda to create a media event that took on a life of its own. The rapidity with which the controversy morphed into the blogosphere, while seeking attention in government offices in Washington, shows that the terms of the complaint were preadapted to American ideological fault lines. Specifically, in the views of the complainant, the program was yet another example of liberal academics, supported by tax dollars, teaching and publishing ideologically driven attacks on America— in this case on the American military. Some of the very same organizations that had written letters to the *Arizona* memorial during the fiftieth anniversary, in 1991, such as American Ex-Prisoners of War and the American Legion, wrote their own letters of protest to the NEH.

The structures of feeling around this case and other museum controversies focus on a perceived insult to national values in national public spaces. Expressions of moral grievance engender a sense of solidarity among those who share the same sentiments, marking community boundaries in the process. The investment in boundaries was evident in the fact that no one involved contacted me to discuss the criticisms—not the unhappy participant, not the American Legion, and not Sean Hannity. Writing in the 1960s, the political historian Richard Hofstadter described something like this when he observed a "paranoid style in American politics," characterized by "heated exaggeration, suspiciousness, and conspiratorial fantasy" (Hofstadter 1964). Marita Sturken (2007b, 45) summarizes Hofstadter's analysis with her statement that "paranoid citizens are those who believe that the government does not have the interests of ordinary persons at heart and is always working to deceive them." Sentiments such as these are best maintained without the possibility of dissonant information. Their value, rather, is reinforced in performances for sympathetic audiences who coconstruct a sense of injury. I assume this is one reason that, decades into the age of Internet-fueled hyperaffect, the kind of moral rhetoric described by Hofstadter seems to be both accelerated and intensified.

In our case, the participant's letter of complaint was addressed to the NEH chairman, to a member of the NEH National Council, and to a congressman, requesting delay in approving the annual budget request for the NEH ($161 million for 2011).[3] As a result, the NEH chairman, former congressman Jim Leach, devoted considerable time to answering the criticism and reassuring the council that the program was conducted within the parameters of NEH guidelines. The controversy did not progress much beyond the initial complaint and response, even though the complainant expressed discontent with the responses received. When written responses from the chairman proved insufficient to end the grievance, the endowment recruited a highly respected author, David Levering Lewis, to examine the content of the program and write an independent report evaluating the merit of the criticisms (Lewis 2011). His report, written after a close review of the details of the program, was submitted to the NEH council and, as far as I know, put an end to further discussion of our program and NEH standards.

Despite its unfortunate effect, placing the NEH and the East-West Center on the defensive, the controversy is a useful way to open this chapter's interest in the tangled and sometimes volatile interrelation of education and commemoration. Despite the fact that most public memorials include education programs ranging from student visits to online projects, such programs are rarely considered in the analysis of memorial memory practices (where attention is often focused on the architecture, aesthetics, and activities in the memorial space itself). At the *Arizona* memorial the first decade of the new millennium saw the growth of a cluster of new educational efforts, taking off just as the memorial was entering into the phase of expansion and rebuilding the visitor center. These included a videoconferencing program ("Witness to History") and summer workshops for teachers and college faculty—all added to the class visits that are a routine part of most national park operations. Similarly, the other three museums among the "Pearl Harbor partners" all have their own educational programs. The aviation museum, for example, runs a summer "Flight School" which, in 2013, consisted of "a 3-day adventure in the history and technology of aviation," in which 161 middle-school boys and girls participated.[4] Such programs are of interest, not only for the nature of the histories they produce, but for the institutional structures that make them possible.

Sacred Histories

As elaborated in previous chapters, the ethnographic study of memorials as social spaces quickly shows them to be much more than sites for commemoration. They are also places where identities are performed, relationships built, and activities ranging from tourism to classroom instruction pursued—all of which may connect larger narratives of history with personal life stories. Memorial sites are places where local, national, and global travelers learn about historical forces that changed lives and, in many cases, still do today. But what kinds of education and what kinds of historical understanding are fostered in such places? Whereas the work of memorializing requires reverence and respect for losses and those tied to them, education inevitably involves critical questioning and debate, openness to new evidence and interpretation, and so forth (Linenthal 1995). Memorial history is always in some way affected by a relationship with the sacred and its affects. Education tethered to zones of sacred space is typically conducted in ways that are deemed consistent with the purposes of remembrance and honoring memory. Even when memorials wish to encourage reflection, they typically avoid critical questions or argumentation. The type of pedagogy that seeks to destabilize dominant narratives through critical reflection or by interrogating basic premises are more comfortable in secular space, at a distance from the sacred.

One of the immediate problems with this conjecture is that it is not always easy to tell where sacred and secular begin and end, even in regard to memorial space. At the *Arizona* memorial, as seen in the previous chapter, certain differences are coded in the separation of museum and memorial. But even though that separation is marked by the architectural and spatial separation of memorial and visitor center, the boundaries between secular histories and sacred memories are almost always blurred in practice. And the blurring, it seems, is evident in the emotions that mark their boundaries. Margaret MacMillan, writing about the aborted atomic bomb exhibit at the National Air and Space Museum, in 1995, put the matter succinctly: "The distinction between museums and memorials is a blurred one and, as a result, gives rise to often angry debates over how the past should be portrayed and interpreted" (2008, 123–24). Similar confusions and tensions surround the new museum at the World Trade Center, as briefly discussed in this book's introduction.

Awareness of the different kinds of discourse possible in zones of memorialization has been an important premise of the educational programs connected with the *Arizona* memorial. With the realization that the combination of remembrance and remembering, of honoring and analyzing, unsettles historical memorial sites, the park service and its partner museum association began to expand educational programs at the visitor center and in classrooms, seminar rooms, and conference halls in Hawai'i and elsewhere. The interrelation of education and commemoration was a constant frame for the teacher workshops, which included visits to memorials, time with survivors, lectures, discussion, and project work. Whereas the very topic of Pearl Harbor is arguably a sacred site for some by virtue of its status as an icon of national loss and sacrifice, bringing teachers to Hawai'i to visit the memorial and discuss educational goals and practices opened up multiple avenues for personalizing the work of history. By conjoining discussion of curricula with opportunities to explore the Pearl Harbor landscape and talk with survivors, the teacher programs necessarily confronted tensions between history and memory as manifest in education and commemoration.

In the course of these programs, we constantly discovered that modalities of learning and remembrance easily intertwined. Memorial ceremonies, for example, create historical understanding, just as historical texts may be a means of memorializing people and events even if we don't label them as such. The fact that textbooks frequently become objects of protest over historical truth is related to their significance as works that not only have the power to say what is regarded as truthful, but to say what is "ours" and who "we" are. As Laura Hein and Mark Selden have written in *Censoring History*, secondary school textbooks in particular attract a lot of attention because "directly or indirectly, they carry the imprimatur of the state" (cited in E. Cole 2007, 22; Hein and Selden 2000, 4) and they speak in a national voice. In this arena, textbooks are usually somewhat cautious in how they represent controversial events, choosing to remain close to "the facts" or to let historical actors do the speaking. Nonetheless, every textbook is involved to some degree in the business of national identity-making. The French parliament passed a national law in 2005 (since rescinded) that mandated that French history taught in high schools should be affirmative in teaching about France's colonial history. Such mandates run the risk of alienating national publics, as found in the Soviet Union and the socialist regimes of eastern Europe, where skepticism ran

so deep after decades of state-directed affirmation that students routinely dis-
counted their texts as propaganda (Wertsch 2002).

Just as they always were at the Pearl Harbor visitor center, the survivors
were the rock stars of the teacher programs—a personable and historic element that consistently captured the imagination of workshop participants. The
poignancy of teacher interactions with the survivors (who ultimately included
civilians and Japanese survivors) was a constant reminder that we were living
through a moment in which that unique first-person voice was fast disappearing. What, then, are the opportunities and liabilities of the kinds of historical
understanding that follow from a focus on personal experience? In the workshops, I was continually struck by the number of teachers who brought their
own personal and family connections to the topics at hand—connections that
motivated and excited interest in engaging with the survivors. And those interactions in turn would show up in research projects and teaching exercises
that the teachers developed in the course of the programs. For educators, these
connections offer both opportunities and risks—opportunities to get people
"turned on," but also risks that the turning on easily hardens into a single, right
point of view, whether patriotic dogma or some other ideological correctness.
Scholars interested in historiographies of war, especially the problems of
representing the Holocaust, have written about the power and danger of
first-person witnessing for historical analysis and writing. Asking what kind of
historical understanding is produced through first-person accounts goes beyond
problems of bias that are often discussed in relation to oral history and its attendant issues of selective perception, distorted memory, and so forth. Rather, we
might ask, What are the different forms of knowledge that follow from listening
to a survivor's voice as compared to tracing events through decades or across re-
gions using not only personal testimonies (if available) but all manner of texts,
voices, and distillations of memory? Dominick LaCapra calls the former "memorial history" and notes that one of its effects is to challenge historical "distantiation": "Remembering such pasts [violent, traumatic] in a mode we might
call memorial history, especially where it occurs in commemorative contexts in
which mourning takes place, challenges historical distantiation by seeking to
re-member or revivify the past and to fuse the people of the past and the people
of the present into a single collective body" (LaCapra 2004, 55–56).

To listen closely to the first-person stories of veterans and survivors is to
think about history in human terms, in the language of personal experience,
through thoughts and emotions that allow us, in the present, to understand
by inhabiting subject positions or identifying with the actors and dramas that
unfold in personal accounts. Something like this seemed to be going on with

participants in the teacher programs, who over and over talked about being moved by meeting and talking with survivors. This is a powerful device for teachers seeking to make history relevant and meaningful to students who might otherwise feel disconnected or disinterested.

But whose voices, speaking in what registers, for what audiences, will create such evocative histories? And how do personal modes of history-making relate to other forms of history, to the kinds of questioning that arise when competing stories vie for recognition? In her book *The Era of the Witness*, Eva Wieviorka (2006) argues that the emergence of survivor testimony in Holocaust memory (as recorded in trials, memorials, films) reshaped the writing of history by making oral testimony or witnessing the centerpiece of historical representation. She sees this shift occurring about midway through the postwar career of Holocaust "collective memory" (which is many collective memories, formed and reformed by different publics around the world, not least Jewish families and nation-states, from Israel to Iran). Given that most teachers regard witnessing, the use of first-person testimony, as a means of enhancing history education, what are its limitations? One answer to this question concerns the issue of who speaks as a witness. Who are the principal actors in the dramas of history that matter?

Other Histories: Articulations in the Memorial Zone

As previous chapters have recounted, the dominant form of witnessing in and around the Pearl Harbor memorial has always been that of the American military survivors of the attack and of veterans and active-duty military. From the moment Congress drafted founding legislation, the voices of military survivors, and of those who died in the attack, have made up the core of Pearl Harbor history represented at the memorial and the visitor center. The centrality of their stories has been continually evident in the honored presence of survivors in anniversary ceremonies, their active presence at the visitor center, and their participation in videoconferencing, school visits, and so on.

Even before the creation of the World War II Valor in the Pacific National Monument and its expanded historical scope, one of the important aspects of the evolution of the memorial was the progressive expansion of the category of survivor to include other survivors—civilians and even Japanese veterans of the attack. Similarly, over time, the educational programs of the memorial traced a microcosm of this evolution, focusing first on the experience of military survivors of December 7th, before then adding testimonies from civilian and (by proxy) Japanese veterans of the attack, and finally creating separate panels of both military and civilian survivors. In a number of ways, these teacher programs anticipated developments at the memorial involved with expanding the museum and commemorative activities.

Thinking back to Sean Hannity's statement that the objectionable workshop was "just miles away from Pearl Harbor" (unaware that a substantial amount of the program was at Pearl Harbor), we might say that the greater the distance from the *Arizona* shrine itself, the greater the possibility of critical historical analysis and debate. The development of Pearl Harbor (and Pacific War) history programs for teachers, conducted in the secular spaces of classrooms and conference halls, made it possible to expand the scope of relevance for Pearl Harbor history to consider other Pearl Harbors—Pearl Harbors relevant to communities such as Japanese Americans, Native Hawaiians, and Japanese military survivors. By connecting the canonical story of the attack—the one most central to the interpretive programs of the memorial—to an expanding range of voices and publics, the teacher programs entered into somewhat unknown terrain.

As architects of the workshops, my colleagues and I wished to bring survivor voices into the mix of the academic program, setting up opportunities for teachers and survivors to interact. After the first year, we broadened participation in this witnessing aspect of the agenda to include civilian perspectives, ultimately creating two separate panels, with military and civilian survivors talking about their war experiences. The teacher programs mixed these panels of first-person witnessing with presentations from scholars addressing a range of topics, including contentious issues such as Hawaiian colonial history and Japanese American internment. Because the teacher programs were being organized and conducted each year during the museum design process (2007 to 2010), some of the workshop speakers became resources for exhibit planners looking for ways to include new subjects and perspectives in the museum.

As might be expected, introducing new topics and perspectives to a museum concerned with sacred history is a process likely to meet with skepticism, if not resistance. Indeed, this proved to be the case even before the complaint in 2010. Here I want to briefly summarize a debate that unfolded around one of the most contentious of those topics, that of Hawai'i's colonial past, as presented from the perspective of the ongoing movement for Hawaiian sovereignty. While the idea of Hawaiian sovereignty still sounds radical to many, particularly those outside the state of Hawai'i who know little of Hawaiian history or politics (see appendix 2), Hawaiian sovereignty is in fact part of mainstream politics in the state of Hawai'i. The best evidence of that is legislation proposed in the U.S. Congress by Hawai'i's senator Daniel Akaka to create a formal treaty relationship between Native Hawaiians and the federal government (something never done after the illegal overthrow of the last Hawaiian monarch, in 1893). The Akaka Bill, as it is called, would resolve land claims and challenges to federal authority by Native Hawaiians—a reason that many activists and organizations now oppose the bill. In short, the topic of sovereignty has become fully integrated into everyday debates and discussions in Hawai'i, even if it remains an emotional and divisive topic for families and communities who differ in their perspectives on the Hawaiian past and future.

Not surprisingly, then, the effort to introduce a critical perspective on Hawaiian history into the Pearl Harbor workshops met with resistance from those who saw such topics as either irrelevant or unpatriotic. In this case, despite initially opposed views, the educational context facilitated a longer conversation about the purpose of teaching Pearl Harbor that ultimately established enough understanding to allow the topic into these programs. Not only was the topic allowed, but the discussion and social networks established would ultimately inform the kinds of history worked into the new museum—a process reviewed in chapter 5's discussion of exhibits about Hawai'i in the museum's Oahu court. The initial challenges and responses to these topics illustrate something about the ways memorials work as social space, as zones of encounter that, at least in some circumstances, facilitate relationship-building.

The very first time that the National Park Service and the *Arizona* Memorial Museum Association cosponsored a one-week teacher workshop, in 2004, the inclusion of speakers addressing topics such as Japanese American internment and Hawaiian colonial history led some of the sponsors to object, saying that these topics were not related to the memorial's primary mission of honoring sacrifices made on December 7th and so should be dropped. Critics saw these other topics as political. In particular, responses to the presentation on Hawaiian history showed how precarious such intrusions are in a national memorial zone.

Whereas it might be possible to conduct a Pearl Harbor history seminar in North America and not think of indigenous perspectives on the harbor and the history of its acquisition by the U.S. military, in Hawai'i such an omission would be quickly noticed by local audiences. In designing the teacher workshops, we wanted to begin the program's lecture discussions with a presentation about the longer story of Pearl Harbor in Hawaiian history. For that, we invited Jonathan Osorio, who proceeded to sing and talk his way through multiple workshops, before eventually publishing his remarks (Osorio 2010). Osorio gave his presentation in a largely personal register—not unlike the testimonials of the Pearl Harbor survivors speaking in other parts of the program. He would begin his presentation by reading a story written by Sarah Keliʻilolena Nākoa, born in 1910, about the area of Pearl Harbor, known to Hawaiians as Puʻuloa, as she experienced it in her youth. Speaking in the collective voice of Native Hawaiians (or Kānaka Maoli), he articulated sentiments that would ultimately work their way into the Pearl Harbor museum exhibit (see chapter 5), saying, "Puʻuloa has become unfamiliar terrain to us" and going on to explain why, for him and many Native Hawaiians, Pearl Harbor, as a naval base, is a symbol of dispossession and sadness because of the feeling that "they [the ships and sailors] belong to that place now and we do not" (2010, 5). One of the strengths of the NEH workshops was that they encouraged questions and discussion. And there were always plenty of both following Jonathan Osorio's talks. However challenging his presentations were for the teachers, evoking a range of responses from puzzlement to agitation and respect, in program evaluations teachers were overwhelmingly positive in their assessments, particularly those who taught American history and found fresh material for linking Pearl Harbor to the longer arcs of U.S. history in the Pacific.

Despite the teachers' enthusiasm, Osorio's criticism of the role of the U.S. military in Hawaiian history struck some of the sponsors as an unwelcome political slant. In the months following, as planners discussed the program for the next year, the organizing committee concluded that no one should be invited to talk about Hawaiian "sovereignty," deemed to be outside the scope of relevance to the workshops. The head of that committee at the time wrote to the program director at the East-West Center (and to myself as program codirector) saying that "there were multiple concerns expressed that the Hawaiian sovereignty movement issue could creep in again . . . this conference is about the Pearl Harbor attack and not the present day." The committee head went on to say that funding could be at stake: "If the conference delves into the sovereignty issue, this issue is beyond AMMA's education direction and could possibly cause negative concern and cloud the issue of continued support" (email from acting chair, education committee, *Arizona* Memorial Museum Association, to director, AsiaPacificEd program, East-West Center, May 10, 2005).

Some of the National Park Service staff involved in workshop planning also expressed reservations about Jonathan Osorio's sovereignty perspective. A follow-up message from the chairman of the museum association emphasized that the "sovereignty issue" was "inappropriate" and stated that the lecturer concerned should not be invited to participate in future workshops (email from chairman, board of directors, AMMA, to director, AsiaPacificEd program, East-West Center, May 10, 2005). This was, to be sure, a teachable moment that not only revealed differing assumptions about history but also about the articulation of education and commemoration in relation to national historic sites. In an email to key members of the museum association board, almost as if anticipating what I would say five years later to the other, more shrill challenge of Sean Hannity, I wrote that

> If we [the workshop organizers] were following the parameters that NPS imposes at the memorial, we would have to stop at Midway. No educational discussion of implications for postwar politics, cold war, September 11, etc etc. All the stuff teachers are looking for to make Pearl Harbor relevant to their contemporary courses.
>
> . . . I have no doubt these views are controversial. But in teacher workshops of this kind, dealing with big historical topics, it is the ability to present and talk about controversial subjects that add to the value of the teaching. I think you'll find confirmation of this in the evaluations done by the participants. (email to acting chair, AMMA education committee, May 11, 2005)

The chair of the association board replied by saying that he wanted to "avoid controversial issues wherever possible," and "when we must address controversial issues, and there is no doubt we will, we must all agree that a balance is being presented." If a balance is not possible, then "the issue should not be addressed or AMMA must consider not participating" (email from board chair, AMMA, to the author, May 11, 2005).

Not long after this communication, a member of the National Park Service team weighed in with reservations, stating his "growing dissatisfaction with the direction that the Pearl Harbor teachers' workshop was headed." He added that he was "not pleased with the sovereignty topic in our last workshop" and that he also had concerns about "the heavy focus on the Japanese-American experience after Pearl Harbor." Like other critics, he saw these topics as political: "I think it's important that one's political beliefs and agendas are left out" (e-mail from NPS staff, USS *Arizona* memorial, to chairman, *Arizona* Memorial Museum Association, May 21, 2005). Anyone not so inclined should not be one of the speakers. Despite the seemingly sharp division of views expressed in this exchange, the conversation continued as a broader, multilateral exchange leading to decisions to include Hawaiian history, and Jonathan Osorio, in future programs.

This exchange illustrates how fragile education is in the border zones of memorial space—fragile, but neither insular nor disconnected from memorial discourse. The concerns raised in these exchanges highlight tensions that mark the interface of memorialization and historical scholarship, an opposition often held up as a dichotomy in writings on memorials and commemoration. But the opposition is anything but dichotomous. In this case, discussions of history draw from both memorial and educational practices. Each is capable of informing and transforming the other. Here history becomes contentious precisely because the principles and purposes of historical representation draw from different discourses, both educational and commemorative, that intersect in complicated and often unexpected ways.

The other insight to be gained from this case is the fact that the contentious topics at hand are not abstract or disconnected from present-day society. The issues are embedded in the social relations and practices that represent them. In this case, unlike other controversies, such as the one around the *Enola Gay* exhibit, continued discussions led to agreement to include an array of subjects, such as Hawaiian history, Japanese American internment, September 11, and other difficult topics on the agenda, with in-depth focus on the bombing attack. As the criticism of the workshop in 2010 showed, however, the decision to include those topics did not mean that the issues concerned were no longer difficult or contested, especially when discussed in programs receiving federal support. In fact, by the time of the workshop in 2010, which became the focus of one participant's bitter complaint, one of the readings singled out for criticism was the published version of Jonathan Osorio's talk (Osorio 2010). Stripped of the context of presentation, the talk became, simply, a target for branding as antimilitary and anti-American.

It is curious that the media-fueled criticism of the workshop homed in on several issues that related to some of these debates that surrounded the first workshop, but completely ignored the fact that the objectionable program was a fully international program, with more than one-third of the thirty-eight participants coming from Japan and Asia, and supported by translators and facilitators. This fact could have lent support in crude fashion to the criticism that the workshop was "un-American." Why would the international aspect of the program be ignored by such a complaint? In my assessment it is because the international composition and goals of the workshop were irrelevant to the critique. Instead, the criticism, addressed to the NEH as a national tax-payer supported agency, was primarily driven by a concern for actions that undermine national values from within, a failure of loyalty or patriotism within the state itself.

War Memory and National and Transnational Pedagogies

Teaching war history (that so often has a commemorative dimension) raises questions about the social context of historical scholarship and its relation to the subjects it seeks to represent. If national histories of war, particularly those represented in war memorials, are deeply embedded in national institutions and frameworks for knowing, what kinds of public history are possible? Memorial sites, protected from the disruptions of inconsistent or contradictory narratives, powerfully evoke national sentiments. Our experience with Pearl Harbor programs for educators shows that, even in regard to international programs, educational systems organize themselves in state-centered ways not unlike the institutional structures that produced the Second World War in the first place. It may seem a truism to say that, in an era of globalized violence fueled by religious and cultural conflicts of all sorts, most educational institutions rely on state-centered epistemologies. The possibilities for disrupting them are discouraged by vast, unspoken, institutional structures (cultural, linguistic, and economic constraints maintained by educational bureaucracies) and, more loudly and directly, by surveillance attuned to the detection of unpatriotic discourse.

Organizing the Pearl Harbor teacher workshops brought home the force of some of the quieter, institutional practices that sustain national histories. The first, obvious point is that historical education at all levels gives priority to telling national stories for national audiences. Curricular structures and economic resources make it relatively easy and natural to organize programs focused on national histories for citizens, as is the case for the great majority of programs sponsored by the NEH Landmarks of American History program. Programs that might seek to cross national boundaries, ranging from study abroad or joint seminars involving teachers and students of different nationalities, are a special breed, more characteristic of higher education, and usually requiring supplementary funding and institutional support. In the world of textbooks, transcultural approaches to history are even more rare. One notable example is the East Asia history textbook *History to Open the Future* (China-Japan-Korea Common History Text Tri-National Committee 2010) produced through an intensive collaboration of a group of scholars from China, Japan, and South Korea, to produce a single text that could be used in all three countries (in translation).

In our experience with the Pearl Harbor teacher workshops, organizing a program that would bring American and Japanese teachers into direct dialogue about their understandings of the Pacific War and the ways they address the topic in their respective educational systems had the feeling, from the very beginning, of working against the grain. Why are occasions for cross-national discussions of war history so rare? As far as I know, the first time a group of American and Japanese teachers came together in a formal program to discuss strategies for teaching about Pearl Harbor and the Pacific War was at a high school teacher workshop we convened at the East-West Center in 2005, with support from the *Arizona* Memorial Museum Association. Why did it take more than sixty years after the war for such an exchange to take place?

In 2004, the first of the NEH Pearl Harbor workshops (titled "Pearl Harbor: History, Memory, Memorial") consisted entirely of American participants (one hundred high school and middle school teachers). No Japanese teachers participated. In fact, the question of Japanese participation did not even come up, because funding came from the National Endowment for the Humanities, which is mandated to use its congressional funds to support and improve education for American citizens. One of the consequences of this mandate is that only U.S. citizens or teachers residing in and teaching in the United States are eligible recipients of NEH support.

It is thoroughly reasonable that educational programs supported by a federal agency like the NEH will emphasize American institutions and events. Like national educational programs everywhere, a prime value and objective of education is to inform students of their own history and heritage. The effect, however, is to limit the learning experience to a domestic conversation among those who share the same national background. When the topic involves international conflict, what is the effect of such domesticated knowledge-making for historical understanding? Here it is patently clear that our understanding of the past is always connected to the present. What might be gained (and what lost) by looking at past conflicts through a different optic, one that moves from monocular to binocular to polyocular vision, constructed through a wider range of conversations?

In the case of the Pearl Harbor teacher programs, we were able to complicate the domestic model for teacher programs because of the involvement of the East-West Center, an organization devoted to international research and education, and the nonprofit organization, the *Arizona* Memorial Museum Association, not bound by federal restrictions. In this case, then, the institutional context supported and encouraged interest in internationalizing the program. Following the first program, the East-West Center's director of teacher programs suggested that in the following year, 2005, the sponsors organize a second workshop that would include Japanese teachers, joining American teachers gathered for a one-week program. The museum association responded by contributing a grant to support five Japanese teachers in the next program. This made for a modest beginning for an international teacher program that would grow in subsequent years, when NEH grants again supported larger numbers of American participants.

It is relevant here to note that when it was first proposed that the museum association fund participation by Japanese teachers some in the association questioned the rationale for bringing Japanese teachers rather than more Americans. Such questions are not surprising, given they came from an American organization concerned with preserving and enhancing the history of the Pearl Harbor attack, a quintessential American story. What is surprising is that such an organization ultimately decided to fund Japanese participation and did so with increasing enthusiasm, even increasing the number of teachers from Japan in subsequent workshops.

What, then, was the added value of turning an American Landmarks of American History program into a transnational program that generated an intercultural dialogue about the significance of those events and the ways they are taught and remembered? From the vantage point of many of the American sponsors, the participation of Japanese teachers could redress the effect of national "amnesia" in Japan with regard to the responsibility of Japan for the attack and the start of the Second World War. For their part, Japanese teachers saw the value of the workshop somewhat differently. They saw an opportunity to go beyond the usual national approach to the Second World War that generally focuses on "why the Japanese military perceived the attack to be necessary and the subsequent impact of the attack on Japan" (Yaguchi 2011). Despite the fact that the workshops brought teachers together who spoke different languages, literally and figuratively, once in the program and engaged in daily lectures, discussions, working groups, and the development of collaborative projects, many of the teachers expressed strong interest in learning from their international counterparts.[5]

Recognizing these difficulties, we worked on developing ways to sustain interaction across national boundaries, one of the few ways to expand on these habits of national knowledge machines. The Pearl Harbor workshops created a program that supported boundary-crossing interactions on the assumption that such practices benefit teachers and students at home by illuminating unspoken cultural models that constrain ordinary historical understanding. In this context, once involved, many teachers responded enthusiastically by developing cooperative teaching plans that implemented a kind of educational reconciliation, affecting the ways histories of the war are taught to future generations. Yujin Yaguchi, who coordinated the participation of Japanese teachers, observed that, during the course of the weeklong programs, "important shifts took place in the attitude of participants from both sides."[6] "Spending hours together every day, the Japanese and American teachers began to communicate while also recognizing and respecting their differences" (2011). As an example, he translated a particularly illustrative comment from one of the Japanese teachers: "I was struck by a drastic change in the attitude of a teacher from the American south. Initially he was clearly hostile to me even though we had hardly talked to each other. Neither did he seem terribly interested in 'multiple perspectives.' But this man said at the time of the collaborative presentation [which took place at the end of the workshop] that even though he had 'never even thought of incorporating Japanese perspectives in class until now,' he had 'learned so many things during the week that now he would like to start including many things.'" The sociality of the workshop facilitated a certain sense of collegiality, if not personal friendship, that motivated interest in exploring collaborative approaches to teaching that might take advantage of the internet and electronic means for linking classrooms and creating joint projects between American and Japanese classrooms. Examples of these projects are discussed in a collection of essays by Japanese alumni of the programs, convened at the University of Tokyo by Yujin Yaguchi (see Yaguchi et al. 2011).

For their part, American teachers responded enthusiastically to their experience with Japanese colleagues. Their endorsement of the international dimension of the workshop reinforced efforts to continue to expand the approach. As an example of the kinds of statements appearing in teacher evaluations, consider these statements from American teachers referring to the value of interacting with Japanese colleagues in the workshop ("Summarize your overall assessment of the experience and the effect you anticipate it will have on your teaching"):

> The experience was very emotional and moving, from the stories of the Pearl Harbor survivors to the interaction with our Japanese colleagues. . . . I want to video conference also with my Japanese colleague and her students. One of the Japanese teachers came up to me this morning and handed me an origami swan she had made for me to symbolize the peace between our countries. It was a very emotional moment for me. [evaluation # 5322]
>
> One of the most significant concepts that came across in this workshop was the idea that Pearl Harbor and the war MUST be viewed and taught from multiple perspectives. I was particularly struck by the genuine Japanese perspective of emphasizing peace, not war. During the tours, I had wonderful discussions with some of the teachers from Japan, and learned that they do not have ships or planes sitting in harbors or airfields from WWII for visitors to view. They do not look back and go into great detail teaching about the war, but instead emphasize the need for peace through their Peace Education programs. [evaluation # 5315]

Similar comments were received from more than a few participants who described a level of personal engagement more typical of memorial spaces than academic ones. The inclusion of American and Japanese teachers in the workshops created a kind of educational analogue to the reconciliation activities initiated by Japanese and American veterans at the memorial (see chapter 2). Just as survivors who participated in the early reconciliation activities faced resistance from others in the community of veterans, so the proposal to include reconciliation as a topic in the teacher programs in 2004 (even before Japanese teachers were involved) also drew criticisms from grant reviewers. A program officer at the NEH passed on comments from the review panel to the effect that "the 'Reconciliation' theme raised some hackles in the review process, as, I think, it appeared to undermine a certain sense of vigorous self-confidence in a strong policy of defending the US against its enemies."

Nonetheless, the more teachers explored areas of difference and agreement while working in close quarters during the weeklong workshop, the more they themselves seemed to inhabit the very narrative of war and postwar reconciliation they had come to discuss. That process even led to the creation of a small ritual of reconciliation created by the park service historian Daniel Martinez during one of the workshop field trips to the Punchbowl National Cemetery of the Pacific. In almost spontaneous fashion, the first year that the workshop group visited the Punchbowl cemetery as part of a day in which teachers visited Oahu war sites, we enacted our own brief "handshaking ceremony" at the plaque that had been dedicated by American and Japanese veterans as part of their handshaking ceremony at Punchbowl a decade earlier (see chapter 2). A veteran himself of many American and Japanese veterans' events, Martinez spontaneously choreographed a short, invented ritual for the teachers as we stood by the commemorative plaque, installed along the edge of one of the cemetery's walkways. Asking the teachers to form two lines facing one another, Martinez asked me to recount a brief summary of the plaque dedication in 1995, and then invited the teachers to walk in single file, shaking hands. What might seem a bit forced turned out to be an activity that many teachers responded to, describing it as relevant to their motivations for participating in the workshop. We repeated that ritual each year of the binational teacher workshops, from 2005 to 2009. In 2010, with college faculty from several Asian countries, we dissolved the dual structure of American-Japanese handshaking in favor of a moment of reflection.

The recruitment of teachers from Japan and the United States with the assumption that they bring two nation-centered points of view had the ironic effect of reinscribing the nation-state as the dominant framework for know-

FIGURE 6.1
American and Japanese teachers in handshaking ceremony, National Memorial
Cemetery of the Pacific at Punchbowl. July 26, 2006.
Photo by author.

ing and feeling history. Yujin Yaguchi makes this point in his commentary on
these workshops (2011). Indeed, in the workshop in 2010, with participants
from other Asian countries, including China, Korea, Taiwan, and the Philippines, the limitation of previous programs' focus on Japanese and American
perspectives became obvious. The more complex, expanded structure of participation for the program in 2010 called attention to the way the oppositional
structure of dominant narratives often simplifies understandings of the war as
a binary, U.S.-Japan conflict (Fujitani et al. 2001).

Just as the teacher workshops created a space for expanding the scope of
Pearl Harbor narrative in ways that ultimately made their way back into the
more sacred domain of the memorial, so the collaborative activities of the
teachers (and the invented rituals of handshaking) somehow managed to
bring commemorative practices and analytic work into the same institutional
space. The transformations in commemorative practices, soon to come at the
World War II Valor in the Pacific National Monument (such as the tea ceremony in 2011 or the Sadako crane exhibit on Hiroshima, installed in 2012)

were anticipated in much of the daily activity of the workshops, whether in the collaborative teacher projects comparing Hiroshima and Pearl Harbor memorials, discussion about differences between peace memorials and war memorials, or in the invented ritual of handshaking at the Punchbowl cemetery. Over the course of several years, then, the Pearl Harbor workshops illustrate well some of the ways the educational and the commemorative intersect in the memorial zone of Pearl Harbor, collapsing binaries and transgressing boundaries—transgressions seen by some as moral outrage and as emotional and moving pedagogy by others.

Conclusion

The story told here of transformations in the memorial landscape of Pearl Harbor would no doubt find parallels in the career of Second World War memorials worldwide. But each story, each history of memory, is embedded in specific locations, histories, and subjectivities. From my own vantage point, as a participant-observer involved with memorial practices at the *Arizona* memorial over the last two decades, the clearest sign of the present moment of transition is the vanishing presence of military survivors. Today most people coming through the entryway of the World War II Valor in the Pacific National Monument will not encounter a veteran survivor. If they do, it's likely to be a sole individual, probably in a wheelchair, signing books, alongside other authors or perhaps the souvenir coin salesman.

Now veteran survivors are present as the primary voices in the memorial's audio program and video kiosks; and they are always an honored presence in ceremonial activities, acknowledged in December 7 ceremonies with standing ovations and a ritual "walk of honor" (figure 2.2) leaving the event. Similarly, the ease with which veterans of other wars and active-duty military personnel move in and out of the spotlight of ritual practice shows that the memorial remains a powerful space for the valorization of U.S. military heritage. The point, rather, is that what was once the dominant perspective in the memorial's history-making activities, its raison-d'être, is now joined by other narratives of the Pacific War and, indeed, other Pearl Harbors, such as that of the Japanese American community and its experience with internment and enlistment, or of Native Hawaiians and their historical perspective on the harbor as a place of dispossession and alienation in the face of an expanding American empire.

This study, spanning the fiftieth anniversary of the bombing to planning for the seventy-fifth, tracks the rise and decline of a period in the lifecycle of the memorial, a period characterized by personal witnessing. The significance of this moment has been discussed most intensively in relation to Holocaust memorials, where an extensive literature has explored the tangle of issues that arise with the passing of living memory. As James Young succinctly asked, "How will the past be remembered as it passes from living memory to history?" (2000a, 40). In what ways, then, are memorial sites that purport to honor the memory of the Second World War transformed by the disappearance of the generation that experienced it?

The analysis developed here has sought to complicate the terms of these questions by tracing ways the very categories "memorial" and "survivor" have themselves been destabilized during this span of time. In this period, the diminished presence of military survivors stands out as the most obvious marker of fundamental changes in Pearl Harbor memorialization. This demographic change, however, is joined by the creation of a new institutional umbrella for the memorial, the World War II Valor in the Pacific National Monument. The creation of a new national monument, grouping together several historic sites of the Second World War, came at nearly the same time as the dissolution of the Pearl Harbor Survivors Association—formally dissolved in December 2012, a year after the seventieth anniversary of the bombing.

These transformations could be read as a grand narrative of change, a kind of passing of the torch of national memory. But that reading would miss the more basic lesson that memorial histories are neither singular nor fixed, but rather social constructions that emerge from the interplay of contending voices, perspectives, and politics. The idea that memorials are sites of contestation has become a cliché in cultural and memory studies. But the focus on contestation is nonetheless useful for emphasizing the social and political dimensions of public history, as well as for resisting the tendency of ethnography to produce an authoritative reading of cultural texts, whether about history or something else. It is not coincidental that this book's investigation of memorial history in ceremonies, film, museum exhibits, and educational programs finds in every case that wherever Pearl Harbor history becomes most meaningful or emotional, it evokes struggles over public memory, over which voices and narratives will be inscribed in the sanctified spaces of memorial history. Nor is it surprising that, in an even more fundamental way, memorial space itself emerges as a fragile construction, vulnerable to forces that variously bureaucratize, commercialize, and commodify the past, in discourses as diverse as military heritage and world peace.

When Memory Becomes History

When the World War II Valor in the Pacific National Monument subsumed the *Arizona* memorial as part of a new institution with a wider and longer historical mandate, the National Park Service was challenged to alter its historical focus from the Pearl Harbor bombing attack to the entire Pacific War. The title of a talk presented by a park ranger in downtown Honolulu in February 2014 captured the essence of this change: "December 7th and Beyond: Expanding the Story at WWII Valor in the Pacific National Monument."[1] As described on the monument's website, the thematic scope of this wider mandate is summed up by the phrase "From Engagement to Peace," introducing a language for the new millennium in which words like "bombing" or "attack" are displaced by the idiom of "engagement."[2]

The administrative change from *Arizona* memorial to World War II Valor in the Pacific National Monument amounts to much more than an expansion of the scope of history now interpreted at the site. As the labeling implies, it is a change from memorial to monument, from an institution focused on a sacred site of military sacrifice to a collection of historic sites, most of which aren't memorials and hence more concerned with preservation and education than memorialization. These are different kinds of institutions, with different kinds of objectives (and the historical practices that go with them). The ranger's presentation about "expanding the story" talked as much about philosophy and an approach to history as about specific events or people. This is a metacommunicative story about changes in the telling of history at the memorial. As the speaker observed, "We tell different perspectives. Now this is a pretty new concept for this Monument. Before we were solely focused on the military story, and now we've incorporated many different perspectives." In fact, as noted in earlier chapters, the interest in different perspectives is a long-standing value, reflected in principles of diversity and balance that guide historical representation in national parks. The tension between representing military history and representing multiple perspectives on the Pearl Harbor attack was evident from the very first discussions of the new museum, two years before the proclamation of the monument, in 2008. The changes associated with the creation of the monument are more a matter of emphasis than a sudden innovation. The monument has created a context that legitimates and encourages multicultural and international perspectives on the past. The great irony in this is that President Bush's proclamation, created to better publicize the history of America's Good War, provided an institutional support for multivocal and balanced history—the very approach that two decades earlier was targeted as "unpatriotic" by editorial critics (Sowell 1991).[3]

The shift from memorial to monument also entails a change in the voices of history and positions from which the past is enunciated. Thus, whereas the December 7 narrative is about a violent attack, articulated primarily from the subject position of its American victims, peace seems to offer some sort of connective tissue in which American and Japanese commemorative cultures intersect (even if the readings of peace in these respective national cultures are likely to have different resonances). The tea ceremony conducted in 2011 and the dedication of the Sadako crane exhibit, in 2012, are examples of collaborative commemorative events that probably could not have been enacted prior to the creation of the monument. As discussed in chapter 2, even the events that brought American and Japanese veterans of the Pearl Harbor attack together in the 1990s and 2000s (and hence fit well within the original mandate of the *Arizona* memorial, to focus on December 7) had to be conducted outside the memorial's sacred space and time. Activities and themes once marginal, controversial, or excluded from the public spaces of the *Arizona* memorial have now become topics for history inscribed in permanent exhibits and performed in ceremonies in the very heart of sacred space, in the shrine room of the memorial. As testimony to the dramatic shift in the memorial's commemorative culture, the ranger who gave the presentation on "December 7th and Beyond" asserted that "our site has now become a mecca for reconciliation of the Pacific War. We've done peace ceremonies for Okinawans, Japanese, and many others who were affected [by the war]."

Daniel Martinez, an NPS historian who has been in the center of memorial activities since the 1980s, brings a historical perspective to thinking about these changes. In making introductory remarks at the ceremony held to dedicate the Sadako crane exhibit in September 2013, he talked about the affective politics of the peace theme in the work of the memorial:

> As the historian for the park, I have seen over the last 27 years remarkable moments. Many people in this audience are responsible for the reconciliation moves that began with President Bush in 1991 with his remarks to the Pearl Harbor survivors. The National Park Service's mis-

sion here is to share the story of the World War II Valor in the Pacific Monument. The major interpretive theme for this site is now "From Pearl Harbor [Engagement] to Peace." This new theme allows us to explore the crucible of the Pacific War and the profound lessons of a sustained peace that has existed between America and Japan for 68 years. Today's ceremony moves us closer to solidifying and celebrating the aspects of that peace. (audio recording, September 21, 2013)

Here, placed in historical perspective, the theme of peace takes on greater meaning precisely because it was once a countermemory, or alternative memory, constructed in the margins of the memorial's commemorative culture, focused on American survivors and veterans of the Second World War. Just a few years earlier, as the new museum was being planned, decisions about the final design self-consciously decided not to include the theme of reconciliation in the newly architected landscape—largely due to anticipated opposition from a segment of veteran survivors who retained wartime feelings about the Japanese (chapter 5). When Martinez said that the Sadako crane exhibit and ceremony were "moving us closer to solidifying and celebrating . . . that peace," he was effectively positioning everyone present in a genealogy of active (and affective) memory-work, spanning the lifecycle of the memorial. In the process, he implies that ritual practice at the memorial is itself a force in creating that reality.

The monument's theme, From Engagement to Peace, also entails a different kind of mythopraxis than the *Arizona* memorial's Remember Pearl Harbor. As made evident in recent ceremonial events, the theme also comes with different publics. With Japanese and local Japanese cosponsors, distinguished guests include leaders in the local Japanese community as well as state political dignitaries. With the dissolution of the Pearl Harbor Survivors Association and the near disappearance of the survivor generation, the presence of veteran survivors at these events has been limited to just a handful of honored guests. In the case of the tea ceremony, three veterans sat in a prominent position and were publicly acknowledged but otherwise had no active role in the ceremony. In the case of the Sadako crane ceremony, in 2012, a sole wheelchair-bound *Arizona* survivor, Lauren Bruner, had an important role in the ceremony as a kind of representative for his generation of veterans. As listed on the program, he gave a "Message on behalf of World War II veterans" and also performed a ribbon cutting when the exhibit was dedicated. Just at the moment in which veterans themselves had virtually disappeared from active involvement in remembrance activities, this ceremony framed Lauren Bruner's remarks as speaking on behalf of World War II veterans. Such a scripted ritual presence, standing in for an entire community of veterans, mostly absent that day, seemed to me similar to the role of Hawaiian kahuna and Buddhist priests at December 7 ceremonies, where they give blessings that perform a ritual presence for otherwise absent communities.

The incorporation of one of Sadako Sasaki's cranes in the World War II Valor in the Pacific museum is full of the same kind of ironic juxtapositions that John Dower (1996) noted in his assessment of the atomic bomb exhibit that was canceled at the Smithsonian Air and Space Museum, in 1995. In that context, Dower observed that plans to display in America's Air and Space Museum a child's melted and irradiated lunch box from the Hiroshima bombing, in the same exhibit as the fuselage of the B-29 airplane that dropped the bomb, could well find that the lunch box evokes an even more powerful moral narrative than that of the B-29, with its awesome technological power. The same ironies are now evident in the tragic image of a twelve-year-old victim of the bomb, a symbol of another kind of sacrifice, both powerful and dangerous because it potentially links with other narratives, narratives of world peace, of civilian suffering, of human rights, and of antinuclear and antimilitary movements worldwide. But that potential has yet to be realized, in part because of discursive practices that contain and compartmentalize the monument's histories.

The various perspectives that cohabit the monument's spaces often seem as parallel worlds with few points of intersection. In this study, I have had little to say, for example, about the ways the U.S. Navy, beyond its cosponsorship of the December 7 ceremonies, uses the memorial for its own ritual and political purposes. In addition to those ceremonies, the navy conducts up to two thousand reenlistment ceremonies each year at the memorial and hosts hundreds of official parties for formal visits. The coordination of use of the *Arizona* memorial for military and civilian purposes is a good example of the way two state agencies, the National Park Service and the U.S. Navy, sustain distinct commemorative cultures in the same memorial space, converging most notably in the December 7 ceremonies, described in chapter 2.

Even the teacher workshops that brought American and Japanese teachers together for the express purpose of discussing the Pacific War in comparative perspective (see chapter 6) may have done more to uncover differences in perceptions of Pearl Harbor and the atomic bombings than to foster any kind of sustained discussion on the subject. In addition to frustrations with having to work mostly in the English language, Japanese teachers in those programs talked about more difficult gaps in understanding. One of the most difficult, as reported by Yujin Yaguchi (2011), coordinator of Japanese participation in the workshops, pertained to differing views of the atomic bombings of Hiroshima and Nagasaki—events that Japanese teachers often linked to Pearl Harbor, seeing both as "testaments to the horror and folly of fighting wars," whereas many of the American teachers saw the linkage as flawed, given that the Pearl Harbor attack was unjustified in comparison to the atomic bombings that, "however unfortunate, were a necessary and ultimately justifiable means to end the war" (cf. Daizaburo 1997).

Such differences point to even more fundamental questions about just what memorials are trying to do. Whereas many Americans understand the purpose of the *Arizona* memorial as a war memorial, constructed to honor military sacrifice and service, Japanese teachers, bringing a perspective that sees the entire war as an unjustified catastrophe, tend to see it as a testimony to the devastation and pointlessness of war, similar to the peace memorials that often mediate Japanese remembrance. In his essay reflecting on the teacher workshops, Yujin Yaguchi notes the marked difference in the place of war memorials in the respective cultures of Japan and the United States. He points out that the controversial, state-run Yushukan Museum, managed by Yasukuni Shrine, is an exception to the dominant culture of peace commemoration, insofar as it is a memorial that honors service and sacrifice in war. As a result, according to Yaguchi (2011), it is a place "where few, if any, [Japanese] teachers would dare take their students for fear of triggering public controversy."

Placed in comparative perspective, transformations in the memorial's commemorative culture resemble trends in the remembrance of the Second World War in Europe and elsewhere. Scholars of memorialization have noted a widespread shift in war memory at the end of the twentieth century, a turn away from state projects celebrating national victories to a more humanitarian focus on the costs of war. Paul Williams, in his book *Memorial Museums: The Global Rush to Commemorate Atrocities* (2007), cites Jay Winter's observation (1995, 9–10) that the horrors of the Holocaust and mass (atomic) bombing of civilian populations in the war brought a sea change in commemorative culture, away from military memorials celebrating state victories to a greater focus on loss. He argues that "the emergence of memorial museums in the last decades of the twentieth century may have hastened an awareness of the cracks and falsehoods of cultural and national unity" (2007, 160). Here's a similar speculation from a study of the Memorial to the Murdered Jews of Europe, in Berlin: "Traditionally, Western monuments have celebrated military victories, heroes, and triumphs. However, years of dictatorship and crimes against civilians have challenged these architectural and political conventions. The

Second World War, and specifically the Holocaust, shifted commemorative practices. The focus on victims moved from soldiers to civilians, and memorial design turned to increased abstraction. Defeated states and perpetrators could choose to present themselves as victims, deny any wrongdoing, or face self-indictment" (Sion 2010, 244).

Whereas the simple reading of the shift from memorial to monument would seem to fit this pattern, a closer look at the range and variety of memorial practices at the *Arizona* memorial contravenes any such singular assessment. Focusing on narratives of death, tragedy, and victimization (expressed in a growing literature in tourism studies on "dark tourism") minimizes the complexity of emotional work done in memorial zones, obscuring moral possibilities that often cohabit such places. It is difficult to reconcile the kinds of history evident at the Pearl Harbor memorial, whether the triumphal narrative of military victory or the uplifting story of constructing a postwar alliance nurturing peace and prosperity, with the characterization of war memorials as places that recognize injustice and suffering. It should be clear from the account of decades of commemorative practice in and around Pearl Harbor that these activities are bound up with an ethos of military service, honor, and remembrance, now joined by narratives of peace and reconciliation—all of which remain closely articulated with dominant national histories. The mythopraxis of military remembrance, the central focus in the military museums of Pearl Harbor, is distinctly different from European commemorative cultures shaped by Holocaust memory, civilian suffering, and, for many, military defeat (what Sharon Macdonald in her study of Nuremburg calls "difficult heritage," 2009). If the Pearl Harbor case is any indication (and it bears many similarities to the memorial museum at the Normandy American Cemetery), practices of memorializing the Second World War in European and American institutions continue to draw upon profoundly different commemorative cultures.

Others have noted these same sorts of contrasts within national cultures. Certainly the rapid growth of interest in "dark tourism" everywhere suggests an emerging global taste for the tragic. One of the few studies that makes domestic comparisons across American memorials of war and violence, *Shadowed Ground: America's Landscapes of Violence and Tragedy* (Foote 2003), argues for a distinction between events that are commemorated "because they could be molded into a heroic view of the national past . . . [and] affirm a sense of patriotism, uphold community values, and honor sacrifices made for nation and community" (these include the Boston Massacre, Harpers Ferry, and Pearl Harbor) and events which are "episodes of tragedy and violence [that] remain unmarked because they conflict with or contradict this message . . . such as the history of slavery and the genocide practiced against Native Americans for centuries." The last category of events the author terms the "shadowed past," because they are "so shameful that it is nearly impossible to cast any positive light on them" (Foote 2003, 284).

And History Becomes Personal

Efforts to typologize or classify memorials (as patriotic, world heritage, military heritage, dark, war, peace, and so forth) usually end up simplifying or mystifying what goes on in such places. Differences between national memorials, especially war memorials, are not explained either by differences in their fixed representations or in the kinds of people who visit them. The portrait of the *Arizona* memorial developed in this study points rather to an ecology of meaning-making in which the past emerges from interactions between visitors and institutional practices. The social and emotional dynamism of the *Arizona* memorial is precisely its generative capacity as a site in which multiple histories, sometimes competing or contradictory, intersect—even if the intersections result in erasure or invisibility. That said, representing the memory-work of memorials has to look both outward to larger structures and histories and inward to the more intimate worlds of the people who traverse such sites, keeping in mind that it may be precisely the absent histories and the people who are not present that may be especially telling of the potentials of memorial history.

Representing the past in the memorial is itself an action that is already in history, adapting and transforming the ways the past is made relevant in the present. As Peter Carrier wrote in introducing the subject of Holocaust memorials in France and Germany, "Since the meanings ascribed to monuments are themselves conditioned by the social and political contexts in which successive spectators formulate interpretations, they are prone to historical relativism" (2005, 32). Since memorial evocations are always thoroughly social, embedded in social relations, the histories they construct and the processes through which they construct them are themselves commentaries on the emergent state of society and its history. Ironically, the story of Pearl Harbor, one of the strongest narratives of national unification in American popular culture, also evokes memories of inclusion and exclusion when told in the public spaces of a national memorial. Not only is the story of the memorial about social relations and identities in the past, telling the story in memorial space in the present (whether in ceremonies, exhibits, or films) enacts and re creates those same social relations. Whether honoring the memorial's histories or challenging them, such actions are performative moments that put the actors themselves into the histories they speak about.

Recognizing that, historically, the *Arizona* memorial had developed as a place with little relevance for the local population of Hawai'i and its histories, one of the stated objectives for the new museum, discussed in chapter 5, was to create a place that would attract residents of Hawai'i. As noted in this book's introduction, comments during a public panel discussion of the new exhibits found Japanese American critics appreciative of the changes that now include stories of internment as well as Japanese American military service. By the same token, a Native Hawaiian resident speaking on that same occasion expressed feelings of alienation, finding no place for himself or his family in the museum history, despite family memories of the bombing. Ironically, his commentary amounted to a performance of the same kind of feeling of dispossession that the new museum now describes in the little-noticed exhibit about Native Hawaiian history (Osorio 2010).

While the inclusion of an exhibit on Hawaiian history that expresses sentiments of dispossession indexes an important moment of change, it is also a placeholder for a much wider range of emotional storytelling in the native Hawaiian community that is absent at the memorial—stories of a past that tell of the loss of native culture and native lands—sentiments presented and sung in teacher workshops by Jonathan Osorio, and uncovered by Ty Tengan (2011) in oral historical work with Native Hawaiian veterans. Tengan writes, for example, of Joe Estores, a Vietnam veteran and retired lieutenant colonel of the U.S. Army, who talks of his childhood growing up on Hickam Air Force Base, adjacent to Pearl Harbor. He notes the way "Uncle Joe's" recollections of living on the base interweave a personal story with a larger history, much as the veteran survivors used to do at the memorial visitor center: "For him, it was also a playground where his Native Hawaiian and Filipino family thrived on the abundant marine resources that have all but vanished now. The personal and familial stories he tells articulate with broader histories of Indigenous engagements with U.S. empire, the traces of which are found in the bones that are unearthed in construction projects and forgotten place names that appear on old maps." Finding the park service and museum histories irrelevant to his experience of Pearl Harbor, Joe Estores uses his base privileges to give his own narrated tours—tours part cultural and part ecological, which constitute a kind of countermemory to the audio guide provided by the park service or private military tours available in the Honolulu tour markets.

Ethnographic and performative approaches to memory (Connerton 1989, 2009; Hirsch and Stewart 2005) place the social, relational contexts of historical representation in the foreground.[4] Reading history from fixed exhibits or architectural spaces alone misses both the dialogic process of meaning-making as well as the social and political process that produces them. To take the example of the exhibit about Native Hawaiian history in the museum, looking beyond the text to the conditions of its production makes it possible to see that, however ambiguous and marginal it may be, the exhibit only emerged because of the evolution of movements for the empowerment of Native Hawaiians and the influence of Native Hawaiian organizations in Hawai'i. In this case, the possibility of obtaining exhibit funding from the state's Office of Hawaiian Affairs occasioned a second look at the exhibit script. Similarly, it was the Japanese American Citizens League and the Japanese Cultural Center of Hawai'i, as well as congressional representatives with roots in the Japanese American community, who were instrumental in changing the memorial's film and in sponsoring the tea ceremony and Sadako crane exhibits. The capacity of such organizations to speak in the voice of cultural memory, combined with the willingness of the park service to embrace diversity, enabled previously marginal perspectives to move into the public spaces of memorial history in ways that would be more difficult, if not impossible, in other, less public military museums.

Recognizing the importance of dissonance or dialogic tensions in memorials does not diminish the fact that hegemonic histories or structures ensure certain narratives and voices occupy center stage. No one could study memory in the environs of Pearl Harbor and not be impressed with the force of U.S. military heritage as both ideology and ritual apparatus devoted to the values of military service, most emblematic in national death. Handelman (1997) and others have discussed the powerful symbolism of violent death understood as national sacrifice: "The placement and commemoration of national death have been central to the molding of holistic collective memory and identity in numerous states of the modern era" (1997, 86; also see Mosse 1990; Tumarkin 1994). Conjoined with images of national death are the stories of veteran heroes who braved death in war or in violent attack and, in so doing, became "models for action, and . . . desired qualities considered useful in future actions against those who threaten the state" (Donahue 2011). And these dramas, in turn, undergird the category of war veteran in American popular culture—a category that has been enlivened at the *Arizona* memorial for decades by Pearl Harbor survivors.

A close-up look at commemorative ceremonies and historical representation in an American war memorial reveals the symbolic potency of the figure of the war veteran in the social life of memorial activities. But that potency is neither static nor monolithic, especially at the present transitional moment. A historical and ethnographic look at commemorative practices at the *Arizona* memorial shows significant shifts in both the institution's memoryscape (its architecture, exhibits, and activities) as well as in the demographics of people traversing the space. The passing of the war generation has had real consequences for the evocative power of veterans' voices in the memorial landscape. While still a dominant focus of Pearl Harbor memorialization, the creation of the World War II Valor in the Pacific National Monument is making institutional histories more complex and varied.

It is not difficult to trace the path through which such voices acquire emotional force with American travelers, at least for older generations. Given that the boomer generation acquires its name from the demographics of returned soldiers starting families, a large proportion of that generation can find personal ties to the Second World War and, by implication, Pearl Harbor. Connections between family memories and national narratives are a common source of sentimentality in memorial spaces of all kinds. For sites of the Second World War, when people talk about being moved, or seeing others moved, by histories of young men (and women) in war, they are saying something about the relevance of those histories to their own lives. The emotionality in these responses is evident in styles of documentary filmmaking that rely on oral witnessing. Ken Burns's series *The War* (2007), about the American experience of the Second World War, is paradigmatic, asking ordinary citizens, mostly veterans, to recall their experience. The end product is a relentlessly nostalgic, if at times brutal, reflection on war through personal narrative, constantly framed as (a diverse) American experience.

In the course of participating in ceremonial occasions, educational programs, and so forth, I have been struck by the number of people who talk about Pearl Harbor by telling stories about the experience of relatives or ancestors in the war. In the December 7 ceremony held at the visitor center in 2013, the secretary of the American Battle Monuments Commission, Max Cleland, a decorated veteran of the Vietnam War and former senator from Georgia, gave one of the keynote addresses (following that of Admiral Harry Harris, commander of the United States Pacific Fleet). His talk, recollecting the experience of his father in the war, was given in a spontaneous, personal register—speaking from the heart in a way that was at times audibly emotional:

> I am the only child of a man who survived the Great Depression, whose only skill at the age of 19 was to plow. In 1934, joined Franklin Roosevelt's CCC Program. . . . That was my father. . . . In December of 1941,

he was employed by an unnamed truck company and had been success-
fully married to my mother . . . [when] their lives were shadowed by the
news of what happened in Pearl Harbor. For them as for their generation
and for the rest of us really, life would never be the same . . .

As a little boy growing up, I would sit by the fire, no kidding, at my
father's knee and look at his album he acquired at a place called Pearl Harbor. And that's how I first learned of the . . . mystical beauty of it, of the incredible attack, and the massive response of the United States where some
60 million fellow Americans like my father [were] drafted and served in
the war in World War II. (audio recording, December 7, 2013)

Throughout the speech, Secretary Cleland wove together his small family story
with the epic history of the war, with the effect of personalizing national history
while at the same time nationalizing family memory.

Secretary Cleland's story would no doubt have resonated with a large
portion of the American audience present for the ceremony that, like most
December 7 ceremonies, included large numbers of veterans and active-duty
military. A prominent feature of the memorial's commemorative culture is the
close coupling of (emotional) historical narratives with contemporary military
service. As traced in chapter 2, this coupling was especially evident during
the years in which the United States moved into an intensified war footing
in the Middle East. The expansion of the U.S. military in the first decade of
this millennium, deploying National Guard units and quickening rotations in
war zones for a large proportion of servicemen and servicewomen had obvious
consequences for the commemorative culture of Pearl Harbor. Just as the flood
of veterans who returned from the Second World War and the Korean War led
to the redefinition and renaming of Armistice Day to Veterans Day in 1954, so
the newly visible presence of the current generation of veterans of the wars in
Iraq and Afghanistan in U.S. society renewed the relevance and intensity of the
figure of the veteran in Second World War ceremonial practices.

This book has traced commemorative activities in one historical epoch,
an epoch that has seen veterans of the Second World War celebrated as the
greatest generation, in the 1990s, passing from the scene as the new generation
of combat veterans emerged. During this same period, leading up to and following the September 11 attacks, the United States executed two wars in Iraq
and one in Afghanistan, pursuing a so-called war on terror while escalating and
withdrawing from three ground wars in the Middle East. The well-established
ritual traditions of honoring the warrior, recounted in this book's account of
ceremonies at Pearl Harbor, also reinforce the kind of unquestioned loyalty to

lines of command required to fight wars.[5] And yet, as Thorsten (2002) astutely observed, creating military minds capable of functioning well in war is not always compatible with the kind of critical questioning required of a citizenry expected to evaluate policies that take nation-states to war.

During this same epoch of remembrance at Pearl Harbor, other civilian histories also gained greater public recognition, including movements to recognize the historic importance of Japanese American internment and the rise of a movement for Native Hawaiian sovereignty. The history of Japanese American internment continues to gain increased visibility through the creation of national historic sites at former internment camps, such as Manzanar, in 1992 (Hays 2003), Tule Lake Segregation Center, in 2006 (before becoming part of the World War II Valor in the Pacific National Monument in 2008), and most recently the Honouliuli internment site, on Oahu, just minutes away from Pearl Harbor (Falgout and Nishigaya 2014). At the same time, the movement for Native Hawaiian sovereignty gained momentum with a number of significant milestones (see appendix 2), including the U.S. Navy's returning the island of Kahoʻolawe to Native Hawaiian control (beginning with an act of Congress in 1993), an outpouring of commemorative activity around the hundredth anniversaries of the overthrow of the Hawaiian monarchy (1993) and the annexation of Hawaiʻi (1998), and the authoring of congressional legislation (the Akaka Bill) proposing a Native American–style treaty relationship between the United States government and a political body representing Native Hawaiians (first proposed in 2000). Thus, during the time of this study, the *Arizona* memorial gained renewed meaning as a military memorial sanctified by the sacrifices of servicemen and servicewomen in the December 7 bombing, while also emerging as a space for inscribing newly significant Japanese American and Native Hawaiian histories, among others. Tracing the paths of the intersections between these histories tells much of the story of the memorial's evolution in recent years.

In his book *The Texture of Memory*, James Young proposed a vision for the future of Holocaust memorials in America in which they could serve as spaces for the production of intercultural or transcultural historical understanding: "Public Holocaust memorials in America will increasingly be asked to invite many different occasionally competing groups of Americans into their spaces. African Americans and Korean Americans, Native Americans and Jews will necessarily come to share common spaces of memory, if not common memory itself. In this, the most ideal of American visions, every group in America may eventually come to recall its past in light of another group's historical memory" (cited in Lippard 1999, 129; Young 1993). The recent history of memorial practice at Pearl Harbor suggests that such a vision is made more difficult when the multiple histories in memorial zones are already entangled in narratives of race and nation. Rather than a forum for expanding vision by learning of other histories, the points of intersection often demand rethinking and revaluing one's own history. And the possibilities for historical rethinking are further complicated by the fact that memorial histories are often personal stories embedded in affective structures of memory built up over the course of a lifetime, hence the privileged relationship that customarily positions survivors and close relatives of the dead as guardians of memory, adjudicators often granted veto power over the narratives allowed into memorial history. Sturken (2007a, 218), writing about the World Trade Center site, described a situation much like the early phases of memorial evolution at Auschwitz or Pearl Harbor: "Any attempt to situate 9/11 within broader historical contexts at the site of Ground Zero, which the canceled International Freedom Center attempted to do, would inevitably clash with the inscription of the site as one of unique and immense loss."

As seen in the case of the *Arizona* memorial, however, these politics of memory are themselves in motion. With the passing of the survivor generation, sacred memory loosens its grip on public memory, allowing space for other narratives and even, to a degree, the desacralization of history, as in the move from memorial to monument. At Auschwitz, the international council that oversees the museum and memorial made a decision in recent years to update the material presented by its exhibitions and tour guides so that it would better address contemporary educational goals. A particular goal is to make the place more relevant for students (an estimated 850,000 in 2010). Driven by the realization that such youthful visitors are not likely even to have grandparents that experienced the war, plans for revamping exhibits aim to provide more context (Kimmelman 2011), even if such diversification evokes challenges from survivors. One of the stated aims of the expansion of exhibits was to provide more understanding of the mechanisms of genocide, making the Auschwitz Museum and Memorial more relevant to present-day crises. One letter-writer reacting to these plans, however, said that he was "appalled at what [he] considered a universalization and dejudaization of the Auschwitz death camp."[6]

Another primary driver of plans for redevelopment at Auschwitz is the rise in numbers of visitors, who must be moved through the site more and more efficiently as time goes by. Tim Cole, in his book *Selling the Holocaust* (2000), writes about the segmentation of the Auschwitz landscape into areas made suitable and desirable for tourist consumption that often have little to do with the history of atrocity there (2000, 110). The ethnographic history of memorialization at Pearl Harbor shows that differences between the *Arizona* memorial and the military museums at Pearl Harbor also represent a segmentation of memorial space into zones that differ in their mix of sacred and touristic histories.

Pearl Harborland

The new visitor center and online ticketing system that offer access to the *Arizona* memorial and other museum sites have significantly increased attendance since opening in 2010. But the greater numbers coming through the entryway are in many cases not visiting the memorial shrine. Whether content with a stroll through the museum and grounds or preferring to spend time at the battleship and aviation museums instead, the proportion of visitors who skip the memorial has risen from a negligible amount before the new visitor center to around 25 percent today.[7] There are many possible explanations for this, including the increase in package-tour visitors from Asia, who either do not have time on their schedules or do not have the interest, or both (see chapter 4). The overall effect for the historic landscape of Pearl Harbor is that the more secular monument increasingly displaces the sacred space of the memorial. The experience of visiting the memorial itself, which begins with the documentary film, carefully scripted to create a reflective mood prior to visiting the shrine room and wall of names, is less and less the focal point for travelers visiting Pearl Harbor.

As discussed in chapter 4 the Ford Island development plan, created to provide more base housing and expand base facilities, came close to creating a Waikiki-style mini-mall, or at least a shore-side restaurant and shopping area in the area of the current visitor center for the World War II Valor in the Pacific National Monument. If the old *Arizona* memorial museum had not become unstable, necessitating a major reconstruction project, it is quite possible that the space would have been filled by a larger and permanent version of the shopping plaza, with a Second World War theme, that occupied the area in 2006 and 2007. Although the current visitor center and museum were designed under the auspices of a federal agency (the National Park Service), the same forces of commodification are at work there as well. The park service is constantly under pressure to supplement federal funding (a responsibility of its nonprofit partner Pacific Historic Parks) and has developed a five-year strategic plan that talks about "customers," rather than just visitors. Sounding very much like the work of a corporate public affairs office, the strategic plan reads, "We provide good customer service—both to internal & external customers.

Our customer service is personalized, we attempt to accommodate each visitor on an individual basis" (National Park Service 2013, 2).

The shift toward concern with universalized customer service is matched by changes in the ways travelers engage with Pearl Harbor history. In the place of rangers and volunteers who once spoke with people about the history of the attack, visitors may now purchase an audio guide and listen to the numerous video kiosks in the exhibit halls. In the past the National Park Service would review items sold in the bookshop to ensure their appropriateness and educational value. Today bookstore visitors find Pearl Harbor mugs and refrigerator magnets selling alongside Sadako crane earrings. The park service with its nonprofit partner recently introduced a new souvenir photo opportunity—something the other military museums had been doing for years and had been available in the short-lived tent mall (figure 4.3) but had never quite seemed to fit at the memorial. Finally, after some vetting, a large mural backdrop showing the USS *Arizona* at full speed off Diamond Head, was introduced in spring 2015, providing visitors an opportunity to pose for $20 souvenir photos (figure c.1).

Educational programs at the monument are also being planned with one eye on capital development. Plans for a new Pearl Harbor Institute envision fee-for-service programs that can be self-sustaining. A planning document drafted by consultants to the park service and Pacific Historic Parks describes the objectives of the new institute as developing the capacity to "market programs, magnify educational impact, build new markets, and leverage the Pearl Harbor brand." Brainstorming for possible programs for the new institute included ideas for a daylong tour that would follow the American narrative of the Pacific War that begins on December 7, passes through the submarine war presented at the USS *Bowfin* Museum, and then ponders the "turning point" of the Battle of Midway at the aviation museum, before ending up on the surrender on the deck of the USS *Missouri*. Travelers could expect to learn about state of the art weaponry recently deployed in America's wars in Asia or the Middle East before concluding back at the World War II Valor in the Pacific National Monument, in the area near the Sadako crane exhibit and Tree of Life. There, one executive surmised, tongue in cheek, guests could hear about the monument's theme of "engagement to peace" before being given a shopping opportunity in the gift store nearby (see map I.1, in the introduction).

In January 2009, before the new visitor center had opened its doors, local newspapers reported that the USS *Arizona* memorial "tops list of favorite visitor sites." The director of tourism programs at the Hawai'i Tourism Authority was quoted as saying that the top ten destinations were all "good family oriented types of attractions" (Dingeman 2009)—something confirmed more recently

FIGURE C.1
Souvenir photo opportunity. Pearl Harbor Visitor Center. May 29, 2015.
Photo by author.

when the park service proudly announced that the World War II Valor in the Pacific National Monument would receive a "2014 FamilyFun Travel Award" as "one of the top ten vacation destinations" in the "historic site" category.[8] The blurb on the Family Fun website describes the monument as a "constellation of historic sites paying tribute to fallen heroes": "This constellation of historic sites anchored by Pearl Harbor traces the dramatic story of the Pacific War and pays tribute to its fallen heroes through moving first-person accounts, photographs, memorabilia, artifacts, and a memorial hovering above the sunken remains of the battleship USS *Arizona*."[9]

It is not surprising that the Good War is alive and well in arenas of family fun. Pearl Harbor survivors were always popular with American youth. As glimpsed in foregoing chapters, they were lively interlocutors, often human-

FIGURE C.2
Shrine room display panel, USS *Arizona* Memorial. March 22, 2015.
Photo by author.

izing themselves when interacting with visitors through stories, jokes, and satire. Less evident on that stage was the type of skeptical or critical talk that one would hear at survivor association lunches or in more private conversations. John Bodnar, writing about the differences between the glow of nostalgia coded in public symbols of the Good War and the realities of veterans' experiences captures some of the dissonance that I noticed in my days of associating with the survivors when he observes, "In the effort to pay homage, however, many of these cultural products emphasize the virtue of the warriors at the expense of the cynicism and confusion many felt when they were young. The National WWII Memorial in Washington, D.C., does this when it erases a legacy of criticism and loss. Visits to the memorial by aging veterans have proven positively therapeutic, but may also trigger emotional reactions that are not well understood today" (Bodnar 2009, 18).

A number of the military survivors I got to know over the years talked about their experience volunteering at the *Arizona* memorial as therapeutic. Now, at the cusp of living memory, the progressive alteration of the memorial landscape has unnerved some of the few who remain. Even though the Pearl Harbor Survivors Association dissolved and turned over its files to the Pacific Historic Parks (PHP) organization, a former officer based in California recently requested a meeting with PHP to inquire about what he saw as an emphasis on commercialization of the site. Another of the local veteran survivors, who at the time of writing continues to volunteer one morning each week, commented that the area feels to him "like a playground." He is disturbed to have heard that the current administration has asked park rangers not to refer to the memorial as a cemetery. In line with these shifts in the affective meaning of memorial space, the lines between sacred and secular now intersect in complex ways. Where the Tree of Life from Alfred Preis's shrine room now stands as an exhibit between the museum and theater at the visitor center (and is represented as a graphic motif on the display for the Sadako crane exhibit), the shrine room itself has recently taken on the feel of an exhibit with the addition of a display panel explaining its history and significance to visitors (figure c.2).

What is perhaps most telling about these developments in recent years is that at least some of those who are most honored in the memorial landscape feel unsettled there. Many never liked the label "park," with its recreational connotations, even though that designation is a necessary part of inclusion in the national park system. The sense of unease is likely less a response to outright commercialization than the more fundamental realization that memory has become history, that memorial space, which for long had extended its sanctity to the visitor center, is now itself increasingly incorporated within a landscape of a find-your-own-meaning historiography associated with discourses of preservation, education, and diplomacy—an ironic if perhaps inevitable twist to the present moment in the history of memorial memory. One of the more profound ironies in this latest phase in the transformation of Pearl Harbor memory is that the lament of at least some of the attack's military survivors would in the end resonate with the sentiments of sadness, loss, and disconnection voiced by Native Hawaiians reflecting on their displacement from the places of their ancestral memory.

APPENDIX 1

Pearl Harbor Bombing Statistics (December 7, 1941)

Japanese attack force: four aircraft carriers, two heavy cruisers, thirty-five submarines, two light cruisers, two battleships, and eleven destroyers, nine oilers. Aircraft: First wave: 183 planes; Second wave: 170 planes. "Remembering Pearl Harbor: A Pearl Harbor Fact Sheet" National World War II Museum. accessed July 16, 2015, http://www.nationalww2museum.org/assets/pdfs/pearl-harbor-fact-sheet-1.pdf.

U.S. losses: Of the total 2,390 U.S. killed, 1,177 died in the explosion of the *Arizona*. Out of a crew of 1,511, only 334 survived. The subsequent fires continued for two and a half days, at the end of which time only 107 of the dead could be positively identified ("People," National Park Service, accessed June 15, 2015, http://www.nps.gov/valr/historyculture/people.htm).

All U.S. ships, except the *Arizona*, *Utah*, and *Oklahoma*, were salvaged and later saw action. The *Arizona* and *Utah* remain in place as memorials to their lost crews. The salvaged *Oklahoma* was lost in transit but a USS *Oklahoma* memorial on Ford Island was dedicated December 7, 2007.

Table Appendix 1. DECEMBER 7, 1941 LOSSES

	United States	Japan
Personnel Killed	2,390	64
Navy	1,999	64
Marine Corps	109	
Army and Army Air Forces	233	
Civilian	49	
Personnel Wounded	1,178	unknown
Navy	710	
Marine Corps	69	

	United States	Japan
Army and Army Air Forces	364	
Civilian	35	
Ships		
Sunk or Beached*	12	5
Damaged**	9	
Aircraft		
Destroyed	164	29
Damaged	159	74

* All U.S. ships, except *Arizona*, *Utah*, and *Oklahoma* were salvaged and later saw action.
** Figures are subject to further review.
Source: "People," National Park Service, accessed June 15, 2015, http://www.nps.gov/valr/history culture/people.htm.

Chronology of Hawaiian Political History, Postcontact

1778	Captain James Cook lands in the Hawaiian Islands.
March 31, 1820	First American missionaries arrive in Hawai'i.
November 28, 1843	Great Britain and France recognize Hawai'i's independence.
1873	Major General J. M. Schofield and Brigadier General B. S. Alexander visit Hawai'i under secret instructions from the U.S. secretary of war to examine the ports of the Hawaiian Islands for their strategic value.
1875	The first Reciprocity Treaty between the U.S. and the Hawaiian Kingdom (King Kalakaua) is ratified, giving mutual free trade rights (takes effect 1876).
July 7, 1887	The "Bayonet Constitution" is forced on King Kalakaua by a mostly white coalition of business interests, the Hawaiian League, or "Annexation Club." The Reciprocity Treaty is extended, giving the United States exclusive naval rights to Pearl Harbor.
January 17, 1893	Queen Lili'uokalani is deposed by a "Committee of Safety," made up of mission and business interests with support of U.S. Marines and diplomatic representative. A "provisional government" is established.
December 18, 1893	President Cleveland asks Congress to restore Queen Lili'uokalani to the throne.
July 4, 1894	Republic of Hawai'i declared by provisional government.
July 7, 1898	Hawai'i is annexed to the United States by congressional resolution.

1899	The United States establishes a naval base at Pearl Harbor.
April 30, 1900	The Organic Act makes Hawai'i a territory of the United States.
December 7, 1941	Japan bombs Pearl Harbor; martial law declared (1941–44).
August 21, 1959	Hawai'i becomes a state in the United States after a plebiscite.
1978	Office of Hawaiian Affairs created by a Hawaiian state constitutional convention.
November 23, 1993	President Clinton signs U.S. Public Law 103 150, the "Apology Resolution," apologizing for the illegal overthrow of the Hawaiian kingdom.
2000	Hawaiian senator Daniel Akaka introduces the Native Hawaiian Government Reorganization Act (the "Akaka Bill") to provide federal recognition for Native Hawaiians similar to that given to North American Indian tribes.
December 16, 2009	A congressional house committee passes the Akaka Bill (S1011/HR2314), where it remains, not passed by the Senate.

Chronology of Internment of Japanese Americans
and Japanese Residents

December 9, 1941   Sand Island detention camp opened in Honolulu to process internees from Hawai'i. With many sent to mainland camps, an estimated 1,440 Japanese, Germans, and Italians would be interned at five locations in the Hawaiian Islands.

February 19, 1942   President Roosevelt signs Executive Order No. 9066, authorizing secretary of war to establish "military areas" and exclude "any or all persons" necessary.

August 7, 1942   Western Defense Commander announces the completion of removal of more than 120,000 Japanese Americans from their homes.

March 1, 1943   Sand Island camp, Hawai'i, is closed and remaining internees transferred to the new 160-acre Honouliuli Internment Camp, where between twelve hundred and fourteen hundred local Japanese would be interned with about one thousand family members.

December 17, 1944   The war department announces revocation of West Coast mass exclusion orders, effective January 2, 1945.

December 18, 1944   In *Korematsu v. United States*, the U.S. Supreme Court rules that compulsory exclusion is justified during circumstances of "emergency and peril," upholding conviction of Korematsu for resisting internment.

July 2, 1948   Evacuation Claims Act passed, giving internees until January 3, 1950, to file claims against the government for damages or loss of property.

February 19, 1976	President Ford formally rescinds Executive Order No. 9066.
June 23, 1983	The Commission of Wartime Relocation and Internment of Civilians issues its report, titled "Personal Justice Denied," concluding that exclusion, expulsion, and incarceration were not justified by military necessity, but rather were based on "race prejudice, war hysteria, and a failure of political leadership."
November 10, 1983	The U.S. District Court in San Francisco vacates the conviction of Fred Korematsu for evading internment.
August 10, 1988	President Reagan signs the Civil Liberties Act of 1988 into law, authorizing payment of reparations to those interned during Second World War.
January 1998	Fred Korematsu, who challenged the constitutionality of the internment policy, receives the Presidential Medal of Freedom.
December 21, 2006	President George W. Bush signs Public Law 109–441 creating a $38 million grant program to preserve and interpret ten internment camp sites.

APPENDIX 4

Very Brief Filmography of Pearl Harbor Official and Feature Films

1943   *December 7th* (long version). Directed by John Ford and Gregg Toland. U.S.
        Navy. 83 minutes. In 1943 John Ford recruited cinematographer Gregg Toland
        (*Citizen Kane*, *The Grapes of Wrath*) to direct the war department's film about
        Pearl Harbor. Despite the lack of actual combat footage of the attack, filming
        on-site in Hawai'i produced an 83-minute feature, including an overview of
        twentieth-century Hawai'i. The film's use of mock footage to re-create the
        battle has been used by many other films. For various reasons it was never re-
        leased. John Ford salvaged parts of it for a short documentary released in 1943.

1943   *December 7th* (short version). Directed by John Ford with film production
        from Gregg Toland. U.S. Navy. 37 minutes. The short version of *December
        7th* was produced by John Ford, editing down the long version for wartime
        fundraising and morale-building campaigns. Released in 1943, it received an
        academy award for best short documentary in 1944.

1970   *Tora! Tora! Tora!* Richard Fleischer, Toshio Masuda, Kinji Fukasaku. Hollywood:
        Twentieth Century Fox. 143 minutes. *Tora! Tora! Tora!* was a binational produc-
        tion that attempts to tell the story from both sides of the Pacific. The American
        director Richard Fleischer worked with the Japanese director Akira Kurosawa,
        before he withdrew and was replaced by Toshio Masuda and Kinji Fukasaku.

1980   USS *Arizona* Memorial orientation film. Produced by the U.S. Navy for Na-
        tional Park Service Visitor Center. Honolulu, HI: 25 minutes. Not for sale.

1992   USS *Arizona* Memorial orientation film. *How Shall We Remember Them?*
        Directed by Lance Bird, American Studies Film Center. Produced by National
        Park Service. 23 minutes. Not for sale.

2001   *Pearl Harbor*. Michael Bay, director; Jerry Bruckheimer, producer. Walt Disney
        Studios. 183 minutes. *Pearl Harbor* created a big marketing sensation in the
        spring and summer of 2001. The film relies heavily on special effects and lots
        of explosions. Randall Wallace (*Braveheart*) wrote the script around a classic
        love triangle involving Ben Affleck, Josh Hartnett, and Kate Beckinsale.

NOTES

Introduction. MEMORIALIZING HISTORY

1. The panel, organized by the Hawai'i Museum Association, included three museum professionals offering critiques of the new exhibits with responses from three members of the National Park Service team who oversaw the design and installation.

2. Except where individuals are identifiable from their public status, I have used pseudonyms throughout.

3. In line with usage adopted in current scholarship on indigenous Hawaiians (Tengan 2008, 229n2), I use the capitalized phrase *Native Hawaiian* to refer to people who self-identify as indigenous based on descent from ancestors residing in Hawai'i prior to the arrival of Europeans. The Hawaiian language term *Kānaka Maoli* is often used to refer to Native Hawaiians to clarify distinctions between those indigenous to the land and those who reside in Hawai'i. However, for purposes of communicability, I opt for the English language phrase, capitalized to distinguish it from the less specific meanings of "native."

4. "Information for 9/11 Family Members," the National September 11 Memorial and Museum at the World Trade Center Foundation, Inc., accessed June 14, 2015, http://www.911memorial.org/information-911-family-members.

5. "The United States Vietnam War Commemoration," U.S. Department of Defense, accessed July 15, 2015, http://www.vietnamwar50th.com.

6. Sheryl Gay Stolberg, "Paying Respects, Pentagon Revives Vietnam, and War Over Truth," *New York Times*, October 9, 2014, accessed July 15, 2015, http://www.nytimes.com/2014/10/10/us/pentagons-web-timeline-brings-back-vietnam-and-protesters-.html.

7. For a recent example, consider the controversy over a revised "curriculum framework" released in the summer of 2014 by the College Board to guide teachers preparing their students for Advanced Placement history exams. A recent article about this began with the very familiar refrain: "Navigating the tension between patriotic inspiration and historical thinking, between respectful veneration and critical engagement, is an especially difficult task" (James R. Grossman, "The New History Wars," *New York Times*, September 1, 2014, accessed June 14, 2015, http://www.nytimes.com/2014/09/02/opinion/the-new-history-wars.html).

8. An estimated one thousand journalists registered to cover the commemoration (*Honolulu Star-Bulletin*, December 6, 1991, A24), producing cover stories in *Time*, *Newsweek*, *U.S. News & World Report*, *The Wall Street Journal*, as well numerous television specials and documentary film projects.

9. A research grant from the Wenner-Gren Foundation supported a collaborative project in which Marjorie Kelly and I worked at the memorial for about one year spanning 1994–95.

10. Wishing initially to call the monument "World War II Victory in the Pacific National Monument," the Bush administration was persuaded to call the new entity "World War II Valor in the Pacific National Monument," toning down the triumphal rhetoric in deference to contemporary alliances and sensibilities. Created through an executive order on December 5, 2008, the monument clusters together nine historic sites of the Second World War in Hawai'i, Alaska, and California (Tule Lake internment camp). Among these, the USS *Arizona* Memorial is by far the most visited and well known, although the inclusion of memorials to two other ships destroyed in the Pearl Harbor bombing, the USS *Utah* Memorial and the USS *Oklahoma* Memorial, significantly expanded official memorial space inside the Pearl Harbor Naval Base. For the full text of President Bush's proclamation, see http://georgewbush-whitehouse.archives.gov/news/releases/2008/12/20081205-2.html.

11. "Accents and Languages" (4:05) on compact disc, *Andy Bumatai, Stand Up Comic*, 1984, 1994.

12. With the creation of a visitor center museum, the memorial had to decide about the temporal scope of its historical mission, originally drawing a narrow bead on one day and the few hours of the bombing and destruction, later encompassing enough history to include the buildup in international tensions and the aftermath of the attack in terms of recovery and counterattack in the Pacific, up to the Battle of Midway (White 1997a).

13. In his book *Spitting Image*, the Vietnam veteran and sociology professor Jerry Lembcke analyzes stories about the maltreatment of returning Vietnam veterans as a kind of self-propagating urban myth (1998).

14. On two occasions, the park service has granted permission to scholars to interview Japanese visitors at the memorial: first, Patricia Masters, a University of Hawai'i doctoral student during the anniversary year 1991, and then in 2002, Yujin Yaguchi, professor at the University of Tokyo specializing in American studies and tourism in Hawai'i. Yaguchi's study, drawing on both interviews and a survey of comment sheets written in Japanese, shows that the Japanese tend to see the *Arizona* as a peace memorial, although with pronounced generational differences. He also found a tendency among many Japanese travelers to link Hiroshima and Pearl Harbor as two parts of the same story, with both serving as centers for learning about international peace today.

15. On September 16, 1991, the *Honolulu Advertiser* ran a front-page story under the headline "VETS: LET'S 'REMEMBER PEARL HARBOR': And 'Get It Right,' Some Say, Angry at Memorial's Version of Story."

16. The individual involved, a prominent member of the local chapter of the Pearl Harbor Survivors Association, would later that same year be invited to sit in a position

of honor near President George Bush (senior) at the commemorative ceremony held on board the memorial on December 7, 1991.

Chapter One. SURVIVOR VOICES

1. For a list of civilians killed during the attack, see "Civilian Casualties," National Park Service, accessed June 15, 2015, http://www.nps.gov/valr/historyculture/civilian -casualties.htm.

2. In the course of our research at the memorial in the 1990s, Marjorie Kelly and I recorded and transcribed thirty of the theater presentations given by rangers and volunteers. We also recorded ten lectures given in the museum during that decade, the majority by Pearl Harbor survivors. We followed up with interviews with most of these speakers to encourage them to talk in an open-ended way about their presentations, their views of the memorial and its messages, as well as their own life stories.

3. Most of the survivors discussed here are presented with real names. They were public figures who, late in life, devoted themselves to telling their stories. My departure from the usual practice of giving consultants pseudonyms is done to honor their intent.

4. Like a number of the veterans' talks, Joe Morgan's is well honed after some years of practice. In fact, not long after the fiftieth anniversary, he decided to print his talk and, with the help of his son, had it photocopied for distribution.

5. I refer to Reverend Joe Morgan and other survivor volunteers discussed here with their first names, because that's how they were known, and are remembered, at the *Arizona* memorial.

6. A number of publications revisiting the history of the 442nd Regimental Combat Team make use of the phrase *fighting two wars.* See also the regiment's website: Go For Broke National Education Center, accessed July 19, 2015, http://www.goforbroke.org /about_us/about_us_educational.php.

7. Stanley Igawa once served as post commander for his local VFW post.

8. The former treasurer of the Honolulu chapter of the association, Sterling Cale, told me that after the dissolution of the PHSA he had dispersed the remaining funds (not a large amount) among the seven or eight members of the chapter still alive and well in Honolulu.

9. "From 5:30 to 7 p.m. at Punchbowl, AARP Hawai'i and the Veterans History Project will honor veterans with a candle-lighting ceremony. About 1,700 candles will be lighted to honor America's veterans, who are dying at a rate of about 1,700 each day" (Curtis Lum, "Commemoration of Pearl Harbor Attack Begins Today," *Honolulu Advertiser*, December 5, 2003).

10. This is how the contents and purpose were described on the tape jacket: "Designed to supplement existing lesson plans and curricula, this teacher's guide provides survivor stories, oral histories, archive photographs, timelines, charts, and maps as tools for use in World War II classroom instruction. Includes a 173 page binder and 43 minute *Pearl Harbor Remembered* video. Video contains survivor interviews of their personal recollections and reflections of December 7, 1941."

11. During this time commercial interests were also busy producing videos and documentaries that featured survivor testimonials, such as the 1990s production *We*

Were There . . . Pearl Harbor Survivors: Eyewitnesses to History. As the jacket says, in bold letters, "PEARL HARBOR SURVIVORS REMEMBER . . . from this scene of unimaginable hell came survivors of the attack. More than half a century has passed yet the events of that day are as vividly painted in their memories as were the flames of Pearl Harbor against the morning sky. That was December 7, 1941. These are their stories" (Panorama International Productions Inc., Burbank, CA).

12. The Witness to History program was launched initially with assistance from the U.S. Navy, which donated the use of its videoconferencing facilities on the Pearl Harbor Navy Base.

13. That website, originally found at pearlharborstories.org, has since been taken down. That site was comparable to www.wwiimemorial.com and www.loc.gov/vets, mentioned in the text above and still accessible as of June 15, 2015.

14. Those videos can be found at http://www.nps.gov/valr/photosmultimedia/videos .htm.

15. Credits for film sponsors appear as follows: Northrop Grumman Corporation / Boeing / General Dynamics / Pacific Historic Parks / Raytheon Company / State of Hawai'i / Triwest Healthcare Alliance.

Chapter Two. CULTURES OF COMMEMORATION

1. Decades after Lyndon Johnson declared December 7 "Pearl Harbor Day," in 1966, on the occasion of the twenty-fifth anniversary, Congress passed Public Law 103-308, in 1994, making December 7 "National Pearl Harbor Remembrance Day" and directing the president to issue a proclamation each year calling on citizens to observe the day in memory of Americans who died in the attack.

2. Naval base commanders spoke in 2005, 2007, 2008 (shared with a veteran of the famous Doolittle Raid), 2010 (shared), and 2012. Federal officials, who often were also veterans, such as Daniel Inouye, spoke in 2002, 2010 (Head of the Fish and Wildlife Service), and 2013 (Head of the American Battle Monuments Commission) while historians spoke in 2004 (Paul Stillwell) and 2009 (Allen Millett), and media figures in 2003 (Ernest Borgnine) and 2006 (Tom Brokaw).

3. Indicative of local Hawaiian attitudes toward the anniversary as an opportunity for expressions of reconciliation, a state planning group, including members of the park service, proposed that American children, led by the governor's wife, and Japanese children, led by a representative from a Japanese sister city, join hands in dropping flowers into the harbor.

4. Beginning in early 1991, in the lead-up to the fiftieth anniversary of the attack on December 7, the Honolulu press began making inquiries to the State Department regarding Japanese participation in the commemoration. In September, in response to an inquiry of Brien Hallett, faculty member in peace and conflict studies at the University of Hawai'i, the State Department read him the following statement (Hallett 1991, 13): "In our commemoration of the anniversary of Pearl Harbor, we will honor the memory of the service men who lost their lives and reflect upon this historic turning point in American history. It would be wrong to interpret this commemoration as directed

against Japan in any way. It is not and will not be an anti-Japanese event. . . . However, we do not intend to extend any official invitations to foreign attendees. Those foreign guests desiring to attend would do so unofficially and their status would be the same as other observers from the general public" (Transcription of U.S. State Department statement, September 4, 1991).

5. The headline of Honolulu's morning paper on December 4 was "JAPAN ACCEPTS BLAME FOR STARTING WAR IN PACIFIC." Immediately underneath, however, another headline read "SOME PEARL HARBOR SURVIVORS SEE JAPAN'S 'REMORSE' AS TOO BELATED." Gerald Glaubitz, head of the Pearl Harbor Survivors Association at the time, said in a television special: "Everybody has said, 'Well, why don't you forgive and forget?' and—for several reasons. Number one, we were not at war. It was not a battle. It was a sneak attack in any way you want to name it" (ABC News Special, December 5, 1991).

6. George Bush's phrasing was actually much the same as that used twenty-five years earlier, when Mitsuo Fuchida, the Japanese pilot turned evangelist, held a Bible with Reverend Akaka "as old memories are revived with old rancor gone" (*Honolulu Star-Bulletin*, December 7, 1991, 1). In 1991 the "end of rancor" again had headline status: "BUSH CALLS FOR AN END TO RANCOR" (*Honolulu Sunday Star-Bulletin and Advertiser*, December 8, 1991, A7), with an article quoting much of the rest of the speech: "I have no rancor in my heart towards Germany or Japan—none at all. I hope you have none in yours. This is no time for recrimination. World War II is over. It is history. We won. We crushed totalitarianism; and when that was done, we helped our enemies give birth to democracies. We reached out, both in Europe and in Asia, and made our enemies our friends. We healed their wounds and in the process, we lifted ourselves up . . . No, I have no rancor in my heart (*Honolulu Sunday Star-Bulletin and Advertiser*, December 8, 1991, B3)."

7. Here Fiske actually said, "When we met in 1941." Because he's talking about the time he and Abe actually met and became friends. I have corrected this to "1991."

8. As an American scholar in Japanese studies doing graduate work in Hawai'i, Marie Thorsten initially volunteered to work as an interpreter and facilitator at the Punchbowl ceremony in 1995, and later coincidentally found herself meeting the same group of veterans in Japan. She then took up the challenge of comparing the political contexts of friendship ceremonies in both nations through the sixtieth anniversary, in 2001.

9. These words are taken from the ceremony's program notes. Specifically, the notes explain the name for the tea ceremony, *Okenchashiki*, as "a sacred tea ceremony to the spirits of the war dead for world peace, conducted without words or music, allows for all participants, regardless of language, nationality or religious beliefs to share in a spiritual communion together."

10. The program listed this as "Kuninoshizume and the U.S. taps." Kuninoshizume is a Japanese military march that, nostalgic to some, is also associated, like all military signs and symbols, with conflicts over the nation's military past.

11. The Hawaiian Urasenke School was convening its own anniversary celebration at the same time, thus making the Pearl Harbor ceremony a prominent symbol of the school's ability to advance the public message of peace. For more than a year following the ceremony, the school's webpage featured a photo of Grand Master Sen performing the ceremony on the memorial (http://www.urasenkehawaii.org, accessed June 15, 2015).

12. An English translation of the remarks was made available on the website of the consul general of Japan at Honolulu, www.honolulu.us.emb-japan.go.jp/en/speech /speech071911.pdf, accessed December 21, 2013.

13. Wesley Pruden, "Crashing the Party at Pearl Harbor," *Washington Times*, July 22, 2011, accessed December 21, 2013, http://www.washingtontimes.com/news/2011/jul/22 /pruden-crashing-the-party-at-pearl-harbor/#.

14. Gary Graybill, "Japanese Tea Ceremony on the USS *Arizona* Memorial," Gary's reflections blog, July 28, 2011, accessed May 21, 2013, http://garysreflections.blogspot.fr /2011/07/japanese-tea-ceremony-on-uss-arizona.html.

15. Associated Press, "USS *Arizona* Memorial to Host Japanese Tea Rite," *Honolulu Star Adviser*, July 18, 2011, accessed July 21, 2011, http://www.staradvertiser.com/news /20110718_USS_Arizona_Memorial__to_host_Japanese_tea_rite.html.

Chapter Three. MEMORIAL FILM

1. The standard response to the question of Japanese American loyalty during the war is that there were no instances of sabotage or even documented spying, with the exception of highly disputed reading of formerly classified Japanese cable communications (Lowman 2001). Perhaps because that view is so prevalent, the Honolulu-based journalist and Pearl Harbor historian Burl Burlingame included the belief in a list of "myths" in a pamphlet written for the media, citing two or three examples, such as John Mikuma, who regularly acted as a taxi driver for the military attaché, gathering intelligence (Burlingame 1991b, 18). Even these, however, have no historical documentation in the form of arrest or trial records.

2. "While we believe that the film provides an historically accurate account of the event in that day in history, we recognize that there are multiple perspectives on how best to interpret and present this information" (Letter from NPS superintendent to Clayton C. Ikei, president, Japanese American Citizens League, Honolulu chapter, June 10, 1999, files of the author).

3. The internment of 120,000 Japanese residents (the large majority U.S. citizens) was determined to be unjust and immoral by the 1988 Civil Liberties Act, signed into law by President Ronald Reagan, that provided reparations to former internees (see Hayashi 1995; Ichihashi and Chang 1997; Taylor 1993; United States Commission on Wartime Relocation and Internment of Civilians 1992 [1983]). Nonetheless, conservative commentators continue to argue for the legality and necessity of internment. Michelle Malkin's book *In Defense of Internment: The Case for "Racial Profiling" in World War II and the War on Terror* (2004), for example, argues for applying Second World War internment policies to Muslim Americans in the "war on terror."

4. "Review of Historical Data of Park Orientation Film '*How Shall We Remember Them*' Sequence Regarding General Walter Short, the Japanese-American Community and Sabotage," by Daniel Martinez, park historian, National Park Service, USS *Arizona* Memorial (H-1815), October 28, 1998, 4.

5. Excerpts of letter from Commander John Ford (Honolulu) to William J. Donovan, head of Office of War Information, Washington, D.C., included with letter of William

Donovan to Frank Knox, secretary of the navy, Washington, D.C., April 13, 1942, National Archives RG 107–47–8, ASW 014.311 Hawaii.

6. The statement released by the War Department reads, "The War Department will be very glad to obtain a motion picture which will present factually the conditions existing in Hawaii prior to December 7 and the story of the Japanese attack there on December 7 and the present conditions in Hawaii as they pertain to preparations for future action." The screen then fills with a note from the secretary of the navy, saying, "I am very desirous of obtaining for the Navy Department a complete motion picture factual presentation of the attack on Pearl Harbor on December 7. As you well know, the president has stressed the highly historical import of this date."

7. *Tora! Tora! Tora!* "treats its material as historical event . . . with meticulous attention to detail, to timings and characterizations that are not controversial. Watching it, it is as if one has picked up a history book and the words one reads become images. It is a docudrama of the sort that is now done regularly on PBS—a 'reenactment' of historical events in a sober manner, as factual as possible, following actual newsreels and photographs" (Basinger 1986, 194–95). See also Thorsten and White 2010.

8. "Lest We Forget!" Hearst Newsreel HNR 2054, 13.242, February 4, 1942, Los Angeles: UCLA Film and Television Archive Commercial Services.

9. Letter from Lowell Mellett, chief, Bureau of Motion Pictures, to James Forrestal, undersecretary of the navy, December 1, 1942, National Archives RG 208, entry 64, box 1433. Censorship of the film was initiated by Nelson Poynter, head of the bureau in Hollywood.

10. Letter from Lowell Mellett, chief, Bureau of Motion Pictures, to secretary of war and secretary of the navy, April 29, 1943, National Archives RG 208, entry 64, box 1433.

11. Letter from Nelson Poynter, chief, Bureau of Motion Pictures, Hollywood, to Lowell Mellett, Office of War Information, Washington, D.C., October 19, 1942, National Archives, RG 208.

12. The film's interest in showing multiethnic America at war is captured in the image of an African American sailor firing a .50 caliber machine gun pointed skyward (Doherty 1993, 259). This image would have been particularly noticeable in 1942–43, when African Americans in the U.S. military remained in largely noncombatant support positions. Here it depicts one of the heroic stories of Pearl Harbor, that of Doris Miller, a mess attendant on board the USS *West Virginia* who, in the middle of the attack, manned a machine gun to fire back. At the time of film production, Miller was already prominently depicted in naval recruitment posters and public ceremonies.

13. "Preliminary Scenario for Motion Picture, 'December the 7th,'" 9, National Archives, RG 226, Entry 133, Box 153, Folder 1280.

14. Letter from Gregg Toland, lieutenant, USNR, to Bert Cunningham, captain, USMCR, OSS, October 23, 1942, National Archives, RG 226, OSS, Entry 90, Folder 382.

15. Letter from Cunningham to Toland, October 28, 1942, National Archives, RG 226, OSS, Entry 90, Folder 382.

16. Superintendent to regional director, Western Region, January 28, 1992, 2.

17. Robert Chenoweth, recorded interview with the author, September 30, 1992.

18. One of the many publications that provoked public reaction was *Betrayal at Pearl Harbor*, a book devoted to the discredited idea that Roosevelt had advance knowledge of

the attack but chose not to issue a warning so that the United States would be forced to enter the war (Rusbridger 1991). The authors had no difficulty turning their suspicions into criticism of the memorial's film: "Presumably to assuage the modern consciences and the economics of Japanese tourism and business interests in Hawai'i, the film has been carefully sanitized so as to play down the treacherous nature of the attack that morning, which was made while diplomatic negotiations were still in progress. . . . Revisionist history is commonplace in communist countries, but it is bizarre to find it so grotesquely displayed in one of America's great shrines."

19. Memorandum from L. Bird to G. Beito, October 2, 1992, files of the uss *Arizona* Memorial Museum Association (now Pacific Historic Parks).

20. Lance Bird, letter to the author, October 18, 1995.

21. See Magee to DeSanctis, March 3, 1994, superintendent's files, uss *Arizona* Memorial.

22. Lance Bird, letter to the author, October 18, 1995.

23. Robert Chenoweth, interview with the author, September 30, 1992.

24. "Status of uss *Arizona* Memorial Film Script," memorandum from Superintendent Donald Magee to Western Region regional director, NPS, January 28, 1992, superintendent's files, uss *Arizona* Memorial.

25. Lance Bird, interview with M. Kelly, April 14, 1994.

26. Memorandum from NPS Chief Historian Edwin Bearss to uss *Arizona* Memorial Superintendent Donald Magee, May 5, 1992, superintendent's files, uss *Arizona* Memorial.

27. Memorandum from NPS Historian Edwin Bearrs to NPS Superintendent Donald Magee, May 15, 1992.

28. Burl Burlingame, "New Dec 7 Film Debuts at *Arizona*," *Honolulu Star-Bulletin*, December 3, 1992, A-10. Evidence of the very different readings of the film evoked among the memorial's diverse audiences may be found in comment sheets that visitors fill out (or used to fill out). Comments left soon after the current film started showing included polar-opposite interpretations of the film's depiction of Japanese people, with some upset that the film gives a euphemistic portrayal of them while others said it is anti-Japanese and xenophobic (White 2001, 289–90).

29. Robert Chenoweth, interview with the author, September 30, 1992.

30. Lance Bird, interview with Marjorie Kelly, April 14, 1994.

31. Burl Burlingame, "New Dec 7 Film Debuts at *Arizona*," *Honolulu Star-Bulletin*, December 3, 1992, A-10; Daniel Martinez, personal communication, 1994.

32. Her voice carries a deep, lilting quality that conveys a sense of historical inevitability and sadness about Pearl Harbor and the mounting losses over the ensuing course of the war. The broader significance of this gendering of voice is suggested in work on Civil War narratives by the historian Drew Gilpin Faust, who has noted differential reactions to the outbreak of war by Confederate men and women, with men speaking of "courage and glory" and women fearing "war's approaching harvest of death" (Faust 1997).

33. "uss *Arizona* Memorial orientation film script," 1980, 8, files of the author.

34. "uss *Arizona* Memorial orientation film script," 1992, 16, files of the author.

1. "TripAdvisor presents travelers' choice attractions," TripAdvisor, Inc. Press Release. June 25, 2013, accessed June 26, 2013, http://www.multivu.com/mnr/57958-tripadvisor -presents-travelers-choice-attractions.

2. An operational report by the superintendent in the early 1990s described the more extreme cases this way, "Some foreign groups are dropped off at the USS *Arizona* Memorial with their baggage while waiting for the availability of their hotel rooms. These visitors have little appreciation or interest in visiting the memorial, cause severe crowding of the facilities, create problems with storage of their baggage, and many fall asleep during the theater program" (Magee 1992, 26). In September 1997, an internal park service memorandum noted that the park had "received numerous complaints from visitors regarding loud talk on the memorial" and gave instructions for identifying tour guides that "will verify for us whether it truly is the 'Japanese' tour groups that so many visitors are complaining of. Or is it the 'Chinese' and 'Taiwanese' groups that we should be concerned about" (Memorandum from Neal Niiyama, tour company coordinator ranger, September 3, 1997).

3. My discussion of Chinese perceptions of Pearl Harbor is drawn largely from research conducted by Kuang-Jung Lai Page in which she interviewed Chinese visitors and guides (Page and White 2011).

4. Kim Murakawa, "*Missouri* Coming to Pearl: Battleship Where War Ended Joins *Arizona* as Visitor Attraction," *Honolulu Advertiser*, August 22, 1996, A1.

5. The late Senator Inouye's interest in the *Missouri* apparently originated with the presence of the ship in the fiftieth anniversary of Pearl Harbor, in 1991, and his view that the ship was also a memorial: "I realize many, many people will visit her. . . . But it should not be a tourist attraction. Just as those who built the Tomb of the unknowns didn't plan on it being an attraction. It's a memorial. You go there to pay your respects" (Gregg K. Kakesako, "Landing Mo Took a Mighty Long Time," *Honolulu Star-Bulletin*, June 16, 1998, A1, A8).

6. See, for example, Gregg K. Kakesako, "Will 'Mo' Be Too Much?: The National Park Service Is Concerned that the USS *Missouri* Might Detract from the *Arizona* Memorial," *Honolulu Star-Bulletin*, October 15, 1997, A3.

7. As Patricia Masters wrote in her report (1991, 4), questions included in her interviewing at the memorial had to be approved by the parent agency of the park service, the U.S. Department of the Interior. "Among the questions rejected were those which asked about comparisons of the Pearl Harbor memorial and those of Hiroshima and Nagasaki. It was felt that such questions were sensitive and would best be avoided."

8. George Sullivan, Chairman, Arizona Memorial Museum Association, "Star-Bulletin Editorial," e-mail March 26, 2005.

9. "USS *Arizona* Center Should be Tasteful," *Honolulu Star-Bulletin* editorial, March 25, 2006, accessed March 27, 2005, http://archives.starbulletin.com/2005/03/25/editorial /indexeditorials.html.

10. Kanahele's hospitalization record shows that he was shot twice, once with entry and exit wounds and another in his groin area with gunshot burns (Waimea Hospital Nurses Record, No. 8934, December 31, 1941).

11. R. Alex Anderson was the composer of a large corpus of "hapa haole" songs, including such classics as "Lovely Hula Hands" and "Mele Kalikimaka."

12. Decades later, when *Honolulu Magazine* ran a story about the Nishikaichi affair, in 1979, it did so with an article titled simply "The Battle of Ni'ihau," concluding with the lyrics of Anderson's song (Nicol 1996 [1979]).

13. And see "The Battle of Niihau," accessed June 15, 2015, http://www.youtube.com /watch?v=yzDpi3TFZ8w.

14. Letter from Admiral Ronald J. Hays USN (ret.), chairman, and Clinton R. Churchill, president, Pacific Aviation Museum, to David Forman, president, Japanese American Citizens League of Honolulu, March 25, 2008.

15. One of the designers of the Aviation museum exhibit also devotes several pages of a recent book to challenging this received wisdom (Jones 2014, 1523–31), citing analyses of wartime intelligence data that have been said to contradict claims of Japanese American loyalty. What he does not mention, though, is that the data he cites and those who have claimed it is evidence of a network of spies in the West Coast Japanese American community have long been a subject of scholarly criticism (Herzig 1984).

16. Despite the fact that the events on Ni'ihau ensnared participants with deep differences in language and cultural orientation, all of the debate about the Ni'ihau exhibit at the Pacific Aviation Museum has been conducted in English, among American critics and defenders. But the Ni'ihau "incident" is also a Japanese story, told in Japan, most important in the hometown of the pilot, Imabari, in Ehime Prefecture, where memory of the Ni'ihau incident connects most strongly with Shigenori Nishikaichi's relatives (even Alan Beekman's original account [1982] includes observations from his travels to Imabari). Although there is not space to address these issues here, I am grateful to the dedicated work of Fumiaki Fujimoto, a Japanese teacher from Nishikaichi's prefecture who participated in one of a binational Pearl Harbor teacher program in 2009, for some understanding of the remarkably different histories of Nishikaichi and Harada that exist across the Pacific.

Chapter Five. MAKING A NEW MUSEUM

1. Since 2010 the base has been "Joint Base Pearl Harbor-Hickam," a product of merging Naval Base Pearl Harbor with Hickam Air Force Base.

2. The project also added six new acres to the memorial's land base. Whereas the original building had been constructed in 1980 on eleven acres of soil that had been dredged from the harbor (making landfill in areas that had once been Hawaiian fish ponds). That ground, however had become unstable, with the building dropping thirty inches instead of the predicted eighteen, requiring an expensive process of reengineering the foundation with deep pilings (Nakaso 2010).

3. Funding for the project came through three avenues: private fundraising, the National Park Service, and the Department of the Navy. Final tally of amounts raised were: $29 million by the Pearl Harbor Memorial Fund, $20 million from the Department of the Navy, and $9 million from the National Park Service.

4. Hill, meeting notes, Washington, D.C., historians meeting, April 23, 2006.

5. This exhibit takes its name from a video documentary developed a decade earlier at the National Japanese American Museum, in Los Angeles (Fujitani 1997).

6. The story of heroism among minority servicemen (and servicewomen) is now well established in the public face of U.S. military service. The issue of diversity in the military has become a moral theme in American history, where the contributions of minority servicemen and servicewomen are now celebrated in museum exhibits, books, and films.

7. A report by the consulting firm Aldrich Pears on the first round of consultations, setting out requirements for the new project, listed "the Park's secondary themes" as

— The salvage operation of Pearl Harbor raised fighting ships, resulting in new technology and salvage techniques
— Military bases and facilities on Oahu continue to serve as a center for military operations in the Pacific
— The Pearl Harbor attack and America's entry into World War II brought about dramatic and lasting effects on the populace of the Hawaiian Islands
— The site of Pearl Harbor, Wai Momi, has evolved from a place of traditional Hawaiian cultural uses (*ahupua'a*, fishponds and *heiau*) to an active military base (Aldrich Pears Associates 2006, 5)

8. USS *Arizona* Memorial Visitor Center Development, USAR226 Interpretive Media Value Analysis—Draft Update November 2006, Aldrich Pears Associates, 8.

9. Recorded interview with development officer, Pacific Historic Parks, February 26, 2010.

10. In fact the decadeslong process of gaining military access and control in Hawai'i was wrapped in secrecy, from the first secret commission sent out in 1873 to assess the value of Pearl Harbor as a naval port, to the act of Congress that annexed the Hawaiian Islands as a territory, in 1898. This is established history that the U.S. Navy represents in its own public histories. See http://www.history.navy.mil/docs/wwii/pearl/hawaii-2.htm.

11. The museum design benefited from the long-standing effort of the National Park Service to video record oral histories with veterans, creating an archive of video productions of survivor testimonials. Videos of recollections of veterans of both sides, as well as civilians, appear in the new museum's multimedia kiosks. The inclusion of civilian and Japanese voices represents a broadening of scope, an intention stated by the NPS historian as the museum was in the planning stage, when he said he still "needed more civilian and Japanese aviator voices" for a DVD in production in 2007 (personal communication, February 26, 2007).

12. Japanese commanders such as Yamamoto, certainly, were always part of the attack story on display in the original museum, where an exhibit with a large portrait of Yamamoto was popular with Japanese tour groups.

13. Aldrich Pears report, September 5, 2006, 35; "USS *Arizona* Memorial Visitor Center Development, USAR226 Interpretive Media Value Analysis—Draft Update November 2006," Aldrich Pears, 12 (with photos of Japanese and American veterans in friendly embrace at sixtieth-anniversary symposium).

14. If one walks further along the shoreside one will encounter three more inscriptions, including one civilian author and Eleanor Roosevelt, as well as another survivor. (See "100% Design Development: Graphics & Text Document," Aldrich Pears, June 23, 2008, 381–82.)

Chapter Six. PEDAGOGY, PATRIOTISM, AND PARANOIA

1. In this chapter, I mostly use the previous name for Pacific Historic Parks, the *Arizona* Memorial Museum Association (AMMA) to refer to the nonprofit partner of the *Arizona* memorial and the World War II Valor in the Pacific National Monument because that was the name during most of the period under discussion, up to June 2010.

2. Full details in the original complaint, including responses from me, the NEH, veterans, and many of the other program participants are available at http://www .anthropology.hawaii.edu/people/faculty/white/NEH_2010/home.html.

3. The National Council on the Humanities provides advice to the NEH chairman. It is composed of twenty-six appointees, largely humanities scholars and authors, selected by the U.S. president with Senate confirmation.

4. NOTAM *Notice to Airmen Newsletter*, issue 19, fall 2013, 4.

5. It is important to mention that practical problems in working across national educational systems also proved a limiting factor in regard to the types of collaborative projects that emerged. Results were necessarily partial and tentative due to the limitations of funding available for translation support and for sustaining interactions beyond the weeklong workshop. Coordinating instructional activities across national boundaries raises an array of practical challenges ranging from translation to matching curricular subjects and academic calendars.

6. Yujin Yaguchi worked closely with Takeo Morimo and Kyoko Nakayama in recruiting, orienting, and advising the Japanese teachers. As he states in a brief published reflection on these programs (2011), the teachers appreciated the opportunity to participate but found it frustrating to find themselves in a program with a large majority of American teachers, working in a mostly English-only environment.

Conclusion. HISTORY'S FUTURE

1. This talk was one of a series of invited talks sponsored by community organizations involved with historic preservation. The series was titled, "Preserving the Legacy of World War II."

2. "From Engagement to Peace," National Park Service, accessed June 15, 2015, http:// www.nps.gov/valr/index.htm.

3. Recall here that the first name floated for the monument was Victory in the Pacific World War II National Monument.

4. And, I would add, the social conditions of research become part of the puzzle. Putting yourself in the habitus of any institution's daily routines creates relationships based on shared interest that develop over time. These sorts of quotidian relations are

very much the same as those that underpin the authoring of history in memorial space. I had this insight brought home to me by the media criticism described in this conclusion. When the board of directors of Pacific Historic Parks, made up mostly of military veterans and business leaders, met to discuss the controversy, discussion quickly turned to ways "we" could deal with the problem. In retrospect, the reason that some on the board who would be disposed to take accusations of antimilitary content very seriously (and who were getting calls from veteran associates on the island) seems obvious: we already had a decade of working together; we knew each other, even if we didn't always have the same politics.

5. It was, no doubt, the ability of some aging Pearl Harbor survivors to see their Japanese counterparts as "military men serving their country" that allowed them to see them in a different light, as persons, rather than simply a treacherous enemy.

6. Menachem Rosensaft, "Reflecting on the Essence of Auschwitz," letter to the editor, *New York Times*, February 26, 2011.

7. Prior to the opening of the new visitor center, less than 5 percent of travelers would skip the trip out to the memorial. That figure jumped to 25 percent or more in the years following the opening of the visitor center, with an artificially high 37 percent not taking the memorial tour in 2013 (655,700 of 1,777,844 who entered that year). That figure was due to a reduction in the availability of boats, caused by federal budget problems that involved a sequestration of funds and government shutdown. These figures are from National Park Service visitor statistics, https://irma.nps.gov/Stats/SSRSReports/Park%20 Specific%20Reports/Park%20All%20Months?Park=VALR.

8. The FamilyFun Travel Awards are tied to a commercial marketing enterprise and given out on the basis of a survey of two thousand parents.

9. Leslie Garisto Pfaff, "Best Family Vacations: 2014 FamilyFun Travel Awards," Parents.com, accessed June 15, 2015, http://www.parents.com/fun/vacation/ideas/familyfun -travel-awards/?page=3.

REFERENCES

Abe, Zenji. 2006. *The Emperor's Sea Eagle: A Memoir of the Attack on Pearl Harbor and the War in the Pacific*. Edited by Michael Wegner. Honolulu: Arizona Memorial Museum Association.

Adams, Michael C. C. 1994. *The Best War Ever: America and World War II*. Baltimore: Johns Hopkins University Press.

Aldrich Pears Associates. 2006. Visitor Center Development: USAR226 Interpretive Media Value Analysis DRAFT.

Allen, Gwenfread E. 1971. *Hawaii's War Years, 1941–1945*. Westport, CT: Greenwood.

Anderson, Benedict. 1991. *Imagined Communities: Reflections on the Origin and Spread of Nationalism*. Rev. and extended 2nd ed. London: Verso.

Associated Press. 2011. "USS *Arizona* Memorial to Host Japanese Tea Rite." *Honolulu Star-Advertiser*, July 18, 2011. Accessed July 21, 2011. http://www.staradvertiser.com/news /20110718_USS_Arizona_Memorial_to_host_Japanese_tea_rite.html.

Bailey, Beth, and David Farber. 1992. *The First Strange Place: The Alchemy of Race and Sex in World War II Hawaii*. New York: Free Press.

Basinger, Jeanine. 1986. *The World War II Combat Film*. New York: Columbia University Press.

Beekman, Allan. 1982. *The Niihau Incident: The True Story of the Japanese Fighter Pilot Who, after the Pearl Harbor Attack, Crash-landed on the Hawaiian Island of Niihau and Terrorized the Residents*. Honolulu: Heritage Press of Pacific.

Beidler, Philip D. 1998. *The Good War's Greatest Hits: World War II and American Remembering*. Athens: University of Georgia.

Bergman, Teresa. 2013. "Submerged Patriotism: Evolving Representation at the USS *Arizona* Memorial Visitor Center." In *Exhibiting Patriotism: Creating and Contesting Interpretations of American Historic Sites*, 31–58. Walnut Creek, CA: Left Coast.

Berliner, D. 2005. "The Abuses of Memory: Reflections on the Memory Boom in Anthropology." *Anthropological Quarterly* 78: 197–211.

Bodnar, John E. 1992. *Remaking America: Public Memory, Commemoration, and Patriotism in the Twentieth Century*. Princeton, NJ: Princeton University Press.

———. 2009. "The 'Good War' Portrayed in Popular Culture." *VFW*, April 2009, 18–20.

———. 2010. *The "Good War" in American Memory.* Baltimore: Johns Hopkins University Press.

Brown, Roger, and James Kulik. 1982. "Flashbulb Memories." In *Memory Observed: Remembering in Natural Contexts,* edited by Ulric Neisser, 23–40. San Francisco: W. H. Freeman.

Burlingame, Burl. 1991a. "Mystery Fighter." *Honolulu Star-Bulletin,* December 7, B1.

———. 1991b. "Remembrance 1941–1991: A Guide for Pearl Harbor Reporting." Honolulu: *Honolulu Star-Bulletin.*

Burlingame, Debra. 2005. "The Great Ground Zero Heist." *Wall Street Journal,* June 7, A14. Accessed June 15, 2015. http://online.wsj.com/news/articles /SB111810145819652326.

Buruma, Ian. 1994. *The Wages of Guilt: Memories of War in Germany and Japan.* New York: Farrar, Straus, Giroux.

Carrier, Peter. 2005. *Holocaust Monuments and National Memory Cultures in France and Germany since 1989.* New York: Berghahn.

China-Japan-Korea Common History Text Tri-National Committee. 2010. *A History to Open the Future: Modern East Asian History and Regional Reconciliation.* Seoul: Minimum Ltd.

Clark, Blake. 1942. "Never Shoot an Hawaiian More Than Twice." *Reader's Digest,* December, 77–80.

Clifford, James. 1997. *Routes: Travel and Translation in the Late Twentieth Century.* Cambridge, MA: Harvard University Press.

Coerr, Eleanor, and Ronald Himler. 1977. *Sadako and the Thousand Paper Cranes.* New York: Putnam.

Cole, Elizabeth A., ed. 2007. *Teaching the Violent Past: History Education and Reconciliation.* Lanham, MD: Rowman and Littlefield.

Cole, Tim. 2000. *Selling the Holocaust: From Auschwitz to Schindler: How History Is Bought, Packaged and Sold.* New York: Routledge.

Cole, William. 2002. "Navy Settles on Restyling Plan for Ford Island." *Honolulu Advertiser,* April 17. Accessed March 15, 2014. http://the.honoluluadvertiser.com/article /2002/Apr/17/ln/ln04a.html.

———. 2003. "Navy Renovation Plans Model for Cooperative Projects." *Honolulu Advertiser,* July 4. Accessed March 14, 2014. http://the.honoluluadvertiser.com/article/2003 /Jul/04/ln/ln13a.html.

———. 2006a. "History in the Air." *Honolulu Advertiser,* December 3. Accessed November 22, 2014. http://the.honoluluadvertiser.com/article/2006/Dec/03/ln /FP612030338.html.

———. 2006b. "Navy Reclaims Controversial Piece of Pearl Harbor Land." *Honolulu Advertiser,* April 5. Accessed March 14, 2014. http://the.honoluluadvertiser.com/article /2006/Apr/05/ln/FP604050350.html.

———. 2007a. "Fewer Pearl Harbor Day Vets in Hawaii." *Honolulu Advertiser,* December 4. Accessed January 18, 2014, http://the.honoluluadvertiser.com/article/2007/Dec/04 /ln/hawaii712040356.html.

———. 2007b. "Pearl Harbor Pauses to Honor Its Heroes." *Honolulu Advertiser,* December 8. Accessed January 18, 2014. http://the.honoluluadvertiser.com/article/2007/Dec /08/ln/hawaii712080358.html.

———. 2012. "New USS *Arizona* Exhibit Will Reflect Upon Peace." *Honolulu Star-Advertiser*, August 7. Accessed December 24, 2013. http://www.staradvertiser.com/newspremium/20120807_new_uss_arizona_exhibit_will_reflect_upon_peace.html.

Connerton, Paul. 1989. *How Societies Remember (Themes in the Social Sciences)*. Cambridge: Cambridge University Press.

———. 2009. *How Modernity Forgets*. Cambridge: Cambridge University Press.

———. 2011. *The Spirit of Mourning: History, Memory and the Body*. Cambridge: Cambridge University Press.

Crapanzano, Vincent. 2013. "The Contortions of Forgiveness: Betrayal, Abandonment and Narrative Entrapment among the Harkis." In *The Interview: An Ethnographic Approach*, edited by Jonathan Skinner, 195–210. London: Bloomsbury Academic.

Cummins, Gary T. 1981. "USS *Arizona* Memorial: Interpretive Prospectus." Harpers Ferry, WV: Harpers Ferry Center.

Daizaburo, Yui. 1997. "Between Pearl Harbor and Hiroshima/Nagasaki: Nationalism and Memory in Japan and the United States." In *Living with the Bomb: American and Japanese Cultural Conflicts in the Nuclear Age*, edited by Laura Hein and Mark Selden, 52–72. Armonk, NY: M. E. Sharpe.

D'Alto, Nick. 2007. "The Niihau Zero." *Air and Space Magazine*, July 1. Accessed November 21, 2009. http://www.airspacemag.com/military-aviation/the-niihau-zero-18029053/?no-ist.

Dingeman, Robbie. 2009. "USS *Arizona* Memorial Tops List of favorite visitor sites." *Honolulu Advertiser*, January 6.

Doherty, Thomas Patrick. 1993. *Projections of War: Hollywood, American Culture, and World War II*. New York: Columbia University Press.

Donahue, Katherine C. 2011. "What Are Heroes For?" *Anthropology News*, September, 6.

Doss, Erika Lee. 2010. *Memorial Mania: Public Feeling in America*. Chicago: University of Chicago Press.

Dower, John W. 1986. *War Without Mercy: Race and Power in the Pacific War, 1941–1945*. New York: Pantheon.

———. 1995. "Triumphal and Tragic Narratives of the War in Asia." *Journal of American History* 82 (3): 1124–35.

———. 1996. "Three Narratives of Our Humanity." In *History Wars: The Enola Gay and Other Battles for the American Past*, edited by Edward T. Linenthal and Tom Engelhardt, 63–96. New York: Henry Holt.

———. 1999. *Embracing Defeat : Japan in the Wake of World War II*. New York: W. W. Norton.

———. 2010. *Cultures of War: Pearl Harbor, Hiroshima, 9–11, Iraq*. New York: W. W. Norton.

Dunford, Bruce. 2001. "Navy Zeroes in on Commercial Development of Ford Island." *Honolulu Star-Bulletin*, May 21, A9.

Dunne, John Gregory. 2001. "The American Raj: Pearl Harbor as Metaphor." *New Yorker*, May 7, 46–54.

Echternkamp, Jörg. 2010. "Memorializing the Military: Traditions, Exhibitions, and Monuments in the West German Army from the 1950s to the Present." In *Memorialization in Germany Since 1945*, edited by Bill Niven and Chloe Paver, 388–98. New York: Palgrave Macmillan.

Edwards, Sam. 2009. "Commemoration and Consumption in Normandy, 1945–1994." In *War Memory and Popular Culture: Essays on Modes of Remembrance and Commemoration*, edited by Michael Keren and Holger H. Herwig, 76–91. Jefferson, NC: McFarland.

Falgout, Suzanne, and Linda Nishigaya. 2014. *Breaking the Silence: Lessons of Democracy and Social Justice from the World War II Honouliuli Internment and POW camp in Hawaiʻi*. Honolulu: Department of Sociology, Distributed by University of Hawaiʻi Press.

Faust, Drew Gilpin. 1997. "The Civil War's 'Riddle of Death.'" *Chronicle of Higher Education*, February 14, A56.

Ferguson, Kathy, and Phyllis Turnbull. 1998. *Oh Say, Can You See?: The Semiotics of the Military in Hawaiʻi*. Minneapolis: University of Minnesota Press.

Foote, Kenneth E. 2003. *Shadowed Ground: America's Landscapes of Violence and Tragedy*. Rev. ed. Austin: University of Texas Press.

Fujikane, Candace, and Jonathan Y. Okamura. 2008. *Asian Settler Colonialism: From Local Governance to the Habits of Everyday Life in Hawaiʻi*. Honolulu: University of Hawaiʻi Press.

Fujitani, Takashi. 1997. "National Narratives and Minority Politics: The Japanese American National Museum's War Stories." In *Public History and National Narrative: Special Issue of Museum Anthropology*, edited by Geoffrey White, 21 (1): 99–112.

———. 2011. *Race for Empire: Koreans as Japanese and Japanese as Americans during World War II*. Berkeley: University of California Press.

Fujitani, Takashi, Geoffrey White, and Lisa Yoneyama, eds. 2001. *Perilous Memories: The Asia Pacific War(s)*. Durham, NC: Duke University Press.

Gedi, Noa, and Yigal Elam. 1996. "Collective Memory—What Is It?" *History and Memory* 8 (1): 30–50.

Gillis, John R., ed. 1994. *Commemorations: The Politics of National Identity*. Princeton, NJ: Princeton University Press.

Golsan, Richard J. 2006. "The Legacy of World War II in France: Mapping the Discourses of Memory." In *The Politics of Memory in Postwar Europe*, edited by Richard Ned Lebow, Wulf Kansteiner, and Claudio Fogu, 73–101. Durham, NC: Duke University Press.

Gonzalez, Vernadette Vicuña. 2013. *Securing Paradise: Tourism and Militarism in Hawaiʻi and the Philippines*. Durham, NC: Duke University Press.

Gopnik, Adam. 2014. "Stones and Bones: Visiting the 9/11 Memorial and Museum." *New Yorker*, July 7, 38–44.

Halbwachs, Maurice. 1992. *On Collective Memory*, edited by Lewis A. Coser. Chicago: University of Chicago Press.

Hallett, Brien. 1991. "The Official Response." *Ka Leo O Hawaiʻi*, 13.

Handelman, Don. 2008. "Commemorating a Suspended Death: Missing Soldiers and National Solidarity in Israel." *American Ethnologist* 35 (3): 413–27.

Handelman, Don, and Lea Shamgar-Handelman. 1997. "The Presence of Absence: The Memorialism of National Death in Israel." In *Grasping Land: Space and Place in Contemporary Isareli Discourse and Experience*, edited by Eyal Ben Ari and Yoram Bilu, 85–128. Albany: SUNY Press.

Handler, Richard, and Eric Gable. 1997. *The New History in an Old Museum: Creating the Past at Colonial Williamsburg*. Durham, NC: Duke University Press.

Harwit, Martin. 1996. *An Exhibit Denied: Lobbying the History of Enola Gay*. New York: Copernicus.

Hawai'i Tourism Authority. 2012. "2012 Annual Visitor Report." Honolulu: Hawai'i Tourism Authority.

Hayashi, Ann Koto. 1995. *Face of the Enemy, Heart of a Patriot: Japanese-American Internment Narratives*. New York: Garland.

Hayashi, Robert T. 2003. "Transfigured Patterns: Contesting Memories at the Manzanar National Historic Site." *Public Historian* 25 (4): 51–71.

Hays, Frank. 2003. "The National Park Service: Groveling Sycophant or Social Conscience: Telling the Story of Mountains, Valley, and Barbed Wire at Manzanar National Historic Site." *Public Historian* 25 (4): 73–80.

Hein, Laura Elizabeth, and Mark Selden. 2000. *Censoring History: Citizenship and Memory in Japan, Germany, and the United States, Asia and the Pacific*. Armonk, NY: M. E. Sharpe.

Herf, Jeffrey. 1997. *Divided Memory: The Nazi Past in the Two Germanys*. Cambridge, MA: Harvard University Press.

Herzig, John. 1984. "Japanese Americans and MAGIC." *Amerasia Journal* 11 (2): 47–65.

Hill, Sheila. 2006. Meeting Notes Re Washington DC Historians Meeting. Memorandum April 23, 2006. AldrichPears Associates.

Hirsch, Eric, and Charles Stewart. 2005. "Introduction: Ethnographies of Historicity." *History and Anthropology* 16 (3): 261–74.

Hirsch, Marianne. 2008. "The Generation of Postmemory." *Poetics Today* 29 (1): 103–28.

Hochschild, Arlie Russell. 1983. *The Managed Heart: Commercialization of Human Feeling*. Berkeley: University of California Press.

Hoffman, Eva. 2004. *After Such Knowledge: Memory, History, and the Legacy of the Holocaust*. New York: Public Affairs.

Hofstadter, Richard. 1964. "The Paranoid Style in American Politics." *Harper's Magazine*, 77–86.

Howes, Craig, and Jon Kamakawiwo'ole Osorio. 2010. *The Value of Hawai'i: Knowing the Past, Shaping the Future*. Honolulu: University of Hawai'i Press.

Huntington, Samuel P. 1993. "The Clash of Civilizations?" *Foreign Affairs* 72 (3): 22–49.

Hutchinson, John. 2009. "Warfare and the Sacralisation of Nations: The Meanings, Rituals and Politics of National Remembrance." *Millennium: Journal of International Studies* 38 (2): 401–17.

Huyssen, Andreas. 1995. *Twilight Memories: Marking Time in a Culture of Amnesia*. London: Routledge.

Ichihashi, Yamato, and Gordon H. Chang. 1997. *Morning Glory, Evening Shadow: Yamato Ichihashi and His Internment Writings, 1942–1945*. Standford, CA: Stanford University Press.

Igarashi, Yoshikuni. 2007. "Kamikaze Today: The Search for National Heroes in Contemporary Japan." In *Ruptured Histories: War, Memory, and the Post-Cold War in Asia*, edited by Sheila Miyoshi Jager and Rana Mitter, 99–121. Cambridge, MA: Harvard University Press.

Infimedia. 2004. "Pearl Harbor: A Landmark in History." Honolulu: *Arizona* Memorial Museum Association.

Inglis, Ken. 1993. "Entombing Unknown Soldiers: From London and Paris to Baghdad." *History and Memory* 5: 7–31.

Inoue, Yasuhiro. 2013. "Significance and Background of Realization of Paper Cranes Sadako Exhibited at Pearl Harbor." *Huffington Post*. September 24, 2013. Accessed December 12, 2013. http://www.huffingtonpost.jp/yasuhiro-inoue/post_5699_b_3979257.html.

Jones, Syd. 2014. *Before and beyond the Niihau Zero: The Unlikely Drama of Hawaii's Forbidden Island prior to, during, and after the Pearl Harbor Attack*. Merritt Island, FL: Signum Ops.

Kajihiro, Kyle. 2014. "Becoming 'Pearl Harbor': A 'Lost Geography' of American Empire." Master's thesis, department of geography, University of Hawai'i.

Kakesako, Gregg K. 1998. "USS *Arizona* and Mighty Mo: 'Together at Last': With the Ships Near Each Other, Inouye Declares 'The Circle Is Now Complete.'" *Honolulu Star-Bulletin*, September 2.

Karp, Ivan, Christine Mullen Kreamer, and Steven D. Lavine, eds. 1992. *Museums and Communities: The Politics of Public Culture*. Washington, DC: Smithsonian Institution Press.

Kelly, Marjorie. 1996. "Enshrining History: The Visitor Experience at Pearl Harbor's USS *Arizona* Memorial." *Museum Anthropology* 20 (3): 45–57.

Kimmelman, Michael. 2011. "Auschwitz Shifts from Memorializing to Teaching." *New York Times*, February 18.

Kirshenblatt-Gimblett, Barbara. 1998. *Destination Culture: Tourism, Museums, and Heritage*. Berkeley: University of California Press.

Klein, Kerwin Lee. 2000. "On the Emergence of *Memory* in Historical Discourse." *Representations* 69 (winter): 127–50.

Koppes, Clayton R., and Gregory D. Black. 1987. *Hollywood Goes to War: How Politics, Profits and Propaganda Shaped World War II Movies*. Berkeley: University of California Press.

Kramer, Carlton. 2011. "Historic Sites Launch 'Passport to Pearl Harbor.'" Honolulu: Pearl Harbor Historic Sites.

Kwon, Heonik. 2006. *After the Massacre: Commemoration and Consolation in Ha My and My Lai*. Berkeley, CA: University of California Press.

LaCapra, Dominick. 2004. *History in Transit: Experience, Identity, Critical Theory*. Ithaca, NY: Cornell University Press.

Laenui, Poka. 1992. "Hawaiian Sovereignty and Pearl Harbor History." Paper given at conference on Cultural Identity and National History, East-West Center, June.

Larsen, David. 1942. Letter from David Larsen to Katherine Larsen. Honolulu: Pacific Aviation Museum binder of documents provided to Niihau Exhibit Review Panel.

Lembcke, Jerry. 1998. *The Spitting Image: Myth, Memory, and the Legacy of Vietnam*. New York: New York University Press.

Lewis, David Levering. 2011. Report to NEH Deputy Chairman Carole M. Watson on the "History and Commemoration: Legacies of the Pacific War" summer workshop, July 24–30, 2010. Washington, DC: National Endowment for the Humanities, February 25.

Lifton, Robert Jay, and Greg Mitchell. 1995. *Hiroshima in America: Fifty Years of Denial*. New York: Putnam.

Lindstrom, Lamont, and Geoffrey M. White. 1990. *Island Encounters: Black and White Memories of the Pacific War*. Washington, DC: Smithsonian Institution Press.

Linenthal, Edward, and Tom Engelhardt, eds. 1996. *History Wars: The "Enola Gay" and Other Battles for the American Past*. New York: Henry Holt.

Linenthal, Edward T. 1993. *Sacred Ground: Americans and Their Battlegrounds*. Rev. ed. Urbana: University of Illinois Press.

———. 1995. "Can Museums Achieve a Balance between Memory and History?" *Chronicle of Higher Education*, February 10, B1–2.

Lippard, Lucy. 1999. "Tragic Tourism." In *On the Beaten Track*, 118–34. New York: New Press.

Lowman, David D. 2001. *Magic: The Untold Story of U.S. intelligence and the Evacuation of Japanese Residents from the West Coast during WW II*. Provo, UT: Athena Press.

MacCannell, Dean. 1992. *Empty Meeting Grounds: The Tourist Papers*. London: Routledge.

Macdonald, Sharon. 2009. *Difficult Heritage: Negotiating the Nazi Past in Nuremberg and Beyond*. New York: Routledge.

MacMillan, Margaret. 2008. *Dangerous Games: The Uses and Abuses of History*. New York: Modern Library.

Magee, Donald E. 1992. "Statement for Management: USS *Arizona* Memorial." Honolulu: National Park Service, U.S. Department of the Interior. July.

Maier, Charles S. 1997. *The Unmasterable Past: History, Holocaust and German National Identity*. Cambridge, MA: Harvard University Press.

Malkin, Michelle. 2004. *In Defense of Internment: The Case for "Racial Profiling" in World War II and the War on Terror*. Lanham, MD: Regnery.

Martinez, Daniel. 1997. "Park Guide Theater Program" (Draft June 26, 1997). Honolulu: USS *Arizona* Memorial.

Masters, Patricia Lee. 1991. "Another Way of Seeing: Pearl Harbor as Memory." Honolulu: USS *Arizona* Memorial, National Park Service.

———. 1992. "The Politics of Memory: Creating Self-Understandings in Postwar Japan." PhD diss., Department of Political Science, University of Hawai'i.

McAvoy, Audrey. 2011. "Snapshots of 1930s Japan Add to Context at New *Arizona* Memorial Visitor Center." *Honolulu Star Advertiser*, April 30. Accessed May 1, 2011. http://www.staradvertiser.com/news/breaking/121046699.html.

Meyers, Gary. 2013. "Blackened Canteen Becomes Symbol of Peace and Reconciliation." *Remembrance* (winter): 7.

Moore, Laurie. 2009. "Why Pearl Harbor?" *Remembrance* (fall): 10.

Mosse, George L. 1990. *Fallen Soldiers: Reshaping the Memory of the World Wars*. New York: Oxford University Press.

Munday, Doug, and Sheila Hill. 2007a. Preliminary Interpretive Schematic Design Round Table Review, Jan.11–12. Meeting Notes. E-mail, January 24.

———. 2007b. Preliminary Interpretive Schematic Design Stakeholders' Review Workshop, Jan. 12. Meeting Notes. Memorandum, January 12.

Murakawa, Kim. 1996. "*Missouri* Coming to Pearl: Battleship Where War Ended Joins *Arizona* as Visitor Attraction." *Honolulu Advertiser*, August 22, A1.

Nakaso, Dan. 2010. "Pearl Harbor Opens New Visitor Center for the USS *Arizona*: Second Phase of $58 Million Project to Be Done by Dec. 7." *Honolulu Advertiser*, February 17.

Accessed February 20, 2010. http://the.honoluluadvertiser.com/article/2010/Feb/17/ln/hawaii2170351.html.

———. 2011. "With Tea Ceremony, Hope Rises to Heal Wounds of War." *Honolulu Star-Advertiser*, July 20, 2011. Accessed July 21, 2011. http://www.staradvertiser.com/news/20110720_With_tea_ceremony_hope_rises_to_heal_wounds_of_war.html.

Napier, A. Kam. 2011a. "Photos: War Stories." *Honolulu Magazine*. Accessed August 27, 2013. http://www.honolulumagazine.com/Honolulu-Magazine/April-2011/Afterthoughts-War-Stories/Photos-War-Stories/.

———. 2011b. "Afterthoughts: War Stories: Visiting the USS *Arizona* Memorial's New Visitor Center." *Honolulu Magazine*, April, 96.

Nash, Gary, Charlotte Crabtree, and Rosee E. Dunn. 1997. *History on Trial. Culture Wars and the Teaching of the Past*. New York: Knopf.

National Park Service. 2013. "Strategic Plan: 2013 through 2017." Honolulu: WWII Valor in the Pacific National Monument.

Neisser, Ulric, and Nicole Harsch. 1992. "Phantom Flashbulbs: False Recollections of Hearing the News about *Challenger*." In *Affect and Accuracy in Recall*, edited by Eugene Winograd and Ulric Neisser, 9–31. New York: Cambridge University Press.

Nicholson, Dorinda Makanaonalani. 2001. *Pearl Harbor Warriors: The Bugler, the Pilot, the Friendship*. Kansas City, MO: Woodson House.

Nicol, Brian. 1996 [1979]. "The Battle of Niihau." In *Hawai'i Chronicles: Island History from the Pages of Honolulu Magazine*, edited by Bob Dye, 251–56. Honolulu: University of Hawai'i Press.

Niiya, Brian, and Japanese American National Museum (Los Angeles). 2001. *Encyclopedia of Japanese American History: An A-to-Z Reference from 1868 to the Present*. Updated ed. New York: Facts on File.

Niven, William John, and Chloe E. M. Paver, eds. 2010. *Memorialization in Germany since 1945*. New York: Palgrave Macmillan.

Novick, Peter. 2000. *The Holocaust and Collective Memory: The American Experience*. New York: Bloomsbury.

Odo, Franklin. 2004. *No Sword to Bury: Japanese Americans in Hawai'i during World War II*. Philadelphia: Temple University Press.

Osorio, Jonathan Kamakawiwo'ole. 2002. *Dismembering Lahui: A History of the Hawaiian Nation to 1887*. Honolulu: University of Hawai'i Press.

———. 2010. "Memorializing Pu'uloa and Remembering Pearl Harbor." In *Militarized Currents: Toward a Decolonized Future in Asia and the Pacific*, edited by Setsu Shigematsu and Keith L. Camacho, 3–14. Minneapolis: University of Minnesota Press.

Otterman, Sharon. 2014. "Film at 9/11 Museum Sets Off Clash over Reference to Islam." *New York Times*, April 23. Accessed November 22, 2014. http://www.nytimes.com/2014/04/24/nyregion/interfaith-panel-denounces-a-9-11-museum-exhibits-portrayal-of-islam.html.

Page, Kuan-Jung Lai, and Geoffrey White. 2011. "The Chinese Visitor Experience at Pearl Harbor: Final Report to the National Park Service." Honolulu: Department of Anthropology, University of Hawai'i.

Paiva, Derek. 2001. "'Pearl Harbor' Steers Clear of Major Commercialization." *Honolulu Advertiser*, May 13, 2001.

Paul, Caroline. 2006. *East Wind, Rain*. New York: William Morrow.

Perez, Rob. 2005. "New Tent at *Arizona* Offensive to Some: Some Say That the For-profit Venture Is Inappropriate at the Pearl Harbor Site." *Honolulu Star-Bulletin*, January 30. Accessed June 15, 2015. http://archives.starbulletin.com/2005/01/30/news/index2.html.

Piehler, G. Kurt. 1995. *Remembering War the American Way*. Washington, DC: Smithsonian Institution Press.

Prange, Gordon William, Donald M. Goldstein, and Katherine V. Dillon. 1990. *God's Samurai: Lead Pilot at Pearl Harbor*. Washington, DC: Brassey's.

Price, Sally. 2007. *Paris Primitive: Jacques Chirac's Museum on the Quai Branly*. Chicago: University of Chicago Press.

Radstone, Susannah. 2008. "Memory Studies: For and Against." *Memory Studies* 1 (1).

Reed, Rob. 2013. "The Battle of Niihau: The Little Known Story of the Pearl Harbor Attack." *Military Aviation Examiner*, December 7.

Renov, Michael. 1991. "Warring Images: Stereotype and American Representations of the Japanese, 1941–1991." In *The Japan/America Film Wars*, edited by Abé Mark Nornes and Fukushima Yukio, 95–118. Langhorne, PA: Harwood Academic Publishers.

Robinson, Greg. 2001. *By Order of the President: FDR and the Internment of Japanese Americans*. Cambridge, MA: Harvard University Press.

Rodriggs, Lawrence Reginald. 1991. *We Remember Pearl Harbor: Honolulu Civilians Recall the War Years, 1941–1945*. Newark, CA: Communications Concepts.

Rosenberg, Emily S. 2004. *A Date Which Will Live: Pearl Harbor in American Memory*. Durham, NC: Duke University Press.

Ross, Andrew. 1993. "Cultural Preservation in the Polynesia of the Latter Day Saints." In *The Chicago Gangster Theory of Life: Nature's Debt to Society*, 21–98.

Roxworthy, Emily. 2008. *The Spectacle of Japanese American Trauma: Racial Performativity and World War II*. Honolulu: University of Hawai'i Press.

Rusbridger, James, and Eric Nave. 1991. *Betrayal at Pearl Harbor: How Churchill Lured Roosevelt into World War II*. New York: Summit Books.

Ryan, Tim. 2000. "Actors, Film Execs Pay Respects: A Ceremony at the USS *Arizona* Memorial Signals the Start of Work on the Disney film 'Pearl Harbor.'" *Honolulu Star-Bulletin*, April 3. Accessed November 21, 2014. http://starbulletin.com/2000/04/03/news/story3.html.

Sahlins, Marshall David. 1985. *Islands of History*. Chicago: University of Chicago Press.

Sai, David. 2005. "American Occupation of the Hawaiian State: A Century Unchecked." Annual meeting of the International Studies Association, Hilton Hawaiian Village, Honolulu, Hawaii, March 5.

Saiki, Patsy Sumie. 2004. *Ganbare!: An Example of Japanese Spirit*. Honolulu: Mutual.

Schickel, Richard. 1991. "Critical Reassessment: *December 7*: The Movie." *Time*, 80.

Schwenkel, Christina. 2009. *The American War in Contemporary Vietnam: Transnational Remembrance and Representation*. Bloomington: Indiana University Press.

Silva, Noenoe K. 2004. *Aloha Betrayed: Native Hawaiian Resistance to American Colonialism*. Durham, NC: Duke University Press.

Silverstein, Michael, and Greg Urban. 1996. *Natural Histories of Discourse*. Chicago: University of Chicago Press.

Sion, Brigitte. 2010. "Affective Memory, Ineffective Functionality: Experiencing Berlin's Memorial to the Murdered Jews of Europe." In *Memorialization in Germany Since 1945*, edited by William John Niven and Chloe Paver, 243–52. New York: Palgrave Macmillan.

Skinner, James M. 1991. "*December 7*: Filmic Myth Masquerading as Historical Fact." *Journal of Military History* 55 (October): 507–16.

Slackman, Michael. 1986. *Remembering Pearl Harbor: The Story of the USS Arizona Memorial*. Honolulu: Arizona Memorial Museum Association.

Smith, Jeffrey A. 1999. *War and Press Freedom: The Problem of Prerogative Power*. Oxford: Oxford University Press.

Sowell, Thomas. 1991. "Park Service Turns Its Back on Patriotism." *Honolulu Star-Bulletin*, December 11.

Stannard, David E. 1989. *Before the Horror: The Population of Hawai'i on the Eve of Western Contact*. Honolulu: Social Science Research Institute, University of Hawai'i.

Sturken, Marita. 1997. *Tangled Memories: The Vietnam War, the AIDS Epidemic, and the Politics of Remembering*. Berkeley: University of California Press.

———. 2007a. "Tourism and 'Sacred Ground': The Space of Ground Zero." In *Tourists of History: Memory, Kitsch, and Consumerism from Oklahoma City to Ground Zero*, 139–64. Durham, NC: Duke University Press.

———. 2007b. *Tourists of History: Memory, Kitsch, and Consumerism from Oklahoma City to Ground Zero*. Durham, NC: Duke University Press.

Sugano, Hiroya. 2001. *Rising Above the Hate of War: If It Had Not Been for the Attack on Pearl Harbor, Shizuoka City Would Not Have Been Bombed*, translated by Jiro Yoshida. Shizuoka, Japan: Zero Fighter Admirers Club.

Sutterfield, Alan. 1992. *World War nIIhau*. Honolulu: Files of Kumu Kahua Theater.

Tajiri, Rea. 1991. *History and Memory*. New York: Women Make Movies.

Taylor, Sandra C. 1993. *Jewel of the Desert: Japanese American Internment at Topaz*. Berkeley: University of California Press.

Teaiwa, Teresia. 1994. "Bikinis and Other S/pacific N/oceans." *Contemporary Pacific* 6: 87–109.

Tengan, Ty P. Kāwika. 2008. *Native Men Remade: Gender and Nation in Contemporary Hawai'i*. Durham, NC: Duke University Press.

———. 2011. "Return to Fort Kamehameha: Martialing Memory in Occupied Hawai'i." Annual Meeting of the American Anthropological Association, Montreal, November 16–20.

Thorsten, Marie. 2002. "Treading the Tiger's Tail: Pearl Harbor Veteran Reunions in Hawai'i and Japan." *Cultural Values: Journal of Cultural Research* 6 (3): 317–40.

Thorsten, Marie, and Geoffrey White. 2010. "Binational Pearl Harbor?: *Tora! Tora! Tora!* and the Fate of (Trans)national Memory." *Asia Pacific Journal: Japan Focus* 8 (52, no. 2).

Tighe, Lori 2000. "*Arizona* Memorial Film Is Trimmed: A Suspicious Isle Japanese Cane Worker in the Film Upset Japanese Americans." *Honolulu Star-Bulletin*, April 24.

Torgovnick, Marianna. 2005. *The War Complex: World War II in Our Time*. Chicago: University of Chicago Press.

Tumarkin, Nina. 1994. *The Living and the Dead: The Rise and Fall of the Cult of World War II in Russia*. New York: Basic Books.

Ubay, Jason. 2014. "USS *Missouri* Memorial Association Looking for New Visitor Markets." *Pacific Business News*. August 29.

United States Commission on Wartime Relocation and Internment of Civilians. 1992 [1983]. "Personal justice denied: Report of the Commission on Wartime Relocation and Internment of Civilians: Committee on Interior and Insular Affairs." Washington, DC: U.S. Government Printing Office.

Wallace, Mike. 1996. "Mickey Mouse History: Portraying the Past at Disney World." In *Mickey Mouse History and Other Essays on American Memory*, 133–67. Philadelphia: Temple University Press.

Wertsch, James V. 2002. *Voices of Collective Remembering*. Cambridge: Cambridge University Press.

White, Geoffrey M. 1991. *Identity through History: Living Stories in a Solomon Islands Society*. Cambridge: Cambridge University Press.

———. 1995. "Remembering Guadalcanal: National Identity and Transnational Memory-Making." *Public Culture* 7: 529–55.

———. 1997a. "Museum, Memorial, Shrine: National Narrative in National Spaces." *Museum Anthropology: Special Issue on "Public History and National Narrative"* 21 (1): 8–27.

———. 1997b. "Mythic History and National Memory: The Pearl Harbor Anniversary." *Culture and Psychology: Special Issue edited by James Wertsch* 3 (1): 63–88.

———. 1999. "Emotional Remembering: The Pragmatics of National Memory." *Ethos* 27 (4): 505–29.

———. 2001. "Moving History: The Pearl Harbor Film(s)." In *Perilous Memories: The Asia-Pacific War(s)*, edited by Takashi Fujitani, Geoffrey White, and Lisa Yoneyama, 267–95. Durham, NC: Duke University Press.

———. 2002. "National Memory at the Movies: Disney's Pearl Harbor." *Public Historian* 24 (4): 97–115.

———. 2004a. "Emotive Institutions." In *A Companion to Psychological Anthropology: Modernity and Psychocultural Change*, edited by C. Casey and R. Edgerton, 241–54. London: Blackwell.

———. 2004b. "National Subjects: Pearl Harbor and September 11." *American Ethnologist* 13 (3): 293–310.

White, Geoffrey M., and Jane Yi. 2001. "*December 7th*: Race and Nation in Wartime Documentary." In *Classic Whiteness: Race and the Hollywood Studio System*, edited by Daniel Bernardi, 301–38. Minneapolis: University of Minnesota Press.

White, Geoffrey M., and Lamont Lindstrom, eds. 1989. *The Pacific Theater: Island Representations of World War II*. Honolulu: University of Hawai'i Press.

Wieviorka, Annette. 2006. *The Era of the Witness*. Translated by Jared Stark. Ithaca, NY: Cornell University Press.

Williams, Paul Harvey. 2007. *Memorial Museums: The Global Rush to Commemorate Atrocities*. Oxford: Berg.

Winter, J. M. 2006. *Remembering War: The Great War between Memory and History in the Twentieth Century*. New Haven, CT: Yale University Press.

Winter, J. M., and Emmanuel Sivan. 1999. *War and Remembrance in the Twentieth Century*. Cambridge: Cambridge University Press.

Winter, Jay. 1995. *Sites of Memory, Sites of Mourning: The Great War in European Cultural History*. New York: Cambridge University Press.

Wood, Edward W. 2006. *Worshipping the Myths of World War II: Reflections on America's Dedication to War*. Washington, DC: Potomac Books.

Yaguchi, Yujin. 2005. "War Memories across the Pacific: Japanese Visitors at the *Arizona* Memorial." *Comparative American Studies* 3 (3): 345–60.

———. 2011. "Remembering Pearl Harbor in Hawai'i: A Reflection on an Annual Workshop for U.S. and Japanese Secondary School Teachers." *Society for Historians of American Foreign Relations online forum*, posted December 3, 2011.

Yaguchi, Yujin, Takeo Morimo, and Kyoko Nakayama, eds. 2011. *Shinjuwan wo kataru— rekishi, kioku, kyoiku*. [Narrating Pearl Harbor: History, memory, and education.] Tokyo: University of Tokyo Press.

Yoneyama, Lisa. 1999. *Hiroshima Traces: Time, Space, and the Dialectics of Memory*. Berkeley: University of California Press.

———. 2001. "For Transformative Knowledge and Postnationalist Public Spheres: The Smithsonian *Enola Gay* Controversy." In *Perilous Memories: The Politics of Remembering the Asia Pacific War(s)*, edited by Takashi Fujitani, Geoffrey White, and Lisa Yoneyama, 323–46. Durham, NC: Duke University Press.

Young, James Edward. 1993. *The Texture of Memory: Holocaust Memorials and Meaning*. New Haven, CT: Yale University Press.

———, ed. 1994. *Holocaust Memorials in History: The Art of Memory*. New York: teNeues Publishing Group.

———. 2000a. "Art Spiegelman's Maus and the After-Images of History." In *At Memory's Edge: After-Images of the Holocaust in Contemporary Art and Architecture*, 12–41. New Haven, CT: Yale University Press.

———. 2000b. *At Memory's Edge: After-Images of the Holocaust in Contemporary Art and Architecture*. New Haven, CT: Yale University Press.

Zinsser, William. 1991. "At Pearl Harbor There Are New Ways to Remember." *Smithsonian*, December, 73–83.

INDEX

Page numbers followed by *f* indicate figures and maps. Page numbers followed by *t* indicate tables.

commemorative practices (*continued*)
military and corporate support for, 32–33;
military remembrance vs. reconciliation
in, 98–99, 125; multiple cultures of, 6,
13–14, 32, 80, 99, 105, 125, 232–33, 242;
origins of, 82; past and present connections
created in, 84–87; peace as intersection in,
268; public and military parts of, 21–22;
reconciliation marginalized in past, 61;
reflections on, 125–27; retail operations as
affront to, 180–82; routinization of, 111–25;
storytelling as, 68–69; transitional mo
ments in, 121–22, 263–64, 276; "Walk of
Honor" as, 23, 83, 85–86, 86f, 265; wreath
presentations in, 88f, 88–89. *See also* anniversaries (December 7); anniversaries,
end-of-war; collective memory; memorialization; Punchbowl National Cemetery;
rose ceremonies; tea ceremony; transnational memory-making
commercial tours, 185–86. *See also* tourism
commodification: commemorative practices
vs., 196–200; history as antidote to, 180; in
military-entertainment complex, 184–85;
potential for, in memorial tourism, 165–71;
of VALR, 280–84. *See also* advertisements
and marketing; attractions; Ford Island;
tourism
controversies and critiques: approach to
studying, 34; different approaches to
history exposed in, 199–200; implications of, 14–15, 266–67; media-driven, 34,
245–49, 257; military remembrance and
new constituents at issue in, 19. *See also*
representations
—SPECIFIC: allegations of disloyal Japanese American residents, 129–30, 132–37,
139–41, 144–47, 165, 186–87, 189–90,
217, 298n1, 299–300n18, 302n15; atomic
bombings exhibition, 4, 27, 106, 196, 212,
237, 246, 249, 270; culture wars, 209,
247–48; expanded, "balanced" interpretation, 26–28, 29, 58, 80, 98, 267–68,
299–300n18; Freedom Center, 3–4, 5, 279;
Hawaiian perspective missing in museum,
1–2, 293n7; Japanese friendship and end-of-
war anniversary, 108–11; *Missouri*'s arrival

and location, 164, 172, 173–77; new orientation film, 299–300n18, 300n28; retail
operations adjacent to *Arizona* Memorial,
179–82; tea ceremony, 120–21; textbooks
and curricula, 209, 250–51, 258, 293n7.
See also cane cutter controversy; Ni'ihau
exhibit controversy; reconciliation and
peace themes
cultures of commemoration: as contact
zones, 80, 94–97; friendship's emergence
in, 92–93; in Israel, 23; multiplicity of, 6,
13–14, 32, 80, 99, 105, 125, 232–33, 242;
zones of intertextuality in, 107. *See also* commemorative practices; memorialization;
multiculturalism

Day of Infamy (Lord), 152
December 7. *See* anniversaries; Pearl Harbor
bombing
December 7th (original and edited films):
Academy Award for short version (1944),
138; cane cutter scene in, 130f, 140–41;
details of, 291; Hawai'i as paradise vs.
foreboding borderland in, 144–45, 152,
223; memorialization in, 148–49; multiethnic America in, 144, 146–47, 299n12;
mythmaking in, 141–43, 223; narrations of,
142, 147; production of, 138–39; rejected as
fictional, 145–46; representation of Hawai'i
and Japanese Americans in, 137, 139, 144
Declaration of Friendship and Peace (1995),
110f, 111, 234
DePrey, Paul, 115
Di Virgilio, John: historical investigations of,
95, 108; Japanese and American friendships
fostered by, 95, 104; Japanese and American veterans ceremony proposal by, 92–93,
105–6, 107; rose ceremonies continued by,
122–23, 125
Disneyland problem (concept), 167. *See also*
attractions; commodification
Disney Studios, 16, 167, 168. See also *Pearl
Harbor* (film)
distinguished visitors (D.V.s), 182, 184, 198
documentary films. *See* orientation films
Donovan, William, 140
Dower, John W., 26, 107–8, 226, 270

294n14, 301n7; planned U.S. exhibition on bombing cancelled, 4, 27, 106, 196, 212, 237, 246, 249, 270; radiation zone in, 94; representation of, 242–43. *See also* Fuchida, Mitsuo; Sasaki, Sadako

Hiroshima (Hersey), 152

histories: accuracies and silences in, 133–37, 192–95; contested ground of, 224–25; as embodied and personal, 22–25, 40–45, 75, 152–53, 184–85, 251–52; emotionality in, 58–63; entanglements of, 1–3, 215–26; homogenized "official," 7; memorialization's tensions with, 3–5, 255–57; memory as, 267–73; multiple perspectives in, 2–3, 8–9, 14, 29, 80, 133–34, 208, 209–11, 234, 239, 261–62, 267–73, 298n2; in museums vs. memorials, 185–86; political and emotional potency of, 31–32; "revisionist" history critiqued, 210, 299–300n18; shift from embodied to electronic memory in, 30, 36–37, 45, 71–75, 265. *See also* memorial history; national histories and identities; oral histories; public history

History and Commemoration program (University of Hawai'i), 34, 245–49. *See also* National Endowment for the Humanities

History to Open the Future (textbook), 258

Hofstadter, Richard, 27, 247–48

Holocaust: Auschwitz site of, 279; collective memory of, 13; commemorative culture shift due to, 271–72; descendants of generation impacted by, 30; fostering transnational understanding of, 278; memorial evocations of, 273; problems of representing, 251; survivor testimonies on, 66, 252; witnessing of, 37–38

Honolulu: consul general of Japan in, 111, 114–15, 118–19; Hiroshima as sister city, 94

Honolulu Advertiser, 174–75, 188–89

Honolulu Magazine, 200–201, 204, 302n12

Honolulu Star-Bulletin, 94, 192

Honouliuli internment site, 278

How Shall We Remember Them? (orientation film, 1992): audiences of, 150–51; changes to, 129–30, 133–34; *December 7th* compared with, 140; details summarized, 291; goal of, 135–36, 142, 203; introduction to, 204; memorial imperative of, 156–58; motiva-

tions in making, 138, 149–50; multiple voices in, 152–54, 300n32; narrator of, 142, 155, 300n32; new visitor center's continued showing of, 206; orientation film (1980) compared with, 151–52, 154–57; premiere of, 154; public responses to, 299–300n18, 300n28. *See also* cane cutter controversy

"hula girls," 152, 159, 218, 223

Hunt Building Company, 179

Husted, Richard, 44

Huyssen, Andreas, 197

Hyland, Everett: in cane cutter controversy discussions, 159; friendship activities of, 73, 238–39, 240; in-person vs. recorded speaking of, 71–72; quotation attributed to, 238; video vignette of, 67

identities. *See* gender; Japanese and Japanese American residents; national histories and identities; Native Hawaiians; race and race relations

Igawa, Stanley: activities of, 295n7; in cane cutter controversy discussions, 135; on emotions in presentations, 60; on larger significance of story, 55–56; race relations in personal story of, 46, 50–55, 62–63; recordings of, 66; VFW activities of, 54, 295n7

In Defense of Internment (Malkin), 190, 298n3

Inouye, Daniel: on cane cutter controversy, 134, 135; Ford Island project support by, 177; friendship exchanges support from, 111; interest in *Missouri*, 174, 301n5; status of, 212; tea ceremony message of, 118

Interfaith Ceremony, 123, 124f, 125, 270

International Freedom Center (proposed), 3–4, 5, 279

internment. *See* Japanese American internment

Iraq War (first; Gulf War), 11, 78, 80, 173, 182, 184, 277

Iraq War (second), 86–87, 112, 277

Israel, commemorative culture, 23

Ito, Fukumatsu, 93

JACL. *See* Japanese American Citizens League

Japan: ambivalence and amnesia about WWII in, 23, 260; animosity toward, 25–28, 29,

Japan (*continued*)
97–99, 131–32, 150; B-29 crew's crash
and burial in, 93; blame accepted by, 98,
297n5; consul general of (Honolulu), 111,
114–15, 118–19; domestic war experiences
and memories in, 107–8, 126, 176–77;
Fukushima nuclear disaster in, 116, 119;
memorial ceremonies in, 107–8; memorials offerings from, 77–78, 79*f*, 123; new
museum's representation of, 226–30; peace
commemoration culture in, 271; rise of
militarism in, 153; surrender of, 106, 154,
173, 176; tea ceremony's meanings in, 115;
teachers from (*see* teacher workshops); U.S.
veterans questioned about feelings on,
99–100. *See also* Hiroshima; Japanese military; Japanese veterans of WWII; Japanese
visitors; Nagasaki; U.S.-Japanese relations
Japanese American Citizens League (JACL):
cane cutter controversy and, 131, 133,
134–37, 139, 147, 158–59, 275, 298n2; new
museum and, 216, 220; Ni'ihau exhibit
complaint of, 186, 193–94; status of, 212
Japanese American internment: cane cutter
representation in relation to, 133–34,
158–59; chronology of, 289–90; continued
debate on, 298n3; locations of, 51, 216, 278;
new museum's inclusion of, 212, 215–17;
presidential order for, 50, 134, 139, 189,
191; rationalization of, 147, 185, 187, 190;
recognition of and restitution for, 185, 192,
215–16, 278, 298n3; silences about, 192–93;
suffering in, 16–17, 50–52
Japanese and Japanese American residents:
animosity toward and alleged disloyalty
of, 14–15, 53, 129–30, 132–37, 139–41,
144–47, 165, 186–87, 189–90, 217, 298n1;
299–300n18, 302n15; *December 7th*'s depiction of, 139–47; immigration of, 94–95;
interviews of, 294n14; Japan's ties with,
112–13, 116–17; new museum's inclusion
of, 13, 212, 215–18, 274–75; Pearl Harbor's
significance for, 2, 136–37, 158; postwar
position and history of, 19, 62–63; resistance vs. enlistment debate among, 52–53;
Sadako crane exhibit and, 241; in unification theme, 146–47; U.S. military service

of, 51–52, 63, 137, 215–16, 217, 218, 295n6.
See also cane cutter controversy; Japanese
American internment; Ni'ihau exhibit
controversy; Pearl Harbor mythos
Japanese Cultural Center of Hawai'i: cane
cutter controversy and, 275; mentioned,
13; multicultural contacts via, 95; new museum and, 216, 217–18, 220; Sadako crane
exhibit supported by, 241; status of, 212
Japanese Diet, 114–15
Japanese military: aircraft of (Zero fighter),
184; midget submarines of, 44; new museum's representation of, 226–30; training
cruise of, 198. *See also* Japanese veterans of
WWII; Ni'ihau exhibit controversy
Japanese Self-Defense Forces (SDF), 107–8,
119–20
Japanese veterans of WWII: anniversary participation of, 92, 93, 94, 100–105, 109*f*, 233,
236; building relations with, 73; canteen
rituals initiated by, 93, 114*f*; Declaration of
Friendship and Peace signed by, 110*f*, 111;
honored in commemorative practices, 85;
new museum's recognition of those killed
in attack, 230–40; organization of naval
vets (Unabarakai), 93, 105, 107–8; outreach
to U.S. vets initiated by, 46, 62, 80–81, 92–
97, 100–103, 233, 268, 305n5; Punchbowl
friendship ceremony and, 105–8; recordings
of, 66, 68, 69; rose ceremonies initiated by,
103–5, 104*f*, 122–23, 124*f*, 125; as speakers
at symposiums, 100; survivor category
expanded to include, 252–53; videoconferencing with, 73; video testimonials
of, 227–28. *See also* friendship exchanges;
reconciliation and peace themes
Japanese visitors: complaints about, 14, 246;
importance of, 150; interviews of, 25, 171,
294n14; Japanese-language signage and
audio program for, 14, 227; number of, 169;
paper cranes exhibit and, 115; recognizing Japanese killed in attack and, 236–37;
research on, 171; welcome for, 233. *See also*
Japanese veterans of WWII
Japan Society, 240
Joe. *See* Morgan, Joe
Johnson, Lyndon B., 296n1

Johnson, Roy, 86
Joint Base Pearl Harbor-Hickam, 163–64, 274, 302n1

Kanahele, Ben, 188–89, 195, 301n10
Kānaka Maoli. See Native Hawaiians
Katogakuen High School, 77
Kelly, Marjorie, 12, 14, 49–50, 77, 150, 294n9, 295n2
Kempthorne, Dirk, 90, 91
Kihune, Robert, 109, 111
Kingdom of Hawai'i: illegal overthrow of monarchy, 3, 16–17, 225, 278; political history summarized, 287–88; Reciprocity Treaty signed by, 3, 17, 224, 225–26, 287; secrecy in U.S. takeover of, 226, 303n10. *See also* Hawai'i
Kinzler, Robert (Bob), 43–44, 96, 135, 159
Korean War, 11, 184, 277

LaCapra, Dominick, 251
Larsen, David, 189
Leach, Jim, 248
Lembcke, Jerry, 294n13
Lest We Forget! (Hearst newsreel), 144
Lewis, David Levering, 248
Lili'uokalani (queen), 3, 16–17
Linenthal, Edward, 4–5, 100
Little Big Horn Historic Site, 231
local experiences. *See* civilian and local survivors
Lord, Walter, 152

MacArthur, Douglas, 176, 177
Maeda, Takeshi, 97, 100–102, 103*f*
Magee, Donald, 151, 155, 301n2
Malkin, Michelle, 189–90, 298n3
Manzanar internment camp (California), 216, 278
Martinez, Daniel: on affective politics of peace, 268–69; ceremonial activities of, 122, 123, 124*f*, 125, 262; on disappearance of survivors, 65; on including Japanese viewpoint, 227; on Japanese veterans as visitors, 95–96; orientation film and, 28, 157; on respectful behavior, 22
Martinez, Rudy, 69

Masters, Patricia Lee, 14, 25, 171, 176, 294n14, 301n7
Matsunaga Institute for Peace (University of Hawai'i), 95, 106–7
Medal of Merit, 188–89
Medals of Honor, 90, 151, 153–54
media coverage: controversies driven by, 34, 245–49, 257; lesser-known commemorative practices missed by, 78, 80, 92. *See also The Today Show; and specific newspapers*
—SPECIFIC TOPICS: cane cutter controversy, 130–32; December 7th anniversaries, 11, 64, 69, 99–100, 294n8, 296–97n4; *December 7th,* 143; "end of rancor" speech, 297n6; friendship exchanges, 96, 100–102, 109–11, 126; Fuchida's peace offering, 94; Gulf War, 11; Japan's acceptance of blame, 98, 297n5; *Missouri's* arrival and location, 172, 174–76; new museum's representation of Japan, 227; new visitor center and museum, 200–201; Ni'ihau incident, 186–87, 188–89, 190; orientation films, 155; Pacific Aviation Museum, 185; *Pearl Harbor,* 167, 168; retail operations near memorial, 179–80, 182; Sadako crane exhibit, 242; tea ceremony, 115, 117, 120–21; typical tourist attractions, 166
Mellett, Lowell, 145, 146
melting pot. *See* multiculturalism
memorial ethnography: approach of, 30–34; performative approaches linked to, 274–76; recordings, transcriptions, and interviews in, 295n2
memorial film. *See* orientation films
memorial history: collective voice in, 44–45; concept, 31–32, 251; ecology of meaning-making in, 273–80; limits of, 207–8; sacred space in, 249; social history techniques in, 209–10; witnesses' personal reality of, 38–40, 39*f*, 64. *See also* educational programs
memorialization: authority over representations in, 7–8, 58–59, 111; collective memory reproduced in, 78, 80; commodification vs., 196–200; contingent nature of history-making in, 206; in *December 7th,* 148–49; ecology of meaning-making in,

memorialization (*continued*)
273–80; education combined with, 5–9; emotionalizing history in, 22–28; film as both documentary and, 141–43; historical scholarship's tensions with, 255–57; kinds of history possible in, 134–37; national cultures and transformations in, 13–19, 271–73; in orientation films, 156–57; politics of, 13–19, 31, 246–49, 279; racial politics in, 50–56; recognition of both sides in, 230–35; reflections on, 125–27; religion and nation intersecting in, 45–50; sacralization in, 19–22; secular sites as displacing, 280, 305n7; shift to humanitarian focus in, 271–72; spatial opposition of sacred and secular in, 19–20, 35, 58–59, 99; threats to, 168; transitional moments in, 121–22, 227–28. *See also* collective memory; commemorative practices; national histories and identities; national memory and imagination; transnational memory-making

memorialization practices. *See* commemorative practices

memorials and memorial museums: definitions of, 73–74, 204; ecology of meaning-making in, 273–80; historical context vs. memorialization in, 3–5, 211–15; museum environment compared with, 185–86, 249–50; particular histories and memories of, 265–66; shift from memorial to monument in, 28, 29–30, 240–43, 267–69, 272, 279; as sites of contestation, 6–7, 209–11, 266–67; social relations underlying, 58–59, 273–75; space intended as, 201–2; transformations and meanings of, 271–73; visitor behavior expected at, 22, 204. *See also* controversies and critiques; representations; war memorials and monuments; *and specific memorials*

Memorial to the Murdered Jews of Europe (Berlin), 271–72

memorial tourism: affect and memory linked in, 58–63; Disneyland problem in, 167; national imagination in, 13–19; Pearl Harbor context of, 9–13; reflections on purpose and propriety of, 196–200; sacred spaces

of, 19–22. *See also* military-entertainment complex

memory: affect linked with, 58–63; changes and distortions in, 24, 231; ethnographic and performative approaches to, 274–76; "flashbulb," 40, 51; generational change and loss of, 29–30, 75–76, 265–67; as history, 267–73; politics of, 13–19, 31, 246–49, 279; professionalized history juxtaposed to, 58–59, 111–12; social frameworks of, 31–32; as unfinished, 240–43; use of term, 30–31. *See also* collective memory; emotionality and emotion work; oral histories; transnational memory-making; witnesses and witnessing

Middlesworth, Mal, 90

Migita, Torao, 148

Mikuma, John, 298n1

militarization, 219, 229, 247. *See also* Hawai'i: colonization and militarization of; United States military

military-entertainment complex: commodification and trivialization in, 184–85, 223; education and commemoration vs., 196–200; "hula girls" in, 152, 159, 218, 223; objects in, 159–60. *See also* memorial tourism

military museums: focus of, 193, 195–96; friendship exchanges support from army museum, 106–7, 111; memorials distinguished from, 164–65. *See also* Battleship *Missouri* Memorial; Ni'ihau exhibit controversy; Pacific Aviation Museum; USS *Bowfin* Submarine Museum and Park; war memorials and monuments

military service and sacrifice: as key theme in *Arizona* Memorial, 70, 73–74, 84–85, 203–4, 234, 238; memorials as signifiers of, 21–22; online access to stories of, 67–69, 296n13; remembered and honored, 76, 84–87, 88f, 90–91, 277–78; symbolism of, 275–76; valorization of, 15; whiteness unmarked in WWII, 40. *See also* citizen-soldiers; veterans and veterans groups

Miller, Doris, 40, 154, 299n12

Mink, Patsy, 134, 135, 212

moral complexities: challenges of representing, 2–3, 26, 168, 192, 195–96, 272; different readings of, 34, 45, 62, 154, 210;

survivors' voices and, 46, 57–58, 59, 60–63, 99–100. *See also* embodiment; film and movies; social relations

Morgan, Joe: photograph, 47f; printed talk of, 295n4; ranger's recording compared with voice of, 74; religiosity and forgiveness in personal story of, 46, 47f, 48–50, 55, 60, 61–62, 94

Morimo, Takeo, 304n6

Moss, Frank, 55

Mosse, George L., 21, 161

multiculturalism: in *December 7th*, 144, 146–47, 299n12; demographics of Hawai'i and, 17–18, 94–95, 130, 225; Japanese American ties to Japan in, 112–13, 116–17; memorial sequence as representing, 148–49; in survivor's story, 46, 50–55, 62–63; unification triumphant over, 146–47, 299n12; VALR's encouragement of diverse perspectives and, 267–68. *See also* reconciliation and peace themes

Munday, Doug, 16, 211, 214, 235

museum exhibits and exhibit design: "accuracy" in, 185; disappearance of WWII veterans in context of, 36–37; "engagement to peace" theme in, 99, 115, 176–77; marginalized histories included in, 222f, 223–26; for memorial museum vs. monument, 240; multiple perspectives in, 2–3, 8–9, 14, 29, 80, 133–34, 208, 209–11, 234, 239, 261–62, 267–73, 298n2; recognition vs. facts in, 232–33; review panels for, 33, 190–91, 193–95; silences of facts excluded from, 191–92; social relations in production of, 215–21, 275. *See also* audio and video recordings
—SPECIFIC EXHIBITS: atomic bombings, 4, 27, 106, 196, 212, 237, 246, 249, 270; "Looking Like the Enemy," 217–18, 303n5; Native Hawaiian history, 222f; "State of Mind Japan," 227–30. *See also* Ni'ihau exhibit controversy; Sadako crane exhibit

museums and museum practices: avoiding "Disneyland" entertainment in, 167; challenge of uncertainties in sources, 195–96; as contested sites of contact, 6–7, 80–81; history as primary goal in, 58–59; institutional forces underlying, 205, 246; memori-

als compared with, 185–86, 249–50; past as personal and, 211; permeability of, 226; reflexivity considered, 207–8; representation of indexical and iconic in, 197; as unfinished memory, 240–43. *See also* memorials and memorial museums; military museums; museum exhibits and exhibit design; visitor center and museum (new); visitor center and museum (original)

music and songs: Ni'ihau incident, 189, 302nn11–12; "Remember Pearl Harbor," 138–39; rose ceremonies, 104f, 122–23; "They Couldn't Take Ni'ihau No-how," 189, 302nn11–12

Nabors, Jim, 185

Nagasaki: atomic bombing of, 4, 81, 106, 112–13, 271; discussion of, banished from memorial, 240, 242, 301n7; planned U.S. exhibition on bombing cancelled, 4, 27, 106, 196, 212, 237, 246, 249, 270

Nakayama, Kyoko, 304n6

Nākoa, Sarah Keli'ilolena, 255

Napier, A. Kam, 200–201, 204

narratives. *See* museum exhibits and exhibit design; representations; survivor voices

National Air and Space Museum, atomic bombings exhibition at, 4, 27, 106, 196, 212, 237, 246, 249, 270

National Council on the Humanities, 248, 304n3

National Endowment for the Humanities (NEH): advice for, 304n3; educational program supported by, 245–46, 262; Landmarks of American History program of, 246, 258, 260; mandated use of funds, 259; media attack on, 247, 248, 257

national histories and identities: anxieties about and safeguarding of, 4–6, 15; connecting self and, 29, 40, 43, 142, 277; embodiment of, 21–24; memory practices in forging, 13; perceived insult to values of, 245–48; textbooks and curriculum standards on, 209, 250–51, 258, 293n7; war memory and maintenance of, 257–64, 272. *See also* survivor voices; witnesses and witnessing

National Memorial Cemetery of the Pacific.
See Punchbowl National Cemetery
national memory and imagination: collective
voice ("we") in, 44–45, 156–57; complexity
of memorial as site of, 27–28; as mediating
cognitive device, 75; memorialization in
film as vision of, 148–49; military memory
as ritual process in, 81–92; monumental
episodes in, 1–3; social construction of,
266–67; social histories interwoven with,
45–57; textbooks embedded in, 209,
250–51, 258, 293n7; transitions in, 80–81;
veterans' role in shaping, 38–40; war
histories embedded in, 13–19, 257–64; war
memorials as embodiment of, 21–22; zones
of intertextuality in, 107. See also collective
memory; memorialization; Pearl Harbor
mythos
National Park Service (NPS): author's relations with, 32, 33, 92; educational program
supported by, 245–46, 255–56; expanded,
"balanced" interpretation as focus of,
26–28, 29, 60–61, 80, 83–84, 91–92, 98,
151–53, 157, 267–68; "find your own meaning" tenet of, 203–4, 211; funding pressures
on, 280–81; goals for Pearl Harbor, 7–9;
historic interpretation as focus of, 58–59,
91, 165; honorary chaplain of, 48; inclusive
history emphasized by, 8–9, 15, 208–9; on
Missouri's arrival and location, 173–75; oral
history programs of, 65–66, 303n11; PHSA
cooperation with, 27, 117–18, 246; "preserve and protect" motto of, 175; on retail
operations adjacent to Arizona Memorial,
179; role in 1992 orientation film, 150; tea
ceremony approved by, 115–16, 117–19. See
also audio and video recordings; controversies and critiques; educational programs;
How Shall We Remember Them?; Pacific
Historic Parks; park historians and superintendents; park rangers/interpreters; visitor
center and museum (new); visitor center
and museum (original); visitor experiences;
World War II Valor in the Pacific National
Monument; and specific sites
"National Pearl Harbor Remembrance Day,"
81, 296n1

National September 11 Memorial and Museum, 3, 5, 58, 131–32, 250, 279. See also
September 11, 2001, terrorist attacks
National Trust for Historic Preservation, 178
National World War II Memorial (Washington, DC), 67–68, 283
Native Hawaiians: dispossession of, 16–17;
erasure of history and storytelling of, 1–3, 6,
159–60, 199, 274, 284, 293n7; Kaho'olawe
Island returned to, 278; in narrative of
disappearance, 7–8; new museum's representation of, 215, 218–21, 274–75; panel
exhibits redrafted to include, 221–26,
222f; Pearl Harbor features important to,
199, 220, 223, 255, 303n7; personal stories
shared at visitor center, 56–57; population
decline of, 17, 225, 226; proposed treaty
between federal government and, 253–54;
role in Ni'ihau incident, 187, 188–89, 190,
191; use of term, 293n3. See also Interfaith
Ceremony; sovereignty movement
NEH. See National Endowment for the
Humanities
Nicholson, Dorinda, 122
Ni'ihau exhibit controversy: approach to, 165;
dual histories of incident, 195–96, 302n16;
exhibit sign and location, 187, 188f; motivation in exhibiting crashed Zero, 186–87;
panel review and changes in exhibit,
190–91, 193–95; in Pearl Harbor mythos,
188–90; silences in, 192–93, 199; symbolism of, 189–90
The Niihau Incident (Beekman), 187, 194
Nimitz, Adm. Chester, 90, 231
9/11. See September 11, 2001, terrorist attacks
Nishikaichi, Shigenori: crashed Zero of,
186–87; death, 188, 189; goal of, 191, 196;
speculation about, 192; story told in hometown of, 302n16
nonprofit (private) organizations: in-kind
funding support for, 182, 184; retail operations of, 181, 182. See also Battleship Missouri
Memorial; Pacific Aviation Museum; Pacific
Historic Parks; USS Bowfin Submarine
Museum and Park
"no rancor in your heart" phrasing, 49, 99,
239, 297n6

park historians and superintendents (*continued*)

    continued by, 122–23, 124*f*, 125. *See also* cane cutter controversy; *How Shall We Remember Them?* (orientation film, 1992); Martinez, Daniel

park rangers/interpreters: on anti-Japanese attitudes, 14, 53; appearance of, 41; basic tour by, 35; film introduced by, 73–75; interpretive dilemma of, 25–28; replaced by recordings, 64; on retail operations adjacent to *Arizona* Memorial, 181; rhetorical devices of, 55–56; on tourists' ignorance, 22; on veteran volunteers, 42–43

patriotic paranoia: accelerated and intensified, 247–48; discourse surveilled and labeled as unpatriotic, 26–27, 258; film as visual of, 140; paradigm shift in, 218; persistence of, 243

patriotism: as central to public memory, 75; critic's version of, 26–28, 29, 58; culture-war in context of, 132–33; effects in Japan, 107–8; evoked in film, 138–39; religion, racism, and memory's intersection with, 45–56, 57; veteran survivors as embodiment of, 85–86

peace. *See* reconciliation and peace themes

Pearl Harbor (film): absence of local in, 16, 212–13; context of release, 178; details summarized, 291; entertainment value of, 167; film crew's attempt to engage survivors, 168; navy's support for, 199

Pearl Harbor (Puʻuloa): commercial tours of, 185–86; as event vs. place, 16; expansion of military museums in, 164; images of cane cutter and Navy vessel in, 129–30, 131*f*; Native Hawaiian features of, 199, 220, 223, 255, 303n7; tourist sites in, 36*f*, 163*f*; transformation of, 171–73, 177–78. *See also* Pacific Command and Fleet; Pearl Harbor Historic Sites

Pearl Harbor bombing (December 7, 1941): absence of the local in narratives, 15–16, 212–13, 215; civilian casualties in, 38, 57, 148, 212, 295n1; commemorative space and time reflective of, 82–83; consul general of Japan on, 119; different meanings for

different people, 215, 270–71; familial connections to, 276–77; Hiroshima and, 264, 294n14, 301n7; historical context of, 211; memoryscapes, mythos, and meanings of, 40–45, 80–81, 97–99, 215, 270–71; moral significance of, 60–63, 99–100; other histories of, 252–57; as personal turning point, 50–51; reconceptualizing story of, 49–50, 55, 60; standard histories of, 1–3; statistics on, 285–86*f*; teacher's guides and materials on, 66, 295n10. *See also* civilian and local survivors; Japanese and Japanese American residents; Japanese veterans of WWII; Native Hawaiians; Pacific War; survivors of Pearl Harbor; survivor voices

"Pearl Harbor Day," 81, 296n1

Pearl Harbor Foundation, 113, 221–22. *See also* Pearl Harbor Memorial Fund

Pearl Harbor Historic Sites: admission and packaging of, 163*f*, 163–64; entrance to, 162, 164*f*, 171–72, 177, 178–79; language gaps for foreign visitors, 169, 301n2; memorial spaces vs. museums in, 164–65; use of term, 162–63. *See also* Battleship *Missouri* Memorial; Pacific Aviation Museum; USS *Arizona* Memorial; USS *Bowfin* Submarine Museum and Park; USS *Oklahoma* Memorial; USS *Utah* Memorial; visitor center and museum (new); World War II Valor in the Pacific National Monument

Pearl Harbor Institute (plans), 281

Pearl Harborland, 280–84

Pearl Harbor Memorial Foundation, 113, 221–22. *See also* Pearl Harbor Memorial Fund

Pearl Harbor Memorial Fund, 302n3

Pearl Harbor mythos: alleged disloyalty of Japanese American residents, 129–30, 132–37, 139–41, 144–47, 165, 186–87, 189–90, 217, 298n1, 299–300n18, 302n15; discredited charge of FDR's betrayal, 299–300n18; "engagement to peace" theme and, 269–70; filmmaking and practice in, 141–43, 152–54, 205; Hawai'i as paradise vs. foreboding borderland, 144–45, 152, 223; heroic narrative, 24, 153–54, 275–76; Japanese military in, 226–27; memoryscapes

and meanings of, 40–45, 80–81, 97–99,
215, 270–71; Native Hawaiians absent
from, 218–19; Niʻihau incident in, 188–90;
other histories entangled with, 215–26;
social relations underlying, 273–75; unification of country, 52, 139, 141, 146–47, 273.
See also military service and sacrifice;
national memory and imagination
Pearl Harbor Survivors Association (PHSA):
as audience for orientation film, 151; cane
cutter controversy and, 135; cap of, 54;
chaplain of, 46; discourse of disappearance
in, 64; dissolution of, 8, 116, 266, 269, 283,
295n8; local Aloha chapter members, 27,
41, 61–62, 72–73; membership requirements, 40; memorial activities of, 12, 41;
multicultural contacts of, 95; NPS inclusion
of, 27, 117–18, 246; reconciliation rituals
opposed by, 61–62, 108–9; response to
Japan's acceptance of blame, 297n5. *See
also* survivors of Pearl Harbor; veteran
volunteers
Pearl Harbor Survivors Project, 68–69, 296n13
Pearl Harbor Warriors (Nicholson), 102, 122
Perez, Rob, 179–80
PHSA. *See* Pearl Harbor Survivors Association
"political correctness," 26–28, 29, 58, 132,
209, 221
politics: of film representations, 129–37; of
memory, 13–19, 31, 246–49, 279; paranoid
style of, 27, 247–48. *See also* representations
politics of pedagogy: ecology of meaning-
making in, 273–80; memory as history
in, 267–73; Pearl Harborland in, 280–84.
See also educational programs; teacher
workshops
Polynesian Cultural Center, 176
Poynter, Nelson, 146
Preis, Alfred, 284
public discourse: gender differences in,
300n32; histories as topic in, 7–8; on
Missouri's arrival and location, 173–76; on
new museum, 1–2, 5–6, 13, 293n7. *See also*
controversies and critiques; media coverage
public history: conversations about, 1–9;
social history techniques in, 209–10; state-
centered forces vs. cross-national discourse

in, 258–64. *See also* memorial history;
museums and museum practices; National
Park Service; oral histories
Punchbowl National Cemetery (National Memorial Cemetery of the Pacific): friendship
ceremonies at, 93, 105–8, 111, 125, 262, 263f,
263–64; Veterans History Project ceremony
at, 64, 295n9
Puʻuloa. *See* Pearl Harbor

race and race relations: in *December 7th*, 144;
multiculturalism in Hawaiʻi in relation to,
17–18, 61–63; national memory's intersection with, 50–56; Niʻihau incident in context of, 190–91, 194–96; OWI concerned
with, 146; in politics of representation and
memorialization, 129–37. *See also* cane
cutter controversy; Japanese American
internment; *specific groups of people*
Raytheon, 182, 184
Reader's Digest, 189
Reagan, Ronald, 185, 298n3
real estate development: collision of history
with, 177–78. *See also* Ford Island
Reciprocity Treaty (1875), 3, 17, 224, 225–26,
287
reconciliation and peace themes: affective politics of, 268–69; in anniversary
ceremonies, 84; ceremonies in *Arizona*
Memorial, 100–104, 103f; declaration of
friendship signed, 110f, 111, 234; "end of
rancor" phrasing in, 49, 99, 239, 297n6;
first act of, 96; hostility to, 61–62; Japanese veterans' fostering of, 46, 62, 80–81,
92–97, 100–103, 233, 268, 305n5; Joe's
story of, 46, 48–49, 60; multiculturalism as asset in, 18; museum planning and
discussion of, 207–8, 230–40; opportunity
for discourse on, 112–13; rituals of, 61–62;
Sadako crane exhibit as fostering, 242–43,
268–69; survivor's conclusion of, 55–56;
symposium as opportunity for, 100, 102–5;
tea ceremony as symbol of, 116f; teacher
workshops as analogue to, 262–64, 263f;
of U.S.-Japanese Joint Memorial Services in
Japan, 93; validation for Japan in, 108. *See
also* emotionality and emotion work;

reconciliation and peace themes (*continued*)
friendship exchanges; rose ceremonies;
Sadako crane exhibit; tea ceremony

religiosity: Interfaith Ceremony, 123, 124*f*, 125,
270; in Joe Morgan's stories, 46, 48–49, 60,
94; justification for inclusion in veteran's
talk, 49–50; orientation film on, 157.
See also Buddhists

"Remembering the Pacific" video podcast
series, 68–69

"Remember Pearl Harbor" (NPS YouTube
videos), 76

"Remember Pearl Harbor" (slogan), 28, 156,
211, 269

"Remember Pearl Harbor" (song), 138–39

remembrance. *See* commemorative practices;
memorialization

representations: in anti-Japanese sentiments,
25–28, 29, 97–99, 131–32, 150; authority over, 7–8, 58–59, 111; contextualized
narratives as, 69–70; exclusions of, 52–53;
in firsthand witnessing at sites of violence,
37–40; history and memory intertwined
in, 58–59; of Japanese residents in Oahu,
129–30; of Japan in new museum, 226–30;
in memorial's context, 204–5; multiple perspectives in, 2–3, 8–9, 14, 29, 80, 133–34,
208, 209–11, 234, 239, 261–62, 267–73,
298n2; political and emotional potency of,
31–32, 216; politics of, in film, 129–37; shift
from embodied to electronic memory in,
30, 36–37, 45, 71–75, 265; transitions in,
75–76. *See also* controversies and critiques;
film and movies; histories; museums and
museum practices; orientation films; Pearl
Harbor mythos; survivor voices

rituals. *See* commemorative practices; Punchbowl National Cemetery; rose ceremonies;
tea ceremony; USS *Arizona* Memorial

Robinson, Aylmer, 189

Robinson, Greg, 189

Roosevelt, Eleanor, 304n14

Roosevelt, Franklin D.: CCC program of, 276;
discredited suspicions about, 299–300n18;
internment ordered by (Executive Order
9066), 50, 134, 139, 189, 191; on sacrifice
and courage, 238; speeches of, 51, 217

rose ceremonies: beginnings of, 103–5; music
for, 104*f*, 122–23; ongoing transformation
of, 122–23, 124*f*, 125

Rosenberg, Emily S., 30, 98–99

Roughead, Adm. Gary, 89, 90–91

sacred space and sacralization: educational
programs in, 249–50; spatial opposition of
secular vs., 35, 58–59, 99; of USS *Arizona*
Memorial, 5, 19–22, 120–21, 168–69

Sadako crane exhibit: dedication of, 81, 99,
240, 268–69; funding for, 240, 241, 275;
peace discourse fostered by, 242–43; photograph, 241*f*; as shared commemorative
event, 268; souvenirs of, 281; symbolism
of, 99, 113–15, 117, 126, 176–77, 240, 270.
See also Sasaki, Sadako

Sasaki, Sadako: inspirational story of, 126,
240–41, 270; paper cranes folded by, 99,
115, 176–77; photograph, 241*f*. *See also*
Sadako crane exhibit

Saving Private Ryan (film), 153

Schick, Lt. William R., 148–49

Schickel, Richard, 143

Schofield, Maj. Gen. John, 221

Schofield Barracks, 67

schools: audio and video recordings geared
to, 66, 295n10; memorial offerings from,
77–78, 79*f*; videoconferencing program for,
67, 248, 296n12. *See also* education

SDF (Japanese Self-Defense Forces), 107–8,
119–20

Sean Hannity Fox News program, 34, 245–46,
247, 253, 256

Second World War. *See* World War II

Selling the Holocaust (Cole), 279

Sen, Genshitsu, 115–21, 116*f*

Sendai Higashi High School, 79*f*

September 11, 2001, terrorist attacks, 3, 5, 40,
87, 120, 190. *See also* National September 11
Memorial and Museum; World Trade Center attack (2001)

Shadowed Ground (Foote), 272–73

Shin, Naomi, 122–23, 125

Shintani, Ishimatsu, 190

Short, Gen. Walter Campbell, 130, 132,
133–34, 141

teacher workshops (*continued*)
    perspectives in, 257–64, 270–71, 304n5;
    Japanese teachers recruited to participate,
    247, 259–63, 263*f*, 304n6; learning and
    remembrance modalities intertwined in,
    250–51; reconciliation ritual in, 262, 263*f*,
    263–64; survivors' role in, 251–53
temporality, 82–83, 184, 294n12
Tengan, Ty Kāwika, 274
The Texture of Memory (Young), 278
"They Couldn't Take Ni'ihau No-how" (song),
    189, 302nn11–12
Thorsten, Marie, 95, 107, 126, 278, 297n8
The Today Show (television show), 96
Toland, Gregg, 138, 139, 140, 144, 148
Tora! Tora! Tora! (film), 143, 291, 299n7
tourism: *Arizona* Memorial as top destination,
    10–13, 161, 166, 281–82; commercial tours
    of Pearl Harbor, 185–86; commodification
    and trivialization potential in, 165–71;
    double attractions in, 161–62; education
    and commemoration vs. commodification
    in, 196–200; global interests in sites of vio-
    lence and tragedy (dark tourism), 196–97,
    272–73; growth of, 10–11, 18, 22; Hawaiian
    imagery in, 218–19; memorial experience
    vs. pleasures of, 25, 61, 154–55; reflections
    on, 196–200; typical attractions in, 166.
    See also attractions; memorial tourism;
    military-entertainment complex; Pearl
    Harbor Historic Sites; visitors
transnational memory-making: diverse
    representations and, 97–99; in friendship
    exchanges, 80–81, 92–97, 105–11, 110*f*;
    military remembrance vs. reconciliation
    in, 98–99; opportunities for, 19, 112–13;
    rose ceremonies in, 103–5, 104*f*, 122–23,
    124*f*, 125; symposiums' role in, 12, 30, 100,
    102–5; variety and fluidity of, 126–27;
    zones of intertextuality in, 107. *See also*
    Sadako crane exhibit; tea ceremony
TripAdvisor, 161
Tule Lake Segregation Center (California),
    216, 278

Unabarakai (organization of Japanese naval
    vets), 93, 105, 107–8

unification theme, 52, 139, 141, 146–47, 273
United States: colonization and militarization
    of Hawai'i by, 5–6, 16–18, 159–60, 219–20,
    225, 253–56; Reciprocity Treaty signed by,
    3, 17, 224, 225–26, 287; secrecy in takeover
    of Hawai'i, 226, 303n10. *See also* U.S.-
    Japanese relations
United States Air Force, 146
United States Army, 442nd Regimental Com-
    bat Team, 51–52, 63, 217, 218, 295n6
United States Congress: Akaka Bill proposed
    in, 253–54, 278; cane cutter controversy
    and, 131, 134, 135, 139; Ford Island project
    supported by, 178; Hawai'i annexed by, 17;
    "National Pearl Harbor Remembrance Day"
    proclaimed by, 81, 296n1. *See also* Civil
    Liberties Act; Reciprocity Treaty
United States Department of Defense (earlier,
    War Department), 4, 98, 143, 299n6. *See
    also* Office of War Information; *and specific
    armed services*
United States Department of State, 98,
    296–97n4
United States Holocaust Museum, 66
United States military: active-duty personnel
    at memorial, 265–66; "be prepared" slogan
    of, 45, 211; critique of role in Pacific, 255–
    57; diversity and heroism in, 303n6; histo-
    rians in, 209; Middle East and expansion
    of, 11, 86–87, 112, 277–78; naturalization
    of role in state, 199; Pacific pivot strategy
    of, 117; ritual apparatus of, 81–82, 270, 275;
    weaponry of, 173, 182, 184, 197, 198–99. *See
    also* military service and sacrifice
United States Navy: assistance after Fuku-
    shima disaster in, 116, 119; as audience
    for orientation film, 151; boat to memo-
    rial operated by, 35, 63–64, 77; Disney's
    cooperation with, 168, 199; expansion in
    Pearl Harbor, 16–17, 18; Ford Island proj-
    ect of, 177–79, 199, 280; funding for new
    visitor center and museum from, 302n3;
    keynote speakers from, 90–92, 296n2;
    local saboteurs feared, 129–30; "man the
    rails" tradition in, 10, 85; NPS cooperation
    with, 206; Pacific Command and Fleet, 11,
    175, 198–99; ritual apparatus of, 81–82,

270, 275; school program supported by, 296n12; tea ceremony approved by, 115–16, 117–18; value of Pearl Harbor memorial for, 11; view of Pearl Harbor base and fleet, 161–62. *See also* Ford Island; orientation film (1980)

University of Hawai'i: Japanese scholars at, 229; Matsunaga Institute for Peace at, 95, 106–7; scholars on Native Hawaiian history at, 224–25; tea master as student at, 116. *See also* History and Commemoration program

University of Tokyo, 228, 261

Unknown Soldiers tombs, 21, 301n5. *See also* war memorials and monuments

Urasenke School of Tea (Japan), 115–16, 118, 297n11

U.S.-Japanese relations: affirmation of ties in, 119–20; *Arizona* memorial as flashpoint in, 149–50; Cold War and, 18, 25, 61, 226; NPS concerns about, 61; Pacific pivot strategy of U.S. and, 117; reconciliation moves in contrast to, 102–5; tensions in 1980s–1990s, 14, 97–99; validating the value of, 107. *See also* Declaration of Friendship and Peace; friendship exchanges; Sadako crane exhibit

USS *Arizona*: iconic status, 9; location of, 19–20; *Missouri* linked to, 173–74, 175–77; oil leaking from, 64; souvenir photos of, 281, 282f; survivor from, 238, 269; survivors' ashes interred at, 21, 48, 50, 69, 75; World Trade Center remains compared with, 3–4, 9

USS *Arizona* Memorial: "*Arizona*'s tears" story at, 64; B-29 crew remembered, 93, 113; behavior expected at, 22, 204; dedication of (1962), 10; different perspectives and diverse audiences of, 209–10, 271–80; genealogy of memory for, 13–19; influences on representations at, 150–51; as international contact zone, 94–97; legislated purpose of commemoration at, 6, 10, 15–16, 78, 136, 205, 233, 235, 243, 252; location of, 161, 206; memorial offerings at, 77–78, 79f, 88f; navy's ceremony held on, 84; number of visitors, 174; as peace memorial, 294n14;

percentage of VALR visitors who visit, 280, 305n7; personal witnessing period in lifecycle of, 265–66; politics of memory at, 13–19, 31, 246–49, 279; as reconciliation space, 233; as sacred space, 5, 19–22, 120–21, 168–69; sacrifice and courage themes in, 70, 73–74, 84–85, 203–4, 234, 238; as secular and sacred, 58–59, 99; as site of intersection, 6–9; spatial separation of, 19–20, 35, 42f, 99; surroundings of, 171–73; tea ceremony held, 113–21, 116f; as tourist destination, 10–13, 166, 281–82; typical visitor's tour of, 35, 63–64, 77, 203–4; VALR founding and administrative changes at, 19, 112, 267–70, 276. *See also* commemorative practices; educational programs; friendship exchanges; orientation films; visitor center and museum

USS *Arizona* Memorial shrine room: Buddhists at, 84, 124f; display panel in, 283f; emotional power of, 202; as exhibit, 284; inscription on wall, 78; Interfaith Ceremony at, 123, 124f, 125, 270; Japanese and American vets' meetings on, 100–104, 103f; memorial offerings at, 77–78, 79f, 114–15; Tree of Life relief in, 204, 281; visitor response to, 77; wall of names in, 20f. *See also* rose ceremonies; tea ceremony

USS *Bowfin* Submarine Museum and Park: access to, 162–63, 178; fundraising of, 182, 184; military and corporate support for, 32–33; as military museum, 165; opening of, 12, 162, 172; preservation efforts for, 172

USS *Enterprise*, 90

USS *Greeneville*, 198

USS *Honolulu*, 67

USS *John Stennis*, 168

USS *Lexington*, 231–32

USS *Maryland*, 88f

USS *Missouri*: *Arizona* linked to, 173–74, 175–77; as memorial, 162, 301n5; surrender signed on board, 106, 154, 173, 176. *See also* Battleship *Missouri* Memorial

USS *Missouri* Foundation, 173

USS *Missouri* Memorial Association, 173–74, 182, 184

USS *Missouri* Restoration Fund, 198

USS *Monaghan* (destroyer), 44
USS *Oklahoma*, 44, 238
USS *Oklahoma* Memorial, 294n10
USS *Pennsylvania*, 67, 70–71, 238–39
USS *Utah*, 69
USS *Utah* Memorial, 88–89, 294n10
USS *West Virginia*, 40, 69, 92, 101, 299n12

VALR. *See* visitor center and museum (new);
World War II Valor in the Pacific National
Monument
veterans and veterans groups: as audience for
orientation film, 151, 153–54; authoritative
voices of, 58–59; cane cutter controversy
and, 131; honored in commemorative practices, 23, 83, 84–87, 86f, 265, 277, 295n9;
of Middle East wars, 86–87, 112, 277; NPS
inclusion of, 27, 117–18, 246; presence at
memorial, 265–66; symbolism of, 275–76;
transnational imaginings of, 126; variety
of valences of, 23–25; of Vietnam War, 23,
86, 274, 276–77, 294n13. *See also* American
Legion; American veterans of WWII;
AMVETS; Japanese veterans of WWII;
military service and sacrifice; survivors of
Pearl Harbor; Veterans of Foreign Wars
Veterans Day, 34, 245, 277
Veterans History Project (Library of Congress), 64, 67, 295n9
Veterans of Foreign Wars (VFW), 54, 295n7
veteran volunteers: appearance of, 38, 41–42,
54; in cane cutter controversy discussions, 135; commercialization concerns of,
283–84; as embodiment of history, 22–25,
40–45; few remaining, 265; orientation
film introductions and talks by, 43–44;
paper cranes presented to, 126; park historian's instructions for, 26; personalized
stories of, 45–57; popularity of, 282–83;
range of opportunities for, 72; roles in
first visitor center, 41–45, 47f; routinized
narratives of, 69–70; strategies for expressing emotions, 24–25; visitors' encounters
with, 38–40, 39f, 64. *See also* survivors of
Pearl Harbor; survivor voices; *and specific
veterans*
victimization narratives, 37–38

Vietnam War: aircraft used in, 184; fiftieth
anniversary of, 4; naval support in, 11;
veterans of, 23, 86, 274, 276–77, 294n13
visitor center and museum (new): absence
of the local in, 15–16, 212–13; admissions
and single entryway for, 162–63, 164f,
280; audio guide and video kiosks in,
71; commemorative function of, 11–12;
commodification forces in, 280–81, 282f;
context of, 177; criticisms of, 200–201,
204; fixed vs. changeable parts of, 113;
funding for, 12–13, 67–68, 113, 181, 207,
221–22, 302n3; mission of, 202; narrowing of kinds of testimony presented, 45;
opening and dedication, 10–11, 113, 207,
240; response to, 217–18; retail operations
adjacent to, 179–82; sacrifice and courage
theme in, 203–4, 234, 238; temporal scope
of, 294n12; as unfinished memory, 240–43;
VALR founding and administrative changes
at, 112, 267–71; view from, 161–62; workshop presenters as resource for, 253, 254,
255. *See also* educational programs; *How
Shall We Remember Them?*; Pearl Harbor
Historic Sites
—DESIGN AND PLANNING: beginnings of,
206–7; broader context vs. focus on battle
in, 211–15; distinction between museum
and memorial, 204–5; goals in, 202–3;
Hawaiian panels rescripted in, 221–26, 222f;
issues considered, 70–71; Japanese American experiences included, 215–18, 220,
274–75; Japanese voices included in, 226–30;
layout, transition points, and themes, 202–4,
213f, 216–17, 234; "multiple perspectives"
vs. "just facts" debate in, 210–11; Native
Hawaiians marginalized in, 215, 218–21,
274–75; reconciliation theme discussed,
207–8, 230–40; reflections on, 240–43;
social history techniques in, 209–10; stakeholders included in, 208–9, 212–13, 220
—SPECIFIC COMPONENTS: "contemplation circle," 204, 211; entrance, 162, 164f,
171–72, 177, 178–79; exit area, 236–37;
map, 36f; Oahu Court, 36f, 221–26, 222f;
"Remembrance Circle," 204, 234–37; Road
to War building, 228; souvenir photo

opportunities, 282f; Tree of Life relief, 204, 281; "walkway of courage and sacrifice," 203–4, 234, 238

visitor center and museum (original): *Arizona Memorial* separated from, 19–20, 35, 42f, 99; exclusions and silences in, 52, 61, 64, 215; layout of, 36f; plans to rebuild, 12–13; shift from personal talks to recorded presentations in, 30, 36–37, 45, 71–75; spatial orientation to, 46–47; structure and land base of, 206, 302n2; survivors' roles in, 41–45, 42f, 47f; transnational memory-making traced to, 93; typical visitor's tour of, 35, 63–64, 77. *See also* orientation film (1980)

visitor center theaters. *See* orientation films

visitor experiences: concept, 161; customer service vs., 280–81; emotional responses in, 58–63; matrix designed for, 70; multiple options in, 36f, 162–63, 163f; museum and memorial distinguished for, 204–5; NPS concerns about, 166–67; personal meaning-making of, 273–80; transformation of, 171–73; transition points in, 202–4. *See also* emotionality and emotion work; memorial tourism

visitors: absence of local, 15–16; anticipated response in recognizing Japanese, 231–33; behavior expected, 22, 204; Chinese visitors' attitudes, 169, 171; complaints about foreign groups, 169, 301n2; creating sacred space with and for, 168–69; as customers, 280–81; distinguished visitors (D.V.s), 182, 184, 198; diversity of, 209–10; encounters with surviving veterans, 38–40, 39f, 64; FamilyFun Travel Awards for, 305n8; increased number of, 166–67, 280; multiple perspectives recognized, 8–9, 15, 35, 208, 210–11; photo opportunities for, 39f, 170f, 180f, 282f; responses to Joe's religiosity, 49–50; typical tour of, 35, 63–64, 77. *See also* Asian visitors; cultures of commemoration; global audience; Japanese visitors; visitor experiences

Vitale, Rear Adm. Mike, 178

volunteers. *See* survivor voices; veteran volunteers

Volunteers in the Park program, 12, 41, 42f. *See also* veteran volunteers

Wai Momi, 220, 223, 303n7

Walsh, Adm. Patrick M., 119

The War (documentary series), 29, 141, 153, 276

war memorials and monuments: authoritative voices at, 37–40, 58–59; complex issues entangled with, 2–6; as contact zones, 80, 94–97; differences among, 164–65; kinds of history possible at, 6, 134–37; memorial to monument transition in, 28, 29–30, 240–43, 267–69, 272, 279; military constituencies of, 32–33, 97–98; military memory as ritual process at, 81–92; military remembrance vs. peace prayer at, 125; national contexts of, 13–19, 271–73; oral history programs of, 65–66; purpose of, 6–7; recognition of both sides in, 229–33; reflections on purpose and propriety of, 196–200; sacralization of, 19–22; teaching history linked to, 257–64; visitor behavior expected at, 22, 204. *See also* military museums; *and specific sites*

Weatherwax, Herb, 39f, 67, 126

We Were There . . . Pearl Harbor Survivors (video), 64, 295–96n11

Wheeler, Lee, 174–75

Wieviorka, Eva, 252

Williams, Paul, 271

Winter, Jay, 271

witnesses and witnessing: effects of firsthand, 37–40; electronically mediated, 30, 36–37, 45, 71–75, 265; passing of living witnesses, 29–30, 266; power and danger of, 251. *See also* memory; oral histories; survivor voices

Witness to History program (videoconference), 67, 248, 296n12

World Trade Center attack (1993), 185

World Trade Center attack (2001), 3–4, 9, 120. *See also* September 11, 2001, terrorist attacks

World War I: European memorialization of, 161; as touchpoint, 39

World War II: aircraft used in, 184; civilian vs. military experiences of, 37–38, 57; European

World War II (*continued*)
memorialization of, 271–72; familial connections to, 276–77; "fighting two wars" in, 51–52, 295n6; as "Good War," 9, 138, 268, 282–83; narrative of U.S. victory in, 199; power of personal narratives about, 152–53; propaganda in, 96, 143; as touchpoint, 39. *See also* atomic bombings; Holocaust; Pacific War; Pearl Harbor bombing

World War II Memorial (Washington, DC), 67–68, 283

World War II Valor in the Pacific National Monument (VALR): anniversary events held at, 84–87; coordination among sites of, 162–63, 164*f*, 280; expanded elements and audience of, 26–28, 29, 60–61, 80, 83–84, 91–92, 98, 151–53, 157, 267–68; FamilyFun Travel Award for, 282, 305n8; makeover of, 1; mandate and mission for, 7–9, 38, 112, 267–70; map, 36*f*, 163*f*; memorial to monument change due to, 28, 29–30, 240–43, 267–69, 272, 279; memoryscapes and meanings of, 40–45, 80–81; multiple perspectives and sites in, 267–73; name of, 199, 294n10, 304n3; opening of, 123; peace and reconciliation themes central to, 61, 81, 269–70; percentage of VALR visitors who visit *Arizona* Memorial, 305n7; presidential proclamation of, 13, 112–13, 199, 268, 294n10; souvenirs of, 281, 282*f*; spatial arrangement of, 11*f*, 19–20; timing of founding, 266; website and video podcast series for, 68–69. *See also* Japanese American internment; Pearl Harbor Historic Sites; reconciliation and peace themes; USS *Arizona* Memorial; visitor center and museum (new)

Yaguchi, Yujin: as consultant for exhibit design, 229; on absence of reconciliation, 239; on changing perspectives, 260–61; Japanese teachers recruited by, 304n6; Japanese visitors interviewed by, 25, 171, 294n14; on national histories and perspectives, 263, 270–71; on Native Hawaiian perspective, 221

Yamamoto, Isoroku, 228–29, 303n12

Yasukuni Shrine (Japan), 271

Yoshida, Jiro, 92–93, 97, 103, 105, 108

Young, James, 30, 266, 278

YouTube videos, 65, 68–69, 76, 191

Yushukan Museum (Japan), 271

Zlatoper, Adm. Ronald, 176